D1124587

States of Union

CONSTITUTIONAL THINKING
JEFFREY K. TULIS AND SANFORD LEVINSON, EDITORS

States of Union
Family and Change in the
American Constitutional Order

Mark E. Brandon

 University Press of Kansas

Published by the University Press of Kansas (Lawrence, Kansas 66045), which was organized by the Kansas Board of Regents and is operated and funded by Emporia State University, Fort Hays State University, Kansas State University, Pittsburg State University, the University of Kansas, and Wichita State University

Library of Congress Cataloging-in-Publication Data

Brandon, Mark E.
    States of union : family and change in the American constitutional order / Mark E. Brandon.
        pages cm. — (Constitutional Thinking)
    Includes bibliographical references and index.
    ISBN 978-0-7006-1923-8 (hardback)
    1. Domestic relations—United States—History. 2. Constitutional history—United States.
I. Title.
    KF505.B73 2013
    346.7301—dc23
                                                                    2013019105

British Library Cataloguing-in-Publication Data is available.

Printed in the United States of America

10 9 8 7 6 5 4 3 2 1

Dedicated to my son Evan
and to the memory of Walter F. Murphy

Contents

Acknowledgments

This book is about the constitutional status of family in the American order and how and why that status has changed through the years. My interest in the subject began when I was a law student, many years ago. *Griswold v. Connecticut* had been decided in the previous decade, and *Roe v. Wade* was announced just a few years before I encountered it in a course in constitutional law. The Supreme Court's attempt to link both of these decisions to older cases resting on a doctrine of substantive due process concerning the autonomy and status of the nuclear family—*Meyer v. Nebraska* and *Pierce v. Society of Sisters*—was intriguing. For one thing, the economic strand of substantive due process had recently been declared deceased. (Recent developments in our own time, however, suggest that rumors of the death of economic liberty were premature.) For another, it wasn't clear to me how family made its way into the Constitution in the first place. This book is the product of my efforts to make sense of this development.

It's a truism (but still true) that scholarship owes much to others. In my case, the list of others is long. Among them are the many scholars who, in myriad ways, have come to the subject before me. The range and quality of that scholarship are humbling, whether it be in American history, family law, religion, feminism, or of course the Constitution. I acknowledge a large debt to them—including (especially) those with whom I've disagreed.

There's also a long list of friends and colleagues with whom I've engaged in fruitful conversation or on whom I've inflicted drafts of chapters or parts of chapters. Linda McClain and Sanford Levinson read a complete draft of the manuscript and shared valuable suggestions and perceptive criticisms. I'm grateful to the both of them. Others have read, commented on, or simply talked with me about portions of the book. Though I'm keenly aware of the fact that I can't begin to name everyone, nor to extend adequate thanks, I do want to mention a few who've been especially generous as I've stumbled through writing: James Booth,

Al Brophy, Kirsten Carlson, Bob Covington, Jim Ely, John Goldberg, Mark Graber, Julie Hardwick, Hendrik Hartog, Don Herzog, Stan Katz, Ann Lin, Stephen Macedo, Wayne Moore, Noga Morag-Levine, Melissa Murray, Julie Novkov, Gretchen Ritter, Arlene Saxonhouse, Kim Scheppele, Tony Sebok, Dan Sharfstein, Suzanna Sherry, Kevin Stack, Lea Vandervelde, Elizabeth Wingrove, and Christopher Yoo. I've learned more from each of them than I've demonstrated in the pages that follow.

I've also learned much from my students through the years. At the University of Oklahoma, where I took my first full-time teaching job, I supervised a directed reading on "the Constitution and the Family" with three students—Bob Carter, Rob Neal, and Mark Highland—who I'm sure would not now recognize the fruit of the seeds that were planted in that seminar. Bradley Welch was another engaging interlocutor, not only at Oklahoma, but later, too, when he was a law student at the University of Texas. I've had several chances to pursue the subject with students in various courses at the University of Michigan and at Vanderbilt. I thank them all. Thanks also to the students who've helped me with research. At Michigan, Ryan Hudson, John Min Kang, Rick Mathews, and Steve Mazie provided assistance. At Vanderbilt, I've been aided by a number of students: Ashley Alfonso, Thomas Boyd, Brent Culpepper, Miranda Davis, David Dunn, Melanie Erb, Diana Janae Goff, Stacy Howlett, Mona Jean-Baptiste, Matthew Koch, Karen Usselman Lindell, Andrea Verney, and Jonathan Wardle. Their labor has made the book better than it otherwise would have been. Of course, none of them bears responsibility for what I've made of their efforts.

Vanderbilt Law School has provided generous financial and scholarly support for this project. The Law School and the Departments of Political Science and History at Vanderbilt have provided forums for talks and roundtables. I'm especially indebted to Princeton University's Program in Law and Public Affairs for a stimulating year of research and writing, without which the book might never have come to completion. I've benefitted enormously from the opportunity to present work outside the confines of my current institutional home. Thanks to the University of Michigan's Department of Political Science, Princeton University, the Rutgers School of Law–Camden, Virginia Tech, the University of Alabama Law School, the University of Texas School of Law, the University of Wisconsin School of Law, the American Political Science Association, the Western Political Science Association, the Law and Society Association, and the Southeastern Association of Law Schools for forums for talking about aspects of the project.

I'm grateful to the University Press of Kansas for the opportunity to publish the book as part of the Series in Constitutional Thinking, edited by Jeffrey Tulis and Sanford Levinson. For the Press, Fred Woodward has been a superb editor—insightful, encouraging, and patient. Thanks also to Martha Whitt, for her keen copyeditor's eye, and to Kelly Chrisman Jacques and Susan Schott for their roles in production and promotion.

Portions of the book appeared previously in two articles: "Family at the Birth of American Constitutional Order," 77 *Texas Law Review* 1195 (1999), and "Home on the Range: Family and Constitutionalism in American Continental Settlement," 52 *Emory Law Journal* 645 (2003). Thanks to both journals for permission to publish parts of those articles.

Finally, heartfelt thanks to my family, both nuclear and extended, who've encouraged (and sometimes badgered) me to write. Special recognition to Kathryn, my patient spouse, and to Rachel and Evan, who show me daily how rich a life in a family can be.

States of Union

Introduction

Family Values

Forms of human relations that are recognizable as families have been around since the beginning of recorded history. Partly because of this longevity and partly because the functions that families have served can be important, we've come to think of "the family" as being basic to human experience, basic even to human flourishing or happiness. Indeed, it is. In fact, it would be difficult to overestimate its significance. But even if it is significant in these ways, is it also, as some have claimed, an institution that is significant for purposes of constitutional structure or constitutional law? By the end of the 1920s, the Supreme Court of the United States had held more than once that family was in fact an institution possessing a constitutional status and that certain relations within that institution were constitutionally protected. This book explores how this came to pass, what it has meant for family to be constitutionally significant, and what the implications of that significance have been (and continue to be) for the polity and for families.

THE MOVEMENT FOR FAMILY VALUES

In the latter half of the twentieth century, the rhetoric of "family values" became a staple of American civic life. Often the rhetoric has suggested a political program, but in truth it's impossible to talk sensibly about a single program, as the specific concerns that animate the invocation of family values are diverse, reflecting the various aims of a large and disparate collection of groups and scholars. Depending on the source, therefore, one might hear about the nuclear family, sexuality, abortion, pornography, adultery, the roles of women, the welfare of children, domestic economy, familial control of education, the law and practice of divorce, and, more recently, same-sex marriage. These concerns are relevant to this book.

I'm interested in two general aspects of the notion of family values as groups and scholars have deployed it. The first is a pair of assumptions about the relation between family and constitutional order: that the forms and functions of family influence the legal, political, moral, and economic constitution of a society, and that these aspects of the constitution influence, for better or worse, the forms and functions of family.

My second interest is a story that some proponents of family values have told about family, constitutional maintenance, and constitutional change—a story that implicates the role of law in managing the relationship between family and constitutional order. The account is essentially this: across the ages, a particular familial form has held—monogamous, heterosexual, permanent, and reproductive. This family is natural and has helped establish and maintain a kind of civilization, including our own. Law, economy, and culture therefore have historically recognized its fundamentality. But beginning in the 1960s, law altered the landscape on which this family had traditionally flourished. As Mary Ann Glendon has put it, "Legal norms which had remained relatively undisturbed for centuries were discarded or radically altered in the areas of marriage, divorce, family support obligations, inheritance, the relation of parent and child, and the status of children born outside marriage."[1]

According to some who have criticized these changes, one culprit has been the Supreme Court of the United States, which, since the early twentieth century, has gradually made certain aspects of familial relations matters of constitutional law. In effect, the Court has converted family into a quasi-constitutional institution. It has done so primarily, though not exclusively, through the constitutional doctrine of privacy. Ironically, from the critics' perspective, this jurisprudence of family—this constitutionalization of the law of family—has weakened the institution of the family by challenging the preconditions for sustaining its traditional forms and functions. And this alteration, in turn, now threatens to unravel the social fabric of the constitutional order.

The concerns of almost all proponents of family values are animated by religious values. In saying this, I am not suggesting that religion in this context is unidimensional. There is a multitude of religious views on the place of family in the world. But a constellation of religious adherents—including orthodox Roman Catholics, conservative Protestants, and traditionalist Jews—has formed around a commitment to a specific vision of family values. Likewise, I'm not implying that the positions are illegitimate by virtue of their connection to religion. John Rawls and other contemporary liberals have been misguided in their philosophical quest to wall off public forums from religious views. Religious perspectives can't easily be eliminated, whether by force or law, nor should they be. By their nature, however, sectarian appeals will tend to be limited in their persuasiveness. That fact is part of the reason secular arguments tend to dominate in the civic "marketplace of ideas" in a pluralist society. As a result, many proponents sometimes offer arguments in secular language, despite their religious motivation. In fact, one striking feature of the current movement for family values is the tendency of some proponents to speak publicly in terms that avoid overt theological language. Still, most positions ultimately rest on a ground of religion. And some are essentially premodern critiques of the values of the Enlightenment.

Consider, for example, a recently published forum sponsored by the Witherspoon Institute, a center for policy that focuses on "the moral foundations of free and democratic societies."[2] Titled *The Meaning of Marriage*, the forum was designed "to promote the truth about marriage."[3] Robert George's essay explains and defends the "traditional" view—which he calls "one-flesh unity"—that the heart of marriage is a form of sex that is (or could conceivably be) reproductive. Although he doesn't acknowledge it explicitly in this particular essay, the view originates in biblical sources and in the Catechism of the Catholic Church. As he describes it, cryptically:

> Marriage, considered not as a mere legal convention or cultural artifact, but, rather, as a one-flesh communion of persons that is consummated and actualized by acts that are reproductive in type, whether or not they are reproductive in effect, or are motivated, even in part, by a desire to conceive a child, is an intrinsic human good and, precisely as such, provides a more than merely instrumental reason for choice and action. The bodily union of spouses in marital acts is the biological matrix of their marriage as a comprehensive, multilevel sharing of life: that is, a relationship that unites the spouses at the bodily (biological), emotional, dispositional, and even spiritual levels of their being. Marriage, precisely as such a relationship, is naturally ordered to the good of procreation (and is, indeed, uniquely apt for the nurturing and education of children) as well as to the good of spousal unity.[4]

This way of seeing the matter has direct implications for the character or definition of family and for who may marry whom and why. I'll return to George's position at the end of the book.

In the same publication, Roger Scruton's essay on "Sacrilege and Sacrament" is less preoccupied than George's with prescribing a particular method for having sex, but he is nonetheless keen to present a specific view of the connection between sex and marriage. From the beginning of the emergence of Christian institutions in Europe, he asserts, marriage was conceived to be a permanent sacramental relationship, secured by the sacred erotic tie between spouses. Although ancient Roman law asserted secular control over the institution of marriage, it conceded much, he says, to "religious precedent." Still, the Roman law did not view marriage as a "radical existential change" of status, as the sacred law did. This defect in Roman law was exemplified by the fact that it permitted divorce. Scruton does not mention Judaic law, which for thousands of years has permitted divorce. In Christendom, however, Scruton argues that the rising power of the papacy "recaptured [marriage] from the secular powers" and "reconsecrated" it as a central institution of the Church. Through the Middle Ages and up to the Renaissance, then, marriage was the subject of both secular and spiritual jurisdiction, but the Church's position that marriage was essentially permanent and indissolvable held sway. The Reformation, especially Henry VIII's in England, chipped away at the "traditional Catholic teaching" that marriage is "an irreversible change of status, not merely within the community but also before God." But, Scruton says, the key historic moment in the "desecration" of marriage was the French Revolution, when "the state declared itself to be the true broker and undoer of marriages." He suggests that this secularization of marriage was illicit. "When the state usurped the rite of matrimony, and reshaped what had once been holy law, it was inevitable that it should loosen the marital tie. For the state does not represent the Eternal." State-sanctioned marriages, he says, are not "real marriages," because, with the possibility of divorce, the secular relationship lacks the dignity, privileges, and duties of the sacred version. What's more, the American state's commitment to permitting contraception and abortion has led the state to "set itself against the goal of reproduction" and has unconsciously led to "the confiscation of hereditary rights." This in turn threatens to undermine social reproduction and the capacity of civilization to preserve itself.[5]

Among proponents of family values, one worry is that divorce is too easy to obtain. Some have claimed in fact that American law now permits "unilateral divorce," as if one spouse might simply decide to leave a marriage and then do it on his or her own motion.[6] This mischaracterizes the laws of the American states. If a spouse wants a divorce s/he must petition a court, allege a proper ground (often that the spouses have irreconcilable differences or that the marriage has irretrievably broken down), and prove the allegation through cogent evidence. Typically, the other spouse may respond to both the allegation and the proof, though the fact that one spouse objects is not in itself a ground for denying a petition for a no-fault divorce. To be sure, the process no longer requires a showing that one or the other party is at fault, although most states still permit an allegation of fault as a ground for divorce. Often, therefore, the process is not overtly adversarial, nor does it require a full-blown trial. But the process is not, in a simple sense, unilateral. Even so, it is easier to divorce than it was a half century ago, and the rate of divorce is much higher than it used to be. Many in the movement have argued that the frequency of divorce has debased marriage, converting it from an enduring sacred covenant, entered in the presence of God, into a terminable legal contract presided over by the state. Marriage, one writer urges, has been redefined as "a bundle of benefits granted by the state." This, says Jennifer Roback Morse, "means the end of marriage."[7]

To inhibit divorce, proponents of family values have devised a range of policy prescriptions. One is the option of covenant marriage, which the states of Louisiana, Arkansas, and Arizona have enacted. The covenant serves as a prescribed prenuptial agreement, which prospective spouses may enter into after a period of premarital counseling. The agreement, which is binding only in those states that recognize covenant marriage, commits the couple to dissolving the marriage only for certain reasons of fault—e.g., adultery, abuse, or conviction of a felony for which imprisonment is imposed—and even then only after undergoing additional counseling. The percentage of couples who have opted for covenant marriage in states that provide for it has been quite low (1 to 2 percent of all marriages).[8] Morse has proposed another device, not yet enacted in any state. She observes that women file the overwhelming majority (around 67 percent) of petitions for divorce in the United States. This was true in the nineteenth century, long before the appearance of no-fault divorce, and continues to be true today. In light of this persistent tendency, Morse wants to address "both public policies and the social climate that steer women to divorce." One policy that she has proposed is to alter the legal rules governing the custody of children. In short, she proposes a default rule that awards custody solely to the husband-father if the wife-mother is the petitioner. Given the affection that mothers tend to have for their children, Morse reckons that denying them custody of their children "would decrease the probability that the mother files for divorce by about half."[9]

Contraception, too, has drawn critical attention as a source for marriage's demise. From Robert George's deontological perspective, contraception interferes with the "natural" procreative purpose of sexual conjugation and of marriage. Viewed this way, contraception is simply wrong. But even from a utilitarian perspective, contraception might be considered problematic, for it can promote (or at least dis-inhibit) the practice of sex outside of marriage. It can do so because it diminishes the risk of certain consequences, especially the fear of pregnancy and sexually transmissible disease. As a result, it may lower the incentive to marry in the first place, even if fornication were to remain technically illegal. But, according to contraception's critics, contraception may also exert an insidious force within a marriage. For one thing, it short-circuits reproductive possibility and therefore diffuses the operation of the reproductive motive in a proper marriage. For another, by enabling spouses to have sex outside marriage with fewer inhibitions, lower bodily risks, and less chance of being caught, it weakens marital fidelity. This not only dissipates the sacred eroticism of marriage but also creates psychic (and real) opportunities for infidelity, which in turn provides incentives for divorce. The legality of abortion may work in similar but not identical ways, especially for unmarried women, though it is potentially less private than contraception and a more palpable threat to the generation of new life.[10]

For proponents of family values, the creation of new life is a moral imperative, rooted in the biblical injunction in Genesis to "be fruitful and multiply." According to some, this command bespeaks the intrinsic value of human life, a value that abortion transgresses. It also suggests a biological basis for the moral obligation running from the present generation to future generations. This natural obligation is the surest guarantee of human welfare, they say, as parents care for their children, and children eventually care for their parents. But concerns about reproduction in the present day go further than these sorts of moral considerations. They embrace also the survival of civilization itself.

On the one hand is a Malthusian worry about the quantity of reproduction. Actually, to say that the worry is Malthusian is in some ways misleading. As Harold James observes, Malthus argued that the central problem of societies was what appeared to be "a perpetual oscillation between happiness and misery." The root of this boom and bust was population, which in times of prosperity tended to increase exponentially, which in turn produced a struggle for scarce resources, a struggle that could be checked only by catastrophe (like famine or war) or by vicious methods (like infanticide or birth control).[11] What could check this cycle? Malthus considered several possibilities. Two keys were property and (especially) marriage, which could help sustain and limit population in societies both prosperous and poor. James argues, however, that "advanced industrial societies" seem to have learned aspects of Malthus's lesson only too well, for they are dramatically limiting the number of children who are brought into the world. One reason is that they have come to see the reproduction and maintenance of children strictly in terms of economic cost and opportunity, which compete with the happiness of the marital couple. Given the undeniable costs of raising children, combined with the socialization of the economic risks of old age in advanced societies, large numbers of people are electing to restrict reproduction. According to James, "We [in advanced western societies] are thus plunging into an opposite version of the trap that Malthus had attempted to predict." The result, he implies, could be catastrophic for civilized society.[12]

A second threat to civilization has to do with worries not merely about quantity, but about the quality of reproduction. The concern here is that too many children are being born and/or raised in circumstances that are less than optimal. Maggie Gallagher blogs and writes extensively on the importance of religion in society and on the "defense of marriage." She argues that the best home for raising children is a two-parent household in which the parents are married to each other, have a biological connection to the children, do not commit violence, exhibit only moderate conflict, and are religious. Because these homes are not violent or severely conflictual, such children will plainly be less likely to be victims of physical and sexual abuse. She says these homes also produce children who will tend to be less likely to drop out of school, abuse drugs or alcohol, suffer from mental health problems, commit crimes, commit domestic violence, or divorce. In short, children from happy, healthy, peaceful, stable homes will tend to develop into happier, healthier, more peaceable, and more stable persons than will children from miserable, unhealthy, violent, and unstable homes.[13] The rise of sub-optimal homes is socially significant because children from these homes are less likely to possess the character required for republican government, less likely to be self-sufficient, and more likely to sap the strength of the polity with material demands or even through incarceration. Republican society will be unable to reproduce itself. And civilized life will cease.[14]

Every one of the critiques of modernity takes the tenor of an apocalyptic struggle for good, a struggle that becomes all the more intense the closer analysis moves to same-sex marriage. Consider one of the most prolific scholarly proponents of family values: Lynn D. Wardle. Through the years, Professor Wardle has expressed concerns about many social and legal developments related to family, but one in particular that has captured his attention is same-sex marriage. He sees in recent moves to formalize recognition of same-sex relations a threat to civilization. In one essay, he invokes Moishe the Beadle, a Jew whose memory and experience Elie Wiesel recalls in *Night,* his bleak and dispiriting account of the Holocaust.[15] Moishe was captured by the Nazis and imprisoned in a concentration camp, but escaped. "Day after day, night after night, he went from one Jewish house to the next, telling his story" and the stories of others who had lost—who were losing—their lives in the camps. "But people not only refused to believe his tales, they refused to listen."[16] In his warnings against same-sex marriage, Professor Wardle likens himself to Moishe the Beadle. I'll not comment on this prophetic self-conception, on Wardle's identification with Moishe the Beadle, nor on his equation of same-sex marriage with the Holocaust, other than to say that each is evidence of just how fundamental opponents of same-sex marriage perceive their position to be.

THE BOOK

This book tests some of the claims of proponents of family values. It does so by examining aspects of the relations between family (or families) and the American constitutional order. I am not attempting, however, a comprehensive or exhaustive history of family in America. Nor do I want to present a systematic normative framework for resolving specific legal disputes among individual, family, and state. Instead I offer discrete glimpses into American familial households across time. I also look at the legal and constitutional norms that have aimed to govern those households and the lives within them. These glimpses will shed light on the relations between family and the constitutional state, and I believe they will also tell us something about the character of constitutional change more generally. Among the things that we'll learn is that relations between family and the constitutional state have been simultaneously sympathetic and antagonistic, depending partly on timing and partly on the form of family that's at issue. We'll see that law is not consistently effective in regulating relations between family and the constitutional order. And we'll see that, to the extent that law is effective, its effects are not always desirable—though much of the judgment about desirability depends on where one stands historically, socially, geographically, and ethically. The book unfolds as follows:

    Chapter 1 asks why people have long considered family, however it's defined, to be important. The answer, as we've seen in the discussion of family values, is that many people have seen it as basic to civilization. This term "civilization" is loaded, of course. The sources for the belief that family is constitutive of a civilized life are at least fourfold. (1) Family is woven into religious accounts not only of a proper life but also of the creation of the universe. These accounts are ideologically meaningful and practically potent. (2) People have also recognized that family has been a central institution in the evolution of human societies. Whether the story of evolution is one of descent, of progress, or simply of change, family has been at the center of the narrative. (3) Family is an arena in which power is exercised, in ways both visible and hidden. Power may be expressed through the accumulation of resources that are used in connection with (or against) the "outside world" and through the regulation of life within the household itself. (4) Finally, family is psychologically significant. It is one of the basic social forces in forming and maintaining human personality.

To make these points, however, is not to explain how or why family might be *constitutionally* significant or even a proper subject for law within the American order. Chapter 2 begins to explain. It traces the origins of the American law of family to the English common law, broadly conceived. The law of England provided a normative template for one traditional view of family. It established and defined status relations within the household. One of these—master and servant— may seem jarring to our eyes, but its legal presence demonstrated the ways in which the familial household was a basic unit of economic production. Other statuses are less jarring: husband and wife, parent and child, and guardian and ward. Each of these statuses entailed specific duties and entitlements, which English law recognized and sometimes enforced. Embedded in these duties and entitlements were assumptions about both gender and class, assumptions so potent that we may fairly call them constitutive. One of the most important areas of legal regulation involved norms surrounding marriage—who could marry whom, what formalities they had to comply with, what privileges and obligations spouses owed each other, and how and why a marriage could be dissolved. Among the benefits (and burdens) of marriage was sex. Technically, sexual acts outside marriage were prohibited. The prohibition was more lax for men than for women, but even for women enforcement was inconsistent. Still the norm remained, in part to be used (when it was used) as a tool for social order and control. Another aspect of social control involved law's linkage of family to property, especially land. The link was apt not only because most land was held in familial households, but also because English rules were peculiarly preoccupied with the intergenerational transfer of wealth (mainly to male children). Chapter 2 describes these aspects of English law in some detail and shows how they were rationalized to maintain a particular kind of patriarchal social order.

The order to be maintained was not merely social but political, too. In fact, familial norms came to a head in the Crown. For one thing, norms of status, sex, property, and inheritance provided guidance for royal succession and governed relations with and within the "royal family." For another, family was a metaphor for political authority generally and the status of the Crown specifically. The metaphor began to lose its resonance, however, in colonial North America. This is not to imply that the metaphor wasn't strained already, even in England. John Locke, for example, had reconceived the relation between family and political authority in the latter half of the seventeenth century. But by the time of the colonial secession from Britain, social conditions and political aspirations in the colonies made traditional English uses of family as a template for politics increasingly incongruous. Three social conditions, occurring largely outside the normative bounds that law prescribed, helped to undermine English uses and to reinforce an ideology of republicanism as it emerged in the colonies: relative class-based equality, modest movement in the direction of equality of gender, and, relevant to both, the increasingly frequent practice of exit from established households. Chapter 3 shows how these changes supplied ammunition for a rhetorical assault on the "mother country" and for creating a new constitutional order. Reflecting these changes, the text of the Constitution contained some provisions designed to stifle the emergence of aristocratic familial forms. And, according to John Jay, part of the reason for the Constitution's new and complex institutional design was to thwart the rise of dynasties and inhibit familial self-dealing, corruption, and aggrandizement in and through government. Some founders hinted, weakly, that families—or a particular social order more generally—might reinforce the status of states vis-à-vis the national government. Although these considerations weren't trivial, they tended to demonstrate just how far the United States had moved away from the ancient notion that polity was built on family.

Still, the Constitution acknowledged and even entrenched one particular form of family: the slaveholding household. To be sure, slavery didn't square neatly with republican values, as it tended to be brutish, despotic, and hierarchical. Even some defenders referred to it as "peculiar."[17] Still, it was legally protected, and, for decades after the constitutional founding, slaveholding households were present in every region of the country. Besides, if it was inconsistent with republicanism, slavery was compatible with other values in the constitutional order. One, as we'll see also in Chapter 5, was patriarchy. Another was the Aristotelian view of the (slaveholding) family as the basic unit of economic production. A third was that the legal regulation of slavery was a device for maintaining and securing a racialist social order, for enforcing formally a view of "the proper status of the Negro in our form of civilization."[18] Chapter 4 describes the slaveholding household, how it fit within the American order, and how slaves carved out forms of family despite the fact that law inhibited them from doing so. The chapter also shows that, despite the nation's constitutional commitment to slavery, the political structure that dispersed the bulk of regulatory authority among the several states ironically became a device for slavery's concentration in the southern region and hence for its gradual marginalization in the country. This geographic division presaged a political and constitutional conflict, which erupted in the form of civil war. That war was waged over competing forms of family. Chapter 4 closes with a discussion of the post–Civil War regulation and prohibition of interracial sex and marriage, even after the Constitution was amended to prohibit slavery and to provide basic rights to all persons whatever their race.

Many of the social changes that had made republican ideology seem sensible in the Revolutionary era occurred beyond the cover of law. Still, family was in important respects a legal creature in the colonies. It was certainly so after the constitutional founding. But, slavery aside, family was largely invisible as a constitutional matter after the founding. One possible reason was that family simply went without saying as a basic social institution. Despite its variations and the changes it had undergone in North America, family was, in various forms and fashions, a presumed part of the social order. Another reason was that the regulation of family fell mainly within the province of the states. This was so even before the Tenth Amendment confirmed the alleged "truism" (we would later be told) that the states reserved those governmental powers that the Constitution hadn't assigned to the nation. As states' regulations unfolded, a version of an old idea surfaced, invigorated, in American law: patriarchy. Its appearance demonstrated that all was not liberty and equality within the American marital family, regardless of what the social prerequisites and the rhetorical point of the Declaration of Independence had been. One way in which law insinuated itself into marital families was its active prescription of gendered roles. It did so in several ways, including but not limited to the common law's disabling doctrine of coverture. Even after the death of a husband, however, a widow's legal disabilities could persist, enforced partly through a variety of legal norms and institutions and partly through formal and informal restrictions on women's access to gainful employment. Though law permitted separation or divorce, statutes imposed barriers to exit. For a variety of reasons, these barriers tended to be felt more keenly by women than by men. Backed by cultural expectations, then, law played a powerful role in reinforcing gender. And gendered families helped maintain the patriarchal republican order.

One reason for the geographic isolation of slavery was a competing form of family—white, nuclear, and largely agrarian—which was the nation's vanguard for settling the western frontier. As Chapter 5 demonstrates, families that participated in westward migration performed ambivalent legal and constitutional functions. On the one hand, migratory families functioned as institutions for extending and maintaining the dominion of the United States across the continent, self-consciously carrying with them a kind of civilization. At the same time, they challenged two important values of the order. First, they resisted the western expansion of slavery. Often, this resistance was for reasons not of high-minded morality, but of material self-interest. Second, they challenged the gendered roles that law prescribed everywhere else in the country. The reasons these families could challenge these roles were complicated, but one prominent reason was the relative weakness of legal norms and institutions on the frontier. This weakness, combined with the relative isolation of migratory households, provided greater degrees of freedom in the forms that households took. For example, same-sex households—some covert, some not—appeared with surprising frequency in the

West. Even within nuclear heterosexual households, formal marriage wasn't always required. In fact, complying with formalities was sometimes impossible, as legally designated authorities were rarities in some places. Still another reason for the practical challenge to gendered roles on the frontier emerged from the privation that households faced there. In short, necessity often required that men's and women's roles be negotiated within the family, instead of comporting with legal norms or cultural expectations. Negotiation in turn promoted a semblance of equality. As law, government, and civilization took hold in the West, women's equality contracted there, but it did not disappear. Eventually, an egalitarian sensibility would make its way eastward, with effects both subtle and substantial.

For many years after the constitutional founding, the nation did not decisively take sides in the competition between slaveholding families and white nuclear families on the frontier. Very early in American history, however, the nation did assert a plain preference in dealing with another familial form—that of the native tribes. Chapter 6 investigates American policy toward native families. From the perspective of the constitutional order, the tribes presented more than one problem. First, they were an impediment to the sort of continental dominion that the nation increasingly saw as its destiny. In short, they were in the way. Second, the tribes had odd notions of property. To put it differently, they had no conception of "private" property, at least not in land. Instead, their approach to land was simultaneously fluid (especially for nomadic tribes) and communistic. This actually made it easier for the constitutional order to seize tribal lands, as there was no messy legal title to consider; ironically, however, tribal lands were more difficult to regulate after tribes were placed on legally prescribed reservations, as title to communal land was not easily alienable. Finally, and most directly relevant to my study, familial forms and practices of whites were unfamiliar to many tribes. Relationships within a tribe tended to be consanguine, not nuclear, and matrilineal, not predominately patriarchal. Divorce was easy. And sexual mores were more permissive than were European-American norms. How to deal with the tribes? National policy took roughly three forms until the end of the nineteenth century. The first was pacification, which the order achieved through treaties or through conquest. The second was to remove and/or confine the tribes on discrete tracts of reserved land. The third was to assert direct national control over the education of children of the tribes. The explicit aim of this third policy was civilization, within two particular senses of the word. It aimed to dismantle tribal associations and property and to replace them with bourgeois nuclear families living on alienable parcels. And it aimed to transform children of the tribes into children of the nation-state, to instill in them a new, particular civic personality. To achieve the first, the nation employed the policy of "allotment." To achieve the latter, the nation interceded directly between Indian children and their families to impose an aggressive policy of native education. This was the first systematic effort by the American national government to provide education for children. And it became in some ways a model for general state-sponsored programs of education that arose in the late nineteenth and early twentieth centuries. As the chapter will show, the consequences for constitutionalism were mixed.

Native households were not the only familial units to face extensive legal regulation in the nineteenth century. Chapters 7 and 8 consider two familial types that found themselves at odds with an increasingly muscular use of law: communalist and polygamous families. Both of these types tended to be religiously motivated offshoots of Protestant Christianity, subject to strong charismatic leaders, with roots in New England. What they also shared—not only with each other but also with the interracial unions discussed in Chapter 4—was that they became objects of a particular moral concern: who was having sex with whom. Chapter 7 and especially Chapter 8 show how a growing preoccupation with sex and sexuality, combined with a heightened sense of what counted as a normal family motivated coercive legal regulation of these uncommon families.

The normalized family received a constitutional stamp of approval in the early twentieth century in two notable decisions of the Supreme Court: *Meyer v. Nebraska* and *Pierce v. Society of Sisters*. It's a popular conception that these decisions marked the beginning of the Court's foray into the business of constitutionalizing aspects of the law of family. In fact, as the opening section of Chapter 1 suggests and the discussion of polygamy in Chapter 8 illustrates, the Court had long been deciding cases that developed and applied an American law of family. Chapter 9 discusses the emergence and evolution of a familial jurisprudence as applied to disputes over property, inheritance, work, reproduction, the status of women, the status of children (including illegitimates), the regulation of sex and sexuality, and the legal limits to and constitutional significance of marriage. Here we return to the discussion of family values with which this Introduction began. Chapter 9 observes that, prior to the 1960s, families in America had not been undisturbed for centuries but had continually been changing, sometimes in significant ways. At times, changes occurred through law. More frequently, they occurred outside legal norms or even against them. What's more, the legal rules pertaining to family had themselves changed well before the 1960s. Consider, for example, the rules pertaining to inheritance, bastardy, adoption, and divorce. To be sure, some ancient rules persisted in some places, rules like prohibitions of interracial marriage, the prohibition against the use of contraception, and cultural and legal impediments to women's access to a full range of employment outside the home. Chapter 9 shows how the Supreme Court's decisions bore on these norms and practices. The chapter argues that, to the extent that the lives of families changed in the latter half of the twentieth century, the Court's decisions were not the sole cause of change. For those decisions were responding to—and in many cases consolidating—antecedent cultural, political, economic, ethical, and technological changes in society. These social changes were not primarily the products of a moral (nor an amoral) revolution in the 1960s, but were consistent with institutions and values to which the American constitutional order was long committed as a matter of principle.

The book's Conclusion returns to another theme drawn from the discussion of family values: the meanings of marriage. This chapter focuses on same-sex marriage, which is plainly the most contentious issue in current battles over family. It considers the development of same-sex marriage as a political and legal issue in our time. Although doctrinal and logical props for holding same-sex marriage to be a constitutional right have been present for some time, it may well be that, if there is to be a secure foundation for same-sex marriage, it will be laid not through constitutional law, but through the gradual accretion of change in law writ small and in a constitutional culture that is partially autonomous from law.

The Epilogue takes up the holding and reasoning of two cases that the Supreme Court decided at the end of the October 2012 term: *United States v. Windsor* (involving the constitutionality of a provision of the federal Defense of Marriage Act) and *Hollingsworth v. Perry* (involving a challenge to California's prohibition of same-sex marriage). This final chapter considers the implications of those decisions for the future of same-sex marriage and for constitutional change.

1
Family and Civilization

THE AMERICAN CONSTITUTIONAL ORDER

David and Lydia Maynard were married in Vermont in 1828. They had two children. In 1850, the Maynards moved to Ohio. From there, David departed, bound, he said, for California. He promised to send his wife money for support during his absence and vowed that, once he was settled, he would return or send for the family. He never sent the promised support; nor did he return or send for his wife and children; nor did he go to California. Instead, he moved to the Oregon Territory, settled on a homestead (claiming the tract as a married man), and petitioned the territorial legislature *ex parte* for a divorce from Lydia. The legislature granted the divorce. Twenty-four days later, David married Catherine Brashears. After residing on the tract for the requisite four years, he petitioned the United States to have title vested in him. (In his petition, he apparently swore falsely that his first wife had died.) The petition granted, David continued to live on the tract with Catherine until he died intestate in 1873, leaving no children from the second marriage. As sometimes happens, the death of a familial relative incited competition for his worldly possessions. Lydia and the children challenged the validity of David's divorce and contested Catherine's title to the land. The first family lost at trial and again on appeal to the territorial supreme court. It lost a third time before the Supreme Court of the United States, but not before the Court pronounced the marital family to be "a relation the most important, as affecting the happiness of individuals, the first step from barbarism to incipient civilization, the purest tie of social life, and the true basis of human progress."[1]

The irony of this pronouncement was apparently lost on the Court. It is tempting, therefore, to dismiss the Court's celebration of marriage as a cynical flourish designed to give the impression that the Court was defending an institution or value that it was actually undercutting. There's much to support this temptation, but let's not give in to it now. It might also be tempting to dismiss the Court's paean to family, not as cynical or hypocritical, but as a quaint anachronism, sincerely expressing nostalgic longing for a bygone era. Here, too, there might be reason for such a view. Even so, the Court has repeated encomiums to family across the centuries, in a diversity of contexts, among an array of otherwise incompatible justices.

One pivotal later decision was *Griswold v. Connecticut,* which addressed the constitutionality of a state's policy prohibiting use of certain contraceptives. In the climactic paragraph of his opinion for the court, Justice William O. Douglas located a right to contraception, not in the individual, but in the marital family:

> We deal with a right of privacy older than the Bill of Rights—older than our political parties, older than our school system. Marriage is a coming together for better or for worse, hopefully enduring, and intimate to the degree of being sacred. It is an association that promotes a way of life, not causes; a harmony in living, not political faiths; a bilateral loyalty, not commercial or social projects. Yet it is an association for as noble a purpose as any involved in our prior decisions.[2]

In short, the marital relation is constitutionally protected because it is private, it is old, it is sacred, and it is noble and enduring.

Lovely as these sentiments may be, we should not take them at face value. First, if the relationship is private, it is also subject to regulation by law—no less so now than ever in the past. Traditionally in the United States, regulation was almost exclusively the province of the states. Over time, the marital relation has become subject to legal regulation—direct and indirect—from other sources, including national legislative enactments, national administrative norms, even international law. Hence, as lots of scholars have observed, law permeates the relationships that constitute marriage. Second, it is true that the marital family is old, even ancient, if not prehistoric. But, if it is old, it has also been changing. The changes have occurred since families first appeared in human experience. Some changes may have been random. Others have been adaptations to various geographic, social, political, technological, and economic conditions. Thus, if family is old, specific elements of the lives of families are variable. Third, many people do view family, especially the marital family, as a sacred relationship, of divine provenance and subject to divine ordinance. There is an alternative view: that marriage is a civil relationship, sanctioned by and governed under civil law (if not private ordering). Frequently, the sacred view does not compete with the civil or private view of marriage. In fact, governments in the United States have taken numerous steps to ensure that civil law does not collide with religious commitment. And various religions have adapted to prevailing views embodied in civil law. But conflicts between the two views—between secular and sectarian domains—have arisen and show little sign of abating. Fourth, there are important ways in which family does embody what we might take to be noble purposes. As Douglas put it, familial relations can promote bilateral loyalty (even multilateral, if children or extended relations are a part), a way of life, and a harmony or self-sacrifice in living that life. But there is also a darker side to family, less noble by our lights. Sometimes family is a locus for control, manipulation, even violence. Sometimes it instills values that many people abhor. Sometimes it sacrifices children to parental neglect or abuse. And sometimes particular relationships are not enduring but temporary. Thus, if families exhibit something of human beings at their best by our lights, they also reveal people at their worst.

In sum, while Douglas's celebration may be inspiring, it is an insufficient explanation for why an important organ of the nation would attribute to a particular form of family a status entitling it to exemption from a general, authoritative policy of government. What, then, might account for the ostensible constitutional status of family, apart from the fact that the Supreme Court has proclaimed it or that family is an institution widely used and sometimes liked? Why, moreover, is it the *marital* family that is constitutionally significant?

The standard interpretive sources and methods of the constitutional lawyer provide only modest help for answering these questions. As we'll see, the text that calls itself the Constitution is largely silent about family.[3] This did not prevent Justice John Marshall Harlan II from creatively locating a right of marital privacy in the Third and Fourth Amendments, among other sources.[4] Justice Douglas in *Griswold* augmented Harlan's analysis, discerning general protections in "penumbras" and "emanations" issuing from the "specific guarantees in the Bill of Rights." On Douglas's reading, the First Amendment's right of assembly connotes association, including intimate associations, one of which is marital family; and the Third Amendment's prohibition of quartering soldiers in time of peace, the Fourth Amendment's prohibition of unreasonable searches and seizures, and the Fifth Amendment's self-incrimination clause all presuppose "the sanctity of a man's home," which might house not only "a man" but a family as well.[5] Text aside, we'll see that intentions of framers or "original meanings" may have interesting things to say about family. But they are conflictual, and the evidence for any particular intention or meaning in this context can be thin. Common law also has something to offer and has the advantage of being thicker than intentions and original meanings, though it, too, may cut in different directions.[6] Other possible sources include tradition,[7] principles distilled from doctrine,[8] structure,[9] "spirit" or purpose,[10] contemporary ethos,[11] norms of civilized nations,[12] and natural law (or right).[13]

We'll see signs of these sources and methods in this book. It's not my aim, however, to explore them systematically, for my purpose is not primarily doctrinal. I want instead to take a different approach to the question of constitutional status—an approach that borrows from the family values movement. I want to focus on three general aspects of the functional relationship between family (or families) and the constitutional order. (1) How has family participated (or how might it participate) in creating, maintaining, or changing the constitutional order? (2) How has the order tried (or how might it try) to shape or use family? (3) How effective has law been (or can it be) in achieving either? For the purposes of this study, I'm interested in family both as an institution and as a political, social, and legal idea. To approach the subject in this way requires moving outside the domain of conventional legal analysis. To be sure, we can't (and won't) ignore the legal, especially in light of the third question I've just offered. But the constitutive relations between family and the constitutional state are not merely matters of law. They are also about basic values, human needs, social practices, and institutional design.

FOUR FRAMES

To illustrate this fact, consider four elemental conceptual frames—religion, social evolution, power, and human psychology—each of which touches on the justifications Justice Douglas offered for constitutionalizing family. Religion deals in realms of sacred values and of people's attempts to understanding the origin of and purposes for human existence. Through social evolution, we can see family as a basic human institution that has both endured and changed across the millennia. Through the lens of power, one can see family as a site for the exercise of control, not only between members and the outside world but also within the family itself. Through psychology, we might appreciate family's role in forming the human psyche and influencing the expression of human personality.

Plainly, there's more than one version of each of these frames. In fact, there are competing versions. To complicate further, the frames themselves are not mutually exclusive, as one or more iterations of one frame may be compatible with a version of another. For now, however, I'll treat each frame as distinct. In doing so, I make no claim to comprehensiveness. Nor do I aim to fill in subtle details. For the present, I'll merely sketch outlines. We'll see, throughout the account that follows, their relevance to the constitutional status of family.

Religion

Among almost all traditions that are recognizably religious, some form of family is primal. It is primal in at least three senses: it was present either from creation or from the beginning of self-conscious human experience; it is of fundamental social importance; and it is an expression of what human beings are to be if fulfilled. To put the point more sharply, family is part of divine order. An aspect of this point appears in the Hindu account of creation, in which the original divinity became a divided self, whose gendered halves united to make a new whole self, free from fear and loneliness.

In the Beginning the (world) was only the self, in the shape of a person. Looking around he saw nothing else than the self. He first said, "I am." . . . He was afraid. . . . This one then thought to himself, "since there is nothing else than myself, of what am I afraid?" Thereupon his fear, verily, passed away, for, of what should he have been afraid? Assuredly, it is from a second that fear arises. He, verily, had no delight. Therefore he who is alone has no delight. He desired a second. He became as large as a woman and a man in close embrace. He caused that self to fall into two parts. From that arose husband and wife. Therefore, . . . this (body) is one half of oneself, like one of the two halves of a split pea. Therefore this space is filled by a wife. He became united with her. From that human beings were produced.[14]

Here we have a psycho-sexual story of the beginning of the world. Divine loneliness incited duality. Duality became sexualized. Through sex, came (re-)union. And this union was the source for all humanity.

More familiar to most Americans are the two Judaic accounts of creation in Genesis. The first emphasized the sexual unity that is the basis for procreation:

Then God said, "Let us make humankind in our image, according to our likeness. . . . " So God created humankind in his image, in the image of God he created them; male and female he created them. God blessed them, and God said to them, "Be fruitful and multiply, and fill the earth and subdue it."[15]

The second account stressed the twin themes of loneliness and companionship that we saw in the Upaniṣad:

In the day that the Lord God made the earth and the heavens, . . . then the Lord God formed man from the dust of the ground, and breathed into his nostrils the breath of life; and the man became a living being. . . .

Then the Lord God said, "It is not good that the man should be alone, I will make him a helper as his partner." . . . So the Lord God caused a deep sleep to fall upon the man, and he slept; then he took one of his ribs and closed up its place with flesh. And the rib that the Lord God had taken from the man he made into a woman and brought her to the man. Then the man said, "This at last is bone of my bones and flesh of my flesh; this one shall be called Woman, for out of Man this one was taken." Therefore a man leaves his father and his mother and clings to his wife, and they become one flesh.[16]

Three of the Ten Commandments to the people of Israel reinforced the constitutive character of family: "Honor your father and mother, so that your days may be long in the land that the Lord your God is giving you. . . . You shall not commit adultery. . . . You shall not covet your neighbor's house; you shall not covet your neighbor's wife, or male or female slave, or ox, or donkey, or anything that belongs to your neighbor."[17] The Mosaic laws also spoke to familial matters, defining through prohibitions the contours of permissible sexual relations: prohibiting bestiality, homosexual relations, many forms of incest (specifying prohibited degrees of biological and social kinship), and sex with a woman who is menstruating.[18] Polygamy, of course, was not a sin in the days of the Patriarchs, but became problematic as social complexity increased, especially as the social and economic significance of property and inheritance expanded.[19]

Christianity's break from Judaism produced doctrinal changes—from subtle to profound—in several directions. According to scripture, Jesus's teaching on adultery was even stricter than Judaic law:

> You have heard that it was said, "You shall not commit adultery." But I say to you that everyone who looks at a woman with lust has already committed adultery with her in his heart. If your right eye causes you to sin, tear it out and throw it away; it is better for you to lose one of your members than for your whole body to be thrown into hell. And if your right hand causes you to sin, cut it off and throw it away; it is better for you to lose one of your members than for your whole body to go into hell.
>
> It was also said, "Whoever divorces his wife, let him give her a certificate of divorce." But I say to you that anyone who divorces his wife, except on the ground of unchastity, causes her to commit adultery; and whoever marries a divorced woman commits adultery.[20]

If his rules were stricter, however, Jesus's regime for enforcement tempered the Judaic law of his day:

> The scribes and the Pharisees brought a woman who had been caught in adultery; and making her stand before all of them, they said to him, "Teacher, this woman was caught in the very act of committing adultery. Now in the law Moses commanded us to stone such women. Now what do you say?" . . . When they kept on questioning him, he straightened up and said to them "Let anyone among you who is without sin be the first to throw a stone at her."[21]

The apostle Paul's gloss on Jesus's teaching promoted marriage neither for procreation nor to assuage loneliness, but to fortify believers against "sexual immorality." "The husband should give to his wife her conjugal rights, and likewise the wife to her husband. . . . Do not deprive one another except perhaps by agreement for a set time, to devote yourselves to prayer, and then come together again, so that Satan may not tempt you because of your lack of self-control." The ideal life, said Paul, was one of solitude. But those "who are not practicing self-control . . . should marry. For it is better to marry than to be aflame with passion." To those who were married, Paul reiterated Jesus's exhortation against divorce.[22]

Ancient Judaic law sometimes spoke of the wife as if she were the property of the husband. Christian scripture mitigated the severity of this treatment but did not dissolve hierarchy. At one point, Paul flirted with an egalitarian notion of mutual ownership: "The wife does not have authority over her own body, but the husband does; likewise the husband does not have authority over his own body, but the wife does."[23] Elsewhere, however, he reinstated hierarchy: "Wives, be subject to your husbands as you are to the Lord. For the husband is the head of the wife just as Christ is the head of the church, the body of which he is the Savior. Just as the church is subject to Christ, so also wives ought to be, in everything, to their husbands." To similar effect were the commandments "Children, obey your parents in the Lord" and "Slaves, obey your earthly masters with fear and trembling . . . as you obey Christ."[24]

Islam both grew out of and helped create its own distinctive social milieux. The Qur'ān retained (but simplified) Levitican prohibitions against incest (again defined in both biological and social terms) and against sexual relations with a woman married to another. It permitted polygamy.[25] At the same time, Islam exhorted believers to sexual restraint. Men were to "lower their gaze and restrain their sexual passions." Women were subject to the same exhortations, plus another: that they cover "their adornment" except to specified members of the family or household.[26] This difference alone need not have entailed hierarchy between the sexes. But, like Judaism and Christianity, Islam did enforce such hierarchy: "Men are the maintainers of women. . . . So the good women are obedient, guarding the unseen as Allah has guarded."[27] Against Christian doctrine, however, the availability of divorce to men and women on equal terms abated hierarchy, at least as a matter of doctrine.[28]

Islamic, Judaic, and Christian scripture agree on certain matters related to family: marriage is good (to avoid loneliness, to promote procreation, and to resist the slide to sexual sin); adultery is bad (especially for women); the regulation of marriage and family is, in important ways, about the regulation of sex; some forms of sex (incest, bestiality, and homosexuality) are dangerous or evil; and masculine supremacy is proper. If they agree on these general matters, however, they disagree on others: the permissibility of multiple marital partners (for men); the permissibility of and grounds for divorce; and, perhaps, the solicitude we owe to children.[29]

Social Evolution

One way of understanding the view(s) from religion is that family's form and functions are timeless. Family was divinely ordained from the beginning of the world. And so it should ever be. On the surface, this way of thinking conflicts with a range of approaches that I characterize as evolutionary. At the heart of evolutionary approaches is the idea that human institutions are neither timeless nor static but continually changing, sometimes fundamentally.

In truth, an evolutionary approach need not be incompatible with a religious approach. Georg Hegel, for example, argued that human history revealed an inexorable progression toward the realization of "Spirit." In Hegelian terms, we might think of this Spirit as the ethical purpose for human existence and action in the world or as the sort of mental activity reflecting intelligence and will.[30] This Spirit had a manifestation that was subjective, individualist, or particularist and a manifestation that was social, communitarian, or universalist.[31] One institutional representation of the first manifestation was the family, in which a person comes to "self-consciousness of one's individuality" and hence comes into an immediate, particular aspect of an ethical life.[32] The institutional representation of the second manifestation was the state, which was the highest form of "the ethical Idea."[33] The substance of Spirit was reason, which was, in a sense, divine.[34]

The moving force of history, according to Hegel, was the dialectical tension between Spirit and reality, or alternatively the universal and the particular. This dialectic engendered dynamic movement: the tension grows into a contradiction; this contradiction incites a dissolution, which entails the creation of a new order; this new order in turn generates and falls victim to its own contradiction. So history unfolds until human subjectivity and community fully express reason.[35]

As I suggested above, this particular evolutionary approach is compatible with the central aim of most religions: establishing and maintaining a human society that reflects divinity. Two intellectual developments, however, both in the nineteenth century, decisively disconnected evolution from religion. One came from Charles Darwin, who reworked the evolutionary model in at least three ways. First, he focused on biology, not ethics. Put differently, his concern was not the ethical life but life itself. Second, he rejected Hegel's simplistic dialectic in favor of a complex process involving the natural selection of biological forms for survival or extinction. Third, this process was not self-conscious; nor did it aim at the expression of reason through either the state or some other institutional form. It was propelled instead by an innate drive in all species to reproduce.[36]

The second development came from Karl Marx and Friedrich Engels. Unlike Darwin, they found Hegel's dialectical teleology attractive as a historiographic method. They parted company with Hegel, however, over his spiritual explanation for the trajectory of history. Marx and Engels materialized history, in the direction not of biology but of political economy (emphasis on *economy*). In short, history was a story of the progressive emergence of new modes of production: each mode generated its own antithesis, which, at a critical juncture, produced a new mode that synthesized the antinomy of the former.[37]

As the base and structure of economy have changed, said Marx and Engels, so too has family, the former changes driving the latter.[38] Of course, the view that material economy is the most important independent variable driving the form, function, and social regulation of family (or, more narrowly, sexual relations) is not strictly Marxist; for it is shared in our own time by mainstream scholars who work from economic assumptions.[39] Indeed, it is part of the conceptual foundation for all capitalist economies. But Marx and Engels were an important source for this scholarship, just as classical scholarship in economy was the source for the Marxist gloss. In their more polemical moments, they argued that capitalism had destroyed family, at least among a particular class: "On what foundation is the present family, the bourgeois family based? On capital, on private gain. In its completely developed form this family exists only among the bourgeoisie. But this state of things finds its complement in the practical absence of the family among the proletarians, and in public prostitution." In a sense, however, even the bourgeois family was something of a fraud: "Our bourgeois, not content with having the wives and daughters of their proletarians at their disposal, not to speak of common prostitutes, take the greatest pleasure in seducing each other's wives. Bourgeois marriage is in reality a system of wives in common and thus, at the most, what the Communists might possibly be reproached with, is that they desire to introduce, in substitution for a hypocritically concealed, an openly legalized community of women." On this view, family is neither sacred nor timeless. Nor, for that matter, will it persist as we know it. The *Manifesto* predicted that "the bourgeois family will vanish as a matter of course when its complement [the proletarian family] vanishes, and both will vanish with the vanishing of capital."[40]

Left to his own voice, Engels deepened (and modified) the *Manifesto*'s empirical analysis, moderated its prophesy, and noted an affinity between the Darwinian-biologic and Marxist-economic positions. He argued that prehistoric human societies had evolved through three distinct stages—primitive society, savagery, and barbarism—each of which was marked by a distinct form of family. The primary engine for change from one stage to another was natural selection. The engine itself changed, however, in the transition from the third stage (barbarism) to the fourth: civilization. The stage of civilization commenced recorded human history, and its predominant new form of family was heterosexual monogamy. Beginning with the transition to civilization, the new engine of social change was economic.[41]

Though monogamous, marriage in ancient and medieval times was not a relationship of what Engels called "sex love." That is, it was not entered into because of mutual attraction between willing partners. It was instead a duty, whose content and performance were dictated by parents (and/or by extended family). The aim of marriage, on this view, was promote "family interests," which were always material and, in the middle ages at least, political. This is not to say that sex love did not exist in these times. Where it did exist, however, was not in marriage (except by accident), but in adultery.[42]

This changed, Engels argued, with the concomitant rise (in Europe) of Protestantism and capitalism. The system of capitalist production "dissolved all inherited and traditional relationships, and in place of time-honored custom and historic right, it set up . . . 'free' contract." This system of contract, however, presupposed "free" and "equal" individuals, possessing "complete freedom of will." These characteristics, necessary for the economy, migrated also to marriage. In Henry Maine's adaptation of Marxist insight, the marital relationship moved from "from Status to Contract." Or, as Engels put it, marriage moved "from [an] inherited to [a] freely contracted condition" that was shared (in principle) by man and woman alike. The difficulty, Engels noted, was that the principle of equality, if not the image of contract itself, failed, at least among "the ruling class." It did so for three reasons. First, prospective partners were preoccupied with "the familiar economic influences." These influences provided an illicit motivation for the decision to marry and tainted the relationship that followed from the decision, rendering both unnatural. Second, bourgeois marriage perpetuated masculine superiority. It did so through violence against women, through laws disenfranchising them and dispossessing them of property, and through practices barring them from gainful economic activity. Third, by perpetuating and tolerating prostitution, capitalism promoted the commodification of sex.[43]

"Full freedom of marriage," said Engels, is possible only after "the abolition of capitalist production and of the property relations created by it." But what will this full freedom look like? In one voice, Engels suggested that it will be the complete realization of monogamy, as the abolition of capital and property will have "all the accompanying economic considerations which still exert such a powerful influence on the choice of a marriage partner. For then there is no other motive left except mutual inclination." In another voice, he suggested that the "transfer of the means of production into common ownership," combined with the socialization of "private housekeeping" and "the care and education of children, legitimate or not," will precipitate the demise of the single family, which in turn will permit "the complete equality of the sexes" and "the gradual growth of unconstrained sexual intercourse." In the end, however, he conceded with yet a third voice that "it is impossible to predict the nature of [the] successor" to the monogamous family.[44]

Joseph Schumpeter, a pro-capitalist economic theorist sitting squarely in the twentieth century, came to the relation between family and economy from an opposing direction. His premise was that a robust and successful industrial capitalism was built on a robust, successful bourgeois family. There was a time, he says, during the heroic age of capitalism, when families of capitalists took a certain form: they had lots of children, which motivated patriarchs to build substantial estates, which in turn motivated them to preserve those estates for the benefit of their offspring, which inclined them to save for the future, which required their preserving their marriages, to better facilitate the intergenerational transfer of wealth. These characteristics of family helped sustain capitalism because they provided the means and motives for increasing wealth via enterprise. The heroic age of capitalism was the dynastic age of capitalism. The heroic age was marked by intense competition, a tradition of familial ownership of the means of production, and the political and social leadership of the bourgeoisie. But, said Schumpeter, those qualities are dissolving. Why? In true Marxist mode, if not for Marxist purposes, Schumpeter posited that capitalism has produced conditions that are undermining capitalism.[45]

In his view, the motivation that once drove capitalism is threatened both from within the firm and from without. From within, capitalism has produced the modern businessman, who has the psychology of a salaried employee in a bureaucratic organization. From without, the bourgeois family, which was an institutional prerequisite to the heroic age, is declining. The upshot is that family life and parenthood are less powerful molders of behavior than they once had been. The reason for this decline comes from capitalism itself. The utilitarian lessons of capitalism have led people to weigh the benefits and costs of any course of action. They soon realize what a burden family and parenthood are, under modern conditions, and what an attractive and varied life they give up in parenthood. They also realize that, except in peasant societies, children are no longer economic assets. This utilitarian calculus ignores the true benefits of parenthood: its contribution to psychic "normality" and its connection to "the hidden necessities of human nature or of the social organism." Thus, people turn their backs to the traditional value of family. At the same time, capitalist production creates new tastes and possible ways of life. To reinforce childlessness, it produces contraceptives. To promote an alternative style of life, it provides alternatives to the bourgeois family home. The spacious, comfortable, dignified family home—capable of supporting a family—is no longer economical. It is therefore being replaced by smaller, more functional homes, or even apartments, that meet necessaries but little more. This in turn imposes an architectural motive for avoiding parenthood. People have come increasingly to realize that they can live more cheaply and comfortably without large families.[46]

Because entrepreneurial capitalism of the heroic age was driven by the man who was motivated to productivity, to the generation of wealth, and to saving for wife and children, this heroic man took the longer and larger view of things. He worked for the future, even if he himself did not live to see the fruit of his effort. He worked, not to consume but to accumulate. This ethic of saving and sacrifice is not the ethic of the modern economic man of utilitarian individualism. Today's individualist bourgeoisie is a consumer who drifts with anti-savings theories and short-run philosophies. Because his life no longer exemplifies the logic that animated the rise of capitalism, he no longer has a practical reason for keeping faith with capitalism's underlying creed. In short, he doesn't really care, as long as he is kept modestly secure in his insular, nonfamilial world.[47]

Recently, one can see approaches to law and evolution that are more directly Darwinian. Witness, for example, the rise of "law and biology" in American law schools.[48] Perhaps surprisingly, it's possible to see echoes of an evolutionary analysis among proponents of family values. Borrowing from Darwin, family is important precisely because (or to the extent that) it is linked to reproduction, which is necessary for the survival of the species we call human. Thus, one way to explain the appearance of family, and specifically marriage, among human beings is that it was evolutionarily advantageous. On this view, family was advantageous because it permitted a generation of children to survive to adulthood, which in turn would permit them to reproduce. Understandably, proponents of family values have not stopped with mere survival as a species-related good. They have also emphasized a connection between the marital family and the ability of societies (and their members) to flourish. As Justice Robert J. Cordy put it in his dissent in *Goodridge v. Department of Public Health,* "the institution of marriage has systematically provided for the regulation of heterosexual behavior, brought order to the resulting procreation, and ensured a stable family structure in which children will be reared, educated, and socialized. . . . An orderly society requires some mechanism for coping with the fact that sexual intercourse commonly results in pregnancy and childbirth. The institution of marriage is that mechanism." One key to the marital family's social importance, said Justice Cordy, is the creation of an enduring relationship between father and child. In this way, among others, marriage provides "an optimal social structure" for making and bringing up children and for preserving society itself. "The alternative, a society without the institution of marriage, in which heterosexual intercourse, procreation, and child care are largely disconnected processes, would be chaotic."[49] The report of the Institute for American Values on *The Future of Family Law: Law and the Marriage Crisis in North America* is to similar effect.[50] Thus, if Darwin's formulation was a far cry from the aspiration to divinity, proponents of family values have shown how an evolutionary approach is not inconsistent with religious virtues.

Still, there's a lurking tension in an evolutionary approach as deployed by the family values movement. For it's plain that the evolution of human societies did not stop when the marital family appeared on the scene. At least in the United States, not to mention other societies that are both similar to and different from American culture, we can see social change on two fronts. One involves shifts in social practices and institutions. The reasons for these shifts include economy, technology, politics, and culture. They've been especially potent because American institutions are, in nontrivial respects, liberal (in the sense that they carve out domains for individual liberty). A second, related front for social change has been ethical not merely in the sense of individual morality, but more as a matter of social ethos. To say this is not to suggest that change must be accepted simply because it happens. But some changes—especially those that are part of basic ways of life or that grow out of the ordinary operation or logic of authoritative institutions—can take on a life of their own. In fact, they can be stubbornly resistant to excision or alteration, even though many people might believe them to be undesirable or even pernicious. Perhaps as a result, law has responded to changes on both of these fronts in a variety of ways, both subtle and obvious, profound and mundane. Proponents of family values have acknowledged the reality of social evolution even as they've decried it.

Power

The argument from power posits that family is a social arena, perhaps like all social arenas, in which the will to dominate others plays itself out—whether in competition for mates, control of children, or the roles spouses adopt within marriage. This notion would seem at first glance to be in tension with the notion that family is a product of divine ordination. In fact, it is not entirely inconsistent with certain religious understandings. One of the central Hindu epics, for example, depicts good Prince Arjuna, who with his army is thrust into armed conflict against forces that include beloved members of his family.[51] Judaic scripture repeatedly represents the complexity, disharmony, hostility, and sometimes treachery of familial relations.[52] In the Christian canon, Jesus denied his mother and siblings in favor of a gathered multitude: "Here are my mother and my brothers! Whoever does the will of God is my brother and sister and mother."[53] He proclaimed, moreover, that the very purpose of his presence in the world was for conflict:

> Do not think that I have come to bring peace to the earth; I have not come to bring peace, but a sword. For I have come to set a man against his father, and a daughter against her mother, and a daughter-in-law against her mother-in-law; and one's foes will be members of one's own household. Whoever loves father or mother more than me is not worthy of me; and whoever loves son or daughter more than me is not worthy of me.[54]

Despite these congruities, there are tensions between a religious approach and the view from power. But, if not entirely compatible with a religious perspective, the view from power is plainly congenial with a version of the Darwinian position and of the economic accounts of Marx, Engels, and others. It has also found a home in feminist legal theory, one branch of which owes less to Marx or Darwin than to Friedrich Nietzsche.

Dismissing Hegel's preoccupation with the divinity of reason and with the ethical life, Nietzsche contended that morality is simply an artifact of culture. Rejecting religion, he claimed that morality does not speak to ultimate questions of right and wrong. It is not concerned with truth, at least not in the conventional religious or ethical sense. Instead, morality emerges only to rationalize the interests of particular groups or classes of people. Nietzsche was preoccupied with two groups: the weak and the strong. The strong develop what Nietzsche called a "Master Morality." This morality posits that strength and arrogance are virtues, while meekness and humility are vices. In short, the strong develop an ethic of dominance. In reaction to the Master Morality of the strong, the weak develop a "Slave Morality" that is basically an inversion of the Master Morality: strength and arrogance are vices, while meekness and humility are virtues. In short, the weak adopt an ethic of submission.[55]

What explains this inversion? Nietzsche said that a person who is weak cannot live up to the dominant values of the culture, because that person is powerless in a culture that values power. The result is that this person is faced with constant humiliation and utter loss of self-esteem. What is this person to do? He develops a psychological mechanism for coping with these self-destructive feelings. The powerless person copes with these feelings by persuading himself that the values of the dominant culture are actually corrupt and that he himself possesses those traits that are truly worthy. If there is more than one such person, then a moral subculture is born. That, said Nietzsche, is how Christianity arose. The dominance and oppression of Rome gave birth to the Christian ethic of love and humility. But that ethic, if religiously followed, will only reinforce oppression and perpetuate submission. The Slave Morality does not overthrow the Master Morality; it merely helps those who are oppressed to cope with their condition.[56]

Unlike Hegel (or Marx), Nietzsche rejected the notion that this antinomy (between systems of value or classes of people) was part of a dynamic historical process in which thesis and antithesis periodically were synthesized. Nietzsche's antinomy was enduring. Despite this rejection, a traditional Marxist might approve of Nietzsche's basic insight. In liberal societies, the Marxist would say simply, the dominant class is the capitalist class, and the subordinate is the laboring class. Family, on this view, is a window onto the effects of class-based divisions, but it is not a causal factor; it is epiphenomenal.

Catharine MacKinnon does not deny that class is an important cleavage in liberal societies, but she insists that Marx's view was partial and therefore flawed. According to MacKinnon, the crucial division in liberal societies, indeed in any society in human history, is the division between men and women.[57] From the beginning, men have been dominant, and women in a state of powerlessness. The relation between men and women is an enduring relation of dominance and submission. And family, far from being epiphenomenal, is the primary locus of this contest.[58]

On MacKinnon's account, men have sustained their dominance in at least three ways. The first is through violence. Second, they have eroticized their dominance. That is, they have made an instrument of domination the very act of sexual intimacy on which the species depends for its survival. Third, they have constructed political and legal institutions that reproduce the dominance that men possess in civil society. These political and legal institutions are embodied in the state. And the state maintains power from the male point of view.[59]

How does the state do this? For one thing, as an empirical matter, men control the institutions of state, and the values they employ are those that serve the interests of men. Domination over women is part of the way that men perceive—or at least preserve—their interests. For another, institutions of state in liberal societies are perfectly insidious. Take law, for example. Liberal law presents itself to the world as the embodiment of objectivity—that is, of neutrality, rationality, universality, and science. But, from women's point of view, this supposed objectivity serves only to objectify them and to perpetuate their subjection.[60] One element of objectivity, neutrality, serves essentially two purposes. One is to preserve the status quo, which is the domination of men over women. The other is to disguise the fact of that domination. Neutrality looks fair, because it purports to be indifferent to who wins and loses. In fact, it preserves the basic inequalities that are built into civil society. For women, said MacKinnon, civilized society is not a state of civility nor of ordered liberty. It is a state of nature. This is not, however, John Locke's state of nature, a state of perfect freedom and equality. It is instead Thomas Hobbes's, a state in which life for women is poor, nasty, brutish, and short. (Regrettably, MacKinnon might urge, it has not been solitary.) Liberalism's private sphere, of which civil society is part, of which family is part, hides these conditions.[61]

Psychology

A fourth frame that can inform an understanding of family's function is psychological, the study of the origins and manifestations of the emotional lives of human beings. The twentieth century produced (in the Western world) two prominent approaches to the relation between family and human psychology. These approaches—expressed antagonistically in the theories of Sigmund Freud and Bertrand Russell—corresponded roughly to paradigms of obligation and freedom. Both repudiated religion. Both embraced an evolutionary understanding of the human condition. But each had a different understanding of power, the role of women, and the relative primacy of freedom and obligation. Whatever its technical merits, each theory has had a profound effect on our understanding not only of human psychology but also of the family.

To comprehend the human psyche, Freud resurrected and reworked ancient Greek mythology. He posited that innate human aggression (manifested most extremely in the death drive) and sexuality (Eros, or the expression of the instinct for life) made civilization necessary (or at least desirable). The precivilized human psyche consisted essentially of two divisions: the id (the completely unconscious part, which is the source of psychic energy derived from instinctual needs and drives, such as sexuality, aggression, and the satisfaction of hunger) and the ego or self (the part that serves as the conscious mediator between person and reality and therefore makes possible the strategic and tactical pursuit of desire). In this precivilized state, human beings unabashedly pursued their primal happiness, which produced conditions of brutishness and insecurity, marked by "the arbitrary will of the individual" and rule of "the physically stronger."[62]

These conditions were incompatible with civilization, whose "decisive step" was to "[replace] the power of the individual" with the "power of the community." "The essence of it lies in the fact that the members of the community restrict themselves in their possibilities of satisfaction, whereas the individual [outside civilization] knew no such restrictions." Civilized society, therefore, provided four sets of goods that were not consistently attainable without it: protection against forces of nature, promotion of cleanliness and order, encouragement of higher mental activities, and regulation of social relations. This last good is crucial, for it is the heart of what Freud identified as the "first requisite of civilization": justice, which Freud defined as "rule of law." This conception of justice is embodied essentially in the notion of general rules, applicable equally to all. The regime entailed by this conception is one of neither consent nor democracy, but of obligation and obedience. It is a regime "to which all . . . have contributed by a sacrifice of their instincts, and which leaves no one . . . at the mercy of brute force."[63]

Even if we conceded that these characteristics are valuable, how to explain the rise and persistence of civilization in parts of the world? The key, said Freud, lay in sex (the act, not the status). Sex was a simultaneous expression of the instincts for life and for death. It was elemental. It could not be obliterated. If it were to be compatible with civilization, therefore, it had to be tamed. The institutional device for taming sex was the family—specifically the monogamous family—which Freud called "the germ-cell of civilization."[64] This cellular enclosure was ingenious. For, while it retained the DNA of sex, including its antithetical instincts, it provided a context in which the antithesis could be resolved in a sociable manner. It provided an outlet for the sexual impulse, an institution for dealing with the products (children) of sexual acts, and boundaries that helped reduce fighting over the objects of sexual desire.

If it was ingenious, however, its solutions were not complete. For one thing, although it directed the sexual urge, it could not eliminate the pursuit or even the consummation of the urge outside the confines of the family. The boundary (if we keep Freud's metaphor) was a cellular wall, after all, not a stone fortress. Still, a monogamous family could protect society from many of the uncivilizing effects of an unregulated sexual instinct. For another, the sexual instinct could find expression *within* the family, between members other than mates, even child and parent. As the story of Oedipus in Greek mythology warned, this expression could have disastrous consequences.[65] The taboo against incest became a constitutive norm, protecting family itself against the instability that the unregulated pursuit of the sexual instinct can precipitate. This combination of monogamous family and a regulative norm against incest made civilization possible, because it engendered a third division of the human psyche: the superego. As conscience, this partly conscious part of the psyche internalizes the authority of parents and, ultimately, the rules of society. It does so because it rewards and punishes through an interior system of moral attitudes and a sense of guilt. It permits, in short, self-restraint. Self-restraint, in turn, promotes peace, and the sublimation of sexual desire permits the redirection of energy into productive (and not merely reproductive) pursuits.[66]

This much is a happy story; but Freud's family needn't itself be a happy one in order to be civilizing. For one thing, the "love" that cements a paired relationship is, in significant respects, a confederation of mutual (sometimes mutually compatible) neuroses. For another, the intergenerational struggle that grows out of the rearing of children produces its own psychic conflicts (and worse), which must be resolved for the sake of emotional well-being. For another, and perhaps more important for my purposes, the rise of civilization itself diminishes happiness because civilization places on people demands that conflict with desires. Usually, the demands are tolerable. Often, however, they produce unhappy and sometimes disabling psychic consequences. Despite these consequences, civilization cannot do without the self-regulating individual, who cannot do without the monogamous family, which makes the self-restrained person civilized but unhappy.[67]

Despite Freud's antagonism toward religion—indeed, he explained the religious sensibility alternately as delusional and as the infantile expression of fear of uncertainty and of longing for the protection of an omnipotent father[68]—and despite his reliance on pagan sources for his psychic framework, Freud's theory was remarkably compatible with a prominent part of the moral codes of the dominant Western religions—specifically, the part that commanded sexual restraint. To put a finer point on it, the soul of civilization, for Freud, was obligation not freedom. "The liberty of the individual is no gift to civilization."[69]

Working largely within a psychological framework, Bertrand Russell challenged Freud's antilibertarian account on several fronts. If for Freud the love that leads to marriage is substantially the unity of complementary neuroses, Russell raised love to a high value among human goods. If for Freud sex is a socially necessary but dangerous impulse, Russell saw it as a desirable expression of humanity. If for Freud marriage is the cement of civilization, Russell saw it as expendable, and properly so for the sake of women and children.[70]

Russell's premise was that human contact is an intrinsic good. The highest and best manifestation of such contact, he said, is the loving relationship. Love is emotional attachment. This is not equivalent to sexual desire, much less to sexual acts. Nonetheless, sex (like food and drink) is an integral aspect of human experience; moreover, it is "connected with some of the greatest goods in human life." Among these goods is "happiness in marriage." But marriage—at least marriage of the obligatory monogamous type—is not essential for society or for any member of society. This is especially so as the state progressively takes on a role as father-of-last-resort. Perhaps soon, Russell speculated, as state and economy develop, the father (as a regular presence in the rearing of children) will be superfluous. This superfluity was already occurring among the lower classes, said Russell, and it would not be harmful if it took hold generally. In fact, the demise of fatherhood tends to the great benefit of children, with respect to enhancing their health and education and with respect to reducing the cruelties inflicted on them. This view of social development suggests that, if people do marry, they should do so only for love. This view, however, requires freedoms for both partners—including the equality of women, freedom to exit marriage, and freedom to have sex with others outside an existing marriage.[71]

We might characterize this third freedom as an aspect of a more general precept: sex without inhibition. On Russell's account, this is not a license for mere sexual gratification, which he considered base and dehumanizing. It is instead a sexual freedom belonging to individuals who are emotionally attached to each other. Sex, in short, has an expressive purpose whose content is the emotional fulfillment of the individual. This, of course, is a far cry from the position of religions that predominate in the West. In fact, Russell rejected most religions because they relied on foundational propositions that are incapable of demonstration. But he objected especially to Christianity, both for this reason and for its Pauline asceticism, which Russell claimed was ironically and inextricably linked to a morbid, excessive, and destructive preoccupation with copulation. This, he argued, was an implicit rejection of the importance of love and an explicit denigration of the virtue of sex.[72]

Freud and Russell, of course, did not represent the final words on the role of family in the formation of personality. Developments since the early part of the twentieth century are too many and complex to recite here. One social theorist, however, is worth noting. In the latter half of the twentieth century, Christopher Lasch kept much of the Freudian story of the connection between family and personality, but inverted Freud's account of unhappiness. With Marx and Engels, Lasch claimed that the nuclear family rose to prominence with the appearance of the bourgeois state. Family's function was to supply a buffer between the self, on the one hand, and work (expressed institutionally as capitalism) and civic life (expressed as liberal-democratic politics), on the other. In short, family's function was to provide a social and psychological "haven in a heartless world." Unfortunately, Lasch argued, this family and its important role in the formation of personality have been decaying for more than a century, subject to the vicissitudes of liberal society. In Freudian terms, the threat to family has come from the very civilization whose survival depends on family.[73]

The four frames we've just considered help explain why we might view family as important—fundamental even—to the lives of human beings and societies. They also show why family might be a source and object of political conflict and contestation. In themselves, however, they do not show how or why family might come to be considered a matter of the Constitution or of American constitutional law. To understand that move, we should consider the place of family not merely in civilization generally, but in the laws of a particular legal order that was in many respects the principal constitutional ancestor to the American order: England.

2

The English Ancestry of the American Law of Family

FAMILY IN "THE COMMON LAW"

It's a commonplace to refer to the English law that preceded the American separation from Britain as "common law." If, by common law, we have in mind rules rooted in custom and made binding by judicial precedent, the English rules were not, strictly, common law. Nor was the English law unchanging. The laws and putative customs of eighteenth-century England had changed considerably since Anglo-Saxon times and, for that matter, since the more recent reign of Richard I in the twelfth century. They changed through a number of vehicles—not only through the articulation and evolution of legal rules in courts of common law, but also through statutes, constitutional compacts like Magna Carta (1215; reissued: 1217, 1225, 1297) and Carta de Foresta (1217; reissued 1225); canon law (enforced chiefly through ecclesiastical courts); equitable norms and principles (enforced mainly through courts of chancery); and norms arising from feudal relations and obligations.[1]

This chapter sketches the contours of the rules of English law that ostensibly regulated familial relations by the time of the American Revolution. I say "ostensibly" for two reasons. For one thing, an enormous amount of familial life occurred beneath the law's radar, unregulated because unseen or simply ignored. For another, most of English law, on its face, regulated only a narrow slice of English families, as it tended to focus on relations of the upper classes, who had the most to gain and lose from legal regulation. Although some rules did pertain directly or indirectly to "the lower orders," relations of huge numbers of ordinary persons were left for the most part outside the law. Still, for reasons described below, it's worth taking account of the English law, even if its content looks strange to our eyes.

By the eighteenth century, the English law of family reflected at least six general areas of substantive concern. First were definitions of statuses and legally consequential relations among persons living in, tracing their origins to, or otherwise connected with the same household. Second were rules regulating various duties and entitlements among (or arising from the fact of) those statuses or relations. Third were rules governing aspects of the creation, maintenance, and termination of an especially consequential status: marriage. Fourth were legally enforceable moral obligations. Of special concern in this regard were rules governing sexual aspects of human behavior. Frequently, though not always, one could trace these rules (sexual and other) to religion. Just as frequently, if not more so, one could trace them to their function in maintaining a kind of social order and control. Fifth were rules recognizing and regulating rights in and to property, including provisions for the intra-familial and intergenerational transfer of property through laws regulating inheritance. Finally were rules that sanctified the status of (and, in some sense, governed relations with) the Crown: "the royal family." All of the preceding areas came to a head, as it were, in the Crown.

These six areas were not discrete or impermeable units. They were logically connected and interpenetrating. Here are three or four obscure examples: The crime of "stealing an heiress"[2] embraced a legally consequential status (heiress), an entitlement (to the benefits of the heiress's marriage), marriage (both for the preceding reason and because the stolen woman often ended up married to the abductor), morality (because the possibility of sexual relations or "defilement" might be one motive for abduction), and property and inheritance (because obtaining these benefits was often the dominant motive for abduction). "Ravishment," or "stealing a wife,"[3] was to similar effect, except that it touched upon marriage in an additional way, for the status of an already married woman converted the injury into one that was suffered by the husband (because husband and wife were considered one person at law), and hence the abduction adversely affected specific entitlements of the (first) husband. A similar action in ravishment or trespass *vi et armis* (an injury, akin to battery, inflicted through the use of direct force) was available to the parent for the abduction of a child and to a guardian for stealing away his ward. Each of these actions on behalf of a child or ward involved a particular set of relations based on status and therefore implicated associated entitlements and expectations. One basis for each action was the interference with the duty of a parent or guardian (to provide for the child's or ward's education). And, in the case of a child, the action might also implicate both property and marriage (in that one injury to the parent was the loss of the value of the child's marriage).[4]

To say that these areas were rationally connected is not to suggest that the logic linking them was seamless at any given time. Anomalies and inconsistencies were present, as they almost always are in any legal system of even modest complexity. Still, the areas were coherent enough and sufficiently strong to create and hold together a world (or at least a worldview) that was, at least in part, legally constituted.

The discussion that follows relies heavily on William Blackstone's Commentaries on the Laws of England. Of course, Blackstone was not a republican (certainly not, in his word, a "zealous" one). On the contrary, he was a committed monarchist and parliamentary supremacist, and he valued the roles that nobility, status, and hierarchy played in the British constitution.[5] In general, he had a traditionalist's appreciation for the institutions and values of olde England, which tended not to be consistent with our present professed commitments. But if he was a traditionalist and a monarchist, he was also in important respects both liberal and modernist.[6] He posited, for example, that liberty was the primary end of government and that the British constitution was designed to preserve and promote that end. He esteemed the rule of law. He not only presumed law's partial autonomy from religion, morality, politics, and economy but also appreciated law's capacity to authorize, order, and constrain. Although he spoke of natural law and sometimes praised it, his account of English law was ultimately positivist, its deity having retired, for most purposes of human governance, into the clouds (or to ecclesiastical courts). He was critical of some ecclesiastical elements of English law. But even those ecclesiastical elements that remained valid parts of the English law, he argued, were binding not because they were religious or moral, but because they were consistent with social welfare and good order. In fact, he urged at one point, ecclesiastical law was binding only to the extent that "the common law *allows* and permits [it] to be so."[7] Thus, the common law or Parliament could at any time trump canonical norms or even the ecclesiastical domain.

The *Commentaries* remain a lucid, logical, and respectably accurate account of the laws of England at the middle of the eighteenth century and capture a great deal of the working logic and mythology of the British constitution since the Reformation. Again, this is not to suggest that Blackstone comprehensively depicted social and administrative practices in England. He didn't. But he did describe not only the public, authoritative, and coercively enforceable norms of his society, but also the basic values and institutions implicit in or presupposed by those norms. More specifically, the *Commentaries* showed how legal rules helped create and conserve an authoritative institutional space called "the family," specified the ways in which these rules prescribed and constrained roles for persons within the family, and therefore sketched the normative structure within which people performed, negotiated, altered, or evaded their roles.[8] And they showed how at least one political system used legal regulation of family to promote specific social ends: channeling reproduction; designating social institutions for the raising of children; facilitating material production; providing for the conservation and transfer of wealth; authorizing and limiting power; promoting a kind of social order; and articulating public norms aimed at regulating moral behavior, especially the sexual kind.

The *Commentaries* also provide a baseline for understanding later developments in the United States. One reason is that American lawyers, jurists, and politicians of the mid-eighteenth century treated the *Commentaries* as an authoritative exposition of the English law and used them to resolve legal disputes. Although Blackstone's reputation in British North America waned in the late eighteenth century (due largely to his monarchist sensibility), the *Commentaries'* influence waxed in the nineteenth century, when they came again to be treated as a faithful account not only of the law from which the colonies broke but also of the common law that the new nation embraced, altered, and repudiated.[9]

STATUSES, DUTIES, ENTITLEMENTS, AND PROPERTY

Legal status was the heart of the English law of family. That is, the law treated people not as individuals but as occupants of social positions with designated social roles. Central to the familial household were four sets of paired statuses, each with its own legally prescribed duties and entitlements: master-servant, husband-wife, parent-child, and guardian-ward. There was in the household yet another paired category that was foundational even when inexplicit: male-female. Hierarchical distinctions on the basis of gender influenced the specification of almost every duty and entitlement in the household, exerting a sometimes subtle but always powerful force in all four of the other paired relations. To say that gendered distinctions were pervasive, however, is not to suggest that gender was the sole source of hierarchy. Other sources included generational status (parent-child and guardian-ward) and class (master-servant). But if gender wasn't everything in English law, it was constitutive, just as it has been the most enduring and pervasive basis for establishing status through time and across cultures. In the English law of family, gender was most visible in two status relations. One was the distinction law drew between male and female children, especially with respect to the right to inherit property. The other, of course, was the marital relation between husband and wife.

Master-Servant

It might not seem obvious that the relation between master and servant was "familial," but English law treated it so. The primary reasons were threefold: relations of property were basic to the English organization of production; family (or the familial household) was a basic unit of production; and much of the productive labor performed by servants occurred within the household or at the direct behest of the head of the household.

Under the laws of England, the most important institution (outside the Church) for possessing, owning, using, conserving, and conveying interests in property was the family. At the heart of this institution's function was the view that certain important familial relations were essentially "private oeconomical relations."[10] (Blackstone's term "oeconomical" linked directly to roots in Latin [*oeconomicus*] and, ultimately, Greek [*oikonomikos*]. Both the Latin and Greek roots refer to household management.) Trading on Aristotle, the household was the primal locus of material production and welfare—whether through survival, subsistence, or flourishing. But, unlike our current market-based conception of economic relations, the household was not a site in which members freely negotiated their roles and activities. On the contrary, members' roles—including their privileges and obligations—were prescribed by law. And many of law's prescriptions concerned the ownership and control of labor and property.

Viewed in this way, the relation between master and servant was actually the most intuitively plausible domestic relation—the one most obviously "oeconomical" by our lights.[11] Blackstone opened his discussion of this relationship by stressing what it was not: slavery. "Pure and proper slavery does not, nay cannot subsist in England . . . whereby an absolute and unlimited power is given to the master over the life and fortune of the slave. And indeed it is repugnant to reason, and the principles of natural law, that such a state should subsist any where." Even conquest, he said, could not justify slavery.[12] What, then, distinguished the servant from the slave? One difference was that legal servitude was for a limited term. Another was that servants were entitled to wages for their labor.[13] Still another was that the legal servant could not be discharged before the end of a term except for cause. A domestic servant, moreover, was entitled to at least "a quarter's warning" before an early termination.[14] A final difference between English servants and North American slaves was that the status of the former was not inherited (at least not in formal legal terms), while the slave's status in the United States was.

According to Blackstone, legal servitude in England was founded on the "convenience" of the parties, under circumstances in which one's "own skill and labour will not be sufficient to answer the cares incumbent upon him."[15] He wrote of four types of legal servitude. Only two of the four were, properly speaking, familial: "menial" (or "domestic") servants[16] and apprentices.[17] In the case of domestics, the law implied a term of service of one year, although, under contract, the term could be for a longer or shorter period. Apprentices were indentured for a term of several years, which presumably was long enough to permit the apprentice to learn the "art and mystery" of a trade. Notwithstanding the claim of mutual convenience, English law did not require that the master-servant relation be consensual. At times, in fact, the law compelled servitude. For example, justices could compel any person who was within a designated range of ages and who lacked "any visible livelihood" to submit to domestic servitude, "for the promotion of honest industry." Similarly, two justices could order "children of poor persons [to be] apprenticed out . . . till twenty four years of age, to such persons as are thought fitting." This meant, of course, that poor families, under law, were subject to being split apart and the households of wealthier families enlarged and enriched.[18]

If English servitude wasn't equivalent to slavery, it entailed substantial legal privileges in the master—including directing the servant's labor, barring a third party from interfering with the relationship, and "correct[ing] his apprentice or servant for negligence or other misbehaviour, so it be done with moderation."[19]

The privilege of correction was strictly gendered, as the master's wife did not share in it. In fact, if she beat a servant, the beating was cause for the servant to leave.[20] On the other hand, a servant who "assaults his master or dame" was subject to a year's imprisonment. One justification offered for the master's power of correction was that he was legally responsible for the acts of his servant. If a servant negligently caused injury to a third party in the course of his employment, the master was liable, just as he was for any negligent harm caused by anyone else in his family. Thus, the master "may frequently be answerable for his servant's misbehaviour, but never can shelter himself from punishment by laying the blame on his agent."[21]

Husband-Wife

The second status relation within the family—and doubtless the most significant—was that between husband and wife, or, under the categories of English law, Baron and Feme. Here, too, the relationship was intimately connected with production and property. At common law, an unmarried woman was free to enter into contracts, to own and convey property, and to sue and be sued.[22] Once she married, however, her liberty in these respects diminished. In short, wives became legally disabled. As Blackstone described it, the device through which most aspects of this disability were enforced was coverture—the legal unity of personhood. "By marriage, the husband and wife are one person in law: that is, the very being or legal existence of the woman is suspended during the marriage, or at least is incorporated and consolidated into that of the husband: under whose wing, protection, and *cover,* she performs every thing."[23]

Looking back from the end of the nineteenth century, Frederick Pollock and Frederic William Maitland disputed Blackstone's account of the legal character of the relation between husband and wife. After noting that the origins of the English law on the subject were largely indecipherable, they urged that the relation was better explained, not by the legal unity of husband and wife, but by the guardianship of the husband over the wife. They cited Henry of Bracton's thirteenth-century treatise, *De legibus et consuetudinibus Angliae,* for this potentially liberalizing characterization—"the husband is guardian as being the head of the wife"—and attempted to explain away the concept of legal unity as a linguistic quirk. But they also noted that if the husband's status and privilege looked like a guardianship, it was "of course a guardianship profitable to the guardian, as all guardianships are." Thus, regardless of whether it was more accurate to think of the husband as merely his wife's guardian or to imagine that husband and wife were a corporate unity, the upshot was essentially the same: the husband was the head of the domestic domain, and he had both authority to regulate the household and "a very large power of dealing as he pleases with the whole mass of property" owned by either or both parties to the marriage.[24]

What was the scope of the husband's and wife's legal privileges and duties in the mid-eighteenth century? Although Blackstone was not oblivious to the relative burdens, he was keen to show how the English law was beneficial to the wife. In a much-quoted passage, he urged that "even the disabilities, which the wife lies under, are for the most part intended for her protection and benefit. So great a favourite is the female sex of the laws of England."[25] Pollock and Maitland were less celebratory. They rejected, for example, the "common assumption . . . that from the age of savagery until the present age every change in marital law has been favourable to the wife."[26] Still, the descriptive details of the two accounts were much the same.

The husband was liable for any debts the wife had incurred prior to marriage.[27] Similarly, the husband inherited liability for torts the wife committed before marriage.[28] As Blackstone explained it, the reason was that "he has adopted her and her circumstances together."[29] And, just as the master was liable for the wrongs of his servant, the husband was liable for wrongs committed by his wife during the marriage.[30] The law obliged him to provide his wife's "necessaries," such as food, clothing, and shelter. In fact, if he failed to provide them, the wife was legally entitled to contract for them herself, and the husband had to cover the debt, but not "for any thing besides necessaries." The primary exception to this conjugal obligation was when the wife left bed and board and eloped to live with another. This occurred frequently enough that several legal rules were devised to address it. Although elopement did not put the formal marriage at an end, it did end the husband's obligation to maintain.[31]

Outside the realm of necessaries, each party's ability to enter into contracts, either as an individual or for the couple, was more complex. Although she was barred from contracting or serving as an attorney in her own name, the wife was permitted to serve as an attorney for her husband—this on the theory that such service was consistent with the legal unity of the couple. In general, however, husband and wife were prohibited from contracting with each other. One reason for this prohibition was that it violated the metaphysical unity of husband and wife.[32] Another possible reason, visible in other aspects of the law of contract, was a worry about the husband's overreaching or undue influence over his wife. Concern about this influence—Blackstone called it "compulsion"—informed at least two other doctrines related to property and contract. In the absence of a "fine" (an ostensibly voluntary agreement that was the product of a fictitious lawsuit whose purpose was to settle or to disentangle title), any deed that a wife executed while married was either void or voidable. And, except under special circumstances, she was prohibited from devising land by will to her husband, the presumption being that any such action was "under his coercion."[33]

The potential for coercion was real, despite the English law's protective doctrines. The power to manage and alienate one's property can be a powerful guarantor of autonomy. But women when married lost this power. For example, even if a wife owned real property in fee and solely in her name, her husband acquired a possessory estate to her land as "tenant by the curtesy of England" for the duration of the marriage, and he could legally alienate this estate without her permission. If the couple bore a child, the term of the husband's tenancy expanded to cover his entire life, even if his wife predeceased him; again, he could convey his interest without his wife's consent. She, on the other hand, was barred from conveying her own property without her husband's consent.[34]

A wife had even less control of her chattels (real or personal). "Whatever movables the wife has at the date of the marriage, become the husband's, and the husband is entitled to take possession of and thereby to make his own whatever movables she becomes entitled to during the marriage, and without her concurrence he can sue for all debts that are due to her." On his death, she could keep any chattels that were not reduced to her husband's possession during his life. But whatever chattels he took possession of were his, and he was free to dispose of them, *inter vivos* or by will, as he saw fit. She, on the other hand, could make no will without his consent, "and any consent that he may have given is revocable at any time before the will is proved." And, if she should predecease her husband without leaving a will, he alone would take her estate by intestacy.[35]

In contrast, a wife had no share in her husband's personalty, even after his death, with the limited exception of "her necessary clothes." She might also retain certain "jewels, trinkets and ornaments of the person" on his death, assuming he had not previously disposed of them, but creditors' claims might still take priority over the widow's interest in such paraphernalia.[36] To be sure, a widow maintained a life estate in one-third of all lands of which her husband was seised in fee at any time during the marriage (that is, lands in which the husband had a possessory ownership interest). The point of the tenancy in dower was not only to provide for the widow but also to support and to educate children of the marriage.[37] Because of his wife's inchoate interest, the husband was prohibited from alienating any of his lands without her consent.[38]

Dower would seem to have provided a measure of security to wives of landed husbands (though not to wives of others). In practice and by law, however, an interest in dower could be barred in many ways, including the wife's elopement with another, the couple's divorce, the wife's being an alien, the husband's treason, and several other specific misprisions or disabilities of the wife.[39] By Blackstone's time the most pervasive method for barring dower was essentially a prenuptial contract designed to evade the status-based obligations of the widow's forced share. The contract was called jointure.[40]

Jointure was a solution to an old problem created by English tenures in land. The problem was that not all interests in land were held in fee. For example, it was often the case that title was vested in one who held the land for the benefit—or use—of another. Under this arrangement, although the use-holder had a beneficial interest in the property, occupying and receiving income from the land, the use-holder technically was not seised of the property. At least two things followed from this lack of seisin or title. One was that the use-holder could avoid paying tax on the property. The other was that the use was not subject to dower. That is, a widow could not assert a dower interest in land in which her husband had a use. (English law did permit a husband to assert a curtesy interest in land in which his wife was a use-holder.)[41] One way to solve this problem of the bar to dower, especially where most of a husband's estate was tied to uses, was for the husband and wife, on their marriage, to enter into a settlement. The settlement was essentially a deed conveying a "special estate to the use of the husband and his wife, for their lives, in joint-tenancy or jointure." Thus, even in the absence of dower, jointure could provide the wife an interest in her husband's use if he predeceased her.[42]

As fate would have it, Henry VIII intervened in a way that would affect jointure. His primary concern was that monasteries were employing uses to maintain their independence from—and to avoid paying taxes to—the Crown. At Henry's instance, Parliament enacted the Statute of Uses, which effectively converted useholder interests into freeholder (seised) interests for purposes of both taxation and dower. As Blackstone pointed out, the logic of this move would have been to permit a wife both to claim a dowable interest in her husband's uses and to enjoy the benefit of any settlement in jointure that she and her husband might make. This would have been the logic, that is, except for a provision in the statute that, if, before her marriage, a wife agreed to a jointure, "she shall be for ever precluded from her dower."[43]

On its face, jointure would seem to have supplied a modernist contractarian solution to a problem created by a loophole in an ancient status-based relation. Sir Edward Coke was of this view, and Blackstone largely approved Coke's assessment.[44] In a lucid and perceptive study, however, Susan Staves argues that, despite various changes in the legal rules pertaining to married women's property across the centuries, women's ability to own and control property did not appreciably increase. Because of "the deeper structures of male domination and female subordination" that were present in both law and society, she says, the rules of law "always functioned to facilitate the transmission of significant property from male to male."[45] Even if this weren't entirely accurate when Staves was writing (the end of the twentieth century), there is reason to believe it was so in the mid-eighteenth century.

Power over property was only one element of the husband's legal superiority in the marriage. The wife's independent ability to assert civil claims and defenses also was limited. If she suffered a legal wrong, she was prohibited from suing in her own name for redress. As the husband was the head of the marital corporation, his name and consent were required on pleadings. If she was a defendant in a civil suit, the husband had to be joined as well. (If the wife was prosecuted criminally, however, she could be tried and punished as an individual. As Blackstone puzzlingly explained it, marriage was "only a civil union.") In many contexts, the requirement that both be joined as parties in civil cases might have been beneficial to the wife, but it also provided a vehicle for the husband to assert effective control over his spouse's defenses. There were two exceptions to these general constraints on the wife's legal independence. One was when the husband had permanently departed or been banished from the realm, "for then he is dead in the law." The other involved actions in ecclesiastical courts. This latter exception was both an inheritance from the civil law, under which "the husband and wife are considered two distinct persons," and a function of the fact that ecclesiastical courts were forums for enforcing canonical requirements for creating or dissolving a marriage.[46]

Doubtless, another aspect of the deeper structure of gender was the husband's quasi-monopoly on the use of force in the household. I say "quasi-monopoly" because, although his power was authorized by law, it was also technically subject to legal limitation. Blackstone noted that, under the ancient common law, the husband "might give his wife moderate [and reasonable] correction . . . in the same moderation that a man is allowed to correct his servants or children[,] for whom the master or parent is also liable in some case to answer." What counted as moderate and reasonable under the old law? Blackstone seemed to have in mind a concrete example: restraint through "domestic chastisement." But the principle he recited for the ancient power was more capacious and essentially circular: the husband was prohibited from using violence, other than as lawfully and reasonably belongs to him for the due government and correction of his wife ("*aliter quam advirum, ex causa regiminis et castigationis uxoris suae, licite et rationabiliter pertinet*").[47] If this might have seemed harsh, Blackstone noted by way of comparison that the civil law (presumably not applicable in England) permitted the husband, "for some misdemeanors," to beat his wife severely with whips and sticks ("*flagellis et fustibus acriter verberare uxorem*"), but confined him to moderate chastisement ("*modicam castigationem adhibere*") for other misdeeds.[48]

Blackstone celebrated neither the old rules of common law nor those of the civil law. Instead, he recited with apparent approval the newer English rule, authoritative since "the politer reign of Charles the second" in the mid-seventeenth century: "with us, . . . this power of correction began to be doubted: and a wife may now have security of the peace against her husband; or, in return, a husband against his wife." Blackstone nonetheless recognized the tenacity of the ancient common-law rule, especially among "the lower rank of people," and admitted that "the courts of law will still permit a husband to restrain a wife of her liberty, in case of any gross misbehaviour."[49]

What to make of this competing pair of rules, one ancient and the other more modern? One obvious point is the class-based distinction built into legal enforcement. Another less obvious thing to say is that, although the husband's power to correct was frequently justified by reference to his potential liability for actions of those in his household, the power was a tool of social control for other purposes as well, regardless of class. Sometimes this tool was to promote material interests. Sometimes, it was (also) about the enforcement of a kind of morality. Either way, it was likely an expression of arbitrary power. Arbitrariness was distinctly possible under the rule and principle of the ancient common law, for the very circularity of the ancient limitation suggested the difficulty of enforcing it. But arbitrary imposition was a risk even under the "politer" later rule. There were at least two reasons for this.

One reason had to do with the operation of the evidentiary rule prohibiting husband and wife from testifying for or against each other. Blackstone noted three principles lying behind the evidentiary prohibition, each of which rested on the foundational notion of the unity of the marital couple: that testimony would be unreliable because of the proximity of interest of husband and wife; that no person should be a witness in his own cause (*"nemo in propria causa testis esse debet"*); and that no one was bound to accuse oneself (*"nemo tenetur seipsum accusare"*). Of course, the unity of personhood or interest tended to be a weak justification in cases involving physical correction. Blackstone was aware of this incongruity. He recited, therefore, an exception to the general prohibition, such that a wife might testify against her husband if he had committed an offense "directly against the person of the wife." One principle lying behind this exception was that "no man shall take advantage of his own wrong." In fact, however, the exception had a much narrower operation than Blackstone suggested. As he pointed out, authority for the exception was a statute dating from the reign of Henry VII. By its terms, the statutory exception applied only to a case in which a wife offered testimony against a man who had forcibly and feloniously abducted and, ostensibly, married her.[50] Thus, the operative reason for the statutory exception was that the abduction vitiated the woman's consent, which in turn undermined the validity of the marriage, which negated the plausibility of any claim to unity of personhood, which was the ultimate basis for the evidentiary prohibition in the first place. In short, the exception to the testimonial bar was potentially so narrow as to be almost useless.

The second reason for the risk that the husband's power of correction might go unchecked was both more and less straightforward than the first. Even if the rule of correction were as polite as Blackstone reported it to be among the higher ranks of people, and even if a wife's legal privilege to testify were broad, there was substantial room for a husband to restrain or punish his wife beyond the bounds of law. The reason has to do with the structure of subordination affecting married women. We've already seen that this structure was largely constituted by law, which extinguished or suppressed wives' legal capacities and constrained their ability to hold, manage, and convey property. Thus, legal norms tended systematically to channel property into male hands, which affected not only wives but unmarried women as well, limiting materially their options for autonomy or independence. Reinforcing these legal strictures were cultural values—including religious precepts—that devalued or cabined women's roles and contributed to an ethos of masculine superiority. Legal limitations on exit from marriage also reinforced gendered strictures. Finally, there was the enclosure of the home.

As early as 1604, one could find a judicial decision supporting the principle "that the house of every one is to him as his Castle and Fortress as well for defence against injury and violence, as for his repose."[51] In *Semayne's Case,* the King's

Bench held that this right of repose was strong enough to entitle the lawful owner to bar even a sheriff who sought to enter under a valid warrant for the recovery of goods held within. This was a significant norm of domestic enclosure, but there is reason to believe that the security of repose was not enjoyed equally by men and women. For in this realm, the husband was lord. Within the close, a multitude of lordly sins might reside without detection and without easy legal redress. The idea of lordship found expression within the criminal law. If a wife killed or conspired to kill her husband, even if she was already divorced from bed and board ("*a mensa et thoro*"), she was deemed to have breached an "allegiance, of private and domestic faith." Consistent with this characterization, her crime was denominated petit treason. Her punishment, "handed down to us from the laws of the ancient Druids," was to be drawn and burned. Blackstone noted that this was "now the usual punishment for all sorts of treasons committed by . . . the female sex."[52]

Parent-Child

In discussing the relation between parent and child, Blackstone embraced natural law in three ways. First, the relation was "the most universal . . . in nature." Second, the reciprocal duties between parents and children were grounded in "a principle of natural law." Third, "providence" has done an effective job of enforcing these duties—at least the duties of parents to their children, if not vice versa—"by implanting in the breast of every parent that . . . insuperable degree of affection, which not even the deformity of person or mind, not even the wickedness, ingratitude, and rebellion of children, can totally suppress or extinguish."[53] Still, he urged, "municipal laws" were necessary, and not merely to address the problem of wicked, ungrateful, or rebellious children. These laws, and not the natural law, were the primary objects of his attention.

The English law's regulation of the parent-child relation rested on a distinctly unnatural distinction between types of children: those who were legitimate and those who were not. A legitimate child was one born while the mother was married. It was not essential to legitimacy that the child have been *conceived* during the marriage. In fact, the law's many and refined provisions hinted that there was a great deal of premarital (even extra-marital) procreation going on. As Blackstone put it, the law made "allowance for the frailty of human nature." But marriage before the child's birth was the prerequisite for legitimacy in the English law. This rule differed from the rule at civil and canon law, under which a child born out of wedlock could be legitimated retroactively by the mother's marriage after the child was born.[54]

Blackstone preferred the English rule. The primary reasons were that it created a stronger incentive to marry (quickly) and therefore promoted more vigorously the basic social purposes for marriage. The most important of those purposes "in all civilized states" was to secure "the natural obligation of the father to provide for his children." The English law made it more likely that the father—"the person who is bound to fulfill this obligation"—would be identified and would assume his obligation to maintain his children in a timely manner. But the point of marriage wasn't limited to securing support during children's minority. The aim of the English law of marriage was also to encourage "procreating lawful heirs," while avoiding the risk of fraud that Blackstone said the rule of civil and canon law created. The bottom line was that the English law solidified a connection between begetting and the orderly descent and distribution of property.[55]

"Every man," reported Blackstone, was legally obliged "to provide for those descended from his loins." With this principle, the English law celebrated genetic connection at the same time its presumption of paternity partially disguised the possibility that some children born to a married woman might not be genetically connected to her husband. Whether genetic paternity was presumed or real, however, legitimate children were entitled to "necessary maintenance" from their father, just as their mother was entitled to necessaries from her husband. The paternal obligation extended only to necessaries and not to "superfluities, and other indulgences of fortune." Thus, at common law, a father had broad discretion as to whether and how to maintain his children. And the duty ceased when a child reached the age of majority, unless the child, from "disease or accident," were unable to work. The reason for the policy permitting the termination of parental maintenance was to "promote industry." Still, the law left it to paternal judgment whether "to maintain idle and lazy children in ease and indolence."[56] Despite the breadth of a father's discretion, statutes imposed targeted constraints on some paternal decisions. For example, if a Catholic or a Jewish father were to refuse to maintain his Protestant children, either as punishment for leaving the faith or an inducement for returning, the lord chancellor could order him to provide "a fitting maintenance, suitable to the fortune of the parent."[57] There was no similar constraint on Protestant parents whose children sought religious independence.

Blackstone noted that fathers also had natural obligations to provide protection to their children and to give them an education "suitable to their station in life." He called the duty to educate the most important of all parental obligations. What to make of a parent, he asked rhetorically, who brings a child into the world but later "neglects his culture and education, and suffers him to grow up like a mere beast, to lead a life useless to others, and shameful to himself?" Though neglect of the duty to protect or to educate might be deplorable, neither duty was legally enforceable under the municipal laws of most countries, England included. This left virtually complete discretion in fathers as to how or whether to protect or educate their children.[58]

There were two notable sets of exceptions to paternal discretion with respect to education. One, already referred to, involved children of "the poor and laborious part of the community." These children, "when past the age of nurture, are taken out of the hands of their parents, by the statutes for apprenticing poor children; and are placed out by the public in such a manner, as may render their abilities, in their several stations, of the greatest advantage to the commonwealth." The rich, in contrast, were left to their own discretion whether to bring up their children as "ornaments or disgraces to their family." The second exception involved religion. If a parent sent a child abroad to a Catholic college or university or for training in Catholicism, the parent forfeited £100 to any person who reported the offense. Under a similar but more punitive statute, both the Catholic parent and child suffered substantial legal disabilities: "to sue in law or equity, or to be executor or administrator to any person, or to enjoy any legacy or deed of gift, or to bear any office in the realm, and shall forfeit all his goods and chattels, and likewise all his real estate for life."[59] The reasoning, of course, was that Catholicism was perceived to be incompatible with the basic values and institutions of the English constitution, at least for most years in the two centuries after the reign of Henry VIII.[60]

Although Blackstone spoke of the power over children as a *parental* power, it is clear that the English law treated it as *paternal:* "a mother, as such, is entitled to no power, but only to reverence and respect." Paternal power was adjunct to the father's duty and was designed not only "to enable the parent more effectually to perform his duty," but also (oddly) "as recompense for his care and trouble." In ancient Roman law, the father had a power of life and death over his children. The law of England was "much more moderate; but still sufficient to keep the child in order and obedience." Thus, as a husband had with his wife and a master with his servant, a father had legal authority to correct his minor child "in a reasonable manner . . . for the benefit of his education." The term of minority was twenty-one years, which was the point at which "the empire of the father . . . [gave] place to the empire of reason."[61]

If a minor child were to marry, the father's consent was required, lest the marriage be rendered void. Blackstone justified this rule in terms of protecting the child from manipulation and ill-considered decision.[62] Structurally, however, the rule may have merely focused the power of manipulation on the father, who, for reason of status or lucre, may have had motive to engineer marriages for his young children. A father might also use the estates of his sons for his material advantage. Technically, he was merely a trustee of such estates and was required to account for his management. But under the rules of law, he was entitled to the profits from his minor sons' estates. He was entitled also to "the benefit of his children's labour while they live with him, and are maintained by him." The principal constraint on this entitlement was that he could ask no more of his laboring children than he could from his apprentices or servants.[63]

In exchange for parental obligations toward them, children owed their parents "subjection and obedience during . . . minority, and honour and reverence ever after." This duty was not merely a moral admonition arising from natural justice, but a legal obligation enforceable under positive law. Thus, children were obliged to support their parents who were "in need of assistance." The reason behind this obligation to support was reciprocity: just as parents supported and maintained their children during the weakness of infancy and youth, children must support parents whom age or circumstance had rendered infirm. Despite the purpose behind the legal requirement, some parents doubtless neglected, took advantage of, or even abused their children. Nonetheless, the English law required that children who could do so support their needy parents, despite parental "misbehaviour." As Blackstone put it, the obligation extended as well to "a wicked and unnatural progenitor, as [to] one who has shewn the greatest tenderness and parental piety." The only exception to the obligation to support needy parents involved "illegitimate children, or bastards."[64]

As indicated above, the distinction between legitimate and illegitimate children was rooted in the point and purpose of marriage: "to ascertain and fix upon some certain person, to whom the care, the protection, the maintenance, and the education of the children should belong." Despite the simplicity of the basic rule for determining legitimacy, there were hard cases. For example, what to do when the child was born more than nine months after the death of the husband, or when the husband had been out of the country for more than nine months preceding the birth, or when the husband and wife had been separated (divorce *a mensa et thoro*) or divorced (*a vinculo matrimonii*) for more than nine months, or when a first husband died and the wife quickly remarried so that the child could conceivably have belonged to either husband, or when the husband was incapable of procreating (e.g., if he was only eight years old when his wife's child was born)? A fairly complex set of rules was crafted for dealing with them.[65]

We needn't go into those rules here. I'll focus instead on the status—especially the disabilities—of illegitimate children under law. I should note at the outset that there was at least one way in which English law was beneficial to illegitimate girls: It protected them against one form of incest. "A man shall not marry his bastard sister or daughter."[66] This prohibition suggested that illegitimacy did not cast children completely outside the domain of family. But in other respects, illegitimacy was a marker of exclusion or of disability. Social stigma was certainly an element of the disadvantage of bastardy. From a legal standpoint, however, the key handicaps were threefold: the illegitimate child's legally designated place of settlement; the child's limited access to property; and the uncertainty of maintenance. These legal impositions were substantial, and they reinforced the tenuousness of illegitimates' social position.

The illegitimate son—it was the male child who, in relative terms, had more to lose at law through a designation of bastardy—was "the son of nobody, and sometimes called *filius nullius,* sometimes *filius populi* [son of the people]." He had no surname and no inheritance, for he had "no ancestor from whom any inheritable blood can be derived." He could receive, however, *inter vivos* gifts from his parents. And he could be retroactively legitimated—and therefore rendered capable of inheriting—but only by an act of Parliament. Parliamentary intercession aside, he was without property, except for what he might acquire with his own hands or through the beneficence of others.[67]

If the illegitimate were children of no one, who would maintain them? (On the matter of maintenance, we can speak in gender-neutral terms, as the obligation to maintain extended to both female and male children.) One obvious answer was that the mother would do so. The problem on this score was that the economic position of an unmarried woman tended to be but a shadow of that of her male counterparts. Technically, she could enter into contracts, hold and convey property, and work. For huge numbers of unmarried women, however, the likelihood of maintaining a decent living for self and child through conventional economic activity was low.

On this point, it probably makes little difference whether Ivy Pinchbeck or Bridget Hill has the better account of whether England's move to industrialization in the eighteenth century was beneficial to women. (Pinchbeck says that it was. Hill argues that it wasn't.[68]) Whether women found greater advantage in the early modern family-based economy (Hill's claim) or in the modern industrial economy (Pinchback's claim), those women who benefitted in either era were more likely to be married than not. Despite her legal capacity, the unmarried woman tended to be an inferior creature. Doubtless, this was partly due to considerations of social and cultural value. But law, too, reinforced (to borrow again from Staves) a structure of subordination that made it much less likely that a woman could maintain herself and her child without support from a man—whether a husband, father, lover, or paying customer.

If the mother, then, could not fully support her child outside marriage, who would do so? Before the English Reformation, support for the poor was a matter of Christian charity. Afterward, it became a matter of public policy and law. The key institution for this policy was the parish, a geographically discrete administrative unit whose "center" was a parish church within the hierarchy of the Church of England. The first systematic effort to address the problem of relief was the Elizabethan Poor Law of 1601.[69] This statute imposed a levy on each parish, authorized a tax for the benefit of the poor on owners of real property, and created the office of Overseer in each parish (an unpaid officeholder who was responsible for administering local "programs," disseminating moneys to proper recipients, and channeling into productive labor those who could work). Concerning productive labor, children might be enlisted for unpaid apprenticeship or other labor at the age of seven, sometimes even younger.[70]

But to whom—to which parish—did a person belong? This was a substantial question for the laboring classes or the poor, who might be mobile and therefore lack settled places to live. It was also a live question for an illegitimate child, who belonged legally either to no one (*nullius*) or to everyone (*populi*). The key to unlocking an answer to the question was the notion of settlement—akin to the present-day concept of domicile. The Poor Relief Act (or the Settlement Act) of 1662 attempted to resolve questions of responsibility in a manner consistent with the English sense of order and place.[71] Technically, there were several ways an adult might acquire a legal settlement, though doing so usually took time. For our purposes, it's sufficient to focus on the simple rules for children. A legitimate child had a settlement in the father's parish, regardless of where the child was born. An illegitimate child, in contrast, had a settlement where s/he was born.[72] The latter rule could frequently result in the child's having a settlement in a place different from the mother's. Thus, children who were apprenticed might well end up separated from their mothers—not only in a different household but in a different parish entirely. This was so because, without a Settlement Certificate (a certificate that facilitated movement from place to place), a person lacking visible means of support could be excluded or removed from a parish other than his/her own.[73]

Partly because of the potential drain on a parish's resources and partly for other, nonmaterial reasons, many in a parish had a keen interest in shifting the burden of support to others. Consequently, a parish's authorities might go to great length to find a husband for a pregnant unmarried woman before her child was born. After a timely marriage, the husband (and not the parish) would be responsible for maintaining the child, regardless of whether he was in fact the genetic father.[74] Even if officials in a parish did not intercede on their own motion, law supplied a procedure through which an unmarried woman might identify and charge the putative father. Either before or after she delivered, she was permitted, under oath before a justice of the peace, to "charge any person having got her with child," and the justice "shall cause such person to be apprehended, and commit him till he gives security, either to maintain the child, or appear at the next quarter sessions to dispute and try the fact." On a finding of paternity, the sessions judge was not authorized *per se* to compel a marriage, but, if the father did not marry the mother, could order "the reputed father with the payment of money or other sustentation for that purpose," or, failing payment, the judge could put him in jail. Marriage might look attractive by comparison, but flight was always a risk in such cases.[75]

Guardian-Ward

If the point of marriage was to designate the person—a father—who would be legally and materially responsible for children during their minority, the primary point of guardianship was to identify a person to assume aspects of this responsibility for children whose father died before they reached the age of full capacity. Who would be responsible for these infant children and their property? As a solution to this problem, the institution of guardianship complexified the traditional and the natural boundaries and relations of the familial household.

Across the centuries, English law became thick with special guardian-like statuses and relations for designated circumstances: the customary mund of Anglo-Saxon England; guardianship in chivalry or in socage after the Norman conquest; and additional guardianships by nature, by nurture, by custom, by election of the infant, and ad litem under medieval feudal law. Technically, several of the nice distinctions among these statuses were eliminated by the Tenures Abolition Act of 1660; but, as was frequently the case in English law, old ways persisted even after abolition.[76] The act permitted the father to appoint by will a guardian for his children until they reached the age of twenty-one. The mother was barred from making an appointment. Antonio Buti notes, however, that guardians were subject generally to the supervision of the Court of Chancery and that the court might take the mother's wishes into account in supervising a father's appointee or in naming a replacement.[77] In the absence of a testamentary appointment, the common-law rule designated as guardian the child's next of kin who was not in line to inherit. Typically, this was the mother. But if she was dead, or if she stood to inherit from the child, then the court would appoint the next qualified kin who could not inherit.[78]

Despite its susceptibility to abuse, guardianship was a useful social institution. For one thing, most minor children suffered from the physical, intellectual, emotional, and judgmental limitations inherent in immaturity. For another, like wives, all minors in England were covered with legal disabilities that made it impossible for them alone to protect their interests or their property fully or effectively (whatever their native or acquired abilities might have been). This, of course, was both an advantage and a disadvantage. An infant could not sue except through a guardian or next friend (*prochein amy*), and could not be sued unless the guardian were joined as a named defendant. A child younger than seven could not be capitally punished for a crime; a child older than fourteen could be; while a child between seven and fourteen was in a zone of "incertainty." In general, a minor child could not alienate property, deed land, execute a contract or do any other legal act during minority; or, if a child did so, s/he could disavow the transaction on reaching the age of reason. One exception was that an infant was bound to contracts for purchasing necessaries—food, drink, clothing, or medical care. Another was that children were free to deed themselves as indentured servants or apprentices for a period of seven years.[79]

As early as the thirteenth century, English law treated the guardianship in socage as a fiduciary relationship, designed for the benefit of the child, and supervised by the ecclesiastical courts.[80] The guardian was responsible for the child's personal safety and for his/her education. The guardian might also be responsible for arranging a suitable marriage. Social class was always a background condition on the exercise of these personal duties. The duty to train or educate, for example, was conditioned on the child's station in life. And the responsibility to arrange a marriage was subject to a duty not to "disparage" the child—i.e., not to arrange a marriage to a spouse beneath the ward's status. Despite the fiduciary character of the relationship, many guardians, like fathers, succumbed to the temptation to arrange marriages that promoted the guardian's own material advantage.[81] The guardian in socage also managed the ward's property. The law obliged the guardian to keep rents current, to prevent land from going to waste, and to keep dwellings in reasonable repair.[82]

The Tenures Abolition Act made the guardian in socage the model for all English guardianships after 1660. Blackstone described guardianship in the eighteenth century as a relation of trust, equivalent to that between a father and his child. In fact, the guardian's obligation was greater than the father's. The guardian not only had to give an accounting of all transactions performed on behalf of the ward once the ward reached adulthood, but also was liable for "all losses by his wilful default or negligence." This latter liability led some guardians—of either well endowed or troublesome wards—to protect themselves by submitting voluntarily to the direction and control of the court of chancery and by transmitting an annual accounting to the court. These voluntary acts reinforced the lord chancellor's ultimate authority as "supreme guardian of all infants." Chancery had authority to punish, remove, and replace any guardian who abused the trust of the guardianship.[83]

"Outsiders"

Although it was not a nuclear relationship, the relation between guardian and ward lay within the legal boundary of the familial household. As we've seen, bastard children straddled the boundary between relations inside the family and those outside. Beyond these, there was a legal hotchpot of various other persons, who either straddled the boundary or fell outside the familial domain. Either way, they were marked as objects for special regulation.

Take "monsters," for example: physically deformed persons "which hath not the shape of mankind, but, in any part evidently bear the resemblance of brute creation." The law's treatment of monsters ratified one of the most ancient forms of eugenics. Without approving murder as the ancient Roman law did, the English law commanded estrangement, which the subjects of the command must have experienced as a kind of social death. One part of this estrangement was that monsters, like bastards, "hath no inheritable blood, and cannot be heir to any land."[84]

"Idiots" and "lunatics" were persons possessing defective mind or memory. Not every mental defect triggered the classification. If a person "hath any glimmering of reason, so that he can tell his parents, his age, or the like common matters," he was technically not an idiot. "But a man who is born deaf, dumb, and blind, is looked upon by the law as in the same state as an idiot; he being supposed incapable of understanding, as wanting those senses which furnish the human mind with ideas." A lunatic, in contrast, "or *non compos mentis*," was a person who once had reason—or who might have "lucid intervals"—but "by disease, grief, or other accident hath lost the [consistent] use of his reason." As persons lacking "discretion enough to manage their own concerns," idiots and lunatics were technically under the eye of the court of chancery, but there is reason to think that the court's supervision was spotty. They were legally incapable of marriage. Nor could they be prosecuted for the commission of a crime, though at one point English law provided no procedure for pleading a defense of lunacy, on the ground that a lunatic lacked capacity to enter a plea of mental deficiency. (Blackstone sensibly criticized this rule as "contrary to reason.") Finally, idiots and lunatics were barred from purchasing, holding, or conveying land. In fact, law provided a procedure, via the writ *de idiota inquirendo,* through which a jury of twelve determined the mental status of an alleged incompetent. If the object of the inquiry were declared an idiot, the court would grant custody of his person and his lands to another person.[85] Doubtless, this procedure provided incentives for ruthlessly opportunistic petitioners.

Among yet another group of outsiders were persons who were legally able to marry, but who chose not to, electing instead to live unattached and undomesticated. To proper society, these people were perceived as miscreants—and as threats to the prevailing order—not only by their actions (some were involved in riots and criminal activities, both petty and serious), but also by their very being (precisely because they were visibly detached from lawful productive activity and from socially useful institutions). One generic label for such persons—appearing in law and political discourse in the sixteenth and seventeenth centuries—was "Masterlesse men."[86] As Don Herzog points out, the label was a misnomer, as Masterlesse men included "women who rejected the patriarchal wisdom of the day." Still, the gender-specific term has stuck.[87]

For most persons, masterlessness was a product of several social and economic developments, including the weakening of feudal tenures and stable ownership of land; the consequent breakdown of feudal relations tied to the land; and the enclosure (read: privatization) of open lands to which there had once been a traditional common right of access for tilling or grazing. (In general, enclosure functioned as a large-scale redistribution of landed wealth from landless persons—or, more accurately, from society in common—to the gentry.) The result was that massive numbers of people were displaced. Displacement bred anger and uncertainty, not to mention penury. But it need not have produced critical social instability as long as alternative means of support were available to those who were dislodged. In fact, wage labor was on the rise as early as the sixteenth century, especially in emerging cities in England. But, despite the fact that many such jobs were required by law to be within an indenture for years, wage labor was often insecure, and not merely because some work was seasonal. The result was a sizable population that was detached from traditional statuses and institutions, and therefore not easily controlled except through overtly coercive means employed directly by the state instead of through proxies in households.[88]

Thus in 1579, Queen Elizabeth issued a proclamation against "Rogues and Vagabonds, and all Idle [and Vagrant] persons and Masterlesse men, having not wherewith to live . . . by any lawfull Labour or Occupation." The targets of the proclamation populated the cities of London, Westminster, Southwarke, and environs. The Queen ordered such persons to leave these cities, to report immediately to their parishes of settlement, and to get lawful jobs. At the same time, she ordered officials to conduct searches in "Tabling houses, Innes, Alehouses, and Tipling houses, and also in all Bowling Alleyes, and other places, where any gaming or play is . . . frequented," to "apprehend & take such suspected persons being Masterlesse men," and to "commit [them] to prison, there to remaine, untill they shall receive such punishment and correction, as by the Lawes and Statutes of the Realme, is and shall be due unto them."[89]

Elizabeth's proclamation rested on legal categories that were already established by 1579 and persisted to Blackstone's day (and after). Idlers, rogues, vagabonds, and vagrants—all names for persons who lived outside legal institutions and lacked visible means of lawful support—could be punished by whipping and up to two years' imprisonment.[90] From the time of Elizabeth, moreover, soldiers and mariners who were detached from service but idly wandering the country for more than fourteen days were guilty of a felony without benefit of clergy.[91] As the descriptions indicate, these were largely crimes of status, not of behavior. But not all idleness was subject to punishment at law. Quoting Sir Thomas Smith, Blackstone observed that *"gentlemen* . . . be made good cheap in this kingdom: for whosoever studieth the laws of the realm, who studieth in the universities, who professeth liberal sciences, and (to be short) who can live idly, and without manual labour, and will bear the port, charge, and countenance of a gentleman, he shall be called master, and shall be taken for a gentleman." Thus, the various crimes of idleness combined two basic elements: they were specific to the lower orders, and they aimed at persons who failed to fit within prescribed roles of the social order. The heart of that order was domestication.

MARRIAGE AND MORALS

The chief domestic(ating) institution was marriage. In England in the mid-eighteenth century, marriage had a dual character, temporal and spiritual. Blackstone bemoaned this duality, apparently preferring instead a secular view of marriage. Marriage, he urged, was a "civil contract."[92] But when "the Romanists" (as he derisively referred to the Catholic Church) "very early converted this contract into a holy sacramental ordinance," the Church asserted jurisdiction over the institution. This jurisdiction included not only enforcement of rules for entering into marriage, but also the regulation of conditions for marital dissolution and the supervision of legal actions involving injuries to "the rights of marriage." In one respect, he said, this jurisdiction was puzzling, for "one might . . . be led to wonder, that the same authority, which enjoined the strictest celibacy to the priesthood, should think them proper judges in causes between man and wife." In another respect, however, Blackstone urged that ecclesiastical presence in this domain made a certain sense, for it "soon became an engine of great importance to the papal scheme of an universal monarchy over Christendom."[93] Regardless of whether Blackstone's critique of papal influence was apt, it was clear that the power to regulate the institution of marriage was among the most potent of all public powers, as Henry VIII had come to realize.

After the Reformation, both ecclesiastic and common-law courts claimed some jurisdiction over aspects of marriage. The former considered marriage to be a matter of "holiness." The latter professed to have no concern about "sin," but to be interested only in considerations of "civil inconvenience." The common law pronounced three basic prerequisites to a valid marriage: that "the parties at the time of making [the contract] were, in the first place, *willing* to contract; secondly, *able* to contract; and, lastly, actually *did* contract, in the proper forms and solemnities required by law."[94]

On the face of it, the common law's criterion of willingness would seem to suggest an element of freedom with respect to a decision to marry, and perhaps even a degree of equality between the sexes. This appearance, however, rests on assumptions about individual autonomy and agency, not to mention social and legal conditions for equality, that did not hold in eighteenth-century England. In fact, there were substantial social, cultural, economic, and legal constraints on decisions to marry. Some constraints would have been felt by both men and women (or boys and girls), although not always in equal measure. For example, both male and female children would have felt the strong tug of parental (or a guardian's) influence in the decision to marry and in the choice of a spouse. Motives of parents might have been several, ranging from dynastic concern or ambition, to a desire to use marriage as a way of improving the social position of the family, to economic insecurity, to an insistence that one marry a lover (or acquaintance) in the wake of pregnancy. These and other constraints were doubtless felt more keenly by women than by men. As already discussed, some combination of economic necessity (or ambition), limited access to property, constricted opportunities for material support, and strictures on social status weighed heavily on most women. Thus, despite its modernist resonance, the element of willingness to contract was circumstantially circumscribed to a substantial degree.

Still, the power of constraint was variable. Certain persons in the middling-to-lower classes—not so poor as to be desperate or destitute, nor so well off to be worried about the disposition of property—would have been structurally less inhibited in deciding when and whom and why to marry. Thus, their motives to marry could have included a heavier dose of the complex set of emotions and attractions that we know as "love." They could do so because the social and economic spaces they inhabited were less confining than the spaces that others, above and below, occupied. And they could do so because they were less tethered to the dictates and incentives of law, whose primary objects were the propertied classes and the desperately poor. Nonetheless, the pull of parental preference could be substantial, even among the middling-to-lower orders.[95]

The second criterion—ability to contract—was extensively regulated by law. Consistent with the dualist conception of marriage, some restrictions or disabilities on entry were ecclesiastical, and others were authorized by municipal law.

Blackstone called out three canonical disabilities for special mention: marriage in which one of the parties was subject to a prior contract to marry another at some time in the future (precontract), marriage between persons within a prohibited degree of blood relationship (consanguinity), and marriage between persons within a prohibited degree of kinship by marriage (affinity). Although ecclesiastical courts enforced these prohibitions, marriages entered in violation of them were merely voidable and not void *ab initio*. That is, they were "valid for all civil purposes" unless a "sentence of separation" were entered "during the life of the parties." Some ecclesiastical courts had attempted to invalidate marriages after the death of one of the parties, but Blackstone noted that common-law courts would not permit the spiritual courts to do so, as it did nothing for "the reformation of the parties" and tended merely to bastardize the children. A statute in the reign of Henry VIII mitigated the reach of the disabilities of consanguinity and affinity and attempted to abolish actions for enforcing marriage by precontract (though Blackstone noted that the validity of the latter provision was questioned in canonical courts).[96]

Marriages that ran afoul of certain municipal disabilities were void *ab initio,* because these disabilities "render[ed] the parties incapable of forming any contract at all." Impotence—the inability of the husband to achieve an erection sufficient for sexual intercourse—was a ground for voiding a marriage at common law and under ecclesiastical law. To put it bluntly, the ability to have sex was a basic prerequisite to the perfection of the marital contract. This reinforced the importance of procreation to the marital relation at law. Two other straightforward disabilities were "prior marriage, or having another husband or wife living" (i.e., bigamy) and "want of reason" (i.e., idiocy or lunacy) of one of the parties. More complex was a set of restrictions on marriage of the young. Disabilities and preconditions based on age were invigorated in 1753 via Lord Hardwicke's Act (also known as the Marriage Act). Specific grounds for age-based disability were: insufficient age (younger than fourteen years old for boys, twelve for girls), lack of parental consent (for parties under the age of twenty-one), or the absence of publication through either banns or a proper license (again for parties under the age of twenty-one). A man who married a "woman child" under the age of sixteen without her parents' consent was guilty of a criminal offense and subject to fine, imprisonment, and the loss of legal access to his wife's estate. In cases in which consent was required but one parent or the other withheld consent, the law provided a procedure by which a judge could supply the lacking consent.[97]

In regulating the marriage of persons under the age of twenty-one, the legal rules balanced two sets of class-based considerations. For landed families, Blackstone noted, "clandestine marriages of minors . . . [were] often a terrible inconvenience," which weighed in favor of legal restrictions. But restraining access to marriage too strictly "among the lower class," in contrast, undermined the public welfare "by hindering the increase of people," weakened religion and morality "by encouraging licentiousness and debauchery," and destroyed one purpose for "society and government," which was to prohibit promiscuous copulation ("*concubitu prohibere vago*"). These considerations weighed in favor of a more permissive policy of access to marriage.[98]

Before Lord Hardwicke's Act, common-law marriage, in which a man and woman simply declared their present intent to be wed and then held themselves out to the community as husband and wife, was both legal and common in England. After 1753, such marriages were forbidden, swept up in the Marriage Act's general prohibition of clandestine marriage.[99] There were two mischievous forms of clandestine unions: the marriage of a minor without the father's consent and the marriage of adults without the state's knowledge. I've already suggested that two of the Act's aims, where minors were involved, were to ensure that the decision to marry was maturely considered and to protect the child from manipulation. As the additional prohibition of secret marriages of adults suggested, however, the reasons for the increased presence of the state in the business of marriage were more complicated than the arguments from deliberation and manipulation implied. Why would the state need to know who was married to whom? Two related and familiar answers were social control and property.

The interest in social control was multifaceted. The policy might well have been part of a general (and growing) preoccupation with demographics and the management of populations. This was partly related to a fear of disorder. This fear was acute, especially where wandering or Masterlesse men were involved. But what could have animated such fear when the ostensible threat was not from detached men but from the union of a man and a woman? One answer comes from the notorious proliferation of "irregular" marriages, performed in taverns and marriage shops by marginal clergymen and charlatans. The practice took hold in the late seventeenth century and spawned cottage industries across England in the eighteenth century. Erica Harth estimates that as many as 300,000 marriages were performed in one shop in London during the sixty years prior to Lord Hardwicke's Act.[100]

The mischief was not merely that these unions were presided over by disreputable persons and for profit. The unions themselves were perceived to be socially disruptive. For one thing, they were easy to enter into and were thus open to the corruption of manipulation or base motives. Because such unions were secret, moreover, the status of the persons and relations involved in them was uncertain. This created social confusion about a status of keen public import (marriage). It also opened the door to multiple marriages. The risk of bigamous unions, of course, was not merely a product of the marriage shops, though the shops did facilitate the possibility of plural unions. From the state's standpoint, the practice was problematic because it ran afoul of a fundamental moral tenet and took advantage of unsuspecting "spouses" (almost always women). Perhaps more fundamentally, it was problematic also because it generated uncertainty about the disposition of property on the death of the bigamist (almost always a man).[101] The "civil inconvenience" that unregulated marriage shops spawned was even greater if children were involved, and not merely in cases of bigamy. For, if there were questions about proof of the validity of a marriage, the legitimacy of a child might well be at issue, which in turn threatened the child's social and legal status and therefore rendered uncertain the intergenerational transmission of property and wealth.

For these reasons, Lord Hardwicke's Act prescribed "forms and solemnities" that plainly and publicly marked a valid marital contract at law. At the same time, the act illustrated the continuing presence of religious institutions—alongside the civil state—in the creation of a marital union. The forms were fairly straightforward. First, the husband and wife must have declared their vows to marry "in words of the present tense" (*per verba de praesenti*). Words expressing an intent to marry in the future were inadequate. Second, the ceremony must have been performed in a parish church or public chapel. (There was an exception from this requirement for Quakers and Jews and for parties who had a dispensation from the Archbishop of Canterbury.) Third, the marriage must have been "preceded by publication of banns, or by license from the spiritual judge." Finally, the ceremony must have been presided over by a church official, although Blackstone urged that this was a requirement solely of positive law and not of divine or natural law.[102]

Under canon law, the power of proper forms was sometimes sufficient to cure defects in a marriage otherwise prohibited, but their power was limited to avoiding bastardizing the children of the ostensible marriage. (The forms apparently could not establish the right to dower in an otherwise invalid marriage.) The doctrine through which this curative power worked was the doctrine of putative (*de facto*) marriage. Suppose, for example, that a pair of first cousins participated in a marital ceremony, though the marriage was voidable on the ground of consanguinity. Under the doctrine of putative marriage, if at least one of the parties was unaware of the impediment (i.e., was unaware of the fact that the two were first cousins), and if the couple had children without that person's being aware of the impediment, ecclesiastical courts could treat the marriage as valid for the limited purpose of sustaining the legitimacy of the children, therefore permitting them to inherit. Bracton urged applying the doctrine even in cases of bigamy, in which one of the parties was already married at the time of the second, putative marriage. Pollock and Maitland noted, however, that although the law courts of England tended to respect the canonical position concerning consanguinity, they stopped short of doing so in the case of bigamy.[103]

We saw above that English law recognized two types of divorce: divorce from bed and board (*a mensa et thoro*), which was equivalent to a legal separation without the privilege to remarry, and "total divorce" (*a vinculo matrimonii*). In the former, the marriage was presumed to have been valid in the beginning, but was dissolved or suspended for some reason arising subsequently. The causes that justified a divorce of the latter (total) sort, however, must have existed before the marriage, and the dissolution functioned as an annulment. These causes were essentially the noncanonical (municipal) disabilities previously mentioned. The chief cause for divorce *a mensa et thoro* was adultery by either party. Beginning in the eighteenth century, Parliament sometimes granted an absolute divorce on the ground of adultery. Parliamentary divorces aside, the typical venue for obtaining either sort of divorce was an ecclesiastical court.[104]

Adultery was not merely a ground for separation. It was also a criminal offense and a tort, although its definition in these legal domains was not neutral with respect to gender. As a crime, it was defined as "criminal conversation with [another] man's wife." Thus, if a husband had sex with an unmarried woman, the act was not considered criminal adultery.[105] In 1650, "wilful adultery" was designated a capital offense. After the Restoration a decade later, however, enforcement of the criminal law of adultery was delegated to "the feeble coercion of the spiritual court, according to the rules of canon law." Blackstone noted caustically that canon law tended to treat the crimes of adultery and incontinence (i.e., unchastity) "with a great degree of tenderness and lenity; owing perhaps to the celibacy of it's first compilers."[106] As a tort, adultery gave (only) the aggrieved husband an action sounding in trespass *vi et armis* against the adulterous outsider, "wherein the damages recovered are usually very large and exemplary." The action was enforced in temporal, not ecclesiastical courts.[107]

Defining the crime of and civil action for adultery in these ways made it plain that one of the values and functions of marriage was the confinement of sexual behavior of the wife and therefore the restriction of physical (especially sexual) access to her by outsiders. This implied a kind of proprietary interest of the husband in his wife. This is not to suggest that he would have been perceived to own her. But the regulation of access did involve a potent element of social control, of which the husband was the primary beneficiary. He was also the front line of enforcement—though, failing in this respect, he could call on the coercive power and institutions of the state to enforce his legal interest. Although the definition of adultery did not imply a relation of ownership, it did connect with other interests that were integral to marriage in the English law: procreation, genetic connection, and the intergenerational transfer of wealth.

PROPERTY REVISITED: INTERGENERATIONAL TRANSFER

Despite the rise of industrial, mercantile, and bourgeois enterprise, land remained the most important source of wealth and status in eighteenth-century England. A century before, John Locke had imagined that, in the beginning, all land was held in common.[108] This, like his labor theory of ownership, was a distinctly un-English view of things.[109] Even in Anglo-Saxon Britain, land tended to be held in families or clans, and the typical way to acquire land was not through productive use (as Locke had fantasized) but through inheritance. Still, there was a kind of commonality to this ancient feudal system of inheritance. For, under the custom of gavelkind, land descended by partition to all sons equally—or, in a very few locations, to all children, male and female. This customary practice changed gradually after the Conquest, to be replaced eventually and almost everywhere in England by a system of primogeniture, in which land descended to the first-born male child.[110] Primogeniture was among the most important devices for promoting an aspect of patriarchy that we've already seen: the systematic channeling of property into male hands. But its history was checkered.

In his newly conquered domain, William I faced a challenge: How to secure and maintain order in this rough and tribal country that was, as he knew, susceptible to invasion? The answer was to use families, whose allegiance and service to the ruler would be reinforced through feudal attachment. William's brand of feudalism was a hybrid transplantation from the Continent, though it could not have flourished as it did had antecedent conditions and practices not been receptive and fertile. One of William's first steps was to establish new honorary titles (or feods) that endowed an inheritable status of nobility. These titles were in their nature indivisible, and primogeniture became the rule of descent for them. A second step was to reconceive landed tenures. Land held in socage, a feudal tenure in which the tenant held land in exchange for agricultural or other nonmilitary service, continued to descend, partitioned, to all sons, consistent with Anglo-Saxon gavelkind. But tenures based on military service (alternatively, knight-service or chivalry) began to be treated differently from socage, and to descend undivided to the eldest son. The reason was fairly straightforward: it was both inconvenient and enfeebling to have military obligations parceled among several sons, some of whom might try to evade their obligation. Better, for securing clear and clean lines of duty and command, if the tenure were transferred only to the son who was first able to perform the family's military obligation. Why not the first-born child period, regardless of sex? Blackstone noted that women were bypassed because they were presumed to be "incapable of performing any personal service" aside from marriage and procreation.[111]

In time, the rule of descent for honorary and military tenures became a model for the descent of other lands. Primogeniture's first expansion into socage came during the reign of Henry II (1154–1189). Socage land continued to be partitioned among all sons, but only if the descending land had been subject to division "by ancient custom." Absent evidence of such a custom, the land descended to the eldest son. The expansion continued gradually over the next century, so that, by the time of Edward I (1272–1307), the first-born male inherited, regardless of whether his tenure was in socage or in chivalry.[112] And so the rule expanded to include the descent of all interests in land, even title held in fee.

There was a brief time during the reign of Henry I (1100–1135), in which the heir had a right to his inheritance, at least to the principal mansion, a right so strong that the father could not during his life convey away the heir's inheritance. As Cecil notes, this strict bar to alienation was "relaxed" under Henry II (1154–1189) so that a tenant-father might convey his interest, "whether the heir liked it or not, to any ecclesiastical corporation." This, no doubt, pleased the church, and gave the father leverage in dealing with his son. The father could also convey a portion of his land along with his daughter on her marriage. This, no doubt, pleased her future family, and gave the father whatever leverage a prospective union might provide. By 1225, the tenant-father was permitted to convey, during his life, any of his interest in land to any lawful recipient, and the heir had no enforceable objection to such an *inter vivos* transfer.[113] This was a great boon to alienability, and was a social benefit, to the extent that freely transferrable interests in land promoted social welfare. But there were limits to the impact of this rule, not least that it was rarely in the father's interest to convey away substantial portions of his wealth before he died.

What, then, of the father's authority to dispose of his landed interests, not *inter vivos,* but by will? The Norman Conquest terminated an earlier Saxon practice that had permitted alienation by will. The Norman prohibition held for around four centuries. After that time, the law came to permit an evasion of the prohibition: a landholder-father was permitted to convey his interest in land *inter vivos* to a person who would then hold the property for the use of another, to be designated in the father's will. The beneficiary need not have been the heir. This development lasted less than a century, when the Statute of Uses (1535) effectively subverted uses as a device for circumventing the prime heir's inheritance. Shortly thereafter, however, the Statute of Wills (1540) revived the pre-Norman practice permitting the landholder to devise his land by will. This new rule made it possible again to impinge on the heir's formerly "rightful" inheritance, subject to one condition: the eldest son retained his inheritance in one-third of his father's land held in knight-service. As we've seen, however, the Tenures Abolition Act (1660) destroyed military tenures and therefore ended the sole remaining claim of the first son against his father's will.[114] But, where the father left no will, the legal rule governing intestate distribution held. That rule was male primogeniture.

This, in simple terms, was the way the rules of inheritance stood into the middle of the eighteenth century. The paternal duty to maintain children during his life did not extend to devising or distributing his property to them on his death. In short, a liberty in property permitted a father to disinherit his children. Blackstone criticized this rule, preferring instead the exceptional custom of London, which provided children an equal forced share of some portion of the father's estate, so as to leave them "at the least a necessary subsistence." Even outside of London, a father's intention to disinherit had to be expressed clearly and unambiguously in his will in order to be legally effective, "there being required the utmost certainty of the testator's intentions to take away the right of an heir."[115] And the right of the heir was determined, in the first instance, by the rule of male primogeniture. Thus, even after its ostensible demise, primogeniture continued to exert an influence over the descent of land in England.

There was one additional legal institution that tended to concentrate wealth and status in families across generations, even if it didn't consistently channel property into the hands of eldest sons. The institution was entail (alternatively, an estate in fee tail or an estate tail). The point of entail was to tie land to a single family indefinitely. A version of it had been practiced even before the Conquest, but Norman feudalism entrenched it, and the statute *De donis conditionalibus* (the Statute of Westminster II, 1285) commanded that restrictive conditions on conveyances be strictly enforced. The method for perfecting an estate tail was to include specific language in a deed of conveyance. For example, the donor (seller) of property would convey the property with the following language: "to the grantee / foeffee and the heirs of his body." Variations on this language could designate specific heirs to succeed to the interest of the previous grantee, and the designated heirs need not have been the first-born male child. The grant could have been, for example, to all children, the female children, the male children, etc. For dynastic reasons, however, there was a clear interest in avoiding dividing land among a number of heirs, for the general perception was that the power of a family persisted (or grew) over time as the land remained intact. For persons who cared about such things (there were more than a few), familial ambition tended to favor narrow grants to one or a few heirs, and the eldest son was the most frequent beneficiary of the restrictive impulse. Not every patriarch was so restrictively inclined. But even for more liberal grants, entailed land was a family's land, potentially forever.[116]

Though its aim was to promote a kind of social order, entail produced disorder, and not simply because of disputes among heirs. As Blackstone put it: "Children grew disobedient when they knew they could not be set aside[;] farmers were ousted of their leases made by tenants in tail; . . . creditors were defrauded of their debts; . . . innumerable latent entails were produced to deprive purchasers of the lands they had fairly bought; . . . and treasons were encouraged[,] as estates-tail were not liable to forfeiture, longer than for the tenant's life." The very characteristics that made entail socially mischievous, however, also made it attractive to the nobility—so much so that the statute *De donis* persisted for two centuries, and Parliament would not repeal it. The beginning of the end of estates tail came from a judicial decision. *Taltarum's Case* (1472) provided a "common recovery" that essentially permitted tenants in tail to convert their estate to one that was alienable.[117]

Despite the remedy of *Taltarum's Case* and the later Statute of Wills, entail did not die completely. As Cecil notes, it survived "in the practice of settlements," which continued to provide "a subsidiary use for entails" well past the eighteenth century. We needn't worry over the complex logic of the legal instruments through which a version of entail survived. The bottom line was that settlements permitted keeping land well within the family, almost always using the eldest son as the tenant in tail.[118]

The legal family of Blackstone's day is a strange sight to modern eyes. It's not that we can't recognize it as familial in certain nontrivial respects. But the various statuses, their relations and duties to one another, the purposes lying behind most legal relations, and the intricate web of differentially regulated and prohibited behaviors don't comport with many present-day values and practices. What does that fact tell us about the constitutional status of family?

It's plain that there was a direct and substantial relation between forms of family and the English constitutional order. Britain regulated families—entry, exit, structure, duties, privileges—to (attempt to) match the perceived needs of the order. Unsurprisingly, maintaining a distinct class structure was a central need. Hence, some rules applied only to the lower orders. The community's authority to remove children from poor families and to place them in wealthier families for apprenticeships or menial labor was one example. The rules governing Masterlesse men (and women) were another. Most of the rules concerning the intergenerational transmission of property were strictly (and obviously) only for families of means. Among the wealthy or high-born, these rules facilitated and reinforced dynastic formation. But some rules applied ostensibly to all—especially rules regulating entry into and exit from marriage. On their face, the legal disabilities imposed on married women applied also to all classes. In practice, however, it's likely that these disabilities were felt most keenly by women of social status and means—not only because they tended to have the most to lose, but also because ambitious men of elevated classes tended to have the most to gain from rigorously enforcing disabilities. In contrast, poor women were in some respects free from some of the burdens of disability.

English families that were subject to regulation were regulated comprehensively. In no small way, then, these families were far from "natural," whether nature refers to the condition of persons without a constraining political authority or to precepts of natural or divine law. English families were products of law and subject to extensive legal supervision, intervention, and direction. On Blackstone's account, legal rules were binding simply because of their authority as positive law, not because they might arguably comport with laws of nature. The one area in which Blackstone came closest to relying on inferences drawn from his understanding of nature was the relation between parent and child. Even here, however, the rules that governed that relation proved to be far from universal or enduring.

Thus, even in the ancient law, the rules for families were not undisturbed for centuries. By Blackstone's day, the history of legal regulation was a history of adaptation and change. Change in fact characterized the law (and practice) of family even as Blackstone himself was writing. Some of the most significant changes were occurring in British dominions an ocean removed from England. Although British subjects in North America invoked Blackstone and the common law to regulate their affairs, they were simultaneously carving out ways of life that deviated from established English law.

3

Family at the Birth of the American Order

Plainly, English law aimed to structure and influence the forms and functions of family in ways that preserved key aspects of the existing order. What was happening in North America was something quite different. This chapter examines new relations between family and the emerging order in the British colonies of North America. We'll look at family as a social institution and as a political metaphor or idea. My claims are essentially these: even before Blackstone wrote, conceptions of family were at the center of arguments of political authority and obligation in Britain. These conceptions tended to coincide nicely with legal rules that regulated English families. In North America, however, families began to look and act differently. Subtle shifts in the forms and functions of (real) families in North America helped engender basic changes in New World ideology, especially with respect to authority and obligation. The shift in ideology pertained to authority and obligation not only within families, but also in the larger colonial polities. In the latter venues, the ideological shift played an important role in reimagining the relationship between England and her colonies in North America. In time, it would spur the colonies' separation from the mother country and eventually the establishment of substantially new political institutions. Thus, sometimes explicitly and sometimes not, assumptions about the forms and functions of family were at the heart of radical political change in British North America. But if republican families helped to create a new order, they would eventually be put to use to preserve it in ways that would both resemble and deviate from the families of England.

SEVENTEENTH-CENTURY ENGLISH POLITICAL THOUGHT

In the century before Blackstone, one familiar model for the English constitution and politics was distinctly familial. We've already seen the ways in which the legal regulation of the social institution of family in England was patriarchal. Explicitly patriarchal conceptions were also present, pervasive even, in English political thought by the dawn of the seventeenth century, with the accession of James I, in whose reign the British colonization of North America commenced.[1] The systematic perfection of the political theory of patriarchy appeared forty-five years after James's coronation, in Robert Filmer's defense of absolute monarchy.[2] Filmer's strategy was to ground political authority in tradition and nature and hence to protect it from assault by upstart Parliamentarians, social contractarians, and libertarians. What could be more traditional or natural than to link politics to the all-but-ubiquitous institution of family? Drawing on the Bible—another traditional and seemingly natural source for justification—Filmer claimed that "if we compare the natural duties of a father with those of a king, we find them to be all one, without any difference at all but only in the latitude and extent of them."[3]

Moreover, said Filmer, political authority was essentially genealogical in character; in fact, it grew out of a lineage running ultimately to Adam. Filmer described the relationship as follows: "Kings are either fathers of their people, . . . or usurpers of the rights[s] of such fathers. . . ." He explained: "It may seem absurd to maintain that kings now are the fathers of their people since experience shows the contrary. It is true, all Kings be not the natural parents of their subjects, yet they all either are, or are to be reputed, as the next heirs [of] those progenitors who were at first the natural parents of the whole people."[4]

What this entailed for the scope and character of the king's authority was axiomatic, precisely because the scope and character of paternal authority in the family seemed so self-evident. Kings "in their right succeed to the exercise of supreme jurisdiction. And such heirs are not only lords of their own children, but also of their brethren, and all others that were subject to their fathers." Lest there be any question on the matter, Filmer insisted that the king—whether he rose to his station as the "true heir" of the father of the people, by usurpation, or by election—possessed "the only right and natural authority of a supreme father. There is, and always shall be continued to the end of the world, a natural right of a supreme father over every multitude, although, by the secret will of God, many at first do most unjustly obtain the exercise of it."[5]

Thus, if kings were obliged "to preserve the lands, goods, liberties and lives of all their subjects," it was not because the laws of the realm commanded it, but because it was "the natural law of a Father" that kings "ratify the acts of their forefathers and predecessors in things necessary for the public good of their subjects." This obligation might have been a burden on the king, but for the fact that he was the sole judge of the public good. Nor were there other limits to his discretion, said Filmer. The king was not constrained by his oath at coronation. Common law did not bind him, as he was the "author, interpreter, and corrector of the common law." An act of Parliament could not direct him, as any authority of Parliament derived from the will of the king; thus, "the King alone makes laws in Parliament."[6] In all judicial cases, he was the ultimate judge. Two notions followed from these claims. First, the king was the source of all authority—executive, legislative, and judicial—in the realm. Second, the king was not obliged to obey the law.

John Locke, who was an intellectual ancestor of American independence, directly challenged Filmer's thesis on several fronts.[7] For one thing, he famously relocated natural law, grounding it not in the patriarchal family but in a hypothetical state of nature.[8] This relocation permitted him to imagine nature as a domain of reason and a source of limits. Reason and limits were captured in his conception of natural rights.[9] Locke's state of nature was a state of perfect freedom and equality,[10] but it was not a perfect state. For one thing, the rights and limits of nature were insecure, in part because some people failed to respect them.[11] These failures were not always intentional, however, for one thing that nature lacked was "an established, settled, known law" capable of governing the particularities of human relations.[12] But, whether violations were unknowing or intentional, another thing nature lacked was "a known and indifferent Judge" with power to enforce norms.[13] Indifference was crucial because self-interested enforcement could lead to excessive punishments.[14] Power was essential because individuals in nature frequently lacked the capacity to carry out punishments.[15] To remedy these deficiencies in nature, people consented by contract to the creation of government, thus giving up their natural legislative and executive authority, but not abandoning limits per se.[16]

As with Filmer, family was central to Locke's conception of politics, authority, and limits. But family as metaphor (and as institution) worked differently for Locke than for Filmer. For example, in contrast with Filmer's invocation of Adam as first father, Locke cited nature as "the common Mother of all."[17] Filmer had claimed that political authority mapped neatly onto authority in the family (or vice versa). In a sense, Locke agreed, but the conclusion he drew from the mapping—that both political and familial authority were *limited*—was plainly not what Filmer had in mind. For Locke, an unlimited parent, an arbitrary parent, was no parent.[18]

Similarly, the sources and implications of Locke's principle of limited authority were radically different from those of Filmer's absolutism. For one thing, said Locke, it was a mistake to think of familial authority strictly as "paternal"; better to call it "Parental," for the mother "hath an equal Title."[19] Thus, authority to rule was divided and shared, not unitary or strictly patriarchal.[20] For another, and this may be the most important point for Locke, parental and political authority had fundamentally different ends: "*Political Power . . .* I take to be a *Right* of making Laws with Penalties of Death, and consequently all less Penalties."[21] In contrast, familial power aimed not at punishing but at nurturing. Its functions were to protect the child, to provide for him, and to educate him intellectually and morally.[22] Thus, the family's function was to bring the child into the exercise of reason—a kind of self-limitation—and therefore to enable him to live under law, which in turn would enable the child to be free, for Lockean liberty was liberty under law.[23] The authority of parents differed also from that of potentates in that the two acted upon different subjects. Parental authority pertained to an uncomprehending child not fully capable of participating in reason and therefore not able to enjoy liberty.[24] Political authority, in contrast, pertained to a comprehending adult who was capable of participating comprehensively in reason and liberty.[25]

Holly Brewer notes how radical was Locke's conception of the (limited) capacities of children. For one thing, against the English law of family, it opened to question the capacity of young children to indenture themselves to servitude. But it also had implications for a political theory of consent. As Brewer puts it, "under patriarchal political theory, obligations did not end or begin at a particular age: obligations depended upon status relationships, upon one's rank in society."[26] Even Thomas Hobbes's version of social contract came to the same end as patriarchal theory, for it mattered little under the Leviathan whether a subject actually consented or not—or, for that matter, whether he was capable of consenting or not. It's not to say that reason played no role in Hobbes's world. But reasoned consent played no practical role.[27] With Locke, things were different, for he established a rational precondition for the subject to have the capacity to consent. (In discussing Locke's formulation, it's tempting to say "citizen" instead of "subject," but it's yet too soon to do so.)

As Blackstone would later argue, among the fundamental purposes for the marital relation itself were procreation and the rearing of children.[28] Unlike Blackstone, however, and well before Charles Darwin, Locke held that the "natural" duration of the marital relation was the time required for "the continuation of the species"—that is, the time it took to bring children to reason and to prepare them to care for themselves.[29] Once the children flew the nest, this natural imperative for the marital relation was at an end, and the marriage was terminable "either by consent, or at a certain time, or upon certain Conditions."[30] In short, marriage for Locke was even more modernly contractual than it was for Blackstone, for whether it persisted or perished, it did so by consent.[31] Apart from the necessities of natural obligation, then, the ties that bound the family were of two types: as between husband and wife, the tie was basically contractual; as between parent and child, the bond was one of obligation, marked by caring and natural affection.

Whatever its duration, the marital family was profoundly implicated in Locke's account of political authority. One of the basic problems of politics, as Locke saw it, was that of sustaining limits to governmental power. He supplied four solutions to that problem. First, government should not violate the basic purposes for which it was established, namely the protection of life, liberty, and estate—or, as Locke called them in aggregate, property.[32] Second, when government acts, it should adhere to basic precepts of what we might call "rule of law." That is, government should act only through a public, known law, adopted in accordance with the majoritarian principle, framed in general terms applicable to all persons, and aimed at the public good.[33]

Third, Locke suggested a distinction between public and private domains—those domains that were inhabited or regulable by government and those that were not. He identified two essentially private domains: property and family.[34] With respect to property at least, its "privacy" was severely restricted, as ownership and use of property were subject to regulation by law.[35] The Lockean family, however, was autonomous to an extent that property was not, for governmental jurisdiction over the marital relation was confined to resolving "controversies that may arise between Man and Wife about them."[36] For example, in contrast with the common law, government might intervene to protect the life or liberty of the wife, including her liberty to exit the relationship.[37] (Protecting her property was apparently *not* within the purview of government.) Where procreation and the rearing of children were concerned, however, the family was almost hermetically autonomous from government.[38]

Related to the family's exclusive control over its children, the fourth source of limits on governmental power was the distinction between society and state.[39] This distinction was politically potent on Locke's terms, because society possessed two residual powers. One was to establish government anew when the standing government had dissolved, whether by fundamentally altering the legislative power or by breaching its trust to protect life, liberty, or estate.[40] The other was to resist government when it became arbitrary or, again, when it systematically opposed the protection of life, liberty, or estate.[41] But how would people in society know when resistance was justified? The answer was twofold: "manifest evidence"[42] and a felt popular sense or opinion that the standing government had engaged in a "long train of Abuses, Prevarications, and Artifices" inconsistent with the public welfare or safety.[43] To that end, it was important that the family, not the state, control the intellectual and ethical development of the child who would be citizen.

COLONIAL TRANSFORMATION

Thus, despite his repudiation of Filmer's patriarchy, Locke did not jettison the relation between family and politics. Sometimes the relation was analogical and mutually supportive, and sometimes it was antagonistic, but the connection between the two was central to Locke's constitutionalist aspiration for politics. Nor did he explicitly challenge monarchy itself. On the surface, at any rate, he merely subjected monarchy to the limits of reason, law, and popular judgment. But it wasn't clear what other practical political purposes his theory might serve, at least in England. Corwin argues that the major impediment to Locke's success in England was the institution of parliamentary supremacy. Things may actually have been more complicated than Corwin suggests. But whatever the reason, the more libertarian and egalitarian elements of Locke's philosophy did not find fertile soil to grow there.[44] Things were different in the colonies.

At first these differences were mainly of degree, not of kind. For one thing, the English monarchy itself was changing, due largely to the normative and institutional heritage of the Glorious Revolution. In fact, Locke's *Second Treatise* is frequently taken to be a justification (or rationalization) for the Glorious Revolution, after which the monarchy was held out to be "mixed" or "limited." Gordon S. Wood calls it "republicanized."[45] Whatever one calls it, the monarchy after the ascendancy of William and Mary was different from that of the Charleses.[46] Even so, life under monarchy retained characteristics bearing a striking familial resemblance to aspects of Filmer's more absolutist model. Patriarchal dependency, patronage, hierarchy, disdain for labor and the marketplace, and commitment to kinship all helped sustain and order the English social, economic, and political world.[47] Thus, if the English system of the day had elements of republicanism, it was still at base a hierarchical monarchy and not, as Montesquieu described it, "a republic, disguised under the form of monarchy."[48]

Much of what characterized English society—specifically with respect to the tension between republicanism and monarchy—was also present in the colonies, even as late as the mid-eighteenth century.[49] But precipitous changes in colonial life exacerbated social differences between England and North America and altered basic political ideas in the latter location, which in turn intensified forces of division. Thus, while England flirted with a brand of aristocratic republicanism congenial to monarchy, the colonies surged to embrace a more radical and democratic brand of republican norms and institutions.

Two important reasons for this colonial attraction were demography and economics. The population of the colonies was increasing dramatically, doubling every twenty years during most of the eighteenth century.[50] This increase was due partly to a natural, procreative rise in the existing population, but mainly to extraordinary levels of immigration, especially from Britain and Western Europe.[51] Migration within the colonies was also extensive. The motives behind this motion varied greatly, but a dominant motive was material. Some people fled creditors. Others simply sought new venues to pursue advantage—whether on farms, in trades, or through other sorts of ventures, such as speculation in land.[52] Prosperity was becoming increasingly visible as a social fact and prominent as a political value.

The philosophical roots of prosperity as a political value extended back at least as far as Locke. It's not simply that Locke valued property, but that he tied its natural origins to "labour" and that a principal aim of the political economy he depicted was to keep as much property as widely in "use" as possible.[53] In relating the experience of Hector St. John de Crèvecoeur, a Norman-French scientist who captured his experience in the American colonies as a corresponding member of the Académie de Sciences and the Royal Agricultural Society of Paris, Vernon Parrington noted that the pursuit of economic independence and material security were plainly motives for immigration to the North American colonies; but more, industry and enterprise became part of what it was to be "an American."[54] The "pursuit of happiness," made famous in Jefferson's Declaration of Independence, was an expansive notion that included an array of human goods. But there's no denying that the phrase included some notion of property, broadly construed, as declarations of various individual colonies before July 4, 1776, made explicit.[55] By the time the Constitution was ratified, prosperity was sufficiently valued that material success on the heels of ratification was one reason for Americans' widespread acceptance of the Constitution.[56]

The consequences of these conditions were substantial. If English society valued leisure, stability, tradition, and order, colonial society was increasingly marked by activity, mobility, innovation, and disarray.[57] In contrast with the English system of dependency, patronage, and hierarchy, the colonial system (if one could call it that) was largely one of independence, initiative, and relative equality.[58] It wasn't that social differences didn't exist in the colonies. They did. But because the colonies lacked both the extravagant wealth and the masses of destitution so prevalent in Europe, the distance between the highest and lowest orders (slaves excluded) was much shorter in British North America than in England.[59] To be sure, there was a kind of aristocracy in America, but it tended to be relatively weak and unexalted, its boundaries were permeable, and in any event it was not the titled and inherited sort found in England.[60] Thus, Gordon Wood notes that to a European, "American society may have appeared remarkably egalitarian."[61]

One crucial area in which these differences played themselves out was the family. The ability of individuals—especially young men—to strike out and seek their own way in the New World not only weakened the English model of patronage,[62] but also loosened the bonds of family itself. Married women left their husbands; in some colonies they left under protection of law, as the law of divorce was more liberal in the colonies than in England.[63] Children also left home, and many insisted on choosing their own partners for marriage, even when such choices flew in the face of traditional demands to sustain (or improve) one's family's pedigree.[64] These developments meant that, in purely practical terms, it was impossible for many colonial fathers—especially among the gentry—to assert the kind of absolute authority that Filmer had insisted was part of the nature of things. Thus, instead of relying exclusively on dependence and command to rule the family, fathers increasingly found affection and negotiation more effective for sustaining authority.[65]

These social changes were the first steps toward producing and privatizing what we now know as the American version of the modern family.[66] Carl Degler locates the inception of the modern family in the period between 1776 and 1830.[67] In fact, the social origins extended even further back, before the Revolution. Jay Fliegelman calls these incipient forms of family a "revolution against patriarchal authority."[68] If this was a revolution, it was one of the longest, slowest revolutions in human history, for paternal authority persisted, even as the devices for asserting it changed. Still, the social changes Fliegelman notes were significant on their own terms, and they portended changes in political ideology.

THE REVOLUTION

Especially after British troops defeated French and Indian forces in 1763, thus extending and (so the colonists thought) securing for settlement the western frontier in North America, colonists became more and more restive. Like women and children in the family, they became increasingly difficult to govern according to established modes. Around the same time, political rhetorical uses of family began to shift. In some quarters, the new uses remained superficially similar to the old. In England, Blackstone could continue to invoke an image of "the king, as *pater-familias* of the nation."[69] Colonists, too, both Whigs and Tories, employed this image.[70] Some colonists petitioned the Crown "humbly look[ing] up to his present Majesty . . . as children to a father," in part, no doubt to placate royal fear of a colonial revolt.[71] Even in England, however, the metaphor of king as father was undergoing a significant shift in meaning, away from patriarchy per se and toward an image of reciprocal obligations between father and child.[72]

Perhaps more significantly, both in England and in the colonies people began using an alternative familial metaphor—not the king as father, but the country as parent, even as mother. If this revision suggested a distinct softening of the authoritarian rhetoric of patriarchy, it did not necessarily absolve the children of obedience. Hence, both English officials and colonial monarchists exhorted colonists to behave, because that was simply the duty that children—the colonies—owed the "mother country," who after all had nurtured her children as any good mother would do.[73] But the softness of the revised metaphor made it especially useful to those sympathetic to the colonial cause, who argued that the mother country should exercise forbearance toward her colonies.[74]

Ultimately, however, this maternal modification of the familial metaphor failed to convince a number of influential colonists, among whom was Thomas Paine. On the eve of the Revolution, he attempted to wrest the maternal image from English hands and turn it against them in such a way as to obliterate the metaphor entirely.[75] If England be the mother country, Paine wrote, "the more the shame upon her conduct. Even brutes do not devour their young, nor savages make war upon their families. . . . This new world has been the asylum for the persecuted lovers of civil and religious liberty from *every part* of Europe. Hither have they fled, not from the tender embrace of the mother, but from the cruelty of the monster." [76]

Two years later, in a pamphlet addressed to the "People of England," Paine returned to the familial theme, insisting that England might have governed the colonies better had she studied more intensively "the domestic politics of a family."[77] But the time was too late for correction, he said, again for reasons touching on the nature of the family, or at least the family as Locke had conceived it and as it was actually emerging in America. Paine explained: "As in private life, children grow into men, and by setting up for themselves, extend and secure the interest of the whole family, so in the settlement of colonies large enough to admit of maturity, the same policy should be pursued and the same consequences would follow. Nothing hurts the affections both of parents and children so much, as living too closely connected, and keeping up the distinction too long."[78] Children, he said, must eventually "have families of their own."[79] Command cannot hold them. Pressing for a new parental role for the emerging polity, Paine urged: "It is now the interest of America to provide for herself. She hath already a large and young family, whom it is more her duty to take care of, than to be granting away her property, to support a power who is become a reproach to the names of men and Christians."[80]

Having seized the rhetorical trope, Paine turned his attention to social, political, and economic reality. The American Revolution and eventually the revolution in France, he argued, were largely about establishing a new conception of the character and place of family in political society. Paine's enemy, most simply, was a system in which privilege, property, and power were determined by inheritance.[81] The beneficiaries of such a system, of course, were the aristocracy and ultimately the monarchy. Paine waged a two-pronged assault, one from within the defense of patriarchal monarchy and one from without.

The internal critique took two forms. The first, which aimed at the heart of Filmer's defense, was biblical. The only permanent succession recognized "in or out of scripture," Paine insisted, concerned original sin, which all persons inherited equally and from which "hereditary succession can derive no glory."[82] The second focused on the historical record. Hereditary succession to the throne of England was little more than fanciful myth, said Paine. The story of English monarchy was a story not of kindred blood but of bloody conquest, in which families fought one another for the throne.[83] One could see this in the historic contests between the Yorks and Lancasters and later between the Stuarts and Hanovers.[84] Paine insisted that "there is no English origin of kings,"[85] for even the mythic line of succession begins with "William the Conqueror, *as a conqueror.*"[86] Thus the English self-conception of a seamless and timeless succession was a lie, and noble titles and the laws of inheritance aimed merely to disguise the truth and hence to preserve the "conquest."[87]

Paine's external critique emphasized the bad consequences of hereditary monarchy, which is to say its incompatibility with things he valued. Borrowing from Locke's account of the state of nature but extending the normative implications of the metaphor, Paine argued that hereditary succession violated nature's basic precepts: "All men being originally equals, no *one* by *birth* could have a right to set up his own family in perpetual preference to all others forever; and though himself might deserve *some* decent degree of honors of his co-temporaries, yet his descendants might be far too unworthy to inherit them." In short, "nature disapproves [hereditary monarchy], otherwise she would not so frequently turn it to ridicule by giving mankind an *ass for a lion.*"[88]

Aside from its being incompatible with nature's precept of equality, Paine believed monarchy suffered from four additional defects. First, what nature anticipated was for intelligence, wisdom, and ability to rise to the top. She did not, however, assign these virtues to a few fortunate families; instead she distributed them randomly across "every family of the earth."[89] As nature anticipated, so should human institutions have followed. But inherited rule subverted nature's beneficence and made government itself incompetent.[90]

Second, Locke had claimed that the legitimacy of government depended on the consent of the governed. In Locke's hands, this standard did not prohibit monarchy, for it was sufficient that consent be tacit, evidence of which was fairly easy to muster.[91] Paine took Locke's notion of consent and pushed it one step further, insisting that hereditary monarchy was inherently nonconsensual and therefore unavoidably despotic. There were two forms of hereditary succession, said Paine: one in which a family "establish[ed] itself with hereditary powers on its own authority," and another in which a particular family was invested with such powers by the nation.[92] The first, he said, was clearly despotism, for it lacked any semblance of consent. The second might have seemed permissible, but it too was ultimately despotic, for "it operates to preclude the consent of succeeding generations."[93] Parents, Paine argued, may not bind their children in this way. Nor could it be said that children may somehow anticipatorily devise their rights to their forebears: "If the present generation, or any other, are disposed to be slaves, it does not lessen the right of the succeeding generation to be free; wrongs cannot have a legal descent."[94]

Third, hereditary monarchy confused the public good with familial interest. The concern of government, Paine insisted, should be the affairs of the nation as whole. Government, then, ought to be the property of "the whole community."[95] But hereditary succession debased government by making it "the property of [a] particular man or family" and in doing so created "a permanent family interest . . . whose constant objects are dominion and revenue."[96]

Fourth, in promoting dominion and revenue, the English system preserved the fruits of conquest, but perverted the proper relation between property and family. At the heart of that system was the law of primogeniture, under which property descended to the eldest son, to the exclusion of other children.[97] Primogeniture thus concentrated the bulk of a family's property and title in a single set of hands. Such a regime, Paine argued, was inconsistent with natural justice: "Establish family justice, and aristocracy falls. By the aristocratical law of primogenitureship, in a family of six children, five are exposed. Aristocracy never has more than one child. The rest are begotten to be devoured."[98]

Aside from violating principles of natural justice, said Paine, this arrangement was problematic for its pernicious consequences. Much of republican thought in the eighteenth century was preoccupied with the problem of virtue.[99] Republican institutions, the thinking went, were sustainable only among a virtuous citizenry. But what made for a virtuous citizenry? According to an agrarian strand of republicanism, virtue implied manliness; and, as Forrest McDonald points out, "manliness meant independence."[100] Independence in turn required that a man own enough unencumbered land to be able to meet the material needs of his family. Thus independence, which would soon become the foundation for full citizenship, signified not the solitary or unattached individual but the person whose autonomy grew out of his connection to the soil (i.e., production) and to family (i.e., reproduction). Primogeniture undermined this social system of virtue by unduly constraining the distribution of land.[101]

Paine advocated two sets of policies designed to break up the "vast estates" of the aristocracy and to redistribute its wealth.[102] One was to require that landed estates be allocated "among all the heirs and heiresses of those families," including "poor relations" and not just the favored few (or one). This, he said, would go a long way toward redistributing land "back to the community."[103] The other policy was to enact a system of taxation, extraordinary for its time, that would supply revenue for three basic purposes: to support the poorest families; to underwrite the education of children of poor and middling families; and to provide for the aged, a provision "not of the nature of a charity, but of a right." These policies would strengthen republicanism by ensuring a wider distribution of property and hence of the structural guarantee of independence and virtue. By educating the young, they would increase the prosperity of the nation and supply the sole foundation for the "character" of individuals.[104]

Paine offered these policies for the reform of England and the European Continent. Perhaps he imagined they were simply unnecessary in America, where even before the Revolution some of the practices Paine found most objectionable were weakening, and after the Revolution most were obliterated. For example, feudal land tenures, which were basic to the English law of property, had never been widespread in the colonies, where almost all title to land was held in fee simple.[105] New England had abolished primogeniture in the seventeenth century, though the southern colonies continued to recognize it up to the Revolution.[106] Fee tail, which tied title exclusively to lineal descendants, was dead or dying in America by the end of the eighteenth century, when state legislatures completely abolished the remnants of feudal incidents.[107]

Inheritance of property and tenures in land were not the only domains in which English law touched the family. In the domain of criminal law, forfeiture and attainder were penalties that English law imposed for treason and certain other capital crimes. Both imposed "corruption of blood," which meant not only that the convicted or attainted person must forfeit his own real and personal property, but also that he could neither transmit his property to his heirs nor inherit from his ancestors. The theory, plainly enough, was that his family's blood was corrupted—a reversal of familial privilege, a kind of familial curse. The consequence was that the family's relevant property reverted to the Crown. Even before the Revolution, Virginia, New Jersey, and Pennsylvania ameliorated the harshness of these penalties, the latter two by abolishing corruption of blood altogether.[108]

Most important, however, was the effective absence of aristocracy in the colonies. Again, this is not to say there was no social or economic hierarchy there.

New England had its "high born" and the southern colonies their planter class long before the American secession from Britain. But, as I've already suggested, American aristocracy was different, and the upshot of the difference was that its members possessed no inherent claim to rule others.[109]

In 1791, Paine praised the revolutions in America and France for rejecting aristocratic familial systems and embracing principles "calculated to call forth wisdom and abilities, and to exercise them for the public good, and not for the emolument or aggrandizement of particular descriptions of men or families." The revolutions, he said, had "renovat[ed] . . . the natural order of things."[110] This notion of renovation was truer in France than in the United States, for many of the principles of the American Revolution merely reinforced trends that had been present for decades in the colonies. Even so, the separation of the colonies from the mother country did entrench certain solutions to problems concerning the family in the polity. In doing so, it created a new set of questions for the new country to deal with. The new questions boiled down to this: What shape—what institutional form—would characterize the new American order?

INSTITUTIONAL FORM AND POLITICAL LIBERTY

Aristotle had observed three desirable political constitutions in the world: kingship (monarchic rule by one person for the "common interest"), aristocracy (rule by a few good persons for the good of "the state and all its members"), and polity (rule "by the mass of the populous in the common interest").[111] He compared those forms with three "deviations": tyranny, oligarchy, and democracy.[112] In the end, Aristotle didn't make much of these forms. For one thing, he abandoned them almost as quickly as he took them up, turning his attention instead to social and economic matters such as the distribution of wealth.[113] For another, he seemed unable to fathom how rule by the many might constitute a desirable regime.[114]

Writing two centuries later, Polybius purported to solve that problem by embracing a form that Aristotle only briefly flirted with, the "mixed constitution."[115] Originating in Lycurgus's constitution for Sparta,[116] this form combined elements of each of Aristotle's three desirable regimes. In Polybius's day, the mixed constitution was visible in the institutional design of the Roman empire.[117] Its virtues were threefold: It embodied an aesthetic quality of balance; as the Romans demonstrated, it was remarkably successful in extending rule over a large expanse of territory; and, because it was resistant (though not immune) to "natural forces" of decline and decay, it tended toward longevity. In short, its strength was stability.[118]

Much later, Montesquieu also celebrated the mixed constitution. Its principal virtue for him, however, was not stability but liberty. As Polybius had Rome, Montesquieu had his own exemplar in England.[119] According to Blackstone, the idea behind English institutions was a single system that combined all the desirable Aristotelian forms: monarchy (a variation on Aristotle's kingship, in the

Crown), aristocracy (in the House of Lords), and polity (in the House of Commons).[120] Aristocracy was the fulcrum, preventing each of the others from tending to its pernicious extreme—monarchy to tyranny and polity to mob rule.[121] The others, in turn, prevented aristocracy from becoming what Aristotle called oligarchy. The result, said Blackstone (and Montesquieu), was English liberty.[122]

The colonists in North America celebrated English liberty and Blackstone's account of balance. But therein lay a problem, for the social and political order of the colonies was different from that of England. The Crown was present in the persons of royal governors, and the people were present in colonial legislatures. But aristocracy was absent, at least as a formally recognized social institution with a distinct political function. Even before the Revolution, some colonists sensed the problem and proposed to solve it by creating not a hereditary nobility but an uninheritable "nobility for life." This, proponents claimed, would secure a "social basis for constitutional balance." The idea was controversial in its time, but the democratic forces later unleashed by the Revolution made it downright insensible. Still, absent Crown *and* a formal aristocracy after separation, where would balance come from?[123]

The answer was not clear. One thing that might have made the absence of formally privileged classes, and therefore the idea of popular government, less problematic in America was what McDonald called "the stabilizing effects of extra-governmental institutions and forces," including the family.[124] Thomas Jefferson thought something more was needed. He imagined a feeble state, whose weakness would guarantee a kind of liberty, combined with a "natural aristocracy" whose benevolent guidance would ensure good order and thus mitigate what he perceived to be the dangers of democracy.[125] Richard Matthews describes Jefferson as a communitarian anarchist.[126] Putting to one side this tension in Jefferson's thought, it was probably unrealistic to expect social institutions alone to maintain an acceptable balance between order and liberty—especially an institution smacking of aristocracy, but even institutions like church, family, and community. This was particularly so, if "government" connoted not merely the inheritors of colonial administration but also a new nation-state. The territorial scope of a national state would require powers sufficient not only to carry out whatever duties the nation might have, but also to resist many of the centrifugal forces that a state of such size could produce. So substantial a government might overwhelm mere informal institutions whose range of influence in any event would tend to be local.

If the new Constitution did anything, it supplied the design for a nation-state. Its familiar answer to the question of balance borrowed from Blackstone, but owed a deeper debt to Montesquieu, who exalted the separation of governmental functions into distinct legislative, executive, and judicial departments that shared powers with one another.[127] This separation of function, in fact, permitted a kind of marriage of Aristotle to Montesquieu. One could have imagined that each of Aristotle's desirable constitutions was present in its own department: monarchy in the executive, polity in the House of Representatives, and aristocracy in the judiciary.

Conceding the presence of aristocratic and monarchic forms was a matter of some delicacy for proponents of the Constitution.[128] The Antifederalists, who opposed its ratification, were quick to point out the Constitution's "anti-republican" elements.[129] But the Constitution's institutional structure came with a twist. The twist was that the states, which had inherited colonial authority, were also represented in the Senate. The result was a strange new oxymoronic contraption—a confederated national democratic republic.

FAMILY IN THE CONSTITUTION?

In theory, the contraption was "a machine that would go of itself,"[130] and the Constitution's incongruous ingenuity would hold in abeyance a range of worries about explicitly maintaining a social basis for constitutional balance. But this mechanistic account disguised a number of ways in which the Constitution was not simply a political apparatus; or, if it was, it presupposed a particular sort of society to make it work. No one can read Madison's treatment of class-based social divisions in *The Federalist* and fail to appreciate the relevance of concerns about social structure to the proper operation of the new regime.[131]

If family was part of that social structure, the constitutional text didn't mention it by name. But several provisions plainly implicated family in at least two republican ways. The two provisions prohibiting the national government and the states from passing bills of attainder (Art. I, §§9 and 10) and the provision prohibiting "attainder of treason" (Art. III, §3) ensured that corruption of blood and inheritable forfeiture would no longer be part of the American order. In the future, guilt and attaint would be individual, not familial. Two other provisions prohibiting the national government and the states from granting titles of nobility (Art. I, §§ 9 and 10) ensured that this marker of inherited status in the English system would not be part of the American system.

It's also worth noting that the Constitution imposed age requirements for members of the House of Representatives (twenty-five years, Art. I, §2), for senators (thirty years, Art. I, §5), and for the president (thirty-five years, Art. II, §1). One reason for the low requirement for members of the House was to ensure that "the door . . . is open to merit of every description, . . . whether young or old, and without regard to poverty or wealth," or familial station.[132] Still, the idea of imposing any requirements at all for minimum ages was significant. As Brewer points out, these requirements reinforced or grew out of the view that human beings weren't born with the capacity for reason but had to grow into it. The worry was that even persons who had reached the age of majority might lack the refining education that experience could provide. Better, thought some founders, to ensure to the extent practicable that holders of office were able to take a longer and broader view of the nation's interest, apart from the corrupting power of self-interest. Age was a marker of such wisdom, though, as experience has shown, it was no guarantee.[133]

These considerations aside, family drew the attention of some prominent members of the founding generation. At one point, Madison even insisted that the nation itself was a family: "Hearken not to the unnatural voice which tells you that the people of America, knit together as they are by so many chords of affection, can no longer live together as members of the same family."[134] Perhaps because the familial metaphor was archaic, implausible, or implicitly threatening to the preserves of power jealously guarded by the separate states, this was the only time we see Filmer's metaphor at work in *The Federalist*.

In fact, contrary to Madison's happy invocation of familial harmony, several of *The Federalist*'s essays worry that family—as a social institution, not a rhetorical prop—was a serious problem for political societies. John Jay was first to raise the issue, in his discussion of national defense. As Paine had observed the previous decade, Jay noted that "absolute monarchs" are often persuaded to go to war for reasons of purely personal ambition, including aggrandizing "their particular families," even "when their nations are to get nothing by it." This observation suggested two worries. The first, which was Jay's primary concern, was that the United States be strong enough to defend against such predators. The second, which related more directly to Hamilton's and Madison's preoccupations, was how to create a system in which personal or familial ambition did not subvert the welfare of the nation.[135]

Still, the worry about parochial interest drew strength from the fact that waging war was not the only danger familial ambition might pose for a polity. Familial ties could also engender corruption, which was perilous especially in international relations—as in the case of a president's making treaties or appointing ambassadors to benefit himself and his family—but even in the appointment of executive officers having no direct connection to international affairs.[136]

Jay suggested that the solution was to ensure that the "private interests" of the executive were "[in]distinct from that of the nation."[137] In truth, however, this unity of interest was not entirely feasible on republican terms. Worse even, it uncomfortably seemed to evoke a type of regime in which the executive's interest was, by definition, the interest of the nation, as when Louis XIV proclaimed (perhaps apocryphally), "L'Etat, c'est moi."[138]

Thus, the more plausible solution, at least for a republican polity that might be unable to rely consistently on the moral virtue of its citizens or on the statesmanship of its leaders, was one of institutional design. First, divide power among independent departments so that legislative power, for example, did not reside solely in the legislature but was shared by the executive, and vice versa. (The judiciary—its place and function—was arguably a special case.) One way of doing this was to give the legislature, specifically the Senate, some meaningful say over the adoption of treaties and the appointment of ambassadors and certain other executive officers. This kind of check would harness ambition by structurally confining it and would depersonalize national policy and international relations by abstracting them from the parochial interest of person or family.[139]

In Hamilton's words, this architectural design would preclude "a monopoly of all the principal employments of the government in a few families, and [would thus preclude] . . . an aristocracy or an oligarchy."[140]

Second, design a system of representation in the legislature that would expand the range of interests to which any single member was accountable. The devices for achieving this goal were to carefully calibrate the size of districts, to maintain a system of regular elections, and to ensure that eligibility for office was not confined "to persons of particular families or fortunes."[141] Thus, the polity would reduce the risk of captivity to selfish personal interest, narrow familial tie, or the advantages of money or status. Third, and to perfect the foregoing changes, abolish hereditary social status within institutions of government. It was partly for this reason that the Constitution prohibited the United States and the states alike from granting titles of nobility. And it was certainly for this reason that the Constitution barred national governmental officials from accepting any title or office from a foreign prince or state, unless the Congress consents.[142]

Article IV's direction that "the United States shall guarantee to every State in this Union a Republican Form of Government" was to similar but more systematic effect.[143] McDonald claims that there was some disagreement over the meaning of "republican," with Hamilton insisting it meant merely the prohibition of hereditary status and Madison arguing more strongly that it connoted a government whose power derived from the consent of the people.[144] In fact, as Hamilton's and Madison's contributions to *The Federalist* indicate, establishing representative democracy and abolishing hereditary status were merely two sides of the same coin; both were fundamental principles of republican government and aimed at the same basic goal: liberty.[145] Lifting the intergenerational curse that corruption of blood had inflicted under English, colonial, and early American law was to similar purpose.

There were two prominent exceptions to the explicit and implicit bans on inherited status and punishment. The first was a provision restricting eligibility for the office of president to "natural born" citizens, thus making the office an inchoate but hereditary privilege of the native population.[146] The second, which we'll take up in Chapter 4, consisted of various provisions providing protection to slavery. These provisions ensured that the American brand of inheritable servitude would persist under constitutional cover. In doing so, they not only belied the republican prohibition of hereditary status but implicated the family in other subtle and peculiar ways.[147]

These exceptions aside, the Constitution addressed most of the dangers of family and hereditary status for which Paine had lambasted the *ancien régime*. Some proponents of the Constitution imagined, however, that the American version of family not only wasn't dangerous, but would actually benefit the proposed system, or at least would mitigate fears about its structure and operation. One pronounced fear—especially among Antifederalist opponents of the Constitution— was that, despite the baroque arrangement of power among departments, the national government would be so powerful it would overwhelm the states' prerogatives and the people's liberty.[148] In part because of recent experience, both colonial and revolutionary, people perceived that states were the primary protectors of liberty. They were forums for dealing with most significant questions of policy and therefore were the place where people most robustly exercised their ancient liberty to govern themselves. And some people perceived the states to be fortifications against the oppression of a distant central power and thus as institutional guarantors of both ancient liberty and an emerging kind of modern liberty.[149]

What might protect against national encroachment on these interests? The answers offered by proponents of the Constitution were complex and in some respects confusing. But at least one answer relied upon the ties of affection and kinship that resided in family and community. Hamilton put the claim this way: "It is a known fact in human nature that its affections are commonly weak in proportion to the distance or diffusiveness of the object. Upon the same principle that a man is more attached to his family than to his neighborhood, to his neighborhood than to the community at large, the people of each State would be apt to feel a stronger bias towards their local governments than towards the government of the Union."[150] Madison made a similar claim: "The first and most natural attachment of the people will be to the governments of their respective States. . . . And with the members of these [States], will a greater proportion of the people have the ties of personal acquaintance and friendship, and of family and party attachments; on the side of these, therefore, the popular bias may well be expected most strongly to incline."[151]

This picture of an organic hierarchy of human attachments borrowed from Aristotle[152] and Cicero,[153] both of whom had depicted the relation between family and polity as happy and harmonious. Indeed, they urged, the bonds engendered in familial settings were essential to sustaining politics. Aristotle insisted, however, that the harmony should not be too close. For one thing, as Locke also urged, familial authority was not identical to political authority. Thus, family was not simply a little polity to which the rules of politics applied.[154] For another thing, it was positively dangerous to try to unify family and state. "Plurality," as Aristotle called it, was crucial to the success of a well-run state, and the unity of family and state undermined plurality.[155] Family, therefore, required a separate space.[156] Nonetheless, Cicero could claim that the home—understood as the center of reproductive life, in which all things were in common—was "the foundation of civil government, the nursery, as it were, of the state." Moreover, he urged, the intensity of human attachment was stronger the closer one moved to the center of human society—the home—and dissipated the farther one moved from that center.[157]

Hamilton and Madison exploited these insights to craft an argument that was rhetorically useful in light of American conditions. The argument was that the institution of family could reinforce the status of the states (which many opponents of the Constitution exalted) and protect against encroachments by the nation (which all opponents of the Constitution feared). This claim was potentially significant, because it imagined for family a practical role in limiting power within a geographically expansive regime.

CHANGE, TRANSFORMATION, MAINTENANCE

As Hamilton and Madison conceived it, this new role was essentially preservationist. That is, it aimed at maintaining a particular type of political order, which they called republican. Ironically, however, family's ability to maintain depended, historically, on its having performed a role that was radically transformative. Locke had partially justified this latter role. He understood that one of the enduring problems of politics was constraining and directing political power. Specifically, in his terms, power should be constrained against arbitrariness and directed to the common good.[158] His solution to that problem was complex, involving natural rights, majoritarianism, and rule of law. Yet another element was his notion that the people possess a residual power to declare government dissolved and to replace it with a new one more consistent with their needs. By maintaining the threat of dissolution—and, of course, by implementing it—the people's residual powers could help sustain limits. And to the extent that attentive and collectively self-interested people presided over the rites of dissolution and replacement (or destruction and creation), they could help direct political power toward the common good.

The powers to destroy and create are important to constitutionalism. In practical terms, if people are to exercise these powers, they must, at a minimum, be able to imagine new ways—both normative and institutional—of ordering their political world(s). This capacity in turn presumes that people possess intellectual and ethical resources independent from the ruler or state. In other words, people must be able to be not merely good citizens but also anti-citizens—or, more accurately, anti-statists—when circumstance requires. They must be able to dismantle existing arrangements and replace them, perhaps with something radically new, perhaps with something that attempts to recapture or reinforce values or institutions that are lost or waning. They must be able also to occupy meaningful spaces that are partially autonomous from the state.

In a complex and highly differentiated society, there may be many such spaces, though they tend to be diffuse, and one's contact with them can be fleeting. Perhaps because of those conditions, the institutions that are politically most useful are ones that are protected by constitutional design against substantial interferences from the state. The Constitution explicitly carves out space for a few such institutions: the private ownership of property, the press (or "media" as it is known today), religion, and the division of power between nation and states. Surprisingly perhaps, certain functions of family resemble those of property, press, religion, and federalism. Like ownership of property, family can contribute to psychic and material security and independence; and, as a kind of economic enterprise, it can promote prosperity. Like the press, it can perform an important educative function. Even more than most modern modes of religion, families may serve as sites for regularly resolving practical moral problems; the sum and substance of these resolutions can constitute a way of life. Like federalism, but with a greater transformative capacity, family's performance of these functions can foster diversity—Aristotle's "plurality"—with respect to resources, knowledge, and values.

By the end of the eighteenth century, North American families had helped to fundamentally alter political relations that had held for more than a century. They could do so, partly because of social and legal changes in family's form and functions in North America, partly because of the new conceptions of politics that the social and legal changes engendered, and partly because those changes were occurring in spaces that were autonomous from English law. If Hamilton and Madison were correct that families were supposed to secure the position of states to guarantee liberty, one might have expected that states would reciprocate—that is, that states would provide a space in which families might flourish as institutions relatively autonomous from governmental control. In fact, autonomy was always at most only partial, even in the colonial period. After independence, as we'll see in Chapter 5, the states took up regulation with renewed vigor. To be sure, primogeniture was gone, as were entail, inherited titles, and corruptions of blood. But many of the old English forms persisted—including the regulation of sex, the imposition of disabilities on married women, and the prescription of gendered roles. In short, states attempted to harness families in ways that suppressed their pluralist potential and reinforced a kind of control by governments. If colonial experience had demonstrated families' capacity to produce radical change, the constitutional founding concluded the period of transformation.

In these respects, the new order would resemble the one it had just overthrown, except that the source of regulation wasn't centralized. And families, which had helped transform the polity, would be regulated in ways that would help to maintain a new patriarchal order. But patriarchal families came in more than one variety. One kind received the blessing of the Constitution.

4

Slaves, the Slaveholding Household, and the Racial Family

The nuclear family was not the only form of family in America. Another was the slaveholding family. It was prolific and prominent. It had ancient foundations, both classical and biblical. It was present in North America almost from the beginning of European settlement. After the founding, it was constitutionally protected. And it would become the subject of intense political debate, which would eventually play a role in the breakdown of the constitutional order. Thus, if a modern form of family had underwritten the American secession from Britain in the eighteenth century, an ancient form would play a role in a second set of secessions by southern states from the American union in the nineteenth. Unlike the first, the second secessions failed spectacularly. One consequence of their failure was the abolition of slavery. Emancipation was, literally, liberating. But it created something of a problem for Americans: how to think of themselves—and the polity—with masses of persons with dark skin now freed to claim rights of citizenship? Freed slaves were not the only persons to incite this question. Since the earliest coming of the Europeans (including, of course, the British), North America had been a place of immigrants. After the Civil War, immigrants began to pour in from virtually all corners of the globe (notably excluding Africa). Like emancipation, the arrival of these new persons led Americans to search anew for their collective identity. In large part, what they found resided in a racialized image of the home and family.

ANCIENT ROOTS

Slavery is as old as recorded human history. It is so old that it might well count as a tradition. By the fifteenth century C.E., when Europeans started trading for slaves in Africa, forms of slavery had been around for at least 2,000 years in the western world. One influential classical thinker, Aristotle, posited that the familial household, not the individual, was the basic unit of political economy. And the members of that unit included everyone who made it economically and biologically viable: a man, one or more women, children, and slaves. Aristotle's slavery, of course, was not identical to the later American version. Greek slavery—which is to say Athenian slavery—was not based on race. And in many cases slavery in Greece was not a status for life, but a process for eventual integration into society. For example, a few slaves acquired a limited privilege to sell their labor in the marketplace, even while technically a slave. Even emancipation and integration did not produce a full-fledged citizen, so a degree of subservience typically followed a slave into freedom. But the slave's arbitrary existence, in those cases, came to an end. The Greek slave's status tended not to be inherited. Thus, a person might become a slave in Greece for a variety of nongenetic reasons. One way was through conquest or capture in war. Another way was to be a baby unfortunate enough to be abandoned, exposed, and left to die by one's parents, but fortunate enough to be found by another and taken into his household; as a member of the new household, the foundling could be treated as a slave. Parental abandonment occurred more frequently than the "natural" parental ethic of nurture and care would lead one to believe.[1]

European exploration and settlement brought slavery to the Americas as early as the fifteenth century and to North America in the seventeenth. Most persons who came or were brought to North America to perform labor in the earliest years of colonial settlement arrived as indentured servants for a term of years. This tended to be true whether the laborers had black or white skin. Eventually, however, when persons came to North America as slaves, they were African. And when slavery became entrenched in colonial years, with the number of slaves far outstripping the number of indentured servants, slaves were always of African descent. Over time, African ancestry became a marker of status, even as it was possible to find free Africans in many of the colonies of British North America. If African ancestry—or race—was to be a marker of status, however, efficiency suggested that the status be inheritable and that it persist for life. And so it came to be in America, with the status of slave passing through the mother for the life of the slave (unless s/he were emancipated by law or by the positive act of the owner).[2]

Not infrequently, the Europeans acquired slaves through conquest, but slavery came to flourish in European territories because it was profitable, and it became profitable in part through the development of markets that permitted commercial exchanges. At first, markets were rudimentary, with African persons being bartered for European products in simple transactions; but from such rudimentary origins arose a complex system of trade within and between Africa and Europe. Eventually, market-based slavery became embedded in American practices. Partly because of demands of the market, slaves in North America had little control over their own labor. By the nineteenth century, slaves were prohibited by law from offering their service or labor to anyone other than the owner. Masters might rent out slaves as labor for others when there was insufficient work to be done in the slaveholding household, and some masters did permit slaves to work for others for a wage, but legal rules did not compel owners to do so.[3]

In these and other ways, American slavery came to differ from the Greek institution. But the two systems were alike in certain ways. Greek slavery was rooted in the familial household. It was central to the city-states' political economy. And it was basic to Greeks' worldview. Even democratic Athenians saw slavery as part of the foundation of their democracy. So it was in America. American slaveholders with a classical bent—and there were many—often came to justify the institution by reference to both Aristotle and slave-based Athenian democracy. This point of view was so pervasive, in fact, that the Supreme Court ratified it as well, essentially adopting the Aristotelian view that slaves were members of the slaveholder's family, for the purpose of law.[4]

This doctrine was inconsistent with English law. As Blackstone noted, "the law of England abhors, and will not endure the existence of, slavery within this nation. . . . And now it is laid down, that a slave or negro, the instant he lands in England, becomes a freeman; that is, the law will protect him in the enjoyment of his person, his liberty, and his property." Even Blackstone noted, however, that a master in England might acquire "by contract or the like . . . the perpetual service" of a laborer, and the law would enforce such an obligation, "for this is no more than the same state of subjection for life, which every apprentice submits to for the space of seven years, or sometimes for a longer term." Still, lifetime race-based slavery was ostensibly incompatible with English law.[5] This was just one of the many English practices from which the American colonies achieved their independence. It was also a practice indicating that America did not embrace Locke's theory in all respects, including specifically his notion that every person in nature has a property in his own person and therefore a natural right to direct the objects of his own labor.[6]

After the American Revolution, the states assumed primary responsibility for regulating their "domestic institutions," a term that referred simultaneously to family and to slavery. But the legal commitment to slavery in America was not merely a matter of law writ small. It was also a matter of constitutional law, even though the Constitution omitted explicit mention of "slave" or "slavery." Instead, the drafters of the Constitution favored euphemisms like "all other Persons," "such Persons as any of the States now existing shall think proper to admit," and "Person[s] held to Service or Labour." If the text was ambiguous, the original understanding of the text might, if we let it, resolve questions about its meaning. It protected a space in which states were constitutionally permitted to maintain slavery, free from interference from or meddling by other states or the nation.

A RELIGIOUS TRUNK

Ancient slavery, of course, neither began nor ended with the Greeks. As the Judeo-Christian Bible notes, slavery was part of both ancient Judaism and the Roman imperial world in which Christianity was born and eventually came to flourish. Scriptural references to the institution were many, in both the Old and New Testaments. So American slaveholders who were religiously inclined—and there were many—often came to justify their institution by reference to the Bible. One of the leading proponents of this type of justification was the Reverend Doctor Thornton Stringfellow, of Virginia. In various writings, Stringfellow argued that slavery was ordained by God for beneficent purposes, was linked to the primacy of the family in any well ordered polity, and was supported by holy writ. If abolitionists, too, sometimes invoked religious arguments to oppose slavery, he urged that they misunderstood the Bible's true meaning.[7]

Stringfellow scoured scripture for approving references to servitude. He found plenty, and concluded that God sanctioned slavery at three critical junctures in sacred history. The first was during Judaism's "patriarchal age," beginning with Noah and running through Abraham and beyond, to his descendants. During this period the Maker of the Universe specifically approved the practice of slavery and bestowed a divine blessing of prosperity on slaveholders. Abolitionists in America were insisting that the form of servitude described in this part of the Bible was merely service-for-hire. Stringfellow countered with textual evidence that the institution God sanctioned was in fact slavery, that these servants were treated as property, and that in a nontrivial number of cases the condition was inheritable. Even "Job, who is held up by God himself as a model of human perfection, was a great slaveholder." And, "like Abraham, Isaac, and Jacob, [Job] won no small portion of his claims to character with God and men from the manner in which he discharged his duty to his slaves."[8]

The second moment of divine approval was when slavery was "incorporated into the only National Constitution which ever emanated from God." This constitution was the Mosaic dispensation, under which God gave the descendants of Abraham "a written constitution of government, a country to dwell in, and a covenant of special protection and favor, for their obedience to his law." Two key moral precepts were part of Mosaic law: to love God and to love others as ourselves. Slavery, said Stringfellow, was not incompatible with these precepts. If it were, then God himself would have been inconsistent, which is impossible. "For the fifteen hundred years, during which these laws were in force, God raised up a succession of prophets to reprove [the Jewish] people for the various sins into which they fell; yet there is not a reproof uttered against the institution of *involuntary slavery*." Stringfellow recited chapter and verse from Leviticus, Exodus, and Deuteronomy to demonstrate the ways in which slavery had been woven into Judaic law. Thus, "from Abraham's day, until the coming of Christit, . . . this institution found favor with God. No marks of his displeasure are found resting upon it. It must, therefore, . . . be in harmony with those moral principles which he requires to be exercised by the law of Moses, and which are the principles that secure harmony and happiness to the universe, viz: supreme love to God, and the love of our neighbor as ourself."[9]

Third, the coming of the Messiah did not alter this arrangement. "Jesus Christ," said Stringfellow, "recognized [the] institution [of slavery] as one that was lawful among men, and [he] regulated its relative duties." In fact, this was an overstatement, and Stringfellow recognized it, for the text of the gospels contains no words from Jesus on the subject of servitude. The most that Stringfellow could claim on this front, therefore, was that Jesus "has not abolished slavery by a prohibitory command." This in itself was weak support for slavery. Stringfellow propped it up with a claim about the authority of the Mosaic law. In short, he said, Jesus "introduced no new moral principle." This meant that the rules of the Pentateuch continued unabated, which in turn meant that hereditary slavery was still approved by God under the gospel dispensation.[10]

If the gospels themselves provided only a slender reed for this position, the epistles were more substantial. The Apostle Paul captured the spirit of the Roman Empire in his letter to the Christians at Ephesus. In a chapter that opened with a discussion of the moral life, free from "fornication, and all uncleanness, or covetousness," the letter sketched the elements of duty in a Christian household:

> Wives, submit yourselves unto your own husbands, as unto the Lord. For the husband is the head of the wife, even as Christ is the head of the church. . . . Children, obey your parents in the Lord: for this is right. . . . Servants, be obedient to them that are your masters according to the flesh, with fear and trembling, in singleness of your heart, as unto Christ; Not with eyeservice, as menpleasers; but as the servants of Christ, doing the will of God from the heart. (Ephesians 5:22–23, 6:1, 6:5–6 [KJV])[11]

Paul repeated these duties in his letter to the Colossians. And in his first letter to the church at Corinth, he warned members to hold fast to the station in life that God had assigned them. "Art thou called being a servant? Care not for it: but if thou mayest be made free, use it rather. For he that is called in the Lord, being a servant, is the Lord's freeman." (1 Corinthians 7:21–22) Paul underscored the point in a letter to Timothy: "Let as many servants as are under the yoke count their masters worthy of all honor, that the name of God and his doctrine be not blasphemed." (1 Timothy 6:1) The first letter of Peter made it clear that it was not merely believing masters who were to be obeyed: "Servants, be subject to your masters with all fear; not only to the good and gentle [masters], but also to the froward." (1 Peter 2:18)

Stringfellow suggested that, in exhorting slaves to obey their masters, Paul was essentially channeling "even the words of our Lord Jesus Christ." (1 Timothy 6:3) This was a stretch. But it was enough, for a nineteenth-century Christian in America, that the apostles placed such emphasis on obedience, especially in light of the epistles' canonical status by the time Stringfellow wrote. To be sure, duties were reciprocal. Believing masters owed a duty to their slaves. But the principal emphasis was on the duties of slaves, at least on Stringfellow's view.

His was not the only view, of course, as a published "debate" between two Baptists, one southern and one northern, revealed.[12] Rev. Francis Wayland of Providence, Rhode Island, president of Brown University, argued that slavery violated human rights and was inconsistent with Christian teaching, correctly understood. Even if the apostles appeared to sanction slavery in scripture, present-day Christians were not bound to the earlier understanding. "The times are changed— our circumstances are not those in which the apostles lived," and people in later times are permitted to adapt earlier doctrines in light of later understanding. In short, slavery was now wrong, regardless of what the apostles may have said on the matter. If Wayland adopted a "living scripture" approach to biblical interpretation, Rev. Richard Fuller of Beaufort, South Carolina, was an originalist. "What if the gospel can by no torture be framed and bent to what anybody and everybody chooses to call 'the times?' Why, then, the gospel is effete, and obsolete, and must be discarded, as it has been by many of the abolitionists." Lest he leave open a possible door, Fuller said, "I deny that there is any such difference between our condition here, and that of Christians in the days of Paul."[13]

MODERN BRANCHES

To say that slavery was moral or advantageous, however, was not necessarily to say that the version of slavery practiced in America was so. If slavery was good or useful, why not simply hold a lottery to decide who would be slave and who would be free? In his "Speech on the Admission of Kansas," Senator James Henry Hammond of South Carolina met this question with the unapologetic claim that Africans were made for slavery. "In all social systems there must be a class to do the menial duties to perform the drudgery of life. That is, a class requiring but a low order of intellect and but little skill. Its requisites are vigor, docility, fidelity. Such a class you must have, or you would not have the other class which leads progress, civilization, and refinement. It constitutes the very mud-sill of society and of political government." Invoking Cicero's theory of natural law, Hammond said that slavery performed this function in the South. "Fortunately for the South, she found a race adapted to that purpose. . . . A race inferior to her own, but eminently qualified in temper, in vigor, in docility, in capacity to stand the climate, to answer all her purposes. We use them for our purpose, and call them slaves." He accused northern antislavers of hypocrisy in disparaging slavery. You, too, have slavery, he said, though it goes by euphemism.

> Your whole hireling class of manual laborers and "operatives," as you call them, are essentially slaves. The difference between us is, that our slaves are

hired for life and well compensated; there is no starvation, no begging, no want of employment among our people. . . . Yours are hired by the day, not cared for, and scantily compensated, which may be proved in the most painful manner, at any hour in any street in any of your large towns.

In short, according to Hammond, industrial capitalism's "free labor" was an oxymoron and no better than the system of labor southerners honestly called slavery.[14]

James P. Holcombe, professor of law at the University of Virginia, sounded a similar theme in a more scholarly voice. "African Slavery in the United States," he urged, was "consistent with Natural Law." For one thing, preserving civilized society and polity was a fundamental and natural obligation of the members of that society. The rule of law was essential to maintaining society and polity, for law restrained the human inclination toward actions that tend to the dissolution of society. It was not enough, however, for law simply and generically to maintain order. Law must maintain a particular kind of order. "The truth is, that the principles which lie at the foundation of all political restraint, may make it the duty of the State under certain circumstances, to establish the relation of personal servitude." What circumstance might give rise to such a duty?

Where two distinct races are collected upon the same territory, incapable . . . of fusion or severance, the one being as much superior to the other in strength and intelligence as the man to the child, there the rightful relation between them is that of authority upon the one side, and subordination in some form, upon the other. Equality . . . could not be established without inflicting the climax of injustice on the superior, and of cruelty on the inferior race.

But why African slavery? Holcombe's answer in short was that the natural character and temperament of the African—"docile, affectionate, light-hearted, facile to impression, reverential"—rendered him a proper object of slavery. "He is far inferior to other races. Hence, subordination is as congenial to his moral, as a warm latitude is to his physical nature." African slavery, therefore, was "no relic of barbarism." On the contrary, it was an "adjustment of the social and political relations of the races," necessary to the preservation of American civilization. It was so woven into the fabric of American life that to abolish it would dissolve the very society and political system of which it is part.[15]

By far the most ingenious and systematic defense of the traditional slaveholding family came from George Fitzhugh. Like some in our own time, he derided his opponents as socialists. In Fitzhugh's case this was ironic for at least two reasons. One was that his own approach combined Aristotelian natural law with Marxism, aiming at a form of domestic communism with slavery at its center. The other was that he actually opposed not socialism *per se* but capitalism and "free society." Thus, his real opponents were not socialists but liberals, in a manner of speaking. "As civilization advances," he wrote, "liberty recedes."[16] And his philosophical ancestor was not John Locke but Robert Filmer.[17]

Liberalism and its political economy, he argued, were either a lie or a massive failure. If we were honest, he urged, we would acknowledge that all of America was engaged in slavery. This was not because the Constitution protected slavery, as some abolitionists argued, but because there were actually two forms of slavery in the United States: agrarian plantation slavery and the wage slavery of industrial capitalism. Of the two, plantation slavery was superior. How so? The classical economists were correct, he said, in showing that labor is the source of material value in a system of production. Profit is the extraction of value from the labor of others. In a real economic sense, urged Fitzhugh, a free laborer receives less from his labor than a slave does on the plantation. That's one reason there is so much profit in capitalism. The capitalist takes the desperate laborer, often an immigrant, and pays him a pittance. The wage is hardly enough for the individual laborer himself to live on, but capitalism expects him to feed, clothe, and shelter not only himself but also his family. This is difficult enough in good economic times. But, when the economy busts, the free laborer is laid off. When he gets old or sick, he is fired. He has no security. The capitalist sucks the life out of the free laborer and leaves him to starve and die, along with his family. Capitalism, urged Fitzhugh, was little better than cannibalism.[18] Put in more modern terms, Fitzhugh's argument was that capitalism treated the welfare of its workers (but certainly not their labor) as an externality, in turn creating massive social costs.

In contrast, said Fitzhugh, slavery on the plantation was not a system of exploitation. It was a system of mutual obligation. In this system, the slave owed his labor (and, presumably, his obedience). But the slaveholder, said Fitzhugh, owed something in return, something more than a mere subsistence wage. The slaveholder owed food, clothing, shelter, and medical care, even when the slave grew old or infirm. These were all expenses and responsibilities that the slaveholder had to internalize but that the capitalist was not required to account for. This was what made slave labor more expensive than free labor, but also, he said, less cruel.[19]

Plantation slavery created a set of relations that resembled (though it extended) the family. It made family central to social order. But liberalism and capitalism—and especially abolitionism—were dangerous novelties that threatened to subvert the traditional family and its social order. "Liberty and Equality are new things under the sun," he urged, an experiment being attempted most rigorously in only three places in the world: France, the northern United States, and the capitalist cities of England.[20] But the experiment was perilous, for it exalted the "Sovereignty of the Individual" above society and government. If left unchecked, he said, it would destroy all government, even "family government and family relations," including slavery. It would do so because liberal individualism undermines traditional social ties that are not only valuable but essential. The glorification of the individual leads to selfishness and the irrepressible pursuit of self-interest. It leads to the corruption and decay of natural social ties that bind people together, not in self-interest but in feelings of love and mutuality. In destroying people's sense of obligation to one another, liberalism replaces that sense with the crass pursuit of commerce and wealth. In the process, it destroys the family, the best expression of ties that bind. Plantation slavery, in contrast, was a form of communism, a kind of conservative socialism, that recognized and reinforced people's natural social ties. Slavery promoted and preserved traditional family values. That's why southerners had nothing but "love and veneration for the family." The logical end of liberty and equality, in contrast, was "an Oneida den of incest, a Greeley phalanstery, or a New York free love salon." (We'll take up the Oneida community in Chapter 7.) Incest and free love are "the distinctly avowed programme of all able abolitionists." It was bad enough, he said, that abolitionists opposed slavery. But in taking down slavery, abolitionists would also take down family itself. "The annihilation of the Family is part the programme of Abolition."[21]

This claim, of course, was overblown. By the mid-nineteenth century, there were several forms of family in America, each distinguished largely by the kind of economic production in which it was engaged. There were emerging dynastic families of enormous wealth, more modest bourgeois families (rich and poor), agrarian families (rich and poor), and families of laboring classes (from middling to desperate). And there were slaveholding families. Only the last did abolitionists consciously want to eradicate.

NORTH AMERICAN SOIL

In an influential history of American slavery, Eugene Genovese concedes several points to Fitzhugh. Southerners did indeed glorify family as being crucial to civilization and spoke of slaves as part of the family. The latter usage was present not only in everyday discourse but also in judicial decisions and laws of the states. After secession, the Confederate Congress, too, committed itself to the view that the plantation was a family. Genovese notes, with understatement, that "this special sense of family shaped southern culture." To be sure, the slaveholding family was patriarchal. Masters viewed themselves as "authoritarian fathers who presided over an extended and subservient family, white and black." Patriarchy, of course, was part of all legally sanctioned families in North America before the late twentieth century. In this respect, at least, families under slavery shared something with nuclear families as regulated by law. And Genovese notes that the patriarchy of slavery did not preclude genuine elements of kindness, affection, intimacy, and reciprocity within slaveholding families, just as it did not preclude them in patriarchal free families. If these elements were interpreted differently by blacks and whites, says Genovese, they were nonetheless negotiated and, in some sense, mutual. Still, this was explicitly and unapologetically a regime of supremacy, not only by sex (as under the common law) but also by race. The various forms of supremacy and of its enforcement meant that affection, duty, and reciprocity were never (and could not be) genuinely equivalent, for slavery's "arrogant doctrine of domination and its inherent cruelty toward disobedient 'children' . . . pitted blacks against whites in bitter antagonism [and] simultaneously poisoned the life of the dominant white community itself."[22] Thus, Genovese's account of families under slavery is substantially less cheery than Fitzhugh's was. Nonetheless, Genovese agrees that the material condition of many slaves was no more debased than that of laborers under industrial capitalism.[23]

Even if slaves were all in the family and even if characteristics of slavery's patriarchy resembled those of nuclear families, the slaveholding family was different. One difference was that it was layered or mixed. That is, slaves not only were part of the master's household but also, in most cases, had families of their own. Kenneth Stampp notes that families in Africa had been regulated within thick tribal moral codes. Preserving (much less enforcing) the norms of such a code was impossible in a new world in which many of the tribal relations, institutions, and incentives of Africa had weakened, if not dissolved entirely.[24] Contributing to this condition was the fact that many owners encouraged their slaves to adopt a semblance of the forms of white families. The strictures of slavery made it impossible for slaves to adhere strictly to white practices and standards, such as they were. But slaves' families often did bear at least a formal resemblance to those of whites.[25]

One aspect of this similarity was that owners not only permitted marriage between slaves but in many cases encouraged it. To be sure, these marriages were not binding under law, for slaves technically lacked legal capacity to enter into contracts, and masters possessed ultimate authority to approve or forbid (and, as we'll see, to dissolve) a union. But marriages did occur. Stampp describes the marital families of slaves as socially impoverished. For one thing, on his terms, they tended to be matriarchal. Thus, he said, the "slave family" was generally perceived to consist solely of the mother and her children. The husband, says Stampp, was reduced to being her assistant and sexual partner, even her "possession." For another, marriages served as a kind of voluntary concubinage, dissolvable either at the pleasure of either party or by direction of the master. Most marriages, therefore, were marked by instability and impermanence. Even in a family with a clearly designated matriarch at the head, the woman in slavery was a wife only secondarily. She was primarily a full-time servant to the owner, with little time to devote to her own household. Slavery's factory-like division of labor required most slaves to labor in groups other than families. This meant that the husband was not the head, protector, or provider for his family. His diminished status in turn led to emasculation. In short, slave families lacked strong, present parents. Stampp argues that there were three consequences of this social and economic dynamic. First, slaves exhibited a casual attitude toward marriage, which tended to inhibit "deep and enduring affection" between husband and wife. As Stampp puts it, a good master was more valuable than a spouse. Second, slave parents demonstrated indifference toward their own children. Third, slaves' lives were marked by sexual promiscuity, neglect, and physical abuse. Stampp notes that some masters tried to enforce a kind of discipline in living together and "behaving properly" by punishing adultery, enforcing obligations between spouses, and imposing constraints on abuse. A few owners ran what were essentially domestic relations courts to manage domestic conflicts. Still, he observes, most owners simply ignored or even accepted unfaithful behavior as long as it wasn't socially disruptive. The bottom line on the plantation, says Stampp, was that, as a legal matter, there was no such thing as fornication or adultery between slaves, nor bastardy, nor rape.[26]

Genovese's study challenges aspects of Stampp's portrait. He paints instead a picture of slaves' families that is both less bleak and more complex and that acknowledges in slaves a more robust capacity to carve out the semblance of a dignified familial life, despite the bonds of slavery. Genovese doesn't deny what he calls the "life-affirming" embrace of sex among slaves. In fact, some of the men—especially those who had privileges off the plantation as drivers or such—did practice polygyny, frequently with the master's permission. Within the plantation, masters would use male slaves as studs for the purpose of breeding. And there was little shame if an unmarried girl got pregnant, and certainly no assumption that she was barred from marriage after the pregnancy. That said, slaves' sexual behavior tended not to comport with the image of promiscuity and license that preoccupied the white mind. Rates of venereal disease were remarkably low among slaves. And slaves themselves actively regulated sexual behavior in the quarters. This was consistent with the view that sin was "primarily a moral offense to the community rather than to God." Slaves (perhaps more than masters, interestingly) looked sternly on extra-marital sex, at least for wives. And, in practice, most wives were faithful. Even men who might not have always behaved faithfully did want to marry for love. In short, says Genovese, "slaves did not separate marriage or sex from love." If the standards of morality and sexual propriety that they fashioned "deviated from prevailing white standards" of the day, we today "would not necessarily . . . judge [them] negatively."[27]

Most slaves who married did so in their mid-teens. Although masters had an interest in encouraging marriage, pressure to marry, especially for girls, came mainly from momma, not master. Owners plainly preferred marriages within a single plantation. Because intra-plantation unions were not always feasible, however, especially on small plantations, many masters relented to slaves' wishes, even if the chosen mate was not within the plantation family. In fact, Genovese reports that masters adopted a general custom of permitting marriage off the plantation. This custom was recognized and enforced at law in North Carolina, at the same time the law refused to formally recognize the marriages as binding. Plainly, says Genovese, "these interplantation marriages rested on affection and commitment."[28]

Another indication of the significance of marriage is that the weddings themselves were conducted with a nontrivial amount of ceremony. Marriages were frequently formally solemnized by a preacher (white or black) or by the master himself, sometimes in a church and most often on the plantation, even occasionally in the "big house." Some were quite lavish, with dresses and food and gifts. A common ceremony involved "jumping the broom." In it, the couple would attempt to jump backwards over a broom, with the broomstick held slightly off the floor. According to nuptial superstition, if only one spouse cleared the broom without touching it, s/he would rule the household. If both jumped cleanly, they would rule equally. Genovese doesn't indicate what followed if neither spouse cleared the broom, but the potential for an equal rule of the household was a significant departure from the common-law template. To be sure, whites often viewed the ceremony with amusement. Slaves, however, attached their own meaning to the proceeding, which lent it a kind of dignity that even whites sometimes acknowledged. The vows in many ceremonies, especially those supervised by preachers, might be recognizable to us today. Usually missing from the vows, however, was the phrase "till death do you part." Everyone understood the significance of the omission. And, even if a preacher might "slip" and recite the phrase from the Book of Common Prayer, slaves understood that the passage, unlike slavery itself, wasn't binding.[29]

Against Stampp, Genovese says that slave families were not matriarchal all the way down. He observes that slave men did often provide for their families, usually by hunting and fishing for additional food. Most masters permitted this, even though it meant that slaves were armed, which was technically a violation of slave states' laws. Some plantations celebrated an "all-plantation hunt," in which every male on the plantation, white or black, participated. As reinforcers of slave masculinity, Genovese says these events (and hunting in general, for that matter) were not inconsequential. In fact, they were part of a larger gendered division of labor that prescribed specific roles to men and, he says, mitigated men's slide to emasculation. The self-interested reason for such policies, Genovese says, was the perception among owners that some "spirit" among male slaves contributed to productivity on the plantation and helped to promote a kind of order in the quarters. Masculine order was not always beneficent, of course. While slave fathers could exhibit "kindness and affection" toward their children, they could also be "stern disciplinarians," even to the point of violence. And as husbands, men could be quite brutal toward their wives. Masters frowned upon the beating of a child. And they generally forbade wife-beating (at least by a slave husband). But slave wives, even when physically abused, often refrained from seeking the protection of their masters. For one thing, they didn't want to see their husbands subjected to physical punishment and humiliation at the hands of the master or his overseer. For another, some wives preferred to handle violence on their own, with the help of their fathers, brothers, or others.[30] One thing is certain: the level of violence in the quarters, even if not the norm, does not amount to supporting evidence for Genovese's claim of healthy masculinity in slave families. On the contrary, it's a sign that a healthy psyche was being undermined by conditions both on and off the plantation.

That said, slave children did have something of a childhood, subject to few demands for labor, and usually free from violence from owners. So if Philippe Ariès was correct that childhood was an invention of modernity, then slave families were, to that extent, modern.[31] As to violence, there were legal limits to the physical punishment or pain a master might inflict on a slave child, and sometimes they were enforced judicially. A master in Georgia, for example, was convicted of manslaughter for whipping to death a slave girl of thirteen years; and in 1857, the Supreme Court of Georgia affirmed the conviction. Typically, slave children did little or no labor before the age of eight. Between the ages of eight and twelve, they performed work that wasn't terribly onerous: tending gardens or trapping animals for food. Another job, at least for older children (usually girls), was to look after and raise the younger children. This provided quasi-parental experience and, for many, a sense of responsibility. In fact, most performed the job conscientiously, and some were so trusted that the mistress of the plantation would leave her own children to be supervised by young slaves. Still, some infant slaves were crippled or killed because of rough or poor care from the elder children. (Supervision of white children was doubtless undertaken with greater delicacy and attentiveness.) By age twelve, the boys at least were often eager to go into the fields to plow. Doing so was a sign of manhood, and it permitted them to finally avoid wearing the "dresses" that were standard issue for slave children, boys and girls alike.[32]

Childhood included games of many sorts. Some would be recognizable today: marbles, hide and seek, stickball, jump rope. But others were more sinister. Games like "whipping with switches" and "auction" reflected the condition to which even children recognized they were subject. White and black children played together on the plantation and, Genovese reports, did so fairly unselfconsciously. Usually, boys played with boys and girls with girls, but if play brought boys and girls together "there [was] little evidence of those postbellum sexual fears [of] . . . lily-white daughters playing with black boys." On the whole, children helped and supported one another across racial lines, and a few became friends. Sometimes, however, a white child would attempt at an early age to aggressively "lord it over" a black child. Occasionally the latter would physically retaliate. At times on those occasions, the master would permit the black child to get away with the retaliation, the ostensible lesson being that there were limits to lordship. Even so, for all young slaves there came a time when they realized their place was not to be a friend or playmate to their white companions but to serve. For some, this realization was unexpected and sorrowful.[33]

Growing up, slave children's biggest challenge was less to please master than to navigate within their own families in the quarters. Physical discipline within slave families could be frequent and severe, even cruel. Even some masters worried that slave parents hit their children "too hard and too often." One reason for adult slaves' physical treatment of children was doubtless a function of the fear, uncertainty, and violence to which most slave parents themselves were subject. This was not merely an expression of the social power of imitation or habit. It was more significantly an example of the ways in which social oppression can produce severe psychic stresses that erupt in violence. There was also, however, a rational parental basis for severe discipline. The adult slave's world was dangerous, and self-control was crucial to survival. In part for this reason, parents taught their children manners, including racial etiquette and "courtesy and deference to adults." If parents backed up the lessons with physical force, it had the corollary benefit of reinforcing both the importance of the lesson and the stakes of neglecting it. Ironically, masters and mistresses typically treated young slaves with gentleness and even affection. Genovese observes that this was often genuine, as revealed in masters' grief over the deaths of young slaves. But it also created a perverse psychological dynamic in which children attached to their owners and scorned their parents. As a result, owners frequently got credit for the good things parents were doing but no blame for parental excesses. And when children grew up, went into the fields, and suffered under the oppressive hand of an overseer or driver, the master could frequently avoid blame because the adult slave maintained a psychic image of him as a kind and fatherly figure. It was an important and effective element of a larger system of social control.[34]

Aging and elderly slaves posed a problem for both the plantation and families in the quarters. Many "old folks" continued to do work—from caring for the young, to capturing and disposing of rats, to administering folk medicine in the quarters. But these were less-than-robust contributions to the life of the plantation. Illness or simple physical decline could mean that even these responsibilities were out of reach for some. What to do with these slaves? If the law was largely silent on that question, there were social pressures on masters to meet some duty of care toward aged or disabled slaves. In the face of social pressure, masters' behavior ranged widely, from "full and kind consideration," to "minimum attention to paternalistic responsibilities," to "indifference and sheer barbarism." Most masters fell into the median category, providing at least a basic level of material comfort. This, they told themselves, was a responsibility that accompanied ownership. And in practice it was often superior to the plight of aging labor under industrial capitalism. But notwithstanding Fitzhugh's happy portrait, some masters shirked, either manumitting slaves in old age and thus leaving them to fend for themselves off the plantation, or exposing them to savage neglect on the plantation. Perhaps unsurprisingly, a capitalist invention—private insurance policies on the lives of slaves—provided masters a material motive to neglect slaves in the decline of old age. If the behavior of masters ranged widely, so too did the behavior of families in the quarters. When masters were neglectful, some younger slaves—children and grandchildren—responded to their aging ancestors with indifference or worse. When they did, others in the quarters would usually step up to provide care. But, with limited resources, the level of care was frequently lower than might be desired or even necessary.[35]

SEVERED FAMILIES

Maintaining a degree of integrity in slaves' families was challenging enough under the "ordinary" circumstances described above. Often, however, families were subject to even greater structural stresses of two types. The first type involved sexual predation by whites. There were several reasons for its proliferation: patriarchy, of course, but also the relative autonomy and insularity of the slaveholding household, the relative lack of autonomy and insularity of the slave household, and the areas of substantially unchecked power that law carved out for masters. The second type involved the susceptibility of slave families to being broken up. Here, too, and to an even greater extent, law was the vehicle through which power over the families of slaves was exercised, for law not only conceded the space for action, but also supplied the means.

If sex between whites and slaves was not the norm in antebellum America, it wasn't a rarity, either. One could find whites at every social level who were involved in sexual relations with slaves. Such relations occurred between white men and female slaves, and between white women and male slaves. (I've uncovered no data on same-sex white–slave sexual relations, though it's possible that they occurred.) The existence of relations between white women and male slaves was evidenced by the fact that some husbands sought divorce on the ground that their wives had "indecent companionship" with a slave. Stampp reports one such proceeding in which the wife admitted the relationship and testified that her paramour had made love to her "better than anybody in the world." Predictably, such relations did not always involve a woman who was married. Less predictably, they were sometimes long-lasting. The more common cross-racial sex between a white and a slave was between a white man and a slave woman (or girl). Quite often, these encounters involved a man outside the plantation. Typically, they were casual and therefore fleeting. The social cost of these relationships tended to be low—partly because they were relatively easy to conceal, partly because, when known, they were received with winks and nods among white men. Occasionally, however, a man might desire a lasting relationship or even a wife, despite prohibitory legislation. If these more ambitious relations were visible, their social stigma could be quite high. Whether the relationship was short- or long-term, the male was frequently "familiar" in the sense that he resided or worked on the plantation. Overseers, for example, could be a source of considerable commotion for their "sneaking about after . . . negro girls." The disruption was all the greater when the "girls" involved were already married, which raised the ire of their husbands, who sometimes reacted by running away. But even if the objects of his desire were unmarried, an unrestrained overseer could create turmoil, siring (and often leaving behind) a number of mulatto children born to more than one woman.[36]

Sex involving white men, however, was not confined to the hired help. Male members of the planter class were involved at a high rate. Stampp speculates, in fact, that interracial sex "was more common among [the males of the planter class] than among the members of any other group." Mary Boykin Chesnut, writing from the South on the eve of the Civil War, provided support for this view: "God forgive us, but ours is a *monstrous* system and wrong and iniquity. . . . Like the patriarchs of old our men live all in one house with their wives and their concubines, and the mulattoes one sees in every family exactly resemble the white children—and every lady tells you who is the father of all the mulatto children in everybody's household, but those in her own she seems to think drop from the clouds, or pretends so to think." Chesnut's suggestion that most interracial children on the plantation were the children of masters may have been overstated. Even Stampp, who is sympathetic to her complaint, indicates that "most of the relationships between slave women and males of the slaveholding class were the casual adventures of adolescents engaged in sexual experimentation, of college students on concupiscent larks, and of older bachelors or widowers periodically demanding the favors of one of their female chattels." Genovese casts still more doubt on the generality of Chesnut's allegation, claiming that, on many plantations, "little or no miscegenation occurred." Relying on census data, he estimates that the percentage of the slave population that was "part white" was one-fourth to one-third that of the population of free Negroes. Having said this, he admits that such data were notoriously unreliable, not least because they were based on observations of skin color and similar traits, and there were incentives to suppress the number of mixed-race persons, both on and off the plantation.[37]

Whichever of the accounts of miscegenation comes closest to the truth, it is certainly the case that there was plenty of sex occurring between slaves and male members of the slaveholding class, including masters—and sufficient numbers on the plantation to constitute, as Genovese puts it, "a scandal." These numbers were despite the fact that married black men did not take lightly white sexual aggression toward their wives. Against great risk, black women (and sometimes their husbands) resisted overtly and sometimes fiercely. Even when resistance wasn't overt, women were often able to set limits to sexual predation, which most masters were at pains to respect. Despite this, rape occurred. As evidence that many masters expected sexual relations, a special segment of the slave market was devoted to sexually attractive women, who were purchased for the plain purpose of sexual access. Interracial sex on the plantation ranged from seduction to rape, and, in general, it tended to be more vicious than miscegenation off the plantation. Still, Genovese notes, even liaisons that began in seduction or exploitation could engender some measure of affection over time.[38]

Two legal decisions are instructive on this score. *Patton v. Patton* (1831) involved a contest of a master's will. The contestants were the master's (white) heirs, who were vexed because the will had liberated several of the decedent's slaves, including one whom the decedent had professed an intention to marry. The heirs' legal claim was essentially that their deceased ancestor's intention to marry a slave was proof that he was insane (and therefore lacked capacity to execute the will). The Kentucky Supreme Court gave the claim the back of its hand. The court noted that the practice of rearing mixed-race children outside the bonds of matrimony was "too common" to justify a conclusion that the white fathers of such children were insane. "White men, who may wish to marry negro women, or who carry on illicit intercourse with them, may, notwithstanding, possess such soundness of mind as to be capable in law, of making a valid will and testament."[39]

A case from Alabama, *Mosser v. Mosser* (1856), was more ambiguous but still informative. The action involved a complaint for divorce, brought by Mrs. Mosser against her husband. The alleged ground was adultery between Mr. Mosser and a young mulatto slave named Holland, owned by Mrs. Mosser. Mr. Mosser's primary defense was that it was legally impossible to commit adultery with a slave. His secondary defense was that there was insufficient evidence that he had engaged in carnal relations outside of marriage. The testimony, coming mainly from a white housekeeper who lived at the couple's house, indicated that Mr. Mosser was fond of Holland, that he persuaded his wife to move to Florida while he stayed behind (with Holland) in Alabama, and that, after Mrs. Mosser departed for Florida, he and Holland became intimately involved. The housekeeper testified that Holland and Mr. Mosser regularly slept together at night on the same bed, behind the closed door of his bedroom. The chancellor below sensibly found the evidence of adultery to be persuasive, and granted Mrs. Mosser's petition on that ground. Although the Supreme Court of Alabama held that a slave was a person for many purposes of law, including for participating in an adulterous affair, a majority of the court reversed the chancellor's judgment. The basis for reversal was apparently that the housekeeper's testimony was essentially innuendo, as she had not actually seen Mosser and Holland *in flagrante delicto*. (She had only heard them through the door and repaired their ruffled bed sheets on subsequent mornings.) The majority's position was curious, not only because it altered the burden of proof in a civil action of this type, but also because it was all too tenderly disposed to protect the interest of the master. If Justice wasn't blind, she did seem to look the other way where hegemonic privilege was involved.[40]

This sort of legal toleration (if that's the correct term) of sex between the races was the norm in antebellum America—including the South. The state of South Carolina, for example, did not formally forbid interracial sexual relations until after the Civil War, when all manner of states entrenched racial restrictions. And black men were not lynched for being sexually involved with white women before the war. Genovese notes that if "meaningful affairs"—relations of some duration in which a degree of caring was present—were not common, neither were they rare, even among the planter class. Still, such relations could produce "emotional confusion," which over time could produce self-loathing and a projected loathing of the other.[41]

If the structure of sexual relations on the plantation created problems for slave families (especially marriages), another phenomenon was potentially catastrophic: members of families could be forcibly separated from one another, thus effectively dissolving those families. This was a notable extension of the common-law principles, identified in Chapter 2, that authorized the separation of children from their impoverished parents for the purpose of distributing labor more efficiently. In the case of slaves, events precipitating a breakup of their families were varied. Some circumstances were necessitous. For example, a master might find himself in financial trouble and would voluntarily sell assets to preserve liquidity or capital stability. Not infrequently, however, creditors used legal process to force the seizure and sale of assets, with proceeds going to creditors. Typically, these sales were of slaves as individuals, not as families, unless it happened that the sale of a family benefitted the creditor. On every plantation at some point, of course, the master died. If the decedent left a will, some wrenching separations of family might be avoided, assuming he had been disposed to avoid them. But not all masters were inclined in this direction, and even those who were couldn't always control the distribution of property from the grave. Without a valid will, division and sale of the estate were often unavoidable, especially if heirs were numerous or disagreeable. Courts presiding over decedents' estates were rarely solicitous of slaves' families. As the Supreme Court of North Carolina put it with unselfconscious irony, breaking up families "must be done, if the executor discovers that the interest of the estate requires it; for he is not to indulge his charities at the expense of others." In fact, the court expressed a presumption against the sale of slaves as a group or family, because the market value of the whole was typically less than the sum of its parts. And any executor who sold slaves as a family, instead of as individuals, "does it at his peril, and must answer for the true value." In this way, efficiency extracted its price through the law. Many familial separations, however, arose neither from financial distress nor from the need to settle a decedent's estate. A master who wanted unimpeded access to a female slave, for example, might sell off her husband. A master who was displeased with a slave for misconduct might punitively sell either the offending slave or one or more family members as retribution or simply as a device for achieving a measure of social control.[42]

Whatever the motive or circumstance of separations, Fogel and Engerman claim that they occurred far less frequently than Stampp alleges. Genovese splits the difference, claiming that Fogel and Engerman's data, derived from controversial quantitative methods, underestimate the rate of forced familial breakups, while Stampp overestimates masters' willingness to separate members of families. If Stampp has overestimated, it's possible that the lower rate of separation was at least partly attributable to law. Louisiana's code, for example, prohibited the separate sale of a mother and her children who were younger than ten. Other states (but not all) had similar prohibitions against selling young children away from their mother. In practice, only Louisiana's law appeared to be effective. And, although Alabama and Georgia had modest restrictions on breaking up families via forced sale to satisfy creditors, those states imposed no restriction when the master sold voluntarily. In states that most heavily exported slaves (mainly in the upper South), children of any age could be separated from their mother. And

Stampp observes persuasively that, even if slaves were sold as intact families at market, it was not uncommon for members to be separated and resold as individuals, especially if the initial purchaser was a slave monger.[43]

If law provided only minimal constraint against separation, and the market none at all, then the primary force for keeping intact the families of slaves resided in masters' moral sense. Genovese claims this sense was often genuine and sometimes powerful. Even Stampp concedes that a nontrivial number of slaveholders recognized and respected the marriages of slaves and attempted to keep slaves' families together. He cites, for example, a Tennessee slaveholder's purchase of slaves, not because he needed them, but because they were married to slaves on his plantation, who implored him to purchase their spouses so they could live in the same place. And there was the master in Kentucky who, facing financial necessity, gave his slaves authority to find a new owner, satisfactory to them, and agreed not to sell them outside the immediate vicinity. Masters' wills did sometimes direct heirs not to separate families, or not to disperse them geographically, or to provide special solicitude or care for individuals (often as a reward for obedience). Stampp argues that these examples were notable because they were so unusual. Genovese counters that the exception was more frequent than Stampp allows. Even on Genovese's account, however, it's clear that compassionate acts (in contrast with the mere profession of a caring sensibility) were not the norm. It is clear also that, for most masters who faced financial trials, material interest trumped moral concerns.[44]

RUPTURE IN THE CONSTITUTIONAL ORDER

As we've already seen, slavery was controversial despite its being constitutionally protected. This was partly a function of values. Just as powerfully, perhaps even more so, it was a function of interest. The geographic setting for one important set of disagreements was the westward frontier, where the interests of slaveholding households would collide with the interests of non-slaveholding households. We'll see in Chapter 5 some particulars of the latter households—how they became the vanguard for expanding the constitutional dominion of the nation. For now, I'd like to foreshadow the conflict of constitutional politics and eventually constitutional law that arose between the two sets of households. In essence, the question was this: To whom did the frontier belong? Was it a domain exclusively for nonslave labor, agriculture, and enterprise, or were slaveholding households permitted as well?

This question had roiled American politics for decades. Almost from the beginning, Congress had attempted to manage it by drawing boundaries. One of the earliest policies that Congress enacted after the Revolution was the Northwest Ordinance, which, among other things, barred slavery from the Northwest Territory (what we now think of as the upper Midwest).[45] In fact, slavery was present in the Northwest Territory well into the nineteenth century, but Congress had drawn a line. The difficulty with this solution, as Jefferson's purchase of the Louisiana Territory from France had guaranteed, was that the nation was expanding even beyond the Northwest Territory. Again, Congress attempted to resolve disputes over the new territory by drawing a boundary. Admitting Maine as a free state and Missouri as a state permitting slavery, the Missouri Compromise allowed slavery in the westward states-to-be south of 36°36′ (Missouri's southern boundary) and prohibited it north of that latitude.[46] Even this settlement did not hold, however, due mainly to the United States' unprovoked invasion of Mexico and seizure of a massive new southwestern territory, including California. Congress enacted yet another, superceding compromise in 1850, but its hold on the problem was proving tenuous. Outright wars between slaveholding interests and non-slaveholding interests were erupting in parts of the country, including especially Kansas.[47]

Into the growing chaos stepped the Supreme Court in *Dred Scott v. Sandford*, which held as a matter of right that slaveholding households could not be excluded from any territory.[48] If there was any uncertainty, the Court declared the Missouri Compromise unconstitutional, despite the fact that it was by then defunct. *Dred Scott* exacerbated cleavages in American constitutional politics in ways that would be fateful for the order. One powerful manifestation of those cleavages appeared in a series of debates in Illinois between contenders for a seat in the U.S. Senate.[49] Like Thomas Paine eight decades before (though for a very different purpose), Abraham Lincoln understood that images of home and family could be rhetorically potent for attacking *Dred Scott*. He invoked the image of home in a speech in Springfield before his formal debates with Stephen A. Douglas began. The United States itself, he suggested, was a metaphorical house for a national family:

> "A house divided against itself cannot stand." I believe this government cannot endure permanently half slave and half free. I do not expect the Union to be dissolved; I do not expect the house to fall; but I do expect it will cease to be divided. It will become all one thing, or all the other. Either the opponents of slavery will arrest the further spread of it, and place it where the public mind shall rest in the belief that it is in the course of ultimate extinction, or its advocates will push it forward till it shall become alike lawful in all the States, old as well as new, North as well as South.[50]

Ironically, the inspiration for this move had come from Fitzhugh, who had written: "One set of ideas will govern and control after a while in the civilized world. Slavery will everywhere be abolished, or every where be re-instituted."[51] Although Lincoln's rhetorical reply suggested a distinct policy toward territorial settlement, his commitments were complex and conflicted throughout his debates with Douglas. At bottom, however, Lincoln's position seems to have been this: the territories should be open to settlement by free labor, to the exclusion of slave labor; on petition for admission to the Union, the citizens of each prospective new state could decide whether slavery would be permitted.[52]

Underlying this position were two sentiments: a belief that free labor was the wave of the future and an aversion to opening the territories to settlement by blacks, slave or free. Lincoln united these sentiments in a depiction of the (white) republican family. The territories, he insisted, should be reserved for "free white laborers, who want the land to bring up their families upon." He affirmed the proposition that Douglas had pressed in an earlier speech, "that this government was made for white men." "No one," said Lincoln, "wants to deny it." Thus, free families in the territories should be racially pure: "As God made us separate, we can leave one another alone, and do one another much good thereby. There are white men enough to marry all the white women, and enough black men to marry all the black women; and in God's name let them be so married." Separation, he said, would prevent the racial "amalgamation" that Douglas feared. "Why, Judge [Douglas], if we do not let [the races] get together in the Territories, they won't mix there."[53] When pressed in southern Illinois, Lincoln said, "very frankly that I am not in favor of negro citizenship." Hence, he opposed *Dred Scott,* not because it denied the possibility of citizenship for blacks but because it permitted slaveholding families to reside anywhere in the nation. By the end of the debates, he denied "the social and political equality of the white and black races." He also disavowed the right of blacks to vote, to serve on juries, to hold office, or to marry whites.[54]

Lincoln's position on race was not static, of course. He would gravitate to more liberal views before his assassination. But it is telling that racialist views of home and family would be so resonant for an antislavery politician and for the people of a state in which slavery had never been legal. Unsurprisingly, such views did not die after the Civil War, after the abolition of slavery, nor even after the ratification of the Fourteenth Amendment.

THE RACIAL FAMILY IN POSTWAR AMERICA

By the end of the Civil War, the country faced two questions. One, which was peculiar to the states that had maintained slavery, was how to treat established familial relations of former slaves. The answer to this question tended to be straightforward on the surface, though sometimes more complicated in individual application. Although some states around this time were beginning to adopt a bureaucratically rationalized process for registering and approving marriages, the companionate relations of former slaves (even those relations solemnized by ceremony) would have failed to meet requirements of the prescribed administrative process. The American institution of common-law marriage provided a vehicle for former slave states to ratify retroactively these relationships and hence to legitimate the children born to them.[55] Often, complications arose. For example, couples whose relationships had been solemnized when they were slaves were sometimes separated, either because of sales or flight during slavery or because of the confusing aftermath of emancipation. For those couples who remained together, however, the institution of common-law marriage promoted both a practical equity and a kind of liberty that an administrative state would have been unable to deliver. And uniformly, the states even of the former Confederacy extended to former slaves the right to marry.[56]

The second question, which extended far beyond the former slave states, beyond even the racial dichotomy of black and white, was whether to permit persons of any "class" to marry outside their presumptive (or legally prescribed) race. Prohibitions against interracial marriage—or even sexual relations—were in place in some colonies, North and South, before the separation from Britain. Penalties ranged from fines, to imprisonment, to corporal punishment, to the loss of freedom (for blacks), to extensions of the period for indentured servitude (mainly for whites). After the Revolution, some states got rid of prohibitory laws. But the tendency was to enact (or to reenact) them. By the beginning of the Civil War, twenty-eight states (out of thirty-one) had enacted prohibitions against interracial marriage. Despite their proliferation, laws prohibiting marriage were wildly under-enforced, and prohibitions against interracial sex were enforced even more rarely. Reasons for the weak enforcement of laws against sexual relations included the frequency of cross-racial sexual relations, the difficulty of detection, and the fact that the practice was so closely tied to prerogatives of white manhood. Reasons for under-enforcement of laws prohibiting marriage were more subtle. As Dan Sharfstein has pointed out, local communities often tolerated such unions because digging too deeply into racial origins would have threatened any number of families who had established themselves as white. Sometimes, it was better not to know nor even to ask. But even when the racial identities of couples were widely acknowledged, it was sometimes the case that communities tolerated violations simply because it could be more socially disruptive to enforce the law than to leave people be. Still, toleration wasn't uniform, and even when officials didn't prosecute, social pressures could be substantial. Rachel Moran notes that black men were especially vulnerable to punishment, whether within or outside of the law, for sexual relations with white women.[57]

By the end of the Civil War, the law again entered a period of change. South Carolina and Mississippi, which hadn't previously prohibited interracial sex or marriage, enacted bans in 1865. The trend, however, ran in the other direction. In recognition of the new citizenship status of blacks, several western states repealed their prohibitory laws, and Pascoe notes that, in the immediate wake of the Civil War, seven of the eleven former Confederate States repealed their antimiscegenation laws, removed them from their codes, or declared them unconstitutional. Still, the war had depleted the number of white men in southern states. That fact, combined with emancipation, heightened fears among some southern whites that racial boundaries were on the verge of dissolution. This fear incited intense scrutiny of sex across color lines, especially sex between black men and white women. Having said that, it would be a mistake to conclude that there was a univocal southern white view on interracial marriage. Southern views, like those in other parts of the country, were complex. But two tendencies emerged. One was a relative tolerance of sex and even marriage of white men to black women, especially when the men were of a lower class. The second was a suspicion of sex and marriage between black men and white women. More often than not, this latter concern was enforced through extra-legal means. In fact, it was one of the central concerns that animated and agitated the newly emerging, and later quite active, Ku Klux Klan.[58]

If the early years after defeat in the Civil War brought a surprising level of moderation in the South, the end of Reconstruction marked the beginning of retrenchment and reaction. Between 1879 and 1894, all five of the Southern states whose legislatures had repealed laws prohibiting interracial sex and marriage had reinstated them. Other states increased punishments, and, by the beginning of the twentieth century, more than half of the United States prohibited miscegenation. A few even entrenched prohibitions in their state constitutions.[59]

States relied on three methods for policing racial lines. One, which emerged with greatest force in the first quarter of the twentieth century, involved the use of emerging institutions of the administrative state. As states began to abjure doctrines of common-law marriage, which had provided ways of uniting outside the watchful eye of government, they adopted formal licensing requirements, which obliged every couple who wanted the cover of law for their relationship to seek *ex ante* the permission of the state. As Pascoe describes this move, states could employ "a virtual army of bureaucrats perfectly positioned to enforce state miscegenation laws" by the simple act of denying interracial couples a license to marry. Virginia was in the vanguard in devising a regulatory apparatus for this purpose. Virginia's scheme involved not only a bureaucracy for imposing mandatory regulations for licensing marriages, but also an administrative agency whose functions included a voluntary system of racial registration. These two instruments of the administrative state were effective in restricting access to marriage.[60]

A second method for enforcing bans on interracial relationships was via civil judicial proceedings. A variety of proceedings, including divorces and inheritance, could involve an allegation that one or another party had violated a prohibition against miscegenation. For example, an allegation in probate that a marriage was void because the parties to the marriage were of different races could undermine claims of dower or other rights to property asserted by black widows of white husbands. The very possibility of having to face a claim of violation made some (though not all) interracial couples fearful of even the most routine appearance in a judicial proceeding.[61]

The third method was to use the criminal law. Criminal penalties ranged from fines to imprisonment at hard labor. Although the criminal law was the most typical prohibition on the books, at least after Reconstruction, its use was sporadic. One reason for its discontinuous use was that criminal enforcement depended on public complaints, which were less frequent than one might have imagined. But even if infrequent, arrest could serve an expressive function, making examples of particular couples, even if it failed to identify every possible violation of the criminal law. In so doing, arrest could also serve to suppress interracial relations, or at least to give reason to keep them invisible. Even irregular enforcement of law can promote interests in social control. So, arrests there were, especially as states began systematically to try to channel sex through licensed marriage.[62]

Although Alabama retained common-law marriage (indeed, has done so to the present day), its criminal regulation of sex and marriage in the late nineteenth century was not atypical. Section 4184 of the post-Reconstruction Code of Alabama prescribed fines and/or jail for "any man and woman [who] live together in adultery or fornication." For a first offense, the fine was a maximum of $100, and jail time (in a county facility) was limited to six months (with the possibility of hard labor). Section 4189 of the Code denominated a separate crime for "any white person and any negro [who shall] intermarry or live in adultery or fornication." "Negro" included "the descendant of any negro to the third generation, inclusive, though one ancestor of each generation was a white person." The penalty for this crime was dramatically higher than for garden-variety single-race fornication or adultery. For violating Section 4189, a person "must, on conviction, be imprisoned in the penitentiary or sentenced to hard labor for the county for not less than two nor more than seven years."[63] Did such a racialist regime run afoul of the Constitution of the United States?

In *Pace v. State of Alabama,* Tony Pace, "a negro man," and Mary Cox, "a white woman," were convicted of violating Section 4189 "for living together in a state of adultery or fornication" and were sentenced to two years' imprisonment in the state penitentiary. On appeal, the Supreme Court held that the differential punishments between Sections 4184 and 4189 did not violate the requirement of equal protection in the Fourteenth Amendment. "The two sections of the Code . . . are entirely consistent," the Court held. "The one prescribes, generally, a punishment for an offense committed between persons of different sexes; the other prescribes a punishment for an offense which can only be committed where the two sexes are of different races. There is in neither section any discrimination against either race." The Court concluded: "Whatever discrimination is made in the punishment prescribed in the two sections is directed against the offense designated and not against the person of any particular color or race. The punishment of each offending person, whether white or black, is the same."[64] More than eighty years later, the state of Virginia would offer precisely this justification to defend its own criminal prohibition.

BEYOND NORTH AND SOUTH AND BLACK AND WHITE

Some of the most elaborate, restrictive, and punitive regulations of interracial relations came not from the South but from western states. Like southern (and other) states, the western states banned sexual relations and marriage between blacks and whites, even though the tiny number of blacks in the West made this specific prohibition less "necessary" than in the South or even in northern states east of the Mississippi River. Out West, the larger concern was with "Asiatic" peoples—especially Chinese but also Japanese and (later) Filipino. Because immigration from China was solely for the purpose of obtaining cheap labor, the Chinese population in the West was almost exclusively male. Prohibitions on interracial marriage, therefore, denied almost all Chinese men the opportunity to legally marry or to procreate. An additional effect of this policy of social emasculation was to make Chinese men terminal denizens, with only a minimal future stake in their new "home." This in turn had the nontrivial effect of protecting the dominance of the newly resident white population.[65]

The states' policies could not have been effective without a parallel *national* commitment to restricting East Asians' access to or enjoyment of the United States. The increasingly articulate assumption behind exclusion was that race was a matter of blood, that blood was a carrier of traits of character (both moral and social), and that certain genetically transmissible traits made certain groups unfit for American citizenship. As with states' enforcement of prohibitions against marriage, the nation's ability to enforce exclusion was fortified by an extensive and potent administrative state, with virtually plenary discretion, to which even federal courts deferred. And concerns about family were near the heart of the nation's policy and method.[66]

The nation's use of race as a criterion for immigration and citizenship extended back to the U.S. Naturalization Law of 1790, which provided a process for naturalizing a resident alien who was a "free white person" possessing "good moral character." Although women could be naturalized, and minor children of a naturalized parent also became citizens, the 1790 Act provided that citizenship could not "descend to persons whose fathers have never been resident in the United States." As a matter of inheritance, then, citizenship ran strictly through the father. The Act also provided that "no person . . . proscribed by any state, shall be admitted a citizen . . . except by an act of the legislature of the state." In short, this ensured that slaves—or, in some places, persons of African descent—could not be citizens without the permission of the relevant state of residence.[67] The Fourteenth Amendment, which was enrolled as part of the Constitution in 1868, guaranteed citizenship to all persons born or naturalized in the United States, regardless of a particular state's policy. This, abstractly, provided a constitutional basis for former slaves and their descendants to be recognized as citizens. The Naturalization Act of 1870 reinforced this guarantee by, among other things, expressly expanding the privilege of naturalization "to aliens of African nativity and to persons of African descent."[68] This Act did not provide, however, a process for naturalization on a nonracial basis. Implicitly, therefore, the Act denied East Asians access to naturalized citizenship.

Immigration policy of the United States reinforced the restrictive implication of the naturalization statutes. The policy was rooted not merely in racial difference per se, nor even in a sense of cultural fit, but also in a fear that white Americans could not compete with East Asian (especially Chinese) labor. In short, it was born of a simultaneously conflicted sense of superiority and inferiority.

Immigration from China had begun in the mid-nineteenth century, especially after the Gold Rush in California. Chinese men were lured by the possibility of prosperity. A laborer on the transcontinental railroad, for example, could earn in wages ten times or more the amount he could earn as a peasant farmer in China. Railroad work was backbreaking, to be sure, but Chinese laborers (in the jargon of the day, "coolies") by the thousands helped knit the nation together with iron and lumber. In gratitude, the United States refused to permit families, too, to immigrate. And in 1882 (after the railroad was completed), Congress enacted the Chinese Exclusion Act, which suspended for ten years "the coming of Chinese laborers to the United States," established an administrative system for registering Chinese aliens in the country, and barred all Chinese from naturalization.[69]

In an age of Social Darwinism, it was telling to hear Senator Charles Miller (of California) argue that Chinese laborers were in fact the "fittest." They were, he said, "automatic engines of flesh and blood." Instead of rendering them superior across the board, however, their brutish fitness made Chinese unfit for American citizenship. Although the senator did not make the connection, these sentiments were similar to those that justified slavery and the exclusion of persons of African descent from citizenship earlier in the century. Representative Romualdo Pacheco (also of California) was less subtle than Senator Miller, as he told a genetic story of cultural difference:

> By the laws of heredity the habits of his ancestors live in his character and are incorporated into his blood and brain. . . . Family ties and obligations and the sweets of home life are naught to him. The long course of training which has gone on for so many generations has made of the Chinaman a lithe, sinewy creature, with muscles like iron, and almost devoid of nerves and sensibilities. His ancestors have also bequeathed to him the most hideous of immoralities. They are as natural to him as the yellow hue of his skin, and are so shocking and horrible that their character cannot even be hinted.

Family and heredity, both physical and moral, were thus sources of debasement and immorality, which disqualified Chinese from civilized life. What, though, of the natural rights and principles of the Declaration of Independence? Like Justice Taney in *Dred Scott,* proponents of exclusion noted that the original understanding of the Declaration referred only to the rights of white men. All others were inferior, for the purposes of citizenship.[70]

In 1884, Congress extended exclusion to all Chinese, regardless of whether they entered the United States directly from China or indirectly from some other place. In 1888, Congress extended the suspension of the immigration of laborers for twenty more years and strengthened the administrative system of registration. In 1892, Congress extended exclusion for another ten years and again strengthened the system of registration. In 1902, Congress extended exclusion indefinitely. In 1917, Congress enacted a literacy test, designed to allow only immigrants of the better sort, and established an "Asiatic barred zone" that excluded immigrants coming from virtually every Asian land. The only lands not included in this zone were China, which was already covered by extensive exclusionary laws, and Japan, which, because it was a nation of some international status, was subject to a softer set of exclusions by "Gentleman's Agreement." The National Origins Act of 1924 entrenched a system of racial quotas on immigration.[71] The Supreme Court did little to blunt these policies.[72] In fact, the Court upheld the Expatriation Act of 1907, which rescinded American citizenship of women (even white women) who married foreign men.[73] In short, even after the Fourteenth Amendment, the citizenship of even a "natural-born" woman was defeasible, and followed the status of her husband.

The racial family was (and, in many ways remains) remarkably resilient in American life. By the end of the nineteenth century, distinctions among races were central to people's understanding of a well-ordered society and to a moral understanding of sexuality and marriage. These understandings persisted despite the end of slavery and the appearance of the Fourteenth Amendment to the Constitution. And they persisted despite social practices and sexual relations that had long been complexifying both families and racial identities. Notwithstanding the nation's longstanding commitment to racial purity, complexity was part of the picture from the inception of the American order. Witness the historical (and continuing) salience of Thomas Jefferson's relations and progeny.[74] Witness also the disorientation that some yet feel when they encounter the racial ambiguity of their families' histories.[75] From the standpoint of the constitutional order, the racial family was integral to the nation's self-constitution. It informed the creation of rules for who could be a full member of the order. And it influenced the enforcement of legal rules concerning who could establish a permanent home, and where. For a long time, and for many intents and purposes, the racial family has been a distinctly American family.

5

Home on the Range

Families in American Continental Settlement

As important as the racial family has been, it would be myopic to view race as the sole constitutive marker for American family. Another type of family has also been central to American identity. It's the frontier family. To be sure, there was no single model for families that pushed westward across the continent to settle the frontier. Still, American lore has produced a potent image of hearty families, independent and self-reliant. Indeed, in many ways they were. But in important respects they weren't completely independent, for they were agents of the nation. They could serve as agents because they were well positioned to play distinctly constitutional roles.

Substantively, they contributed in fundamental ways to the political, economic, and moral constitution of the expanding nation. National policy profited from these substantive contributions. On the political and economic fronts, however, there was a complication: nineteenth-century American culture housed at least two distinct conceptions of political economy—one agrarian republican (espoused by Thomas Jefferson), the other liberal capitalist (whose articulate early proponent was Alexander Hamilton). Each posited its own values and its own place for family. The United States' policy of territorial expansion embodied the tensions between these two conceptions, as Congress pursued both simultaneously. Although this ecumenical embrace partially reconciled the two conceptions, it didn't suppress conflict entirely. For one thing, there was a persistent political cleavage between homesteaders and speculators. This division, which grew out of competing material interests that were tied to conflicting notions of political economy, pitted an image of the familial farm against that of an individualist market of free laborers. The cleavage was visible not only in Congress, but also on western turf. For another, national policy toward settlement was inextricably bound to the growing sectional conflict over the status and fate of slavery in the order. On the frontier, as we've already seen, sectional conflict pitted two versions of the agrarian family against each other. One was the slaveholding household, which viewed its landed entitlement as prior to the nation. The other was a white, non-slaveholding household that traced its landed entitlement directly to the national government.

Even on the eve of the Civil War, members of Congress and the president were engaged in political pugilism on both the class-based front and the sectional front. Despite the adoption of the Republican Party's Homestead Act after Abraham Lincoln's election in 1860, which would seem to have been a victory for white homesteaders against both speculators and slavery (or, if not slavery, against black settlement), western agrarians criticized national policy as wed to capitalism.

Amid all the commotion, however, Congress was clear and consistent about one thing: family's function was to maintain (and extend) political dominion into the territories and across the continent. Would family comply with Congress's expectations? Western families did indeed help maintain and extend the authority of the nation across the continent. They were both essential and useful to this task. They were essential for two reasons. first, agriculture was the primary mode of production on the frontier; second, the means for pursuing agriculture tended to make family, not the individual, the basic unit capable of material self-sufficiency. Families were useful to the task, because connections among families created communities, which were the basis for a rudimentary form of politics, which in turn was the foundation for political control of the territories and their admission into the union.

If families helped maintain the order, however, they also changed it. There were several reasons for this. Environmental exigencies, the weakness of law, and the paucity of established social ties permitted—in some respects required—changes in family. Among the changes were subtle alterations in relations between wives and husbands. It would be a mistake to make too much of the significance (or longevity) of some of these alterations, but it's fair to say that they had two consequences that were relevant to constitutional order. First, families in the western territories helped produce a political movement whose expressed aim was to challenge the Hamiltonian conception of political economy. Second, alterations of roles within western families helped revise people's conception of who could be a political member of the constitutional order. In short, western women exploited their moral role, expanded their economic role, and were much less excluded from a political role than were their sisters back East. As a consequence, women began to acquire some basic rights of citizenship. This western innovation would eventually echo eastward, beyond the frontier, back to "civilization."

There was yet another social change on the frontier, though it was often (but not always) hidden. It involved the establishment and maintenance of same-sex households as functioning families. Its normative implications for the larger polity were suppressed for even longer than those growing out of the status of women.

POLITICAL ECONOMIES: JEFFERSONIAN REPUBLICANISM AND HAMILTONIAN LIBERALISM

As we saw in Chapter 3, James Madison claimed that the structure of government and constitution of society in the United States would promote the common good. He had no illusion that the system would always run smoothly or that threats to the stability of the order would be absent. One of the chief threats involved the relation between property and government. It wasn't that Madison disbelieved in the desirability of private ownership of property, nor that he conceived of no role for government in the protection of ownership. But he lived at a time that permitted him to see some of the fruits of Lockean liberalism. He saw the development of commerce from a simple mercantile system to one that was dynamic and complex. Even in its rudimentary form, the capitalism that Madison saw by the end of the eighteenth century was marked by material diversification and social differentiation.

Thus, while Locke could see in property a reason for drawing people together into political society for mutual advantage, Madison saw property driving them apart:

> The diversity in the faculties of men from which the rights of property originate, is not less an insuperable obstacle to a uniformity of interests. The protection of these faculties is the first object of Government. From the protection of different and unequal faculties of acquiring property, the possession of different degrees and kinds of property immediately results: and from the influence of these on the sentiments and views of the respective proprietors, ensues a division of the society into different interests and parties.[1]

Such divisions, said Madison, inflame passion, promote injustice, produce instability, and threaten to extinguish popular government itself. His familiar solution was not to posit a vision of the good life, but, as we have seen, to construct a political apparatus that could mitigate the corrosive effects of faction. He understood that structure alone would not prevent conflict over the ownership and regulation of property. Nor would it preclude competition among various forms of property. But he anticipated that the extended republic could knit together a diverse country full of tensions.

Still, some divisions ran deep. One reason was that certain forms of property or of enterprise were integral to ways of life that in turn bore upon the political constitution of the nation. And family was implicated in all three. One constitutive division—which has persisted for much of the life of the nation—was between agriculture on the one hand and commerce and industry on the other. The conflictual stakes of this division were apparent from the earliest years of the republic in the political thought of Thomas Jefferson and Alexander Hamilton.

Jefferson was a famous progenitor of a strand of American ethos known as agrarian republicanism. At its heart was the Aristotelian notion that the foundation for political order was social. That is, the form and character of society were constitutive of polity. For that reason, republican government could flourish only under social conditions congenial to the virtues that collective self-government required. As we saw in Chapter 3, two of the principal virtues in this strand of republicanism were independence and self-sufficiency. Frequently, these traits were combined under a single rubric: manliness. Almost always in this context, a "man" was not a detached individual but a person bound to soil and community, usually through the institution of the family. A man needed enough land to support himself and his family.[2]

But this was a particular sort of family—republican, not aristocratic—that in turn suggested a particular relation to the land. In his "Summary View of the Rights of British America" (1774), Jefferson depicted the historical roots of this theme. "Our ancestors," he said, like "their Saxon ancestors" before them, "possessed a right which nature has given to all men, of departing from the country in which chance, not choice, has placed them, of going in quest of new habitations, and of there establishing new societies, under such laws and regulation as to them shall seem most likely to promote public happiness."[3] The Normans and their progeny destroyed that freedom, he said, imposing instead a yoke of feudal burdens. "Our Saxon ancestors held their lands . . . in absolute dominion, disencumbered with any superior." But if feudal relations were imposed by "William, the Norman," they did not negate the original allodial ground for landed tenure in England, which remained at common law even as subsequent kings and parliaments attempted to usurp it. In any event, he said, "America was not conquered by William the Norman, nor its lands surrendered to him, or any of his successors."[4] "America was conquered, and her settlements made . . . at the expense of individuals," not of the Crown or Parliament or "the British public."[5] If Americans have seemed to acquiesce in the notion that the Crown dispensed their land, it was merely because they were "farmers, not lawyers."[6]

Two years later as a member of Virginia's legislature, Jefferson sponsored two measures designed to shed the Norman yoke. One abolished entail, a condition on property, as we saw in Chapter 2, that restricted its descent to a particular class of persons and not to all heirs.[7] The other abolished primogeniture, under which, as we saw from Thomas Paine, aristocratic families "exposed" most of their children.[8] In tandem, Jefferson's proposals, which the legislature adopted, aimed to throw off feudal burdens, revive the ancient common law, and hence recover the notion of freehold, which alone could sustain free government. They also would redistribute land more equitably, so that families could support themselves as households.[9]

It was important that these households be engaged in a particular type of enterprise: agriculture. "Cultivators of the earth are the most valuable citizens. They are the most vigorous, the most independent, the most virtuous, & they are tied to their country & wedded to it's liberty & interests by the most lasting bonds."[10] Because of the domestic benefits that farmers bestowed, because fishing the oceans risked international conflict and war, and because commerce in general entailed similar risks, Jefferson advocated converting the energy of as many citizens as possible to farming.[11] Thus, in assessing the proposed Constitution, Jefferson approved, but only conditionally:

> After all, it is my principle that the will of the majority should always prevail. If they approve the proposed Convention, in all it's parts, I shall concur in it chearfully, in hopes that they will amend it whenever they shall find it work wrong. I think our governments will remain virtuous for many centuries; as long as they are chiefly agricultural; and this will be as long as there shall be vacant lands in any part of America. When they get piled upon one another in large cities, as in Europe, they will become corrupt as in Europe.[12]

As much as anything, this concern for constitutional order may explain Jefferson's willingness to purchase Louisiana from the French, though he believed the Purchase violated the text of the Constitution.

Given his commitments, Jefferson's quarrel with Alexander Hamilton's fiscal policies during George Washington's administration was unsurprising. Jefferson didn't despair, however, for he hoped that the people would repudiate Hamilton's "corrupt" policies.[13] When, a decade later, Jefferson was elected president, he repeated his commitment to the primacy of agriculture. Among "the essential principles of our Government," he said in his First Inaugural, was "encouragement of agriculture, and of commerce as its handmaid."[14] The upshot of Jefferson's philosophy, for purposes of political operation, was distinctly democratic. The upshot, for purposes of political structure, was decentralist. And the upshot, for purposes of principle, was libertarian. And beneath all three lay a faith in the capacities of ordinary people: "I believe . . . that morality, compassion, [and] generosity, are innate elements of the human constitution."[15]

Within the world of republican thought, Alexander Hamilton opposed Jefferson at almost every turn. To begin, Hamilton's deepest instincts were anti-Aristotelian. He rejected the need for or presumption of an organic unity between society and state. His assumption and aim, with respect to the emerging political order after the Revolution, were that a constitutional machine could (and must) rework society in its own image. Thus, although he shared Locke's individualist intuitions in matters of economy and his attachment to material prosperity as a fundamental value, Hamilton did not embrace Locke's felicitous conception of the social and natural orders antecedent to the creation of government. Hamilton's image of stateless society was Hobbesian, in which chaos reigned. The purpose of government, then, was to cure those defects and to force people to behave, even against their baser native inclinations.[16]

The problem with relations among the states under the Articles of Confederation, he said, was that they were in utter disarray, each state going its own way, for its own purposes, with little disregard for the rest. The dangers here were akin to the Hobbesian dangers that plagued societies without any government at all.[17] But how to correct this condition? Hamilton's answer was twofold.

First, because he distrusted republican governments that depended on the virtue of their citizens and because he especially despised popular government,[18] Hamilton espoused a vigorous national government possessing power sufficient to unify, stabilize, and strengthen the nation and to override the discordant "passions . . . of avarice, ambition, [and] interest." What, though, of the states? Frankly, he suggested, "if they were extinguished, . . . great oeconomy might be obtained by substituting a general Govt." States, he said, "are not necessary for any of the great purposes of commerce, revenue, or agriculture," though he conceded that "subordinate authorities" would be required for efficient administration. Regardless of the role of states in the day-to-day administration of government, "Two Sovereignties can not co-exist within the same limits." Ultimate authority must reside in the nation. In this regard, he said, the British model of government "was the best in the world. . . . It is the only Govt in the world 'which unites public strength with individual security.'" For these and other reasons, the national will should supercede the local.[19]

Second, Hamilton urged that the general government must attend to the nation's economic health in at least two ways. One was to solidify the fiscal condition of the nation by securing and centralizing national credit and by tying the interests of public creditors and banks to the national government.[20] The other was to encourage domestic manufacture, especially among "infant industries." Doing so, he said, would encourage development of the nation's resources, promote economic and political independence, and provide protection in time of war.[21] Although he advocated "leav[ing] industry to itself,"[22] the system that Hamilton imagined was not a scheme of laissez-faire. In this respect, therefore, his thinking deviated from both the Physiocratic ideas that informed Jefferson's agrarianism and the new libertarian economics of Adam Smith. What Hamilton required, again, was an active, paternalist central government, capable of directing material development and enforcing disciplined obedience by citizens.[23] What he required, in short, was a Leviathan.

As for the role of family in the mechanical beast the Constitution created, Hamilton was conflicted, at least on the surface. At one point, as we saw in Chapter 3, he seemed to embrace the Aristotelian notion that ties of kinship and affection would play an important role in limiting the power of the nation.[24] There is reason to believe, however, that this was primarily a rhetorical move, aiming merely to defuse Antifederalist opposition to a strong central government. Hamilton's more genuine political commitment lay with the nation, disentangled from parochial interests. His economic commitment resided with commerce and capital. Although his conception of commerce was not antiagrarian, especially because agriculture was an apt instrument for occupying "uninhabited and unimproved" territory,[25] Hamilton's political economy was unfettered from traditional (including familial) ties and hence contained none of the romantic localism of Jefferson's republicanism. As we've already seen, one aim of the complex configuration of institutions in the new order, on his account, was to inhibit familial influence over the operation and output of government. The bottom line, for Hamilton, was that the nation's government should not concern itself with family, except to counter its potentially dangerous tendencies.

DOMESTIC ECONOMY

There was a second sort of economy at work in the nation and on the frontier. Less grand than political economy, and in some ways less visible, the domestic economy of households was nonetheless a concrete aspect of the lives of persons who resided in the United States (or its territories). We've already seen how English law regulated domestic relations. As much as the ideology of the American Revolution challenged English norms and assumptions, and even though the colonies (and later, the states) repudiated aspects of English law (especially concerning property and inheritance), American law retained elements of English law. For example, the law of family in the American order incorporated the English common law's disabling doctrine of coverture. American law also revived by statute formal impediments to separation and divorce. It's not that divorce was barred, as it had virtually been under the English law. But, in many jurisdictions, divorce could be difficult to obtain. Even after divorce or the death of a husband, women's legal disabilities could persist—enforced partly through law and partly through formal and informal restrictions on women's access to gainful employment. Among the more interesting formal restrictions in America was the institution of the "family meeting," through which five relatives, almost always male, would legally assume supervening responsibility over a widow in administering the financial affairs of her minor children. This institution was an artifact of the civil law, so it was no accident that it appeared in Louisiana (and persisted until 1950).[26] In general, backed by cultural expectations, American law continued to play a powerful role in prescribing gendered families. After the creation of the new constitutional order and the emergence of states with competent regulatory powers, it was within this legal structure that the social dynamics of American families played out.

Still, these were not in all respects identical to families that were creatures of English law. These were "modern" families. Carl Degler has argued that the "modern American family emerged first in the years between the American Revolution and about 1830."[27] In fact, as we've seen, this change was under way before the Revolution. But, whatever their temporal origins, modern families exhibited at least three characteristics, according to Degler. First, they tended to be initiated by the free choice of the prospective partners and maintained through "affection and mutual respect" between them. In short, the relationship partook of individualism, contract, and love. Over the course of the nineteenth century, these elements increasingly implied the freedom to leave the marriage, albeit within limits set (though unevenly enforced) by law.[28]

Second, modern marriage began to deviate from patriarchy to this limited extent: men and women occupied separate spheres of life—husbands the spheres of work and production and politics, and wives the spheres of home and reproduction and morality. Alexis de Tocqueville asserted that Americans viewed each sphere as equally worthy:

> Thus Americans do not believe that man and woman have the duty or the right to do the same things, but they show the same esteem for the role of each of them, and they consider them as beings whose value is equal although their destiny differs. They do not give the same form or the same employment to the courage of woman as to that of man, but they never doubt her courage; and if they deem that man and his mate should not always employ their intelligence and reason in the same manner, they at least judge that the reason of one is as sure as that of the other, and her intelligence as clear.[29]

Despite such rhetoric, the truth is that the spheres were neither distinct nor equal. For one thing, the husband inhabited both, the wife typically only the domestic. For another, the husband's presence in the domestic domain usually meant that the wife's authority was circumscribed. But, to the extent that the ethos of domesticity mattered to people's view of the world (whatever their practices might be), "the wife, as mistress of the home, was perceived by society and herself as the moral superior of the husband, though his legal and social inferior."[30]

Third, children began to occupy a new and special place in the life of the family. Adults began to perceive the child as a different sort of creature, "more innocent." We saw a crabbed version of this among the young children of slaves. Unsurprisingly, nonslave children had vastly larger and more promising horizons. Under modernity's ethos of child rearing, and unlike the assumptions that informed the rules of English law, nonslave children were considered to be valuable in themselves and not simply vessels for the transmission of wealth, instruments of production, or devices for extending familial influence. And "childhood itself was perceived . . . as a period of life not only worth recognizing and cherishing but extending." In a way that John Locke would have applauded, a basic function of family was to care for and nurture children, to educate them in practical industry and morals. And the person in charge of this function, according to the doctrine of separate spheres, was the wife and mother.[31] The doctrine cut against two traditional "common-law" notions that we saw in Chapter 2. The first was that the husband-father possessed comprehensive authority over the home, including the care of children. This was an authority that grew out of his primary legal responsibility as provider and caretaker (though it also entitled him to the benefits of his children's labor). The second was that the wife-mother was "entitled to no power [over her children], but only to reverence and respect."[32]

If the doctrine of separate spheres was, from the perspective of many women, an advance over the old law, it, too, was problematic, in part because it had such a powerful hold on the popular imagination. One reason for this was that it integrated seamlessly into emerging cultural conceptions of the proper role of "the modern woman." Barbara Welter has mined nineteenth-century popular American literature—especially novels and the new genre of women's magazines—to uncover a consistent ideal depiction of women's role. Welter characterizes the depiction as "the Cult of True Womanhood."[33] Rooted in religion, the Cult itself was quasi-religious in character. It depicted women as saints of society. Their virtues were "piety, purity, submissiveness, and domesticity." And their principal role was to preserve civilization, whose moral roots were divinely sanctioned.[34]

This was no small burden. That fact aside, the doctrine of separate spheres (including the Cult that it underwrote) was susceptible to two sorts of criticism. For one thing, it functioned as a kind of nineteenth-century version of *Leave It to Beaver*. That is, it was too neat and clean to describe the experience of many families, especially those that were not of a certain (elevated) class. For another, the image conjured by the doctrine, liberalizing though it was, was confining. Hence, at midcentury Margaret Fuller could invoke biblical sources to extol women's domestic virtues, while pressing a distinctly liberal value: "the emancipation of Woman from the burdens and disabilities" that tend "to merge her individuality" into family.[35] Fuller urged, therefore, that all occupations be opened to women, and she argued that promoting women's independence would strengthen their connection to men, because doing so would reinforce the interests the sexes hold in common.[36] She suggested that women's emancipation, their "liberty" as she also called it, would come through law.[37] It didn't, at least not in the short term. But domestic economy on the frontier would alter women's status in ways that were consequential.

POLITICAL-ECONOMIC CLEAVAGES: HOMESTEADERS AND SPECULATORS

Jefferson and Hamilton embodied distinct strands of American ethos. The two strands were entwined in the fabric of the politics and policy of the new nation. One area in which the strands were both visible and fraying involved the acquisition and settlement of new territory.

From the inception of the American order, national policy aimed at extending political dominion westward. There were at least two challenges to this ambition. The first was that portions of the continent were already occupied by native tribes. We'll see in Chapter 6 how the nation dealt with the "Indian problem." The second challenge was to extend political dominion into "vacant" land. Competition between agrarian republicanism and liberal capitalism was an impediment to formulating an effective national policy of settlement. In fact, a great deal of rhetoric during the first half of the nineteenth century—especially among agrarians—implied that the central cleavage in disputes over the national policy of settlement was between the settler-farmer and his family, on the one hand, and the capitalist-speculator, on the other. There is much to this picture.[38] But matters were more complex than appeared on the face of the image.

Disputes over territorial settlement antedated the Constitution. Even before the Revolution, one of the substantial conflicts between Crown and colonists involved British resistance to settlement on the western frontier after the defeat of French and Indian forces in 1763.[39] During the Revolution, the Continental Congress adopted a resolution calling on the various states to cede their western lands to the national government.[40] Virginia complied soon after the Peace of Paris was signed.[41] By the beginning of the nineteenth century, all of the eastern states with westward claims to territory had ceded their claims to the United States.[42]

One of the first pieces of business in the post-Revolution Congress was to plan for territory "ceded by individual states" or "purchased of the Indian inhabitants." Jefferson introduced a proposal to do just that. As revised and adopted by a special committee in Congress, the plan's primary aim was to install settlers in the territories. The method proposed for pursuing his aim would promote three purposes, one strategic, one political, and one fiscal. First, the physical presence of settlers would help to secure the land. Settlers not only would stake their claims to individual ownership, but would serve as surrogates for the nation's claim to sovereignty over the territory. Second, settlers would comprise the basic ingredient for "establishing a temporary government," including townships, counties, and a legislature. Once the population in each territory was large enough, these institutions would provide the means for establishing "permanent governments" that were "republican" in character and for integrating the territories into the existing constitutional order. Third, because the method for procuring settlers would be for Congress to sell off parcels of land, the plan would shore up the national treasury.[43]

The resolutions did not commit to a particular model of political economy. Perhaps, given the character of the existing economy and because Jefferson had authored the proposal that was the impetus for the resolutions, he (and others) assumed the agrarian republican model would hold. Events would complicate matters.

The Land Ordinance of 1785, for example, provided for surveys and sales of western lands.[44] In the precision of the directions for surveying the territories, one can see the hand of Jefferson. And a particular provision underscored the Jeffersonian ambition to supply the means by which settlers might establish communities in which to raise families: One lot in each township was reserved for maintaining public schools. But other provisions, concerning the sales themselves, suggested an alternative orientation, more congenial to Hamilton's favored interests. At $1 per acre, the minimum price seemed accessible enough even to persons and families of meager means. Congress, however, set an entire section of land, or 640 acres, as the minimum size for purchase. The effect was to promote sales not to individual or familial settlers, but to speculators who had the cash or credit to buy such sizable lots.[45]

"Encouragement" from speculators, in fact, was an impetus for enactment of the Northwest Ordinance.[46] Though it, too, followed Jefferson's model for surveying and organization (including his proposal, which Congress had rejected in the Ordinance of 1785, to prohibit slavery in the territory), speculators typically were the conduit through which lands were distributed. The Land Act of 1796 raised the minimum price to $2 per acre. While this policy was not overtly pro-speculator, it did intensify speculators' relative advantage as compared with prospective settlers; even more, the Act suggested that raising revenue was superior to both settlers and speculators in the Congress's hierarchy of interests.[47]

None of this is to imply that settlers as a group were repositories of civic virtue. The Ordinance of 1785 and subsequent acts disposing of lands prohibited settlement in territories until after the lands had been surveyed.[48] Among the reasons for this restriction were to ensure the orderly transfer of title to land and to encourage the establishment of communities. Greed and the absence of meaningful governmental authority, however, undermined these purposes, as squatting was a significant problem from the beginning. It grew only worse over the course of the nineteenth century. In an early effort to deal with the problem, Congress adopted the Anti-Trespassing Act of 1807, punishing squatting on the public domain with fine and imprisonment.[49]

This Act reinforced a sentiment among potential settlers and even among those already settled that Congress was concerned more with protecting revenue and speculators than with promoting settlement and the welfare of settlers. In fact, however, Congress was increasingly responsive to pressure from settlers throughout the nineteenth century. The Land Act of 1800 had aimed to attract settlers by reducing the minimum size for sale to 320 acres and by providing for sales on credit over a period of four years, with a down payment of only $160.[50] The Land Act of 1820 liberalized even further, lowering the minimum size to 80 acres and the minimum price to $1.25 per acre.[51] Although this Act rescinded provisions of the Act of 1800 concerning sales on credit, the Relief Act of 1820 aimed to give purchasers relief from debt. Specifically, the Relief Act permitted anyone who had made the first payment on four quarter-sections (640 acres) to retain title to one of the quarters by relinquishing the other three to the United States. Alternatively, if such a debtor wanted to try to hold onto all four quarter-sections, the Relief Act extended credit for up to ten years.[52]

Beginning in the 1830s, moreover, Congress began flirting with a policy that was a logical corollary to the Jeffersonian ambition to make land easily available to settlers.[53] At the same time, however, the policy effectively subverted the sort of ordered settlement that, on the Jeffersonian ideal, would have facilitated the development of republican communities in which families could flourish. The policy was preemption. Its purpose was to ratify squatters' premature seizures of public land. Its effect was essentially to quiet title to such land, permitting premature squatters to sell their homesteads to a new wave of settlers.[54] Congress's first formal foray into preemption came in 1830. The Act was tentative, in that it operated prospectively and expired after one year.[55] Congress wrestled with extensions to this temporary Act,[56] but a more enduring commitment to preemption was not long in the wings.

Reflecting on the Whigs' victory in the national election of 1840, Stephenson claims that it was fundamentally a response to "a great change in sentiment relative to the public domain." More strongly, he suggests, the election marked the victory of preemption as national policy.[57] Even if these claims exaggerate our capacity to interpret elections, they are defensible enough. The election produced a Congress that quickly enacted, with President John Tyler's blessing, the Pre-Emption Act of 1841.[58] The Act aspired comprehensively to resolve conflicts over both settlement and revenue. With respect to settlement, the Act permitted squatters—heads of families, widows, and single men over the age of twenty-one—to settle on a quarter-section (160 acres) of land, with the right to purchase at the minimum price once the land was put up for sale. With respect to revenue, proceeds from sales were to be distributed in this way: 10 percent of revenues to states in which the land sat, remainder to the rest of the states, except in time of war or if tariffs were levied above 20 percent on any given import.[59]

With these political developments in mind, Daniel Feller argues that "the dichotomous images of settler and speculator were essentially fallacious."[60] For one thing, says Feller, the moral qualities depicted in the stereotypes—settler as virtuous and productive, speculator as vicious and idle—were not simply exaggerated but wrong. The speculator was not an idler, extracting wealth from others' productivity, but "a doer, a booster," who promoted growth in the West through "cities, farms, roads, canals." For another, and more importantly, "the interests of settler and speculator actually joined at many points." Often, the speculator was not an eastern (nor a foreign) capitalist, but a westerner, like the settler. Both settler and speculator had an interest in cheap land, with rising prices spurred by growth and development. And, he urges, the conventional distinction—"that the settler wanted to work the land, while the speculator acquired it only as a commodity to be held for profit"—is erroneous. Farmers, says Feller, "habitually claimed more land than they could farm." In fact, "the purchase of land for resale was commonplace throughout the West."[61] It is also true that farmers frequently were not the civic-minded husbands of the soil depicted in romantic republican rhetoric, but enterprisers, many of whom worked the soil until they depleted it and then moved on, abandoning both communities and large expanses of exhausted land.[62]

There is value in correcting the demonic image of the speculator. Even so, and notwithstanding the suspicious way in which Feller's rehabilitation transforms speculators from rapacious demons into model citizens, it is a stretch to attribute to them the same interests and capacities as farmers. For speculators tended to have resources and access to credit that most farmers could but dimly imagine.[63] Thus, most speculators could easily purchase land out from under squatters, even after the rise of preemption as national policy.[64] Moreover, because the early land acts lacked ceilings on the amount of land one could purchase, speculators frequently could reconnoiter a vast domain and buy the most desirable land. In some places, like the Yazoo Tract in what is now Mississippi, they could corner the market, if not through legitimate purchase, then through bribery.[65] Frequently, then, potential settlers had to go through speculators to acquire land. These conditions not only put speculators generally at a competitive advantage, but permitted some to operate as predators.

Andrew Jackson's Specie Circular did address some of these excesses. Specifically, it aimed "to repress alleged frauds, and to withhold any countenance or facilities in the power of the Government from the monopoly of the public lands in the hands of speculators and capitalists, to the injury of the actual settlers in the new States." The circular required (1) that payment for public land be made only in gold, silver, or, with respect to certain lands, Virginia land scrip; and (2) that other, less solid modes of payment would continue to be accepted from any "purchaser who is an actual settler or bona fide resident in the State where the sales are made," but only on plots of fewer than 320 acres.[66] The circular did in fact suppress the sale of lands, but its effect in this regard was temporary. Its longer-term effect was to concentrate financial control over sales to eastern banks, whose terms were frequently onerous. And, as an indication of how powerful Hamiltonianism was becoming as a description of the operating logic of American political economy, the collapse in sales contributed to an economic panic in 1837, forcing many who were deeply invested in land to liquidate and hence to lose it.[67]

CROSS-CUTTING CLEAVAGES AND NATIONAL EXPANSION

Regardless of whether less-than-flattering images of speculators were accurate, Feller is correct that political divisions over national policy toward settlement cannot be explained entirely by competition between settlers and speculators. One powerful alternative explanation is sectionalism—specifically, the overlapping and divergent interests and values of North, South, and West.[68] Sectionalism at bottom was a generic surrogate for considerations of political economy, public morality, and ways of life. Although tensions between farmers and speculators were present in all three considerations, sectionalism was never reducible to them, nor to any simple explanation from class-based antagonism. Nonetheless, policy over westward settlement was one arena in which regional differences sometimes became open hostilities. This was so at least as early as the crisis over the tariffs of 1828 and 1832.[69] As the elaborate provisions of the Pre-Emption Act of 1841 demonstrated, moreover, Jackson's nationalist resolution of the crisis did not unify regional preferences.[70]

After 1841, sectionalism became increasingly visibly connected with the status of slavery in the nation and under the Constitution. But debates over slavery were rarely isolated from debates over the western territories and hence did not remain battles simply between North and South. Divergent conceptions of the agrarian family were always just beneath the surface, for the conflict pitted two types of agrarian family against each other: the southern slaveholding household and the northern white nuclear family.[71] Few people understood this better than Abraham Lincoln, who, as we've seen, pressed his understanding to great effect in his debates against Stephen A. Douglas. The sources of sectionalism in which slavery was implicated were many and longstanding. One source, which altered fundamentally the terms on which sectional battles were fought, was the Mexican War. Although the Mexican Cession perfected the nation's continental aspirations, it also provided extensive new turf for politicians and others to fight over.[72] These battles were not always explicitly over slavery's expansion, but slavery was lurking persistently in the background.

One famous battle involved the construction of a transcontinental railroad, which implicated not only slavery but also the tension between homesteaders and capital. The most visible conflicts involved the railroad's location: would the Congress endorse (and finance) a northern or a southern route? Thanks largely to the acumen of Stephen Douglas, the northern route prevailed, but not without piquing sectional jealousy.[73] Less visible than the fight over the railroad's route was resentment over the fact that Congress chose to subsidize construction through grants of land to the railroad corporations. The Hamiltonian logic behind these grants was that government would fulfill its obligation to underwrite prosperity, but would also protect the treasury by requiring settlers who followed the railroads to pay a higher price ($2.50/acre, compared with $1.25) for public land. Even among westerners who coveted internal improvements, this logic seemed perversely to tax agriculture for the benefit of corporations. A better policy, some reasoned, would be to open the land to homesteading (at the lower price) and permit the corporations—which had the means and incentive to pay their own way—to follow the settlers.[74]

Another battle, also pitting homesteaders against monied interests, grew out of the Mexican War. Congress became decidedly generous in offering land as a bounty to soldiers who had served in the war. On its face, this policy would not have seemed especially controversial, but many settlers opposed it. Fueling their opposition was the fact that soldiers frequently neither wanted nor were able to resettle in the West, and so sold their bounty to speculators, who were able to purchase extensive tracts for a pittance.[75]

A similar antagonism grew out of the Graduation Act of 1854. The policy of graduation was straightforward: land that had gone unsold for more than thirty years would be offered for sale at 12.5 cents/acre.[76] The policy was attractive to the national government mainly for fiscal reasons. Selling these "problem" lands would generate a small amount of revenue, but, more importantly, would permit the government to shut down land offices, which were expensive to maintain even when relatively inactive. The states of the Old Northwest tended to favor the policy, because it meant that empty land, when sold, would finally be taxable. Many northeasterners, however, opposed the policy. Their argument was that bargain-basement prices would reward, in Horace Greeley's words, "thrift-lessness and improvidence" and would send westward persons who were ill-fit to suffer the rigors of pioneering life, much less to flourish in it. The material motivation for Greeley's position was a longstanding eastern antagonism to any policy that might soften the supply of labor. Western homesteaders opposed graduation because they said it rewarded laggards (sometimes with very desirable parcels), while effectively penalizing the industry and perseverance of the first families of pioneers, who had endured hardship and uncertainty. Graduation, they argued, might lower the price of all land and not merely that of the parcels for sale. Southerners tended to support the policy, perhaps at bottom because easterners opposed it. With southern support, the policy prevailed.[77]

As the course of the Free-Soil movement, the collapse of the Whigs, and the rise of sectional Democratic and Republican parties in the 1840s and 1850s demonstrated, however, sectionalism, slavery, and territorial settlement were larger and deeper than concerns about bounties, railroads, and graduation. This is precisely why Lincoln and the Republicans could press the issue of homestead so strenuously and effectively. The issue was close to the ethical and institutional heart of America. Through 1859, the southern delegations to Congress were strong enough to defeat any bill promoting homestead. After 1859, however, the tide for homestead surged and soon became unstoppable. During debates over a homestead bill in the Senate in 1860, Senator James Doolittle of Wisconsin offered arguments substantially similar to Lincoln's in his debates with Douglas. By preventing the "Africanization [of the territories] through the introduction of negro slaves," he said, homestead would preserve the territories for free white men and promote a "final settlement of the whole negro question." None of these consequences was attractive to southern members, but a Congressional Conference produced a bill that both houses approved overwhelmingly. President James Buchanan acceded to southern resistance and vetoed the bill.[78]

This veto would prove politically damaging to Buchanan's party in the presidential election of 1860, as northern Democrats tried to deal with fallout from an action that southern Democrats had insisted upon. Propelled by the kind of self-interest that obliterates self-interest, the two factions soon divorced, then adopted substantially similar platforms, then suffered a staggering loss at the polls.[79] The Republican platform, in contrast, pressed for a policy of homestead for the benefit of "actual settlers."[80] Two years later, a substantial Republican majority pushed through Congress a comprehensive Homestead Act, which President Lincoln happily signed.[81]

The Act would be the rhetorical touchstone for national policy on the settlement of public lands for the rest of the nineteenth century. It provided that "any person who is head of a family, or who has arrived at the age of twenty-one years" may enter a quarter-section or less of land and file a claim of preemption on that land; that the claim must be "for the purpose of actual settlement and cultivation"; and that a patent for the land may issue at the maximum price of $1.25/acre or, if a family had settled the entire parcel continuously for five years, for free. Agrarian romantics at the time might have dreamed that this policy signified an unambiguous victory for Jeffersonian republicanism as against Hamilton's political economy. As if to squelch such sentiment Congress passed the Pacific Railway Act two months later.[82]

AGRARIAN DISCONTENT

Thus, the ambivalent national embrace of homesteading families and speculators persisted into the latter half of the century. Some observers have argued that the Hamiltonian strand of American ethos was actually victorious in the end. For one thing, the Homestead Act did not succeed unequivocally on Jeffersonian terms. George W. Julian, a devoted republican of the day, offered three reasons for its failure. First, the Act lacked adequate safeguards against speculation. This meant that speculators could often gain through the back door what they could not through the front. Such is the nature of markets. Second, under a new policy concerning the disposition of lands formerly held by various tribes, these lands were not conveyed to the United States but were released directly to monopolists, railroad corporations, and speculators. Viewed through an agrarian lens, this policy engendered corrupt ties between capital and the national government. Third, the land grants to railroads placed in corporate hands massive amounts of land, which, again through an agrarian lens, should have gone to settlers.[83]

With respect to the last point, Hildegard Johnson points out that "fewer acres were passed on to settlers under the Homestead Act than were sold by the railroads for four dollars an acre."[84] Similar patterns appeared in Texas and the lands of the Mexican Cession, where large-scale ranching overwhelmed smaller-scale familial farms.[85] In parts of the Far West, national policy ensured that vast amounts of land and resources found their way to corporations and speculators.[86] In 1875, Congress resumed the policy of accepting payment for land by specie.[87]

These considerations aside, the Homestead Act intensified a trend that the earlier preemption acts had provoked: the diffusion of agricultural settlement.[88] Although diffusion promoted the national ambition to secure sovereign claims to vast territories, it undermined agrarian republican goals of assuring settlement through families in nuclear communities and therefore of extending a polity knit together through webs of communitarian attachment.[89]

An agrarian republican might have predicted that diffuse settlement would generate diffuse political attachments, which in turn would undermine the capacity of people to sustain any sort of political life. This aspect of the organic account of the character of politics would not hold entirely in the American case, for it did not fully appreciate the presence or function of the nation-state. Weak local attachments might not lead to the dissolution of politics if there were a nation-state sufficiently powerful to sustain political forms in the absence of such attachments.

Although correlation does not establish causation, there was such a nation-state in the United States, at least where matters of political economy were concerned. We've already seen that in the preceding century, Alexander Hamilton had posited that the development of a market-based economy required a vigorous national government. Jeffersonians had opposed this view, partly because they feared the consequences of a strong central state and partly because they distrusted an economy built on a commercial capitalist base. Daniel Feller claims that the abolition of the credit system, the policy of preemption, and the Homestead Act were ultimately unsuccessful because the Hamiltonian logic of the political economy — including the ethos that underwrote the commodification of land — was too powerful to resist.[90] Perhaps the only way Jeffersonian policy could have prevailed was through a government strong enough to make the policy stick. That condition, of course, was incompatible with the premises of Jeffersonian thought.

Notwithstanding agrarian pessimism about the trajectory of national policy, however, there is reason to think that principles of agrarian republicanism persisted, if not in formal national policy, then in disparate settlements on the frontier. But, from the standpoint of maintaining the existing order, the fruit of those settlements would be surprising.

FAMILIES AND LAW: UNCONVENTIONAL ROLES

Lawrence M. Friedman argues that westward settlers carried the law with them. On their journey, although they "were outside any formal institutions of law and order[,] . . . the wagon trains and emigration companies were surprisingly lawful in behavior. . . . Out in the trackless wilderness, hundreds of miles from police, courts, and judges, the fundamental rules of property and contract were followed, just as they were in Illinois or Massachusetts." The persistence not simply of a legal sensibility but of concrete legal norms, he says, was a function of habit and necessity. In transit "and in the midst of strangers, there was hardly an opportunity for new 'customs' to develop. The 'law' that prevailed was 'the taught, learned, accepted customs' of the people; it was part of the baggage they brought with them."[91] Even more strongly (and more problematically), Friedman argues that "the immigrants were Americans, who 'tacitly' brought common law with them to an empty country."[92] Once settled, he argues, the new inhabitants rigged a rough combination of old and new legal norms.

The persistence of old norms in new settlements may well have been due partly to the ethical "baggage" that settlers carried with them, but other explanations may be even more powerful. For one thing, Congress had authority to establish policy in the territories and to regulate the admission of territories into the union as states.[93] For another, some territories were carved from existing states, whose enactments were transplanted onto the territories. Finally, territorial settlement attracted lawyers. If they did not always meet the highest standards of the profession—in terms of ethics or ability—they nonetheless practiced modes of thought and argument that reinforced the reach of law in territories.[94]

The theme of Friedman's picture is that westward settlement and the establishment of law were coextensive and simultaneous. The point, where family is concerned, is that migrant families strongly resembled their eastern counterparts, both because of the ethical habits of immigrants and because of the normative constraints of law. There is something to these claims, but it would be a mistake to make too much of them, especially where family is concerned.

In fact, families on the frontier frequently looked different from those back East. This was the case not only in transit but also after settlement. One reason is that the frontier's harsh conditions posed challenges that defied solution through habitual modes of behavior or established categories of law. In short, necessity incited innovation. Another reason is that, if law accompanied or even preceded the immigrants, its influence on the frontier was comparatively diffuse. This was because, in many places, effective formal institutions of law were weak or nonexistent. Both environmental exigency and the inadequacy of law permitted—in some respects compelled—families to make their way in their own way, as best they could, in a sometimes hostile world. If this world was not a state of nature (of either a Hobbesian or a Lockean variety), neither was it a condition comprehensively ordered by law. This condition produced subtle shifts in relations and expectations within the marital family. Those shifts involved the respective roles of wives and husbands; and they suggested a view of marriage rooted less firmly in legal status, more strongly in an informal kind of contract.

People's motives for moving West were many.[95] For men at least, a prominent motive was economic: they wanted their own land on which to support themselves and their families.[96] For women, motivations were less straightforward, sometimes more conflicted. Certainly, some wanted to go for economic reasons, to pursue prosperity or flee failure. Some sought a better, healthier climate. A few—some men, too—may have harbored romantic visions of life in the West. Many, perhaps most, went to preserve their families. The aim in this respect was not entirely altruistic, for many, faced with husbands bent on going, mistrusted their untethered mates or feared their own loneliness. Some, no doubt, were propelled by affection for their spouses. Wives of ministers frequently accompanied their husbands with an appropriately missionary zeal, to claim the West for God and goodness.[97] In general, however, women were less enthusiastic than men about moving.[98] Some wives blocked their husbands' plans to emigrate. One suspects, however, that most did not, even if they had wanted to do so. Some apparently used resistance as a means for negotiating terms for emigration, extracting from husbands an acceptance of "familial responsibilities" as part of the bargain.[99]

One thing is certain: women went West in large numbers. Census data indicate that many men went first on their own, soon followed by wives or fiancées. Single women, too, went West, especially after the first wave of settlement. Few who wanted to marry found themselves single for long. But wives frequently accompanied their husbands and brought their children. One reason for all of these trends was that men could not fulfill their economic ambition alone. They needed help. In Aristotelian terms, the household, not the individual, was typically the smallest economic unit capable of self sufficiency on the frontier. The sensible assumption was that "married persons are generally more comfortable, and succeed better, in a frontier country, than single men; for a wife and family, so far from being a burden to a western farmer, may always prove a source of pecuniary advantage in the domestic economy of his household."[100] More often than not, then, migration was a familial affair, frequently an extended familial affair.[101]

For those who journeyed as a family, the westward trek was a severe test of established roles in the marital relationship and of the marriage itself. The trek both reinforced and challenged aspects of the eastern template for familial roles. Certain obligations that had been the province of women before the journey—like cooking, making and mending clothes, caring for children, and of course giving birth—tended to remain so in transit.[102] But harsh conditions impelled departures from convention. Some duties that women took on, as when they performed presumptively masculine tasks like pitching tents, yoking cattle, and loading, unloading, and driving wagons, positively defied convention; and a few of the new responsibilities, like collecting buffalo chips for fuel, were not only unfeminine but distasteful.[103] Men, too, flouted a few conventions—by washing clothes and cooking, for example—but, on the evidence available, most men seem to have done so irregularly and out of a masculine sense of courtesy or because they had bargained for the obligations.[104] On the surface, these changes were so subtle as to seem insignificant, but they bespoke an altered sense of the marital family, not simply as a status, but as a kind of partnership, whose members' roles were somewhat fluid, set partially through pragmatic accommodation.

After settlement, some of these unconventional practices persisted, especially during the earliest years, sometimes longer. As on the trail, if the diaries are accurate, women were more likely than men to take on new roles.[105] To be sure, much of what women did on the homestead remained recognizably women's work. They washed and cooked and cared for children.[106] But they also hunted, chopped wood, plowed fields, and carried guns—all of which distinguished them from most of their more civilized sisters back East.[107] When their husbands were away, which was not infrequently, wives assumed responsibility for managing the entire homestead, not merely the home.[108]

Women assumed responsibilities outside the home as well. Teaching was one job that fit the feminine responsibility, by modernist convention, for educating the young. But other activities, like commercial entrepreneurship (of the petitbourgeois variety) or substitute preaching, were distinctly nontraditional.[109] As Deborah Fink puts it, "farm wives' labor placed them in the thick of the productive economy,"[110] rudimentary though that economy was. This did not mean that women were developing a mentality (or status) resembling that of men;[111] but women's labor did reinforce relationships of mutual dependence and partnership between husbands and wives, relationships at odds with the eastern model of strictly segregated spheres and domesticated wives.[112] Both within and outside the family, women pursued new outlets for labor while retaining one important responsibility that Locke had prescribed and that eastern notions of domesticity had delegated to wives: the practical, intellectual, and moral education of children.[113]

WESTERN FAMILIES AND CONSTITUTIONALIST FUNCTIONS

Homesteads on the frontier seemed to vindicate the agrarian-republican conception of the constitution of politics. Households provided the means for material subsistence; connections among households created communities; communities produced what came to resemble a collective way of life; that way of life, in turn, was the locus for an incipient form of politics. This was a politics with a difference, however, for its ultimate aim was not the organic creation of an autochthonous state but the formation of bonds of a particular sort with a preexisting nation-state. This aim and the means for achieving it made westerners directly reliant on the nation, not least because the very presence of homesteads and homesteaders was due to the largesse—not to mention the military, economic, and imperial ambition—of the United States. If homesteaders were dependent on the nation, however, they also found themselves in conflict with it, especially with the Hamiltonian tendencies of its political economy. This ideological antagonism would become a political movement, which traced its roots to Jeffersonian republicanism.[114] One catalyst for this conversion was the frontier family.

What might explain family's participation in the movement to challenge the dominant political economy in the latter half of the nineteenth century? One possibility is that women's contribution to material production on the homestead permitted wives to "relegate their second-class status to the fringes of their reality," thus converting economic power into familial power and then into political power.[115] Another is that "sharing between the sexes," especially with respect to the rearing of children, promoted an intra-familial equality that "enhanced female status and autonomy," which underwrote women's public activity in the community.[116] Each of these accounts is problematic. For one thing, with respect to women's power, status, and autonomy, the accounts seem too happy to be entirely accurate. For another, they rest too heavily on a single causal element; social change is typically more complex, multifaceted, and multidirectional than any single variable can explain. But, if we weaken the assumptions and complicate the causal connections, it does seem true that subtle shifts in women's roles produced political consequences of some significance.

As noted above, there was in modern America an ethos that acknowledged a role for women in maintaining morality in society.[117] According to the doctrine of separate spheres, this role was confined within the home. In the West, however, the role extended beyond those bounds. This extension was not simply a function of the fact that women on the frontier (properly) became teachers.[118] It grew, moreover, from a sentiment that women had a general responsibility for "civilizing" society and for doing so even outside the confines of the home.[119]

Second, therefore, the process of creating communities on the frontier was one in which women were intimately involved. In part, this involvement was a natural outgrowth of the fact that creating community entailed establishing connections among families, in which women had an undeniable role. But even in established communities, women had an active and visible role in the communities' associational life. This was certainly the case for informal activities like dances, barn raisings, quilting bees, and communal butcherings.[120] It was also true for more formal institutions and voluntary associations, especially those, like schools and churches, that fell within women's acknowledged ambit.[121] But, especially after the Civil War, it was true even of associations residing within more conventionally masculine domains like farming and politics. Among these associations were the Grange and the Farmers' Alliance, whose aims included promoting agriculture, as an economic venture and a way of life, and protecting it against what the organizations saw as the predations of capital in general and the railroads in particular.[122]

Typically, women's connection to men's associations was through auxiliaries of the principal organization. Thus, women occupied a separate space for social and other appropriately feminine pursuits.[123] But the Grange and the Farmers' Alliance admitted women as members, officers, and delegates to conventions. Elizabeth Jameson notes that the Alliance encouraged women's membership "because they had a direct economic interest in reform."[124] The source of that interest, of course, was the micro-economy that was the familial household. The Alliance, in fact, presented itself as an extension and embodiment of the farming family. "And like the family farm, the Alliance offered a productive role for every member of the household. Its leaders assumed that mothers, fathers, sons, and daughters would reproduce within the . . . organization the cooperative model of family labor found on the farm."[125] The goal was not simply to reform national policy, but to transform the family itself. "If the family was a microcosm of the country, then the family had to be transformed, 'improved,' and all its members remade into model citizens." The instrument for this transformation was education—for all the family's members.[126]

As Michael Lewis Goldberg points out, although the Alliance's rhetoric and its metaphorical uses of family insinuated sexual equality, the association was not able to sustain the insinuation. Egalitarian commitment was compromised most profoundly, he argues, in the move to the Populist Party as a vehicle for political action in the late 1880s and early 1890s. In short, men controlled the party.[127] This control made a certain sense, in light of the party's strategic emphasis on electoral politics; women, after all, could not vote in most places and times that were relevant. But the effect was to exclude women from the central mission of the organization—a mission that implicated one of the basic duties of citizenship.[128] Perhaps as important, the Populists altered the Alliance's familial metaphor from one of equality and inclusion to one of masculine supremacy, to which the husband's common-law duty of support was central. The reason that corporate exploitation and governmental corruption were so dangerous, the new argument went, was that they undermined the ability of husbands and fathers to provide for their families.[129] Thus, the party's strategic aim and method tended to push women back to an auxiliary role.

The Populist Party also compromised agrarian republicanism's traditional orientation toward localism. Although the party had "grassroots," its agenda was nationalist. This made sense for at least three reasons. First, as noted above, homesteaders west of the Mississippi were connected directly to the nation in ways that settlers in older states back East had not been. According to the Constitution, congressional statute, and the explicit acquiescence of states, the territories belonged to and were subject to regulation by the nation.[130] Thus, the policies that permitted, even encouraged, western settlement were national in origin and purpose. Second, the principal levers of political economy were national. This was due in no small part to the power of Hamiltonianism as a description of and prescription for many aspects of the regime, especially after the Civil War. To put a sharper point on it, if Populism's enemies were national corporations possessing substantial economic power, the remedies must be national as well. Third, the circumstances that propelled Populism as a political movement in the late 1880s and early 1890s—high interest rates, falling prices for farm products, failed farms and foreclosures on mortgages, and the Panic of 1893—were beyond local control.

Populism's platform rested on this central premise: primary authority over the political economy was vested not in enterprise (the "millionaires") but in "the people." The political justification for this position was that democracy demanded it. The people presupposed by this version of democracy, however, were not merely a local (nor necessarily an agrarian) people, but a national people, rural and urban. The economic justification returned to John Locke's labor theory of ownership, but turned it against Hamilton's abstract political economy. Wealth, the platform stated, is created by labor and "belongs to him who creates it." Capitalists, who siphon wealth from its creators, commit "robbery," straight and simple.[131] Almost all the remedies the Populists proposed aimed to enhance governmental presence in the economy—through nationalization of crucial industries, federally financed low-interest loans, postal savings banks, a graduated income tax, and monetary policies like unlimited coinage of silver.[132]

Populism's cause would be coopted by the Democrats, most vividly in the elections of 1896, in which William Jennings Bryan was crucified. After this, the movement's war against capital and the railroads went moribund.[133] There is reason to believe, however, that the agrarian movements that gave rise to Populism helped western women enjoy at least two important entrees into traditionally masculine preserves. The first concerned higher education. Western territories and states embraced coeducation far sooner than those back East, though it is also true that most coeducational institutions prescribed segregated courses of study for women and men—women being directed to courses related to teaching and the economy of the home, and men to other broader studies.[134]

The second entree involved suffrage. Partly through women's associational activities (including their work in the pro-suffrage Women's Christian Temperance Union) and partly through the active agitation of the Populists, women first acquired the right to vote in the West.[135] The reasons for these successes are complex. Jameson argues that support for suffrage came not from among men of the "genteel upper classes" but from "farmers and miners who endorsed political philosophies that supported equality."[136] Although there is something to this claim, the record is actually more tangled and, in some respects, less idealistic. In Wyoming, for example, proponents had a variety of motives: some wanted to embarrass the Republican governor, who they mistakenly thought would veto the measure; others argued that the measure would attract more women to the territory (which at the time had 6,107 males and only 1,049 women over the age of ten).[137] In Utah, extending the suffrage was promoted zealously by a member of Congress from Indiana, who argued that if women had the right to vote in the West, they would discourage sexual promiscuity and outlaw polygamy.[138]

Perhaps the most we can confidently say is that, in the states that were manufactured from the frontier, certain political actors saw their interests to be congruent with women's. These were not always high-minded motives, to be sure. But two possible lessons stand out, one concerning constitutional values, the other concerning the constitutionalist function of family. First, it is notable that actors—men, for the most part—who wanted something for themselves pursued their own interests by promoting a version of constitutional liberty and equality for others. Second, and more modestly, perhaps the fact that these actors perceived women to be worthy or useful political partners—on the model of the marital family on the frontier—was something of an achievement in itself.

UNCONVENTIONAL HOUSEHOLDS

We shouldn't close this discussion without noting that marital families were not the only households on the frontier. The reasons were not mysterious. One was that people could find themselves drawn together—and drawn toward establishing a household—at unexpected times, places, and circumstances across vast tracts of wilderness or proto-settlement. Another, related reason was the paucity of judges, civil officers, or clergy who might legalize or sanctify unions. So nonmarital households and highly fluid movement into and out of households were common on the frontier. This fact alone underwrote an unregulated liberty and a vigorous individualism increasingly forgotten back East.

But a particular form of nonmarital household was present in the West with a frequency that might have surprised easterners. This was the household in which two or more persons of the same sex came together in ways that were functionally familial. Same-sex relations were prevalent across the West, especially in mining camps, logging camps, and communities of wandering tramps and laborers (who, by the end of the nineteenth century, had come to be known as "hoboes"). These "homosocial" places and groups were overwhelmingly male. Some communities of hoboes, in fact, aggressively excluded women. In some respects, each place created a social subculture unto itself, largely cut off from direct contact with cities and towns. Still, there were common themes. In mining camps, for example, one could find all-male "sprees" or "balls," marked by strenuous drinking and exuberant dancing. Some of the men were cast as women, to serve as dancing partners.[139] These dances could hardly count as familial. But some coupling relations did occur within communities of loggers and hoboes. These relations were structurally and functionally domestic and, on some reports, physically intimate.[140]

Cowboys sometimes worked in conditions even more isolated than miners and loggers. They were often assigned to work in pairs, and strong emotional bonds could arise between partners, not least because they depended on each other for survival. One aspect of that dependence involved sleeping together as "bunkies" on cold nights.[141] There's scholarly debate about whether these relations were sexual. Relying on circumstantial inferences from private correspondence and poetry, Walter Williams argues that they were. Quoting from the 1974 memoir of a man who had been a cowboy in Oklahoma around the time of statehood, Williams suggests that attraction between cowboys "was at first rooted in admiration, infatuation, a sensed need of an ally, loneliness and yearning, but it regularly ripened into love."[142] Dee Garceau dissents, describing claims of homoerotic relations between cowboys (or between cowboys and Indians) as "revisionist." She acknowledges that partners shared intense emotional bonds, including both "affection and annoyance, much like [those] between long-term married couples." And sometimes the bonds were poignantly on display, as when a partner died. But Garceau denies that those ties counted as evidence of sexualized relations, and she emphasizes the heterosexual licentiousness, mainly with prostitutes, that was a large part of cowboy culture and identity. The only evidence of homoerotic sentiment in song or narrative, she reports, involved cases of "mistaken identity." "Cowboy myth is hypermasculine, avoiding any hint of homosexual themes."[143]

If so, it's notable that cross-dressing was a theme of cowboys' culture and lore. As with miners and loggers, cross-dressing cowboys took on feminine roles at dances and public skits. Garceau describes these episodes as "public spectacle, a focus of group hilarity," and sometimes a tweaking of Victorian (i.e., eastern) social norms. The episodes were not, she insists, erotic.[144] It is possible that the differences between Garceau, on the one hand, and Boag and Williams, on the other, are partly due to the types of evidence they're examining. In short, Garceau's evidence is public, and Boag's and Williams's is largely personal or private. Perhaps the most we can say is that most evidence of sexualized relations between cowboys is circumstantial. But, given what we today know about sexuality, it would not be surprising to find that some relations between some cowboys were erotic in some respects.

Cross-dressing was not confined to homosocial settings of loggers, miners, and cowboys. It was also present—and socially significant—in frontier settlements and homesteads. Unlike those in homosocial communities, cross-dressers in settlements and homesteads could be of either gender and typically did not publicize their biological sex. When discovered, however, they made headlines. Newspapers, courts' records, and early sociological studies documented the phenomenon and showed it to be widespread through the nineteenth and early twentieth centuries. Peter Boag has uncovered dozens of accounts of cross-dressing women in frontier settlements. Their stories reached a simultaneously titillated and mortified public via newspapers and other sources.[145]

There seem to have been several motives for women's donning men's clothing in the West. Some women did so for simple—and sometimes transient—reasons, like enhancing their safety while traveling or wanting to visit places generally off limits to women. One woman explained to a local judge that "the only way for a girl to see the Barbary Coast (a red-light district in San Francisco) was in male attire." Other women posed as men to gain longer-term access to a lifestyle or pursuit that was otherwise unavailable to them. If they could convince the world that they were men, they might earn higher salaries, work in traditionally male occupations, and be more independent. In a famous example, Babe Bean was so accepted by the male community in Stockton, California, that she was permitted to join the local Bachelor's Club even after she was revealed to be a woman. In an open discussion in the local paper, other women asked why Babe Bean was allowed to cross-dress and work as a man, when other women were not. Bean's reply included information about where women could purchase men's clothing, and for how much. With a male lifestyle sometimes came vices. News stories occasionally included descriptions of how cross-dressing women drank, swore, and chewed tobacco. A few succeeded in voting. One, Joe Monahan, not only voted regularly but also served on more than one jury.[146]

Cross-dressing was not confined, however, to dances, larks, or strategic attempts to find a place in the world. It was also present in sustained ways in households, both married and nonmarried. In these cases it's likely that feelings of sexual difference helped explain at least some of the "passing" that occurred. Many of the women who lived as men for substantial periods carried on flirtations and courtships with and, on occasion, even married other women. One, Milton Matson (born Louise Elizabeth Myrtle Blaxland Matson), dressed as a male for twenty-six years, saying he had always simply felt more like a boy than a girl. When he was arrested for obtaining money under false pretenses, authorities discovered that he was biologically a woman. This was news to Helen Fairweather, a local schoolteacher who was in a romantic relationship with Matson at the time. She reported that she had thought Matson was a man, but had reconciled herself to his biological sexuality. She was reported to have said, "I was loved, and that it was not a man is no fault of mine." Matson seemed almost to take delight in being discovered. "Yes, I like the ladies. . . . It was lots of fun carrying on flirtations . . . and a real joy to make love to them." Eugene DeForest described himself as "a woman with the soul of a man." After a Platonic marriage to a man, who died during the marriage, DeForest took on the clothes and identity of a man, and married a woman. That marriage ended in divorce. The endings to some stories, however, were not merely unhappy but tragic. Nell Pickerell took on the name Harry Allen and romanced women in Minnesota. Two conquests, Dolly Quappe and Hazel Walters, fell hopelessly in love with Allen. When they discovered Allen's true sex, both of them committed suicide.[147]

Communities' reception of the news of cross-dressing could be mixed. Charles Vosbaugh, for example, lived for decades in rural Colorado with his wife, working in the livestock industry and running a family restaurant. When he was hospitalized for pneumonia later in his life, and his biological sex was revealed, those around him continued to treat him as male, much as Babe Bean's acquaintances had done in San Francisco. Others came in for massive amounts of ridicule and shunning. Many found their names in sensational stories of scandal in newspapers of the day. A few stories made their way even into national papers. Explanations for the "masquerades" varied. Some accounts emphasized the disadvantages and hardships that women had to endure in the West, making cross-dressing a rational adaptation to those conditions. Several of these accounts emphasized feminine features of masquerading women. One story described how a woman posing as a man was revealed to have "a swelling bust, beautiful, expressive blue eyes, handsome features, and teeth of pearly whiteness." Doubtless, this story line not only appealed to many male readers, but also normalized the cross-dresser and suppressed any social anxieties about sexuality. In popular culture, such women could be transformed into gun-toting Calamity Janes and Annie Oaklies, as characters in dime-store novels and Wild West shows. Other stories were more difficult to normalize in these ways. Cross-dressing women who were married to or had engaged in same-sex affairs with women, or who strongly identified as male, tended to threaten norms of both sex and gender. By the late nineteenth century, newspapers began to label such persons as "man-woman," emphasizing their masculinity, or calling them "sexual inverts."[148]

Male-to-female cross-dressing outside homosocial environments was more socially explosive than was female-to-male. This was partly because explanations of disadvantage and hardship didn't apply in the same way to men. But it was also partly for other, subtle reasons that made male nonconformity more threatening. And, as we'll see in Chapters 7 and 8, they were caught up in a time of increasing preoccupation with sexual behavior and sexual deviance. Thus, men who chose to live as women were branded as "freaks" and "hermaphrodites" and were consistently marginalized from society when they were discovered. Even when despised, however, their publicity helped produce a public awareness of sexuality that extended beyond the nineteenth century and expanded well outside the West.[149]

CONCLUSION

Frederick Jackson Turner argued that the driving forces and political legacy of westward settlement were individualism, democracy, and nationalism.[150] Their importance is undeniable, even if we might quibble over what they entailed. There was, however, another force whose constitutional legacy Turner undervalued. Families on the frontier were intermediate associations, neither liberal nor democratic, that altered the terms of both liberalism and democracy, while extending the authority of the nation.

In functional terms, nineteenth-century marital families on the frontier did not play the subversive and radically creative roles their eighteenth-century colonial predecessors had played. Perhaps this should come as no surprise; for, despite the presence of familial forms and practices that deviated from what was increasingly considered the conventional norm, these families by the end of the nineteenth century were becoming rationalized as part of the constitutional order. Even on the frontier—where environmental challenges were substantial, and legal and social constraints were thin—these were *republican* families, emulating their eighteenth-century prototypes. Their role, however, was not to revise the political world, but to secure the United States' military conquests over Indians and Mexicans, while inhibiting the expansion of slavery (and the migration of blacks). They would accomplish these tasks by serving as social and political instruments for extending the nation's political authority over the conquered territories.

For many reasons, these families were largely ineffective in limiting the Hamiltonian elements of American political economy. This failure was not for lack of trying. Many families on the frontier, especially in parts of what we now call the upper Midwest and the Great Plains, were active participants in social and political movements whose aim was to challenge, in the name of an agrarian republicanism identified with Jefferson, the individualist and centralizing tendencies that Tocqueville feared. By the end of the century, however, the Hamiltonian logic of political economy was too powerful to be successfully resisted.

If western families failed in this respect, they succeeded in another unexpected direction, and did so in ways that challenged the masculine presuppositions of the common law. To be sure, the West did not liberate women. But it did work substantial change, largely without the aid of law, as environmental and ethical conditions impelled women to take on new roles in families, communities, and the larger society. At first, these roles were informal and social in character. Later, they were formal and overtly political. Eventually, they solidified two entitlements of significance for western women: expansive access to higher education and the right to vote. As a matter of constitutional text and doctrine, however, the question of women's status in the nation as a whole would not be fully joined until well into the twentieth century, long after the frontier ceased to be.

6
Tribal Families and the American Nation

In the process of helping to extend the authority of the nation-state across North America, white families on the frontier performed an additional role: they helped solidify the displacement of the native tribes, who had occupied vast portions of the continent for centuries before the coming of the Europeans. The tribes were not collections of "individuals" in the modernist sense of the word. They were genuine collectivities, constituted by arrays of subgroups, including relations that even we today would recognize as familial. If we might recognize them, however, we would also understand immediately that these were families of a different sort—not the nuclear form that has become such a prominent part of contemporary rhetoric, identity, and practice. This is not to say that sexual pairing didn't exist among the tribes. It did. But, as we'll see, tribal households were not organized around the modernist model. Among the tribes one could see a variety of arrangements. Still, most tribes customarily recognized households formed and organized around complex and sometimes indirect lines of consanguinity, with children's identity and inheritance derived largely from their mother.

The story of the tribes' displacement began well before the late nineteenth century, of course, carried out first by the colonists and eventually by the constitutional order. It is a story that includes broken treaties, brute force, and the rationalizing gloss of the rule of law. It includes also systematic programs, whose chief purpose was to dismantle the tribes. These programs worked in several ways on several fronts—political, military, and social. Ultimately, however, gaining control of the tribes and their members required gaining control of tribal families. An indispensable method for pursuing this project of social control was education, through which the nation aimed to separate Indian children from their families and seize control of children's identities and character. By the late nineteenth century, then, the nation self-consciously aimed to destroy the tribes by destroying their families and replacing them with families whose structure was nuclear, whose members were individuals, and whose function was to reinforce the productive and political needs of a post–Civil War capitalist democracy.

EDUCATION AND CONSTITUTIONAL ORDER

Autocratic systems of government may rely substantially on force or the threat of force to maintain themselves. Constitutionalist orders are different, at least in theory. They depend for their authority on the voluntary attachment of citizens. And, because citizenship is a consequential status in a constitutionalist order, citizens (or at least a significant number of them) must possess the virtues and capacities appropriate to their position and functions. It's easy to see why the education of children might be an attractive approach to inculcating civic competence. Historically, political systems of many sorts have tended to rely on families to provide an appropriate education, not only for civic functions (if any) but also for moral, intellectual, and vocational purposes. We saw this responsibility expressed in the English law of family and in Locke's *Second Treatise*. Some polities, however, might perceive families not to be consistently reliable purveyors of civic information and values.

The United States was not such a polity, at least in the beginning, when the citizenry (not necessarily to say the population as a whole) was fairly homogeneous: white, Western European, and Christian. Even the Deists of the founding generation tended to embrace an ethos that was recognizably Protestant, though they were not Trinitarian, and their worldview was more strongly influenced by the Enlightenment than it was by religious dogma. By the latter half of the nineteenth century, patterns of immigration had changed, as growing numbers of immigrants came from Eastern Europe or outside Europe entirely, and many were non-Christian. Incorporating these recent arrivals into the polity was a challenge. The challenge was all the greater because the United States relied more heavily than most political orders on a degree of civic participation—or at least of civic attachment—and because "America" was as much an idea as it was a geographic place. Increasingly after the Civil War, the several states turned to the common school, supported by various forms of taxation, to educate the young. This move was as much self-interested as it was humanitarian, for it ensured the production of citizens who possessed a basic level of education and literacy. And, in providing civic training, it Americanized the nation's youth—not only the children of immigrants but also children whose familial ancestors had long resided in the United States.[1]

To be sure, many children of wealthy families as well as of Catholics opted out of common schools.[2] But, by the early twentieth century, the common school was the dominant institution for educating the young and for making them Americans, albeit often with a local stamp. The effects of the states' assertion of authority over education were essentially twofold. One was to partially displace the authority of families for educating their children. Another was to make children, at least to some degree, "creatures of the state," in the words (but against the point) of *Pierce v. Society of Sisters*.[3] In short, the United States began to regulate and use education to reproduce its own citizenry.[4]

BEFORE THE CONSTITUTION

The Europeans who first arrived in what came to be known as North America faced a basic question: what to do with the various tribes of people who already lived here? As arrival morphed into invasion and settlement, the question became all the more acute, even as its possible answers multiplied. Plainly, military conquest was a basic element of the European strategy—especially for the Spanish, but also for the English, French, and Dutch. Where conquest stopped short of physical annihilation, however, the question persisted. One answer was education.

The viability of this answer, of course, assumed that Indians were both educable and worthy of education, assumptions that many Europeans contested. In truth, the image of the Indian in the European mind was conflicted—vacillating between felicity and debasement. Some of the felicitous images were imaginary, antedating Columbus's expeditions. But others drew on evidence available from European contact. The image was of people who lived in harmony with both nature and one another—an idyllic life, as if uncorrupted by the biblical fall from grace.[5] A passage from Locke's *Second Treatise* is suggestive in this regard: "In the beginning all the world was *America*."[6] The debased images, on the other hand, became equally potent. They depicted Indians as not only untutored, but positively treacherous, amoral, barbaric, and savage. In short, on this view, Indians lacked the capacity for civilized discourse, intercourse, and life.[7]

Fairly early, however, those who mattered, for purposes of policy in European nations, decided that members of the tribes were capable at least of education even if they remained culturally or otherwise inferior. From the beginning, and regardless of the identity of the colonizing nation, education included at least three elements: religious, linguistic, and economic. From Europeans' perspectives, native education served several purposes: salvation, ethical correction, pacification, social control, and commercial intercourse and exploitation. The relative primacy of these purposes varied, depending on temporal, geographic, social, and military contexts. But it's possible to summarize all in a single word: civilization. Education could illuminate and elevate. In the process, it might enable Indians to learn to coexist with civilized peoples and nations.

Religion—specifically, instruction in Christianity—was central, for reasons metaphysical, ethical, and political. It is clear that their religions were important to the tribes. For some, religion suffused almost every aspect of daily life—from hunting, planting, and harvesting food, to the passage of members to adulthood, to responsibilities across generations, to tribal identification. In short, religion was the foundation for a tribe's view of itself, its members, and the rest of the world. It is clear also that the cosmology, metaphysics, and rites of tribal religions differed from those of Christianity (or, if not of Christianity per se, then of European norms). It has been reported, for example, that in at least one native language there was no word for "sin." And it's clear that some of the ethical relations, obligations, and constraints of tribal religions differed from those of Christianity. Europeans were struck, for example, by aspects of Indians' familial lives. Matrilinearity was typical (and, from a European perspective, problematic). Extended familial relations and norms of inheritance struck Europeans as odd. In some tribes, divorce was common. Some permitted polygamy. Christian missionaries worried that Indian girls had an inadequately developed sense of sexual inhibition. And, outside the realm of familial ethics, missionaries worried about the civility of certain groups who practiced cannibalism or torture or others who, even if "gentle, loving, and faithfull," went without clothes.[8]

In British North America, white settlers assumed that Christianity was the key to civilizing the Indians. Religious efforts in the British colonies were models of disorganization. In New England in the mid-seventeenth century, the Puritans found Indians on the whole to be an unreceptive audience for Christianity. This did not deter some ministers in Massachusetts from attempting to proselytize among the tribes or from establishing towns for "praying Indians." With financial support from the Society for the Propagation of the Gospel and its successors (all chartered by Parliament), colonists distributed books that were translated into Algonquian, including an Algonquian edition of the Bible. These efforts met but limited success, however, and the British decided that the best way to civilize Indians was not only to Christianize them but also to Anglicize them. The British employed two methods to attempt to accomplish this. One was armed force. The other was education.[9]

In the final decade of the seventeenth century, the charter for the College of William & Mary provided for the establishment of an Indian school, with one teacher, whose duty was to teach English language, mathematics, and religion. The school attracted few students until the mid-eighteenth century, when young hostages from the military campaigns against the Cherokee and Shawnee tribes were brought to Williamsburg to study. Despite having a (literally) captive audience, the school fell short of its founders' vision, as many students died from disease, others resisted the course of instruction, and still others "relapsed" into Indian ways when they returned to their tribes.[10]

Schools for Indians were also established in the early eighteenth century in New England. Probably the most famous was Moor's Indian Charity School, founded in Connecticut by Congregationalist minister Eleazer Wheelock. He eventually moved the school to New Hampshire, renamed as Dartmouth College. Harvard College also made provision for the education of Indian boys. Some New Englanders decided that educating native children would be even more effective under conditions that encouraged the creation of families on the English model.

One strategy, which Cotton Mather and Joseph Talcott proposed, was to remove Indian children from their tribes and apprentice them to "English and Godly families." This proposal failed when the tribes refused to cede their children. Another strategy was to establish boarding schools for boys and girls. The boys, after all, would eventually need proper wives if they were to become (part of) families that were self-sustaining and could resist the allure of uncivilized tribal ways.[11]

FROM SOVEREIGN NATIONS TO WARDS OF THE NATION

The aims of the United States' strategy for dealing with the tribes varied with time and circumstance. Initially, American policy aimed at pacification (whose immediate motive was domestic security) and at regulating trade with Indians.[12] There was a geo-strategic aspect to this policy, playing friendly tribes against less friendly ones and against competing powers—the French, Spanish, and British. This was especially the case around the time of the Revolutionary War, as the Continental Congress attempted to appease the tribes either to keep them neutral in conflicts with European powers or simply to maintain good relations with friendly tribes.[13] But this strategic aim continued well into the nineteenth century.

As early as the constitutional founding, however, the United States began aggressively to chase another aim that would alter the new nation's approach to the tribes: territorial expansion. To pursue this aim the Americans employed two strategies. One was conquest, or at least control by the use of armed force. The other was geographic displacement or, as it came to be called, removal. Given these strategies, it was no accident that, in the first seventy years of the republic, the job of supervising and implementing relations with the tribes was the delegated responsibility of the Department of War. (This jurisdiction was transferred in 1849 to the Department of Interior's Office of Indian Affairs.)[14]

If, by the mid-nineteenth century, the United States' approach to "the Indian question" was in some respects "uncivilized," there were nonetheless ethical and practical limits to the new nation's ability to answer it. To put it coldly, it was neither possible nor politically expedient to kill all the Indians. What to do with those who survived? Before the twentieth century, citizenship was not a comprehensive option. For legal and constitutional purposes, the possibility of citizenship for Indians was not assumed. In fact, a strong reading of the Constitution suggested that citizenship was positively prohibited.[15] Treaties and statutes awarded citizenship in limited cases, but didn't recognize citizenship for Indians generally. Even after the adoption of the Fourteenth Amendment, the Supreme Court of the United States held that an Indian who was born on a reservation could not become a citizen, despite the fact that he had separated from his tribe and sworn allegiance to the United States.[16] (In 1924, the Citizenship Act would remove the legal impediment,[17] though not to unanimous acclaim among Indians.[18]) Because of barriers to citizenship and for other reasons, robust economic integration was unlikely, even if it had been desirable. For reasons both altruistic and self-interested, white America espoused education as part of its strategy for dealing with the tribes. Education could promote pacification, secure social control, underwrite an alternative form of economic survival, and encourage acculturation.

In the early years, the United States considered the tribes to be distinct peoples and independent nations. The new republic, therefore, tended to conduct political relations through treaties with specific tribes. Well into the nineteenth century, it was not uncommon for treaties to include provisions for educating Indian children.[19] The first general statutory policy (if it can be called a policy) of education, however, was adopted in 1819. Its unsurprising title was the Civilization Act. Its stated purposes were to inhibit "the further decline and final extinction of the Indian tribes" and to "introduc[e] among them the habits and arts of civilization." To these ends, the Act provided an annual appropriation of $10,000 for education. By its terms, the statute provided for instruction in agricultural production and for more traditionally academic schooling in reading, writing, and arithmetic. Like the nation's policies involving the use of force, the policy of education was administered by the Department of War.[20]

It's possible to read the instructional and civilizing purposes as being benignly motivated; but President Monroe's message to Congress four months prior to the Civilization Act's passage revealed a slightly different spirit:

> Experience has clearly demonstrated that independent savage communities cannot long exist within the limits of a civilized population. . . . To civilize [the Indians], and even to prevent their extinction, it seems to be indispensable that their independence as communities should cease, and that the control of the United States over them should be complete and undisputed. The hunter state will then be more easily abandoned, and recourse will be had to the acquisition and culture of land, and to other pursuits tending to dissolve the ties which connect them together as a savage community, and to give a new character to every individual.[21]

President Monroe's version of the "house divided" was an early step toward the notion that "civilized" meant Americanized. This entailed at least three things: basic minimal schooling in the 3 Rs, training in a manual or petit-bourgeois occupation, and profession of an approved system of religious ethics. Communal property was anathema. Identification with tribe was discouraged. Polygamy was scorned. And promiscuity was condemned (as a matter of public rhetoric, if not as a matter of consistent social practice). The American model was individualist monogamous restraint and self-sufficiency.

In implementing the Civilization Act, officials amplified it in significant ways that made the model Christian, gendered, and patriotic. John C. Calhoun, who was the first secretary of war to administer the Act, committed to using the appropriations to finance the efforts of "benevolent associations" that worked or proposed to work among the tribes. This term was restricted to religious organizations. Calhoun expanded the program of study to embrace (for boys) "such of the mechanic arts [as] are suited to the condition of the Indians" and (for girls) "spinning, weaving, and sewing." He also specified that organizations or schools receiving funds teach patriotism (to the United States)—"to impress on the minds of the Indians the friendly and benevolent views of the Government toward them, and the advantage to them in yielding to the policy of Government, and co-operating with it."[22]

Benevolent or not, the Congress in 1830 enacted a statute to "remove" eastern tribes to reserved land west of the Mississippi River.[23] Although removal had been practiced repeatedly "in a haphazard manner for many years," as Lucille Griffith puts it, the Removal Act committed the United States systematically and comprehensively to the policy.[24] For the tribes, the consequence of removal was catastrophic. This included the impact on programs of Indian education. Tribes that had invested in the conversion to agriculture—attempting, as the United States had encouraged them to do, to root themselves in cultivated soil—saw their investment vanish. By the end of Andrew Jackson's presidency, almost all tribal Indians in the southeastern states were driven under military supervision to the region that would become Oklahoma.[25]

In the wake of removal, the American approach to Indian education altered subtly. One change was a shift in "curricular" emphasis. In the 1840s, officials began to encourage the religious groups that ran Indian schools to deemphasize scholastic and religious instruction and to stress manual training. The reasons were both practical (to encourage economically viable occupations) and racist (that, as savages, manual occupations were the only ones within the Indians' grasp). It's doubtful that ministers and missionaries ever forsook religious instruction, which they viewed as the primary purpose of their mission; but there is some evidence that a greater emphasis on manual training, as against scholastic instruction, was real.[26] Another change concerned the type of school that certain commissioners of Indian Affairs preferred. By the 1860s, at least one commissioner expressed disdain for day schools operating in tribal "neighborhoods" and a strong partiality to boarding schools. The justification was simply that Indians could not be properly acculturated—civilized—if not uprooted from their tribes.[27] Each of these changes was more a shift in sensibility than of direction, but both would become dominant aspects of policy after the Civil War.

From the first day of his presidency, Ulysses S. Grant acknowledged that U.S. policies toward the tribes had produced an unhappy history of predation and carnage (mostly by whites) that had steadily transformed relations between government and Indians. No longer were the latter sovereign peoples. No longer were relations to be managed by treaties.[28] Now, invoking the familial terminology of Blackstone's common law, the Indians were "wards of the nation." This status called for governmental responsibility—to place Indians on the path to "their civilization." What civilization amounted to, however, had changed. Pacification was no longer its principal aspect—and, for the most part, no longer necessary. To be sure, there were still bands or tribes at war with the United States, but these tended to be few and relatively small. By 1870, almost all the tribes had been subdued, defeated, or decimated. (General Custer would realize in 1876, however, that the Sioux and Cheyenne had not been.) The primary aim of civilization, according to Grant, was now citizenship.[29] And citizenship entailed or presupposed assimilation.

Schools were essential to assimilation, but only if they were effective. In truth, most Indian schools were a travesty. White indifference aside, part of the reason for this was that schools were inadequately funded, and the process for supervising them, vested in Indian agents, was susceptible to breathtaking corruption. In an effort to clean up the process for appointing agents, Grant delegated this authority wholesale to Christian organizations (both Protestant and Catholic), which as late as 1870 continued to receive almost all appropriations for operating Indian schools. President Grant also attempted to achieve administrative efficiencies in the management and supervision of schools. And in 1870 Congress began appropriating unprecedented sums for education. The appropriation in 1870 was $100,000. Appropriations after 1870 continued to be comparatively large. Because these amounts dwarfed the $10,000 annual appropriations provided for in the Civilization Act, that act was repealed in 1873.[30]

What made these efforts both feasible and desirable was that most tribal Indians were now confined (or were in the process of being sent) to reservations. Confinement undoubtedly made it easier to implement Grant's administrative efficiencies. It also focused attention on government's legal responsibility for these "wards." This is not to suggest that the United States became more benevolent in all respects. It is only to say that government became more attentive. From the standpoint of the tribes, attention was a double-edged sword; for, having sequestered most of the tribes, the United States now tried to demolish them. The assault was two-pronged. One involved property (and its relation to citizenship), the other a distinct shift in the character of and control over Indian education.

PROPERTY, MANHOOD, AND FAMILY

The General Allotment Act (also known as the Dawes Severalty Act) authorized the president to order that any reservation be surveyed, divided into lots, and allotted among the Indians living there, with the largest parcels going to heads of families, smaller ones to various "single person[s]." Congress amended the Act two years later, to permit nonreservation Indians, too, to select parcels. In theory, an allottee became a citizen when he took possession of his parcel. This status was merely inchoate, however, as the allottee lacked full privileges of citizenship. In fact, he lacked also full rights to the parcel, for the United States held it in trust for twenty-five years. After this period, the allottee would ascend to full citizenship, and the government would convey title to the land, unless the president decided to lengthen the period of trust.[31]

In its own way, the Dawes Act was designed to be an educational enactment. Its aim was to provide individual Indians a powerful set of incentives. In the immediate term, the allottee would be impelled to assume responsibility for his and his family's material welfare. Over time, he would begin to acquire values of the "Protestant ethic"—thrift, energy, and productivity. In short, he would learn to become an individual, not a tribal member. The lessons of responsibility for property would also transmit a capacity for citizenship, and the twenty-five-year trust would provide time for Indians to practice (or imagine practicing) citizenship. In this way, the ownership (or possession at least) of property united liberal individualism and democracy. From the standpoint of the United States, allotment would generate ancillary benefits, too, for the subdivision of property into individual parcels would dismantle the communal property that was the reservation. Having destroyed the material base supporting communist ethical conceptions, which were in turn the foundation for tribal ways of life, the government aimed to destroy the tribes' capacity to sustain themselves as tribes. In their place would arise, the logic went, a new American way of life for Indians.[32]

Hiram Price, the Commissioner of Indian Affairs, had anticipated this logic in his Annual Report in 1881. In what was becoming an American political habit, the report invoked a trope that President Monroe had employed more than sixty years before:

There is no one who has been a close observer of Indian history and the effect of contact of Indians with civilization, who is not well satisfied that one of two things must eventually take place, to wit, either civilization or extermination of the Indian. Savage and civilized life cannot live and prosper on the same ground. One of the two must die. If the Indians are to be civilized and become a happy and prosperous people, . . . they must learn our language and adopt our modes of life. . . . The few must yield to the many.[33]

Allotment, he said, would help to civilize the tribes. It "tends to break up tribal relations. It has the effect of creating individuality, responsibility, and a desire to accumulate property. It teaches the Indian habits of industry and frugality, and stimulates them to look forward to a more useful life, and, in the end, it will relieve the government of large annual appropriations."[34] The Annual Report of the Board of Indian Commissioners in 1881 agreed: Allotment would "secure to [the Indian] the integrity of the family and the home[,] . . . the unit of Christian civilization."[35]

Merrill Gates, president of Rutgers College and a member of the U.S. Board of Indian Commissioners, reiterated some of these themes and gave them a gendered cast, in a speech in 1885. The tribe, he said, had perverse effects on its members. "The highest right of man is the *right to be a man,* with all that this involves. The tendency of the tribal organization is constantly to interfere with and frustrate the attainment of this highest manhood."[36] How so? The answer implicated family and property.

The family is God's unit of society. On the integrity of the family depends that of the State. There is no civilization deserving of the name where family is not the unit in civil government. Even the most extreme advocates of individualism must admit that the highest and most perfect personality is developed through those relations which the family renders possible and fosters. And from the point of view of land and law, students are generally at one with Sir Henry Maine when he says, in his latest work, "I believe I state the inference suggested by all known legal history when I say there can be no material advance in civilization unless landed property is held by groups at least as small as families."[37]

The tribal conception of property—specifically, the institution of communal property—"cuts the nerve of all that manful effort which political economy teaches us proceeds from the desire for wealth." It makes people lazy. And it inhibits the accumulation of wealth that might have been used "for the benefit of children." As an example of the lethargic effect of communism, Gates noted the absence of theft in tribes: "The fact that robbery is said to be almost unknown among Indians within the tribe is largely explained by the fact that property, too, . . . is almost unknown. There is an utter barbarism in which property has almost no existence."[38] Oddly, then, robbery was a marker of civilization, and the Indians were the poorer for its absence.

The solution, said Gates, was law, propagated by the nation-state. Law should work toward family and property. It should do so by promoting private property, "punish[ing] offenses against purity, and . . . abolish[ing] polygamy. . . . These laws enforced will help still further to develop true family feeling. Family feeling growing stronger and stronger as all the members of the family work on their own homestead for the welfare of the home, will itself incline all toward welcoming the reign of law, and will increase the desire of all for systematic education." But perhaps it was too much to expect that all would desire education. "We must as rapidly as possible break up the tribal organization and give them law, with the family and land in severalty as its central idea. We must not only give them law— we must *force* law upon them. We must not only offer them education—we must force education upon them!" And so, through the law of severalty, "the family and a homestead [will] prove the salvation of those whom the tribal organization and the reservation were debasing."[39]

The Dawes Act was terribly effective in wresting land from the tribes. It did more than this, however, for it also led to the loss of land even from allottees. Understood in one way, law became an instrument for defeating legal rights. It is estimated that, before the Act, Indians held 138 million acres of land, either as individuals or through tribes. By the end of the period of allotment forty-five years later, they had lost more than 60 percent of those tracts. One reason is that initial allotments were either too isolated or too small to support productive grazing. Another is that laws of inheritance frequently worked to break up holdings.[40]

Still another reason has to do with white settlers and agents. Unscrupulous or coercive bargaining was commonplace; but it was also not uncommon for whites who coveted desirable Indian land to have the allottee declared incompetent and so to force the sale of his land.[41] All of these consequences were traceable to the Dawes Act. This experience, in itself, was a kind of civic education for Indians, though not the precise lesson intended by the Act's most benevolent proponents.

INDIAN EDUCATION AGAINST FAMILIES

In the schools, the United States made two significant changes. One was the gradual move away from federally funded sectarian schools, toward schools that government both funded and ran. Sentiment for secular schools had begun to surface in the mid-1870s, especially among governmental administrators in Indian affairs, and gathered momentum in the following decade. It is difficult to know whether the dominant motive for this change was a belief that government-run schools would be more effective, an unreflective succumbing to the rising tide of common schools, a principled objection to the use of public money to support sectarian activities, or a desire to draw more responsibility (or power) under a bureaucratic umbrella. Whatever the motive, secularization happened. In 1889, the new Commissioner of Indian Affairs Thomas Morgan announced his intention to terminate federal contracts with religious schools. Most religious organizations responded by getting out of the business of educating Indians. One exception was the Catholic Church, which, indignant, fought the policy intensely on several fronts. In the end, however, the Church conceded the inevitable and severed ties with governmental programs.[42]

Regardless of who ran the schools, there was still a question about their character. One option, long practiced especially by the churches, was the day school, located on the reservation. In the 1870s, as we saw above, commissioners of Indian Affairs grew disenchanted with these schools, and not merely because they were run by religious organizations. Truancy was rampant, partly because of parental resistance. The quality of instruction was generally low. And officials (and others) worried that the environment to which students returned at the end of the day were subverting the lessons of school.[43]

Another option resurrected an approach with which English settlers had flirted in colonial times: the boarding school. The idea, plainly, was to have children take up residence at the school. The earliest versions of this arrangement were located on or near reservations. One challenge, of course, was getting students. If some Indian parents resisted day schools, wouldn't they be even more reluctant to send their children to boarding schools? The answer is that they were. Frequently, agents and officials who ran the schools resorted to deceit, coercion, and (sometimes) kidnaping to generate a clientele.[44] But even when parents voluntarily sent their children, many parents would not stay away. They visited frequently and expected their progeny to come home at every available holiday. Almost immediately, therefore, critics argued that these schools suffered from some of the same limitations as day schools.[45]

Some critics advocated and began to experiment with boarding schools located far from the reservation. As proponents of off-reservation schools saw it, this approach had several advantages. With students unable to return home, it would be much easier to compel attendance and enforce discipline. Learning, therefore, could be more rapid. Schools could require all English all the time. And they could more effectively deemphasize academic subjects in favor of a more systematic exposure to "industrial" training. As we've already seen, for boys this training was in agriculture and mechanical trades; for girls it was in domestic pursuits like sewing, cooking, and cleaning. The aim at bottom was to ensure that students acquired the "habits of civilized life."[46] Commissioner Morgan was specific about what this life entailed:

When we speak of the education of the Indian, we mean that comprehensive system of training and instruction which will convert them into American citizens. . . . Education is the medium through which the rising generation of Indians are to be brought into fraternal and harmonious relationships with their white fellow-citizens, and with them enjoy the sweets of refined homes, the delight of social intercourse, the emoluments of commerce and trade, the advantages of travel, together with the pleasures that come from literature, science, and philosophy, and the solace and stimulus afforded by a true religion.[47]

The prototype for and most famous of the off-reservation industrial boarding schools was the school in Carlisle, Pennsylvania. The Carlisle School was established in 1879 by a former Indian fighter, Capt. Richard Henry Pratt, in vacant army barracks.[48] Pratt was a committed assimilationist. He believed that, as individuals, Indians were plainly educable; their disability was their culture, which was, in a word, "savage."[49] The aim of a civilizing education, then, was to kill the savage person. "We accept the watch-word. There *is* no good Indian but a dead Indian. Let us by education and patient effort *kill* the *Indian* in him, and save the *man!*"[50] Removal—this time removal *from* the reservation—was essential to education.[51]

The Carlisle School's program combined systematic acculturation with formal learning. Every aspect of the program aimed at killing the Indian. Acculturation commenced as soon as students arrived on campus. The school cut their hair, gave them "civilized" clothing, and renamed them. The most immediate purpose for renaming was that it enabled (white) teachers to become more familiar with students more quickly, which promoted both pedagogy and discipline. But it served, too, as a general device for the transmission of culture. And it was also the case that, if students were to become owners of property someday, they would have to have proper surnames that could be efficiently registered in the records of probate courts. Exposing students to western food played a (universally despised) role in acculturation. But perhaps the most thoroughgoing effort at acculturation was the militarist, Spartan regimentation imposed throughout the day—from waking, to taking meals, to studying, to working, to sitting in the classroom, to sleeping, to participating in regular marching drills. In more than one respect, this way of life was both illiberal and undemocratic. The justification for the militarization of citizenship boiled down to the centrality, not of deliberation or choice, but of obedience: Military regimentation cultivated the ability to follow orders; following orders was a necessary condition for personal discipline; discipline was a fundamental prerequisite to life under law. To this extent, the rule of law was antagonistic to individualism and democracy.[52] The curriculum reinforced militarism, but also other values. Much of the curriculum, of course, covered the standard academic and vocational subjects whose aim was "self-reliance." But a significant part of the training was in citizenship, inculcating a patriotic respect for the American nation and its values, and suppressing the history of conflict between whites and Indians.[53]

No matter how rigorous the discipline or refined the instruction, the school was in its way still separated from white society. Thus, if Pratt criticized reservations for their inherent segregation, his school was susceptible to a similar criticism. Pratt recognized this tension. The best system, he believed, would be to take every Indian child on the continent and place him/her permanently with a white family, who would send the child to public school, teach by example the requisites and regularities of a civilized life, and prepare the child for a lifetime of productive labor. This would be consistent with the child's best interest as a human being, not an Indian.[54]

In most cases, Pratt acknowledged, permanent placement wasn't possible. But there was a "second-best" alternative that borrowed from the eighteenth-century fantasy of transforming Indian children by apprenticing them with "English and Godly families" in New England. Pratt adopted a version of this vision. He called it "outing." Although outing was voluntary, it was thoroughly integrated into the rhetoric and operation of the program. The school extolled and encouraged it (for the right students). Holding to Jeffersonian notions of the republican virtue of agrarian life, Pratt preferred to place his students on farms with white Christian middle-class English-speaking families. There, students would have an opportunity to participate in the daily lives of host families, attend local schools, work on farms (for a wage), and go to church—all the while immersed in English. The typical outing was for the summer months only; but Pratt favored, where possible, placing his students for one or two years. On occasion, the school would place students in cities, to learn nonagrarian trades. But Pratt disliked these placements. "We prefer good country homes or homes in the suburbs. . . . Almost every time we have placed students in a city they have dropped into the servant class and became the victims of some degeneracy, unless they happened to be our especially advanced and capable students."[55]

The Carlisle School was a model for similar schools across the country. By 1902, there were twenty-five off-reservation schools[56] and even more boarding schools located on reservations. As early as 1887, 76 percent of Indian children who attended school were in boarding schools; and 94 percent of federal appropriations for Indian education went to such schools.[57]

The boarding schools operated with varying degrees of success. At many, even the most basic of buildings, sanitation, and food were inadequate. The level of instruction at some was quite low. And more than a few schools were poorly managed and maintained.[58] At some schools in the West, the outing program was essentially a device for farming out cheap, pliable labor to locals.[59] These operational deficiencies aside, it was also the case that boarding schools ultimately failed to achieve the results their most ardent proponents had predicted.[60] Pratt had urged, "To civilize the Indian, get him into civilization. To keep him civilized, let him stay."[61] As it happened, most students did not stay. For a variety of reasons, they went home after their time at school had ended. (In the parlance of the day, they "returned to the blanket.") On going home, many graduates, again for a variety of reasons, did not practice the bourgeois lives for which their education had ostensibly prepared them.[62] This fact was a source of bitter disappointment for Pratt and others who had proclaimed boarding schools to be effective vehicles for assimilation. In part because of these failures, the United States would eventually rescind the program of allotment, retreat from using boarding schools, move to community day schools, and renounce assimilation as a goal.[63] By then, however, the United States had decimated tribal ways of life.

EDUCATION, PERSONHOOD, AND AMERICAN FAMILIES

By the late nineteenth century, the various policies for educating children of the tribes tended to share at least five characteristics: maintaining the constitutional order, employing coercive methods, creating civic persons, suppressing certain ways of life, and assimilation. First, the educational program for the tribes was a device for maintaining the constitutional order. One way of maintaining was to control the native populations. From the perspective of the regime, physical control was the first priority. But after achieving that goal, the regime used education to provide an added layer of control, for education not only reinforced pacification but also began a process that made dramatic uses of physical constraint unnecessary and that aimed to strengthen and extend the power and reach of the regime.

Second, in order to be effective, the policies had to reach their targets. To that end, the policies were coercive in several ways. For one thing, the nation required that Indian children receive an education provided by the nation-state. For another, the methods of instruction were coercive—to some extent, perhaps, unavoidably so. And for another, just as English law had permitted children of paupers to be taken from their families and placed in others for the purpose of extracting productive labor, American policy facilitated coercively taking Indian children from their tribes and families in order to place them in boarding schools for the purpose of making of them productive persons.

Third, the policies were designed to create a new, civic personality. Thus, teaching was not confined to skills of expression (reading and writing) or analysis (arithmetic). It also concerned the transmission of values and culture. These values were "civilizing," within a particular meaning of the word. That is, they aimed to cultivate the basic elements (or virtues) of a civilized life, from the perspective of the regime. For British North Americans and eventually for the early United States, those elements were religious, linguistic, and economic in character. After the constitutional founding, the economic element eventually became forthrightly liberal in ways it was not (could not have been) in colonial times. And over time, explicit commitment to religion gave way to ostensibly secular values. By the end of the nineteenth century, the United States would adopt another civilizing element that was overtly political in character, related specifically to citizenship. This is not to suggest that the nation was then prepared to welcome Indians as full citizens. But it was prepared to prepare them for the possibility of citizenship. This new civic element coincided with several disparate elements of American history related to the clarification and intensification of nationalism: a tendency toward increasingly democratic norms, the suppression of the southern secessions, the conquest and containment of the tribes, and the rise of secularization in common schools. With respect to the last trend, overtly religious expressions of value gave way to a language of civic values, which encompassed two competing sets of commitments: democracy and liberalism. Perhaps ironically, adding citizenship as an element of civilization enhanced and expanded the state's control over persons.

A fourth aspect of the program of Indian education was a suspicion of nonconforming associations. In this context, "non-conforming associations" connotes familial, religious, or tribal groups whose values and practices—ways of life— were perceived to contradict in some substantial way the prevailing commitments of the regime. In the beginning, these commitments were monarchic, colonial, mercantile, and Christian. By the nineteenth century, they became liberal-democratic, imperial, capitalist, and formally secular. Despite their differences, however, each regime attempted to suppress nonconforming associations. The American policy—expressed in institutions of education, in the dismantling of tribal lands, and in the redistribution of that land to bourgeois families—sought to limit the influence of incompatible tribal and familial ways of life and ultimately to eliminate or transform them.

Fifth, civic education's function was assimilative. That is, it aimed to render children productive members of society, or at least to prevent their being threats to or drags upon it. Assimilation had not always been the point of policies for educating the tribes. In the early years, there was doubt about Indians' ability to become, for example, proper Englishmen or Americans. Thus, the Europeans and early Americans focused primarily on moral instruction and economic integration, skills designed to promote accommodation, not outright integration. Later, however, the American policy became aggressively assimilationist. The rise of nationalism and the importance of citizenship were part of this shift. In important respects, the larger American project for the formation of citizens through education, independent from families, began with the education of Indians.

In the United States' policies toward the tribes, too, lay the seeds of yet another significant development related to recognition of the nuclear model of family. In his sweeping anthropological-historical study of family, published in 1891, Friedrich Engels claimed that the rise and victory of the monogamous family in human societies marked the victory of private property over communal property and the victory of man over woman.[64] In a world-historical context, Engels may have been onto something. But in the American context his claims were an overstatement, as the legal inheritance from English law had already entrenched both private property and male domination long before the tribes were overrun. Still, American policies toward the tribes did place the constitutional order on a potentially fateful path, in which the model of the bourgeois monogamous nuclear family became by the end of the nineteenth century not merely an objective of local regulation, but also a national commitment. The national commitment would harden, however, over Christian families of European descent who themselves experimented with uncommon familial forms.

7
Uncommon Families, Part 1
American Communism

From an improbable but fertile mix of plentiful cheap land, immigration, religious and associational freedoms, opportunities for communal self-sufficiency, and millenarian Protestantism, uncommon experiments with familial forms sprouted in America. The experiments began to appear even before the constitutional founding of the nation, but they proliferated during periods of social complexification and religious ferment in the nineteenth century. In this chapter and the next, I'll be concerned with two general types of experimental reformation of the family: communal families and polygamous families. They are "uncommon," not in the sense that they were rare, but in the sense that they departed from the legal template that the common law (broadly conceived) presumed to impose. In fact it's interesting that these experiments were as frequent as they were. It's also notable that the seedbed for experimentation was New England, that the expanding western frontier became a place for transplantation, and that southern soil tended to be inhospitable to these experiments. And it's worth examining the ways in which legal and political institutions tended to deal with each form and why they dealt distinctly with each. From an institutional standpoint, the larger process involved the gradual nationalization and constitutionalization of the morality of family. In this chapter, I'll focus on communal families.

Perhaps surprisingly, communism is as American as apple pie. At least it was at one time. Communal forms of social organization were present from the beginning of the English arrival in North America. As we saw in Chapter 6, many of the native tribes had long been essentially communist. But some of the early English settlements, too, possessed communal elements, usually animated by commitment to a religious idea and identity. The Plymouth Colony is merely one example. Still, these settlements were chartered by the Crown as trade-related (and hopefully profit-making) enterprises, and they tended to be punctuated with rights to property, the legal foundation for which was transmitted through common law.

Both characteristics made these associations less than thoroughly communal in character. In any event, in this chapter I'm interested in neither the tribes nor the primal chartered English settlements. I'm interested instead in associations of English or European (and later, American) settlers who self-consciously organized themselves into communities that repudiated or limited certain forms of private ownership and in which boundaries circumscribing nuclear families were either permeable or nonexistent. There were many such associations through the end of the nineteenth century. Two of the most famous were Robert Owen's atheist community of free love in New Harmony, Indiana, and Brook Farm in West Roxbury, Massachusetts. The latter attracted such New England notables as Nathaniel Hawthorne, Bronson Alcott, and Ralph Waldo Emerson. I won't be able to discuss all the communal experiments here. Instead, I'll consider briefly three that formed before the American Revolution and take up in greater detail two other significant associations that appeared in the first century of the New Republic. The strand that ties together all five is that they were religiously motivated.

COMMUNAL FAMILIES PRIOR TO NATIONHOOD

The earliest communal associations in the part of North America that would become the United States could only loosely be characterized as familial. But they shared with one another certain basic elements. They were ascetic, pietist, millenarian, and Protestant. Bohemia Manor was the first. It was established on the northern reaches of the Chesapeake Bay by followers of Jean de Labadie, a lapsed Jesuit who had converted to (and then defected from) Calvinism, moving from France to Holland to Germany in search of toleration. The band that found its way to North America in 1683 adopted an intentionally Spartan way of life, hoping for perfection, which the group pursued by abjuring worldly values, just as the earliest Christians had retreated from the values of imperial Rome. In this way, the believers were preparing for Christ's second coming and for their own spiritual rebirth in the kingdom of heaven. Although the commune permitted marriage, it celebrated as "Perfect" those who were celibate, following the doctrinal lead of the Apostle Paul. The community began to dissolve for at least two reasons. One was that Peter Sluyter, who became the group's spiritual leader, was a tyrant, inflicting harsh discipline on members. The other was that Sluyter permitted private ownership of property alongside the communal settlement. Private property resided uneasily with the settlement's animating ideology, especially as Sluyter himself, with the help of slaves, grew tobacco for profit on private tracts. In the mid-1720s, the commune died, even as tobacco survived.[1]

In the Christian Bible's Book of Revelation is the record of a vision of "a woman clothed with the sun, and the moon under her feet, and upon her head a crown of twelve stars." According to the vision, she gave birth to a male child, "who was to rule all nations with a rod of iron." As protection against "a great red dragon, having seven heads and ten horns, and seven crowns upon his heads, . . . the woman fled into the wilderness, where she hath a place prepared of God," waiting for the descent of her son from heaven, the second coming of Christ.[2] From this vision came the name for a commune of forty German Baptists, fleeing persecution in northern Europe. The forty called themselves the Brotherhood of the Contented of the God-loving Soul. Their site became known as The Woman in the Wilderness, which they established in 1694 on Wissahickon Creek, near Germantown just west of the Quaker village of Philadelphia.

The Brothers were waiting, like the woman in the vision, for the return of Christ to the world. To that end, they committed to a life of piety, celibacy, collective self-sufficiency, and watchful waiting. Each night, the Brothers searched the heavens from the watchtower above the roof of their dwelling for signs of the return of the Son of God. Their leader Johann Kelpius was a mystic Rosicrucian. He had at first calculated that the millennium would arrive by the end of 1694. Each subsequent year after the expected millennium failed to arrive, the Brothers ever watchful, Kelpius would extend the prophesy. As they waited, the Brethren were curious about their neighbors. Corliss Fitz Randolph noted, for example, that "they made a persistent effort to find out whether the Indians were descendants of the ten lost tribes of Israel." Curiosity extended also to sex, as one of the Brothers broke his vow of celibacy and married. This was socially disruptive, especially after other Brothers followed his lead into marriage and made their way into the secular world. Kelpius died in 1708, his prophesies unfulfilled.[3]

Word of Kelpius's demise did not reach Germany. So when Johann Conrad Beissel arrived in Philadelphia from Germany in 1720 with a company of pietists intending to join the Brethren on the Wissahickon, he was surprised to find the commune there essentially dissolved. After a year in Germantown, he trekked west, eventually joined by three companions. They settled on a tributary of the Conestoga River in what is now Lancaster County, where Beissel took up preaching. He also set up a religious school for the children of Mennonites who had settled in the area years earlier, having fled Germany branded as heretics by Catholics and Lutherans alike. (The Catholic Church had charged the Mennonites' European ancestors, the Anabaptists, with several grievous sins. One was rebaptizing adults who had already been baptized as infants. Another, so the rumor went, was holding wives in common.) Beissel soon decided that the traditional Christian celebration of Sunday as the weekly day of rest and contemplation was unbiblical. Relying on scripture, he concluded that the proper Sabbath was Saturday, the biblical "seventh day." At first, his companions kept the Sabbath with him, but, for whatever reasons, each of them soon abandoned him. In the face of this loss, he pushed farther into the forest, alone. He would eventually find spiritual regeneration in the company of others—German Baptists—who preached the doctrine of adult baptism. In 1725, he was dunked in the frigid water of the Pequea River, baptized into the first congregation of German Baptists in America.[4]

Beissel returned to Conestoga where he continued to lead services for his flock at the homes of different members. The core group of pietist men began to call themselves "the Solitary." Aside from simple survival, the early challenges were essentially twofold. The first involved sex and gender. In 1726, two sisters, Anna and Maria Eicher, arrived, having left their parents' home to join and live among Beissel's congregation. The presence of young, unattached women posed potential trouble. For one thing, their living among solitary men provoked gossip among surrounding neighbors, who doubtless harbored images of sexual scandal. For another, it was something of a social (and spiritual) challenge to the self-denying men in the congregation. How to handle these two women, spouseless as they were? Beissel's answer was to admit them, though he had a separate cabin built for the two. Perhaps provoked by the women's presence, Beissel wrote his *Book on Matrimony*, a religious justification for celibacy that Benjamin Franklin's press published in 1730. When the Eicher sisters later became the objects of still more gossip, Beissel angrily wrote another book on marriage. Whatever their motives, even more women, almost all of them with husbands, made their way to Conestoga to join the flock.[5]

The second challenge was doctrinal and surprisingly more explosive than rumors of sex. It involved the Sabbath. Even before the *Book on Matrimony*, Beissel had published his *Book on the Sabbath*, in which he presented the Sabbatarian position. Observing different days of rest, of course, physically separated his congregation from those of other German Baptists. In time, many Baptists in the region came to consider Beissel's Sabbatarian observance to be doctrinal error, and a suspiciously Judaic error at that. Even more, they (and some Quakers, too) urged that the celebration of a different Sabbath was a positive threat to public order. In this way, they rehearsed an emerging theme in American history: those who had fled persecution in Europe became themselves intolerant in America. Two Sabbatarians were arrested, fined, and imprisoned for performing manual labor on Sunday. In the wake of these events, combined with internal dissent among his own Sabbatarian congregation, Beissel dramatically resigned in the winter of 1732 and retreated to a secluded spot still farther into the forest. He paused on Cocalico Creek, at a cabin inhabited by Emanuel Eckerlin, the son of a member of his old congregation. Beissel stayed. In the spring he built his own cabin, where he apparently intended to remain in devotional solitude.[6]

His solitude didn't last long. Beginning in the fall of 1732, a trio of men, including a brother of Emanuel Eckerlin, showed up and built a third cabin. The Eicher sisters followed. Some of the men objected, but they eventually built a cabin for the sisters on the opposite side of Cocalico Creek. In the next two years, still others arrived. Two more Eckerlin brothers were among the new arrivals. So was Maria Heidt. Young, beautiful, and betrothed, Maria left her family and fiancé to take up residence with the Eicher sisters at Cocalico. Scores of German Baptists arrived from Germantown when the patriarch of one of the congregations there died. And Peter Miller, the well-educated pastor of a Reformed Lutheran congregation, departed from his church (along with a few of his congregants) to join Beissel's Camp of the Solitary. With more people, the camp became less solitary and more social. In 1735, the group built a large three-story building — named *Kedar* — at the center of the settlement. It contained a large general meeting hall, several sizable rooms for "love feasts," and a number of small cells where some of the Solitary men resided and prayed. The next year, the group raised an even larger structure — *Bethaus* (House of Prayer) — adjacent to *Kedar*. With a people, a shared purpose, a discrete geographic place, and common architectural spaces, the foundation was laid for communal life. Recognizing their transformation (and demonstrating that the line between individualism and community in early America was finer than one might imagine), the settlers renamed their place: the Camp of the Solitary became the Community at Ephrata.[7]

The constitutive elements of communal life were threefold. The first involved a way of life devoted to worship and self-denial. Over time, the ethic of asceticism was increasingly attached to a strong strain of mysticism, at least for Beissel and a few others among the Solitary. Mysticism aside, music, prayer, common meals, midnight services, and individual confessions were components of everyone's life. Evangelism and education, too, played active roles in the Community's mission. Over time, the Community offered a writing school, a music school, a general elementary school, a classical (Latin) school, and a Sabbath school (mainly for indigent children in the area). The second element involved the common ownership of property that was central to the life of the Community. This element did not preclude members' privately owning property. In fact, some members, not among the Solitary, owned their own plots. Unlike in Bohemia Manor, this dual system of ownership seems not to have created significant tensions among the early faithful. The third, predictably, involved relations between the sexes. The animating ideal was celibacy. As I've already indicated, the celibate ideal did not entail the exclusion of women, for they were present in the settlement even before the emergence of community. Their presence, however, did make sexual segregation an institutionally attractive way of suppressing *eros*. So celibate men and women maintained sexually distinct associations — men with the Brotherhood of Zion and women with the Spiritual Order of the Roses of Saron (alternately, the Order of Spiritual Virgins) — each with its own distinct architectural spaces. If celibacy didn't exclude women, some of the faithful believed that it went hand-in-hand with the repudiation of marriage. One prominent "house-father" offered biblical proof "that the marriage state originated in the fall of man." For the group as a whole, however, the aspiration to celibacy did not preclude the presence of marital families. Although marriage was discouraged, married couples were permitted to join the congregation. But even married members were sexually separated for most collective activities, including worship and common meals, just as the celibates were. Thus, the group's "love feast" was not the kind of carnal event that the term might suggest to the modern mind, but a celebration of *agape*, a divinely inspired self-sacrificial love, spiritually superior even to philial affection.[8]

Communism per se in Ephrata was never a cause for suspicion among civil authorities or surrounding populations (as long as sex was not suspected). In fact, the members tended to be respected outside Cocalico as intelligent and honorable, even if they dressed and behaved strangely. But the Community did run into conflict with civil authorities on at least two occasions. The first involved an attempt by the local constable to collect a "single men's tax" from the Solitary Brethren. We've seen the dominant motive for such a tax in Chapter 2, in Queen Elizabeth's attempt to identify and control "masterlesse men." When the Brothers refused to pay, the constable had six of them arrested, transported to Lancaster, and jailed. Before a local magistrate, they pledged allegiance to the King but refused to pay the tax, both because a "head tax" violated their belief that there was no worldly authority over their bodies and because they objected to being placed in the same class as rogues and vagabonds. If the judge would consider the Brothers to be "a spiritual family," they urged, "they would be willing to pay of their earthly possessions what was just." Hearing this plea, the judge accepted a bargain and imposed a reduced fine on the Community as a whole, making Ephrata the first officially recognized communal same-sex family in North America.[9]

The second conflict involved the practice of voluntary divorce. From the early years of the commune's history, some married couples had agreed to separate, the better to pursue spiritual celibate lives. In the early 1740s, the Eckerlin brothers, who had become a dominating presence in the community, devised a plan to encourage and formalize spiritual divorce. To that end, they constructed a building—*Hebron*—that was divided into two sections, one for (former) husbands, who would commit to the Brotherhood of Zion, and one for the wives, who entered the Roses of Saron. In 1744, the Eckerlins presided over the building's dedication, the climax of which was a formal exchange of "letters of divorce." This ceremony provoked a civil investigation into these extra-legal divorces. Beissel had initially agreed to the Eckerlins' plan. When he learned about the investigation, however, he recanted and ordered the couples to return to their previously married lives. Even on the fringe of European settlement, the civil authority was jealous of its control of marriage and divorce.[10]

There's reason to believe that the motive for the experiment at *Hebron* was only partly about spiritual purity. The Eckerlins' plan had been that each couple, on entering a newly celibate life, would convey its property to the Brotherhood, which the Eckerlins controlled in a discrete, closely held profit-making entity within the community. As it happened, many couples refused to divest themselves of landed property, which was one more reason the experiment failed. But the Eckerlins' interest in material matters extended beyond the venture at *Hebron*. From the beginning, they were an industrious, energetic, enterprising, and ambitious family. Largely at their initiation, the community developed a diverse portfolio of industrial ventures. They began with a bakery, then developed a grist mill, a saw mill, a paper mill, an oil-making mill, a weaving loom, a fulling mill, a tannery, a bark mill, a shoe-making operation, a pottery, quarries, a printing press, and a bookbindery. The bakery distributed bread in the community and beyond for free — to each according to his needs. But the Eckerlins planned and eventually utilized their other enterprises for profit. They established agents in Philadelphia and other places to facilitate the sale and purchase of supplies and products. By all accounts, they were wildly successful, bringing an impressive level of material prosperity.[11]

Material economy often swamps moral commitment, and so it did at Ephrata for a time. The Eckerlins' enterprise became so potent that they gradually gained governing control of the community. For a few years, they displaced Beissel and even had him confined to a marginal cabin in the settlement. This offended Beissel for reasons personal, proprietary, and spiritual. The personal and proprietary concerns were easy enough to understand. The spiritual concern, too, was fairly straightforward. Beissel worried that, under the Eckerlins, the community had lost its way, as concern for Mammon overwhelmed devotion to God. Despite his marginal status and location, Beissel remained at least nominally the community's spiritual leader, which meant he was not without leverage among at least a portion of the community. Spying an opportunity in the fall of 1745, Beissel used one Eckerlin against the others, and then had them all demoted and eventually ousted from the community. To avert temporal temptation, he then summarily closed most of the mills (though the printing press continued), canceled all future contracts, and disbanded the Brotherhood of Zion under whose auspices the enterprise had operated.[12]

With the end of the businesses, austerity returned, and Beissel's leadership became intensely autocratic. Still, the community prospered into the 1750s, then declined, as Beissel himself deteriorated from tuberculosis and longevity. He died in 1768. His successor was Peter Miller, an intelligent, talented, and well-connected leader. (He was an elected member of the American Society of Science in Philadelphia.) Despite his talents, and despite the establishment of other settlements modeled after Ephrata, the community steadily declined through the 1790s, when it perished after Miller died.[13]

THE SHAKERS

As the commune in Ephrata was on the verge of dissolution, a new communal group was forming in the wilderness of upstate New York. Notably, it was led by a woman, Ann Lee. (Her surname at birth was Lees, but she later shortened it.) She had emigrated from Manchester, England, where in 1758 she attached to a millennialist Protestant sect that had originated in France as a radical offshoot of Calvinism. A small contingent from the sect had fled to England in the seventeenth century in the wake of French religious persecution. Under the leadership of a pair of Quakers in Britain, the group gradually took on elements of Quakerism and Methodism. Among the group's distinguishing practices were ecstatic rites in which participants displayed "violent trembling and agitation of body and limbs." They earned the derisive moniker "Shaking Quakers," later shortened to Shakers.[14]

In England, Lee latched on to the group's rapturous worship, its reliance on visions and revelation, and its practiced devotion to ascetic purification and self-denial. Her attachment as a young uneducated working-class woman may well have been one of desperation, for she and her parents lived in relative poverty, and there's little doubt that the sect provided respite from her soulless labor in a cotton mill, not to mention her conflictual relationship with her family. She soon became a central figure in the group. Although the Shakers' doctrines encouraged celibacy, Ann married Abraham Stanley (also reported as "Standley"), a local blacksmith, in 1761. The marriage may have been motivated partly by acute material need, partly to escape her parents' household, partly for other hidden reasons. Whatever her reasons, the marriage proved to be unhappy, not least because she gave birth to four children, none of whom survived infancy.[15]

Her unhappiness as a wife and her grief as a mother were searing. It's likely that they played a role in her eventual public rejection of "lustful gratifications of the flesh." Distancing herself from her marriage both psychically and physically, she came into her own as a charismatic figure in the little sect. In meetings and on the street she railed against carnal pleasure, social inequality, economic privation, and established religion. Because Shakers' meetings were so boisterous and Lee so aggressively militant, the group incited complaints, which led to legal intervention. In the early 1770s, constables repeatedly broke up meetings on the ground that they were a breach of the Sabbath. On two occasions, Lee was imprisoned. Her message steadily sharpened: "to be born again into the kingdom of Christ, one must repent and forsake all that [is] carnal." And she could show the way. Many people may have been put off by Lee's claim that she was the incarnation of a new sacred dispensation. Others doubtless stumbled over the sexless imperative. Whatever the reason, her message never gained traction in England. In 1774, she sailed with eight others (including her husband) for North America.[16]

On landing in the city of New York, the first order of business was to survive. The trekkers did so, not by banding together but by dispersing and finding labor to support themselves, mainly in upper New York, in and around Albany. Abraham Stanley did what many husbands did in North America: he left his wife and went into the world on his own. There is no evidence that Lee was rocked by her abandonment. Instead she remained in the city of New York, residing in the home of a local family, and making a living doing laundry.[17]

The timing of the Shakers' arrival was propitious. For one thing, it occurred during the run-up to the American secession from Britain. For another, and more important from the standpoint of the Shakers' success, was the fact that they arrived in the midst of one of the periodic religious Awakenings that swept New England. Among those whose spiritual hearts were awakened were "New Light" revivalists, drawn mainly from among Free Will Baptists in the area around

Niskeyuna, New York, where the Shakers had eventually settled. The revivalists were interested in salvation and were watching for signs of the second coming. Some of them found their way to meetings led by "Mother Ann," as she came to be called. The emotive forms of worship that were on display were curious even for Baptists. Another curiosity was the messenger: a woman, a self-described millennial prophetess, whose very presence repudiated the Pauline appeal for women to be silent and submissive. Still another was the message: that the Shakers had already risen with Christ, but the cost of resurrection was to "forsake 'the marriage of the flesh.'" For some revivalists, the package was captivating and convincing. In 1780, Lee's group held its first public meeting. People came. Thus in America, unlike in England, Lee found converts.[18]

Still, many of their neighbors were less taken with the Shakers. Exuberant forms of worship and extremity of belief bred suspicion. In fact, at one point during the Revolutionary War several members, including Lee, were jailed by patriots who suspected (wrongly) that the Shakers were attempting to deliver sheep to British troops. On occasion, as in England, members of the group were physically assaulted. And, of course, they were denounced in both pamphlets and casual conversation as apostates. Among the accusations were that they engaged in witchcraft and danced naked. Another was that they threatened American civil authority, perhaps because they rejected war and refrained from politics. Some critics attacked celibacy, confession, and belief in miracles as being uncomfortably close to Catholicism. And William Plummer, who would later become Governor of New Hampshire, worried that the group was too communal: "Several persons who had valuable farms have sold them and given the money to support the common cause."[19]

Lee's approach softened with time. As she put it, "Once I served God through fear, but now I serve Him by love." At the same time, her ideas broadened beyond the intense preoccupation with carnality. She repudiated material excess of all sorts (covetousness, gluttony, drunkenness, waste, and abuse of wealth). She preached against the sin of deceit. She began to emphasize the danger of idleness and the value of industriousness. And she elevated charity, especially to the poor, as a constitutive element of Christian duty. Still, she had not yet articulated a vision of communism. Members had practiced communal sharing of property since their arrival in America, mainly as a means for survival. By the 1780s, the practice was beginning to gel as a doctrinal commitment. The number of faithful had grown steadily by this time, enhanced especially by the attachment of a group of devoted New Light Baptists, led by Joseph Meacham. And Shaker communities were emerging in other sites in New England, due largely to Lee's energetic proselytizing.[20]

Mother Ann died in 1784, not long after the death of her beloved brother. The passing of the woman believed to be the second coming of the Messiah was a blow to the communities. Some members left, disillusioned. Unlike the communes that had gone before, however, the Shakers not only survived but flourished after the death of their founder. Most members stayed on and reconstituted themselves into the United Society of Believers in Christ's Second Appearing. James Whittaker, who had traveled with Lee from England, assumed leadership of the group after her death. He moved administration from Niskeyuna to New Lebanon. And he emphatically preached Christian communism. "The time is come," he said, "for you to give up yourselves and your all to God—your subsistence, your temporal property—to possess as though you possessed not." He died in 1787. Joseph Meacham (now "Father Joseph") assumed dual leadership of the Society, along with Lucy Wright ("Mother Lucy"). Their accession was notable for at least three reasons. One was that they were the first American-born leaders of the United Society, making the Shakers the first communal group to make the transition from immigrant to "American." Second, they commenced a process of bringing disparate Shaker groups within the new, united organization. In this way, they were able to integrate existing Shaker communities and to organize new ones in various locales in New England and upstate New York. In fact, by the early nineteenth century there would be communities in Kentucky, Indiana, and Ohio, and by the end of that century even in Florida and Georgia. Finally, their joint leadership was a visible expression of a basic tenet of the Shakers: equality of men and women. Perhaps it's ironic that this tenet came not from modernist institutions of the New Republic, but from a group that rejected many aspects of modernity.[21]

Ironic or not, the Shakers' commitment to equality was both practical, in the sense that it was woven into their way of life, and theological. As interpreted by Benjamin Youngs, an early Shaker theologian, the Bible recognized that male and female were created from the same matter, and so they were equal in their "rational faculties and governing powers." But the extent of their equality in scripture was limited: "As the man was first formed, and afterwards the woman, to be a helper with the man; therefore she was dependent on him for her counsel and instruction, and was not *first,* but *second* in the headship of MAN, and second in the order and government of all the inferior creation."[22] Still, even Christ's appearance in the world could not fulfill the various promises of the Old Testament. In order for God to "*shake* the heavens and the earth," to achieve a "full and final manifestation of Christ," and to redeem a church that had succumbed to the Antichrist, a second appearance was required. And, in order for it to perfect the first, this appearance had to be in the form of a woman: Ann Lee.[23] The Shakers' beliefs and practices reflected this doctrine of sexual equality. The Shakers' conception of the Creator was not a Trinity but a duality, in some ways akin to the Hindu conception of creation described in Chapter 1. As a deacon of the United Society put it in the mid-nineteenth century, "And why the Trinity? [The Book of Genesis] says nothing about the Trinity[.] It states expressly that 'God created man in his own image; male and female created he them.' Is it not evident from this that there exists in the Deity the likeness of male and female; forming the unity of that creative principle from which proceeds the work of father and mother?" When challenged that the Shakers did not act on that principle, the Deacon responded,

"Yes, we do—we associate woman in everything: in our government, in our religion, in our social affairs, she stands beside us—not as our *property,* but as our *equal* and helpmate."[24]

Sexual equality was only one of five related tenets of the United Society. The others were separation from the world, community, voluntarism, and the abolition of individual property. Meacham spoke of separation from the world as "taking up the cross of Christ." This involved two elements. The first was behavioral, the denial of "all ungodliness and worldly lusts." The faithful should repudiate "the world, flesh, and devil," confess all sins, and repent, turning away from the world and toward a godly life. Plainly, one aspect of this imprecation drew on Lee's denial of sexual activity.[25] The second aspect, and following from the first, was relational. A tract first published in 1830 clarified this element. Having turned from ungodly ways, believers should "withdraw from the communion and fellowship of the world." This required disowning not only status and material goods but also family. "No worldly honor, no earthly interest, no natural affection, is taken for an excuse." The tract pushed home the point, quoting from Jesus in the book of Matthew: "If any man come to me and hate not his father and mother, his wife and children, and brethren and sisters, yea, and his own life also, he cannot be my disciple.... He that loveth father or mother more than me is not worthy of me; and he that loveth son or daughter more than me, is not worthy of me; and he that taketh not his cross and followeth after me, is not worthy of me."[26]

As the excerpt from Matthew suggested, the aim of separation was not merely "the end of sin," but also "establish[ing Christ's] kingdom on earth."[27] Individuals in isolation from one another, however, could not achieve that kingdom. They must come together in community, organized as a new spiritual family whose practical aim was "to assign to each individual the lot and place which he is best qualified to fill, and in which he can improve his talents to the best advantage." This, in Christian incarnation, was a variation of the marriageless family for the guardian class depicted in Plato's *Republic.* The Shakers understood that their practice of "disorganizing [nuclear] families, and dissolving the ties of nature" was controversial, but insisted that it was necessary for attaining "the gospel relation" required of the kingdom.[28] The institution of marriage itself came in for special attention. Shakers refrained from marriage for several reasons. It tended to incite debased motives of jealousy and partiality and to undermine higher sentiments of unity and universal benevolence.[29] It tied the marital couple together in a fleshly way. And it was inconsistent with the example of Christ, who abjured marriage for himself and his followers. "Christ condemned [marriage in the flesh], both by precept and example; ... saying, that in the kingdom of Heaven they neither marry nor are given in marriage."[30] Monogamous marriage, then, was "a civil right and a civil institution, properly belonging to the citizens of the world, and therefore the privilege of every man who chooses to use it." But it was not an institution with a connection to Christianity, properly understood.[31] Better, in the Shakers' view, to practice a form of family that more readily produced a "community of interest," a "united interest in all things," and inhibited the baser sentiments that not only tied people to the world but also reinforced sin.[32]

Shaker families were comprised of 25 to 150 persons, men and women, who lived together. They were the basic self-sustaining social and economic units of the United Society. Each had autonomy from the other units with respect to its economic activities, thus permitting families to specialize as members' talents and local resources permitted, but all were organized and administered under the same model. Each was governed by a central ministry, consisting of two men and two women. The dwelling was divided into three courts, consistent with the Shakers' understanding of the ancient Jewish temple in Jerusalem. In the inner court was the order of persons possessing "the greatest faith and abilities" in sacred matters. In the second court were those whose spiritual abilities were not as mature. Typically, these members were young and able to carry out manual labor. In the third, outer court were the elderly, whom the family attentively cared for, as well as members who conducted business with the rest of the world. Prospective members resided in a distinct novitiate order, in which they were permitted to continue to live with their worldly families during their "partial relationship" with the Society.[33]

Membership in the United Society was purely voluntary. Any adult person of faith, commitment, industry, thrift, and good will—who was free from material debt or relational encumbrance—was welcome to join as a full and equal member after serving a period of novitiate.[34] And any existing members who wished no longer to remain in the Society was free to leave. For an organization that saw its root and purpose in the experience of the primitive church, these commitments to free will and to freedom of entry and exit were notably liberal. For Shakers, however, they were not incongruous, for they grew out of Shakers' understanding of the logic of the Reformation. Freedom of conscience and freedom from compelled belief were basic tenets of the Society. So, just as Shakers expected the world to respect their "free choice" to live together outside of marriage—"Do such people violate any principle of free government in so doing?" John Dunlavy asked—the Society itself respected the same options of choice and exit for its members.[35]

Those, at least, were the norms that pertained to adults. As John Locke had posited, children were different, for they lacked full capacity. The Covenant for the church at New Lebanon, therefore, prohibited receiving children as members and even barred their being placed under the direct authority of the church, unless all relevant parents or guardians of the child consented, "together with the Child's own desire."[36] Still, children came to communities from a variety of routes. Frequently, their parents simply brought and left them there. As we'll see below, this was not strictly speaking an informal prototype of adoption, but an indenture, akin to the old English model. Marianne Finch reported that, during her sojourn with the community in New Lebanon, a widow left her "two little girls," to be brought up as members of the Society. Men, too, would take their children (and sometimes their wives) to the Shakers. Any child who wanted to leave the Society was free to do so on reaching the age of majority. Many did leave, but a number of them stayed. Finch noted one case in which a father, who had left his two young sons, returned for them when they were nearly grown. When they refused to go with him, he sued, but the court gave the sons liberty to decide for themselves. They elected to stay with the Shakers, after which the father abducted the elder son by force.[37]

The fifth element of Shakers' ideology involved production and property. Production was simple: everyone worked who could do so. Property was more complicated. The Shakers' commitment to withdrawing from the world required that each member give up his or her property to the United Society. Children, of course, typically came without property. Adults brought their property, but not their debts, with them. Finch noted that the Shakers "will not allow any one to join them as a member till his debts are paid, and his affairs with the world settled."[38] Property was held in common. In the terminology of the Society, each member held a "Joint Interest" in the Society's property, not as a legal joint tenancy or tenancy in common, but as a "consecrated whole." If the form and terminology of joint interest sounded slightly capitalist, in the sense that each person held a share in an entity that resembled a corporation, the operative ethical basis was communist: from each according to his possessions and abilities, to each according to his needs. The Covenant for the Church in New Lebanon put it this way: "All [members] should have Just and Equal rights and Priviledges, according to their needs, in the use of all things in the Church, without Any difference being made on account of what any of us brought in, so long as we remained in Obedience to the order and Government of the Church." The Society generously devoted resources to charity, "for the relief of the poor" in surrounding communities, and it unflinchingly supported those among the flock who could no longer contribute productive labor. These practices didn't mirror precisely the radical command of the Gospel: "If thou wilt be perfect, go and sell that thou hast, and give to the poor, . . . and come and follow me." (Matthew 19:21 [KJV]) But the Shakers did generously support the poor, the old, and the disabled, both within and outside the Society.[39]

According to the Society's governing norms, when a member transferred property on entering the Society, the property belonged irrevocably to the Society as part of the "consecrated whole." In practice, if a member left the Shakers, the Society would hand over an equivalent sum to the departing member, after s/he executed a "discharge," which served as a legal release from additional claims by the member against the Society. Occasionally, departing members would sue the Society for the return of the specific property they had donated, but courts tended to uphold the legal sufficiency of the donation and discharge.[40]

More delicate than the legal status of communal property under the Covenant was the matter of children. Complications over children's status arose in at least two contexts. One involved the practice of non-Shaker parents who deposited their children with the Society. Parents' motives varied. Some necessitous parents were simply unable to care adequately for their children, and the Shakers provided an attractive, caring community. Others were motivated less nobly by a desire to be rid of children whom they perceived to be burdens or nuisances. In either case, the Shakers would accept these children only under a legally binding indenture. (Early American law retained the English practice permitting children's indenture.) Under the Shakers' standard formal agreement of indenture, parents agreed not to interfere with their children during the term of the contract. Parents agreed also to take back, without charge to or prejudice against the Shakers, any child who "obstinately refuse[d] to perform and conform in and to" the duties the Society's trustee might impose. For its part, the Society agreed to provide each child food, clothing, shelter, a general education in reading and writing, and instruction in a skill or trade "best adapted to his genius and capacity." The Shakers committed to acting for "the present good . . . [and] the future benefit and welfare" of the child. The indenture ended when the child reached the age of twenty-one, at which point s/he was free to remain in the Society or leave.[41]

The second complicating context involved "divided" nuclear families in which one parent attached to the Society but the other did not. The Society's Covenant prohibited receiving children except by the consent of both parents, and its rules barred one spouse from deserting the other in order to join the community.[42] Still, conflicts arose when both spouses joined the Society but one became disaffected. Under those circumstances, an aggrieved spouse could find resorting to the civil law attractive, especially when the grievance was intense. In the first half of the nineteenth century, complaining (usually "nonbelieving") spouses frequently prevailed. Often this result was because of institutional prejudice against the Shakers. In one case in New York, for example, Eunice Chapman petitioned the state's legislature for an order granting her custody of her three children, who were then living with their father in a Shaker community (where Eunice had also lived for a short time). In the process of awarding her custody, the legislature also granted her a divorce and enacted a law providing that, if a man joined the Shakers, custody of the children would automatically go to his dissenting wife. Around the same time, Kentucky enacted a statute that provided for an immediate divorce if one spouse joined the Shakers.[43] Technically, neither of these laws on their face would have covered the Chapmans, as both spouses had joined the Society, but the statutes demonstrated the suspicion in which the Shakers were held.

Not all aggrieved spouses were successful, however, even in the first half of the century. Mary Dyer had joined the Shakers' community in Enfield, New Hampshire, in 1813, with her husband, Joseph, and their five children. On her account, she was a hesitant "convert," having joined only because her husband became enamored of the Shakers (after the couple failed to find a Baptist preacher in their area) and because military maneuvers on the Canadian border during the War of 1812 threatened the safety of her family. But join she did. She was miserable from the start—less from the loss of conjugal relations with her husband than from forced separation from her children, who were placed with other households in the community. Despondent, ill, and aching over separation from her children, she made several fitful attempts to leave, drawn back each time because neither the Society nor Joseph would let her take any of the children with her. After two months she did leave, without children or husband.[44] She petitioned New Hampshire's legislature for custody but was unsuccessful, primarily because she and Joseph had signed the standard agreement of indenture ceding to the Society the care and control of their children. The legislature did later enact a statute providing a ground for divorce from a spouse who joined and stayed for at least three years with a sect that professed that "the relation between husband and wife [is] unlawful." On the basis of that statute, the Supreme Court of New Hampshire granted Mary a divorce from Joseph in 1830. The court noted that one reason for granting a divorce in such a circumstance was that, in refusing to cohabit with his wife, Joseph had failed in a duty that was "the great end of matrimony, the continuation of the species."[45] Mary spent the rest of her life writing and speaking against the Shakers—that they were devoid of "natural affection" and destroyed the family.[46]

She also said they abused children.[47] In this regard, she was doubtless projecting a mother's anguish over the loss of her children. To be sure, Shakers were strict with their children, especially by standards of the twenty-first century. It's also the case that their living conditions were in some respects severe. But the Shakers treated their children as well as the bulk of agricultural and working-class nuclear families did in the nineteenth century. For the Society, education was the key to raising children. The purposes of a proper education were threefold: "to instil into the mind the principles of virtue, to store it with useful instruction, to form practical habits of goodness, and to regulate and bring into operation every useful talent." To achieve these purposes, education proceeded in three stages. The first was to ingrain in children from the youngest age the "habits of self-government," of which obedience was primary. Next was to provide "moral and religious instruction" to the self-regulating child. Third was to furnish a scholastic education whose content was guided by moral and religious truth. Children possessing "traits of genius" were provided a literary education appropriate to their ability.[48]

To these ends the Shakers opened day schools for their own children and for children in surrounding communities whose parents consented. The curriculum was basic and practical—including instruction in reading, writing, and numbers.[49] It was also moral, in that it was designed to reinforce in students the elements of a Christian life:

> to [display] honesty, punctuality and uprightness, in all their conduct; to keep a conscience devoid of offence towards God and all men; to be neat, cleanly and industrious; to observe the rules of prudence, temperance and good economy in all their works; to subdue all feelings of selfishness and partiality; to let the law of kindness, love and charity govern all their feelings towards each other; to shun all contestation and strife . . . ; [and] to conduct themselves with civility, decency and good order before all people.[50]

The culmination of this education was to participate in a life of productive, nonsexual harmony and happiness.

Toward such a society, the judgment of modernity could be harsh. Charles Dickens visited a Shaker village in New York, as part of his tour of America in 1842. He dismissed the community as irredeemably "grim," describing one elderly Shaker's eyes as "hard, and dull, and cold as the great round metal buttons on his coat." Dickens mocked the Shakers' architecture ("like English barns, and . . . English factories"), their worship ("unspeakably absurd" and "infinitely grotesque"), and their ethos ("which would strip life of its healthful graces, rob youth of its innocent pleasures, pluck from maturity and age their pleasant ornaments, and make existence but a narrow path towards the grave"). He also ridiculed Shaker women's appearance. Commenting on "the Spartan model" of the Shakers' community, he noted that rumors persisted that the lives of men and women were not celibate as Shaker doctrine required. Indeed, Mary Dyer had hinted that sexual relations existed among the Shakers, quoting one to say that "the world's people think we are afraid of each other, but they do not know the liberties which we take. Mary, you must not be afraid of loving the brethren, we think it a privilege for the brethren to love the sisters, and the sisters to love the brethren." Dickens dismissed these reports out of hand, based mainly on Shaker women's appearance, calling them "hideously ugly." Recalling a brief stop at a Shaker store during his visit, he said "the stock was presided over by something alive in a russet case, which the elder [man] said was a woman; and which I suppose *was* a woman, though I should not have suspected it." Later he wrote, "If many of the sister Shakers resemble her, I treat all such [rumors of sexual activity] as bearing on [their] face the strongest marks of wild improbability."[51]

Putting aside his modernist critique, Dickens conceded that the Shakers were capable artisans, good farmers, good and humane breeders of cattle, and "honest and just in their transactions, even in horse-trading."[52] Other observers, including socialists like Friedrich Engels and Robert Owens, were even more charitable.[53] Engels cited the Shakers as an example of the social, moral, and economic vitality of a communist society in which marriage, statist law, and bourgeois property (but not religion, alas) had been abolished. He praised their dwelling, their farms, and their way of life.

> Amongst these people no one is obliged to work against his will, and no one seeks work in vain. . . . [A]ll their needs are met and they need fear no want. In their ten towns there is not a single gendarme or police officer, no judge, lawyer or soldier, no prison or penitentiary; and yet there is proper order in all their affairs. The laws of the land are not for them and as far as they are concerned could just as well be abolished and nobody would notice any difference for they are the most peaceable citizens and have never yielded a single criminal for the prisons.[54]

It's not so clear that Engels's claim that the Shakers could have dispensed with "the laws of the land" was accurate. For much of the Shakers' collective security depended on the law's protection of property, contract, association, and enterprise, not to mention its respect for them as a quasi-corporate entity. But he was correct that the Shakers were able to maintain an ordered and respectable society partially autonomous from law.

In an article on the virtues of capitalism and property, however, Associate Justice Henry Brown, of the Supreme Court of the United States, challenged this happy picture. He criticized the Shakers as "a simple-minded sect" that was "content with a plainness of living and severity of dress that would be intolerable in a community of high intelligence and aspirations." And he predicted that, without vigorous institutions of property and marriage, the group would soon die out, testament to the poverty of the idea of socialism.[55]

Regardless of the grand debate over the relative merits of capitalism and socialism, most Americans by the middle of the nineteenth century extended to the Shakers a sincere if sometimes grudging respect for the way of life they produced. If they were odd, they were productive, honest, and essentially harmless. If many young members left the community, many others remained. Of Mary Dyer's children, for example, only one left the community when he came of age, though he was never close to his mother, and he (along with his siblings) repudiated his mother's attacks on the Society.[56]

Judicial decisions, too, began to display a surprising level of tolerance toward the Shakers. Notwithstanding the New Hampshire Supreme Court's (correct) assessment that the Shakers' way of life was incompatible with New Hampshire's procreative and monogamous view of marriage, the Michigan Supreme Court held, in a case involving benefits under an insurance policy, that Shaker communities were families. The court noted that the word "family" in the relevant state statute was "an expression of great flexibility" that could be "applied in many ways. It may mean the husband and wife having no children and living alone together, or it may mean children or wife, . . . or blood relatives, or any group constituting a distinct domestic or social body. It is often used to denote a small select corps attached to an army chief, and has even been extended to whole sects, as in the case of the Shakers." The court held that a woman who had lived "under the same roof" as the insured, had been treated by him as a daughter, and was part of "the same social and domestic circle" was entitled to claim as a beneficiary under the insured's policy.[57]

At the very time the group was flourishing and coming to be tolerated, however, it was already in decline. As might have been expected in an asexual society, its numbers were dwindling through deaths and departures, despite the fact that the United Society was acquiring members through conversions. Into the twentieth century, in fact up to our own time, there remain communities that grew from Ann Lee's visions, but they are mere remnants of the more vital Shaker communities that thrived before the Civil War.[58]

Before the Shakers' decline, there were scores of other communal experiments in America. Some of these communities—including those inspired by Robert Owen and Charles Fourier—were predominately secular in orientation. Others, like

George Rapp's society in Harmony, Pennsylvania, and later New Harmony, Indiana, remained rooted in Central European Protestantism. It's beyond my purpose to cover all of these here. Instead, I want to close out the discussion of communal families with one that both embraced and rejected basic aspects of the Shakers' Society. Like the Shakers, the Oneida Community espoused a communal family that repudiated marriage and committed itself to sustained economic self-sufficiency. But Oneida publicly parted company with the Shakers on the matter of sex.

THE ONEIDA COMMUNITY

The seeds for the Oneida Community sprouted from the rocky crevices of New England in the 1830s. John Humphrey Noyes was born in Vermont in 1811 to a well-placed middle-class family. He grew to be a shy and insecure young man. By the time he graduated from Dartmouth College in 1830, he was dissatisfied and searching for a path in life. After attending a revival meeting the following year in Putney, Vermont, he was inspired to enroll in the Andover Theological Seminary, but soon transferred to the Yale Divinity School. There he stumbled onto the doctrine of perfectionism—the notion that human beings are not fatefully fallen from grace, but are capable of achieving perfection in this world. Within two years, he obtained his license to preach, joined the New Haven Anti-Slavery Society, and was appointed pastor at the Free Church in New Haven. In 1834, he announced to his congregation that he had achieved "full salvation from sin." After this announcement, he promptly lost his congregation and his license to preach. Emotionally shaken but relentlessly searching, he began to seek converts to his perfectionist views among communities in New York and New England.[59]

In the next three years, Noyes would collaborate on the publication of a periodical (*The Perfectionist*), leave that venture after a disagreement with his collaborator, begin a Bible institute in Putney, start publishing a second journal (*The Witness*) in Ithaca, and lose the affection of his beloved follower Abigail Merwin, who left him to marry another. All these activities were part of a spiritual and intellectual ferment in which he was beginning to formulate his ideas on marriage. Between the frenetic activity and the collapse of his relationship with Abigail, Noyes himself was near collapse. Friends and family worried that he was on the verge of insanity. His life grew even more challenging after a third journal (*Battle-Axe and Weapons of War*) published a private letter that Noyes had written to his friend David Harrison. The journal was published from Philadelphia. Its name was lifted from the biblical book of Jeremiah: "Thou art my battle-axe and weapons of war; for with thee I will break in pieces the nations; and with thee I will destroy kingdoms." (Jeremiah 51:20 [KJV]) Its editor was T. R. Gates, who was committed to a revolution in sexual relations.[60]

Noyes's letter fell into the editor's hands through an improbable chain of events, but once Gates held it, he found it irresistible. He published the letter, without permission, on page one of the second issue of *Battle-Axe*. The bulk of the letter contained a defense of perfectionism and of Noyes's claim to being the leader of the establishment of the kingdom of God on earth. But the closing paragraph included a glimpse into Noyes's early thinking about sex and marriage:

> When the will of God is done on earth as it is in heaven, there will be no marriage.—The marriage supper of the Lamb, is a feast, at which every dish is free to every guest. Exclusiveness, jealousy, quarreling, have no place there. In a holy community, there is no more reason why sexual intercourse should be restrained by law, than why eating and drinking should be—and there is as little occasion for shame in the one case as in the other. God has placed a wall of partition between the male and female during the apostacy [*sic*], for good reasons, which will be broken down in the resurrection, for equally good reasons. But wo [*sic*] to him who abolishes the law of apostacy before he stands in the holiness of the resurrection. I call a certain woman my wife—she is yours—she is Christ's, and in him she is the bride of all saints.[61]

Put less cryptically: under Noyes's doctrine of perfectionism, those who are purified, and who are in society with others who have been purified, may enjoy here and now the fruits of the resurrection. One condition of the resurrection is the abolition of marriage. He argued that marriage is an impediment to holiness, because it creates an artificial separation of the sexes. Those who have achieved holiness, therefore, are freed from the convention of marriage and from the conventional sexual constraint that marriage imposed.

Predictably, the letter was controversial. Because Gates had published it without attaching Noyes's name, Noyes briefly considered remaining anonymous. Honor, glory, and recognition are seductive, however, and he soon decided to publicly avow his authorship.[62] The risk of social (or other) repercussions was dampened by the fact that neither Noyes nor those in his circle were prepared immediately to act on the doctrine. Within a year he married Harriet Holton, a wealthy follower who had converted to perfectionism after reading some of Noyes's pieces and sent him several donations to finance his work. There's scholarly disagreement about whose idea the marriage was. Oved reports that she proposed to him. It's an appealing account, but appears not to be accurate. More persuasively, Robert Thomas recites that Noyes proposed to Harriet. It's a more conventional mode, but Noyes's proposal wasn't exactly the stuff of conventional romantic myth. For one thing, he did it in a letter. For another, the letter was more in the form of a business arrangement than a romantic overture. He offered Harriet a partnership, apparently asexual, in which each would permit the other to freely enjoy the "fellowship of God's universal family." In a grudging concession to the Apostle Paul, he admitted that conventional marriage was indeed necessary for some persons, but, even if a necessity, still "honorable." Harriet quickly accepted (also by letter), in a spirit of obedience and cooperation. The two then exchanged a series of letters in which they worked through an understanding of the nature of their marriage. They married in 1838, fewer than three weeks after his proposal.[63]

One immediate benefit of the marriage, at least for Noyes, was that he could rely on Harriet's material assets to further his work. With her money, he recommenced publishing *The Witness,* which he had suspended the previous year for lack of funds. Even with Harriet's support, the new effort soon ended again, because resources were inadequate to sustain the enterprise. If her money didn't solve all his problems, it appears that she provided nonmaterial benefits that had been missing from Noyes's life up to that point. Among the most important was emotional stability, which provided the psychic space and energy for Noyes to engage actively and productively in new ventures. It also helped that Noyes received an inheritance from his father. Noyes committed his resources (and Harriet's) to building a perfectionist community.[64] Over the next decade Noyes found fellow travelers scattered in New England and as far south as New Jersey. But the core flock was in Putney, where Noyes eventually maintained two farms and a store. With this group, denominated the Society of Inquiry in 1841 (or, as some have called it, the Society of Believers), he clarified his ideas about sex, marriage, and the kingdom of God. The group devoted itself to religious study and the formation of a community consistent with Noyes's ideas about the earthly kingdom of God. When one member suggested that the intensive focus on religion was distracting from the business of work and profit, Noyes responded as Johann Beissel had done to the Eckerlins in Ephrata, that devotion to spiritual matters was the heart of their commitment to perfection. "I would much rather that our land should run to waste than that you should fail of a spiritual harvest." Noyes won the day.[65]

Still, he was exaggerating, for material production played a large role in the life of the community from its inception. Production aside, it was no mystery that spirituality was not merely about spirit. It was also about channeling sexuality. As his ideas evolved on this front, they included three revolutionary notions about the form and functions of family and the roles of its members: complex marriage, male continence, and "stirpiculture." Complex marriage was the cornerstone, in part because it was the idea to which he had given the most thought. This doctrine presupposed the abolition of coverture, the equality of men and women, and the belief that in the kingdom of God people's sexual relations need not be monogamous. As Noyes put it, "The New commandment is that we love one another, not by pairs, as in the world, but en masse." Persons outside the community would call it "free love." Noyes insisted that this characterization was inaccurate, because sexual intercourse in a properly constituted community was subject to social controls and spiritual purposes. Central to this regulatory framework was the idea of "ascending and descending fellowship." Those who were new to complex marriage were introduced to the practice by coupling with one who was above them. "Above" in this context meant both spiritually advanced and practiced in the sexual norms of the Society. This suggested that young men would be introduced to proper modes of coupling by women who had been through menopause, and young women were typically introduced to sexual practice through the guidance of an older man. Connections between two partners were facilitated by a mediator, who would transmit a proposal from one party to the other. As Noyes put it: "This method is favorable to modesty and also to freedom. It allows of refusals without embarrassment. If the third party is a superior, . . . one in whom the lovers have confidence, calm wisdom will enter, . . . to give needed advice and prevent inexpediencies. The third party will also be helpful in arrangements. This method excludes selfish privacy and makes love a Community affair." It also, in his view, drew "upward" those companions who were novices. Complex marriage was the idea that made the Society distinctive and that propelled conversion and "immigration" into the community.[66]

If sexual practice in the system of complex marriage were to avoid an explosion of the population in a community with limited resources, however, its propagative potential had to be regulated. Early on, the key component of regulation was the practice of male continence, which became the community's method of birth control. Essentially, the male partner was instructed on how not to ejaculate, either during or after sexual relations, unless the pair were intending to achieve a pregnancy. Perhaps surprisingly, it appears that the method was effective in reducing births. Between 1848 and 1861, only thirty-one babies were born in a community of roughly 200 adults.[67]

Besides managing the size and character of the Society, there may have been several reasons for Noyes's interest in preventing unwanted pregnancies. One was that control of reproduction was philosophically consistent with the norm of sexual equality. There are limits to this explanation, because the commitment to sexual equality, while real, was also thin and honored inconsistently. Another explanation, and probably more potent, involved Harriet's experience with pregnancy. In the first six years of their marriage, she gave birth to five babies, all but one of whom were stillborn. These experiences were existentially searing, and not only for Harriet, for they led Noyes to virtual despair. He questioned his role as a spiritual leader, and, as a man, he felt a sense of shame for his procreative failures. Yet another reason for the practice was that continence helped avoid the feeling that intercourse, in his words, was merely "a momentary affair, terminating in exhaustion and disgust," which in turn bred "self-reproach and shame." As Noyes saw it, ejaculation was the source of disgust and shame. For community, not to mention for individual personality, this was a problem. Continence supplied a solution. It permitted the lovers the enjoyment of, again in his words, "the *simple presence* of the male organ in the female," without the "crisis which expels the seed." Like some in our own time, Noyes viewed the nonprocreative spilling of seed to be not only needless but debasing. But, unlike some in our own time, he said the practice enhanced and sustained the "enjoyment" of both lovers. To perform in this way required a high degree of self-control. Hence the need for the ascending and descending fellowship—not merely to "draw upward" spiritually, but also to provide practical tutelage.[68]

Self-control of this type was one thing. Controlling social consequences was another, for sex can be socially explosive, as Noyes knew quite well. He had had to intercede in 1840 to manage consequences when a member, Mary Cragin, wife of George Cragin, became intimately involved with a man who wasn't her husband. Noyes's intercessions eventually put an end to the affair.[69] But five years later Noyes would find himself spiritually-physically involved with Mary Cragin. When they revealed their relationship to their spouses, George, feeling cuckolded again, was less than enthusiastic, but eased his mind when Harriet admitted that she had feelings for him. This, in 1846, was the beginning of the practice of complex marriage. Aware of the delicacy of the practice, Noyes introduced it slowly, deliberately, and selectively to others in the community, seeking (and receiving) communal affirmations of his untrammeled authority to regulate affairs. Still, things were rocky at first. Mary began to display (and act on) interest in yet another member of the community (Noyes's brother-in-law), which provoked both George and Noyes. But by 1847 Noyes preached that the time for the kingdom of God had arrived and with it the end of private property and conventional marriage, and among the chosen, he established a "testing committee" for regulating access to sexual intimacy. Even with the committee, Noyes retained a firm hand in supervising decisions and resolving conflicts.[70]

Almost immediately, Noyes misstepped. After spiritually healing Harriet Hall, who had been bedridden for months, he took into his confidence her husband, Daniel. Noyes explained the sexual freedom that he and a small group of members were now enjoying, and he sought to bring Daniel into "full membership." Daniel thought it over for a couple of days, and then went straight to the local state's attorney's office to press criminal charges for adultery and fornication. At first, Noyes was oddly upbeat, seizing on the charges as an opportunity to expound publicly on his views of sex, marriage, and spirituality. What he didn't anticipate was that some of the townspeople of Putney were inflamed against his community, not merely for offenses against morality but also for Noyes's role in a failed faith-healing in which the patient ended up dying. Instead of presenting Noyes an opportunity, his arrest posed a genuine threat to the survival of his Society. Still, Noyes thought the matter would soon blow over, until his brother-in-law Larkin Mead, an attorney in a nearby town, confided that some in Putney, including clergymen, were openly discussing mob action against the community. Mead recommended that Noyes leave Putney, along with several other members, including the Cragins. Noyes left Vermont immediately, first to Connecticut, then to New York City. During his sojourns, threats of mobs subsided, but agitation continued in the town. There was talk of prosecuting all the men in the community for "offenses against chastity, morality, and decency." Nothing came of the charges, but unrest persisted. Noyes bided his time until a new convert to perfectionism offered his land in upstate New York as a new home for the "heavenly association." The spot was Oneida, formerly the reservation of the Oneida Indians, recently ceded to the state of New York and sold to whites at bargain prices.[71]

Noyes soon invited the Cragins to purchase twenty-three acres of land across the road. They did in 1848, and brought Harriet and her children with them. Still others followed, not only from Putney but also from other towns and villages in New England and New York, and by the end of the year the newly organized Oneida Association had eighty-seven members, some of whom were unaware that perfectionism included complex marriage. The foundation for the Association was communism, based on the first Pentecost: "All that believed were together and had all things in common; and sold their possessions and goods, and parted them to all, as every man had need." (Acts 2:44–45 [KJV]) "The family," as they came to call themselves, set to work, building farmhouses and a Mansion House. They began experimenting with complex marriage, they raised children in common, and they shared all material goods. And Noyes relentlessly continued to publish his ideas, dividing his time between Oneida and a communal outpost in Brooklyn, where most of the tracts were produced.[72]

The early years in Oneida were challenging. For one thing, there was the onerous task of organizing material production. For another, controversy followed. Between 1850 and 1852, local courts in Oneida and Madison Counties, New York, commenced separate grand jury investigations into the Association. Members were called to testify, and the threat of criminal indictments loomed. The *New York Observer* also piled on, comparing the Oneidans with polygamous Mormons and agitating for more investigations and prosecutions. At the same time, the community was under threat of civil suits from families of young women who made their way into the group. Noyes made sure that he and the community were represented by respected local counsel, who deftly handled the suits. Almost all of the cases were settled, as Noyes preferred. As he put it, "Our policy is to give the enemy a bridge of money, over which to make a decent retreat." One of the most dangerous of the legal proceedings occurred in the 1850s, when a member, Henry Seymour, was indicted on a charge not involving sex, but of assault and battery for physically whipping his wife Tryphena. Tryphena's father, Noahdiah Hubbard, initiated the indictment. The Hubbards threatened more indictments the following year, but Noyes announced that he would disband the community before going to trial. "I am satisfied that our true policy is to avoid a trial, as we did at Putney, by paying whatever is necessary. . . . A trial, if public and reported in the newspapers, converts a local difficulty into a general scandal. We are dealing with the enemy on the field of public opinion, and our hope is that we shall finally overcome prejudice by common sense, sound reasoning and good behavior."[73]

The community weathered the storm. Capable counsel and tactical settlement were two reasons why they were able to do so. Also crucial, however, was Noyes's bold strategic management of relations with the outside world. For example, in March 1852, he announced that the community was suspending complex marriage. There was no need, he suggested, to make a fetish of forms. Better to adapt in the pursuit of "spiritual freedom." In dealing with the Hubbards, Noyes effectively enlisted the townsfolk on his behalf. He publicly announced to surrounding neighbors that he would disband the community if they insisted that he do so. The only condition was, strangely, that the neighbors attend an ice cream party at the community. He also invited the Hubbards. Three hundred neighbors, including the Hubbards, attended. By all accounts the party was a smashing success. After it, Noyes offered to pay $150 to Mr. Hubbard, if he would provide a certificate "honorably discharging [the Association] from further claims and expressing his wish that the indictments be dropped," and offered to pay $150 more if the indictments were in fact dropped "so that we shall have no further trouble." Hubbard provided the certificate and took steps to assuage animus toward the Oneidans. Noyes paid the money and also paid for Tryphena's psychiatric bills. (She would later overcome her illness and return to the community, where, after mothering a child with Henry Seymour, she would live until her death.) Animosity dissipated. One neighbor publicly declared in writing that "the people in this vicinity will not consent to have you disperse." Soon after, the community resumed the practice of complex marriage.[74]

Thus commenced a period of stunning prosperity for the group, which now had communes not only in Oneida but also in five additional cities. The community initially supported itself through agriculture. Over time, its material pursuits diversified, pursuing economic ventures on a number of fronts, including a massively successful trap-making business, a canning business, an enterprise producing silk thread, and a silverware business (which exists today as Oneida, Ltd.). They invented an agitating washing machine. Uncomfortable with high-heeled laced boots, the women invented a low, comfortable, laceless shoe with an elastic interior to keep it snug. They also jettisoned the traditional circular garter, and invented what would become the garter belt, which they said was more comfortable because it didn't restrict circulation in the legs. And they adopted simpler, shorter, more comfortable dresses, getting rid of the long, elaborate, and binding garb that typified women's dress in the day. Business exploded. By 1864, Oneida was becoming one of the most productive and prosperous communities in the nation.[75]

The community took enormous pride in its children. As in Plato's Guardian class, "children between the ages of two and twelve were housed . . . with their nurses and teachers," in a building denominated the Children's House. Beginning at age twelve, both boys and girls were assigned to "employments" in the household, on the farm, or in the various business enterprises in which the community was engaged. Biological parents could visit their children, but were discouraged from being too attentive to them. One justification for this policy was to free parents to pursue their own work and to engage in spirit-enhancing amative pursuits. For the children, the policy was designed to avoid spoiling them. It also reinforced a structure of authority in the Children's House, which was designed to promote good behavior, sociability, and spiritual well-being. And, as Noyes's granddaughter Constance Noyes Robertson would later put it, the policy helped "to 'communize' the children, . . . 'making them the property of the whole Community.'" Still, the children had time to be children, in the modern sense of the status. They could roam the grounds, play games, play with toys, swing on ropes, ride on sleds, swim, run, and otherwise enjoy the pursuits of childhood.[76] They also received what seems to have been a decent scholastic education. Reports suggested that children were reasonably well adjusted and productive. Many went on to study at some of the nation's most prestigious institutions of higher learning. Some returned to the community with ideas from the larger world.[77]

One of those ideas was eugenics—the social control of reproduction to promote the genetic improvement of the race. Noyes himself had anticipated a theory of "scientific propagation" in his essay on *Bible Communism,* published in 1853, a few years before Darwin's *On the Origin of Species.* Unlike Darwin, Noyes linked his ideas with women's freedom to control their own reproduction:

> Our theory, separating the amative from the propagative, not only relieves us of involuntary and undesirable procreation, but opens the way for *scientific* propagation. We believe that the order to "multiply" attached to the race in its original integrity, and that propagation, rightly conducted, and kept within such limits as life can fairly afford, is the next blessing to sexual love. But we are opposed to *involuntary* procreation. . . . We are opposed to excessive, and of course oppressive procreation, which is almost universal. We are opposed to *random* procreation, which is unavoidable in the [traditional] marriage system. But we are in favor of *intelligent, well-ordered* procreation. . . . We believe the time will come when involuntary and random procreation will cease, and when scientific combination will be applied to human generation as freely and successfully as it is to that of other animals. . . . And at all events we believe that good sense and benevolence will *very soon* sanction and enforce the rule, that women shall bear children only when they choose. They have the principle [*sic*] burdens of breeding to bear, and they, rather than men, should have their choice of time and circumstances, at least till science takes charge of the business.[78]

Many of the community's youth who attended university latched on to Darwin's theory of evolution. One such young man was Noyes's eldest child, Theodore, who completed his study of medicine at Yale. When he returned to Oneida, he found a receptive audience in his father. In 1869, stirpiculture (the cultivation of the race) became Noyes's experiment, through which science took charge of the business of reproduction.[79]

Robertson reports that the community voted unanimously in favor of the experiment. It was borne of prosperity, a growing collective self-confidence, a commitment to science, and a belief that "Motherhood . . . was not the chief end of a woman's life; she was not made simply for the children she could bear. She was made for God and herself." Under the program of stirpiculture, however, this belief yielded to other considerations. Fifty-three young women voluntarily signed resolutions committing themselves to the experiment: "we do not belong to ourselves in any respect, but . . . belong first to *God,* and second to Mr. Noyes as God's true representative." They disavowed "rights [and] personal feelings in regard to child-bearing." And they forswore "all envy, childishness, and self-seeking" concerning which of their number would be "chosen as candidates; . . . we will, if necessary, become martyrs to science." Thirty-eight young men signed a similar statement, offering themselves "to be used in forming any combinations that may seem to you desirable. We claim no rights. We ask no privileges. We desire to be servants of the truth." Decisions about fitness for reproduction were delegated to the Association's central committee. Robertson notes that "this meant that in reality John Noyes directed the mating, and in certain cases strictly forbade it." In 1875, a formal Stirpicultural Committee was appointed for this purpose. This Committee sat for only fifteen months, however, after which authority reverted to the central committee (and to Noyes).[80]

The result was a baby boom, at least by Oneida's standard. Robertson says that in the ten years in which the experiment was conducted, eighty-one of the participants in the experiment became parents, and they produced fifty-eight live births—"Stirpicults" as they were called. By 1921, more than a half-century after the experiment commenced, only six of the fifty-eight had died. For the time and place, this was a stunningly low mortality rate. They were raised in the standard Oneidan way. They were placed in the common nursery of the Children's House when they learned to walk. They stayed there until they reached adolescence, at which point they began to participate in the productive life of the community. As adults, Stirpicults gave birth to ninety-eight children of their own. Among these, there were no stillbirths. Only three did not survive a full year.[81]

The Stirpicults survived, but did they flourish? At least one of their number reports that they did, though he notes that life became tense by the late 1870s, and the children sensed it.[82] What they sensed but didn't fully comprehend at first was that the community was unraveling. The sources for the unraveling stemmed partly from dynamics within the community and partly from events and forces outside. It might seem natural to imagine that one internal source had to do with competition, jealousy, and unhappiness over stirpiculture. In fact, this seems to have had little to do with the disintegration. More salient was the rise of a division between the founding generation and the generation of children who came after. Many of those children were able to take advantage of opportunities for higher education outside the community. Even when they returned, they were changed by their time away and by the ideas to which they'd been exposed. Many of those ideas, if not most, were secular. Some ideas inclined some younger adults, including, it seems, Noyes's son Theodore, to subversively entertain the desirability of conventional marriage. Hence, in a society whose cohesion, from the beginning, had depended on an emphatically religious ethos and worldview, the influence of secular ideas was corrosive. In short, societies that are thickly constituted by morality tend to be unstable over time, especially if subject to nonconforming ideas.[83]

One thing that can hold such communities together, aside from the inertial force of a shared way of life, is strong leadership. Leadership doesn't have to be totalitarian to be effective. But it does need to rest on authority. Noyes possessed authority—partly because of the strength of his association with the community's animating ideology, but also partly because of his skill and charismatic leadership. Being human, however, he grew old. Recognizing that fact, and desirous of extending his legacy, he arranged to have his eldest son, Theodore, ascend to the leading position in the community, and then he left so as not to overshadow his son. Theodore's rule was controversial. One reason, about which he could do nothing, was that he simply wasn't his father. But the way in which he wasn't his father was important: he was religiously agnostic in a society built upon commitment to religious faith. This produced ideological disorientation. Besides this, his style of leadership was both aloof and authoritarian (in the totalizing sense of the word). This engendered personal resentment. Discontent, even rebellion, were the products of that resentment. Within a year, the elder Noyes returned, but the damage was done, and even he had to accede to sharing his leadership with another, not his son.[84]

The external forces were sharp, and exacerbated those within the community. In 1873, Anthony Comstock, an influential New York Congressman, successfully agitated for morals legislation in Congress. The Comstock Law, enacted that year, criminalized the mailing of "obscene, lewd, and/or lascivious material," including information about contraception or abortion. This prohibition barred no small segment of the Society's tracts, dealing frankly as they did with subjects of birth control (even if only involving voluntary continence), not to mention conventional adultery. Comstock's New York Society for the Suppression of Vice organized pressure on a number of fronts, including against the Oneida Community. Pro-Comstock forces, including the Congregational Church of New York, adopted resolutions condemning the community as a "pernicious institution which rests substantially on a system of organized fanaticism and lust." Later, the Baptist Church and a select committee of the Presbyterian Church, headed by John W. Mears of Hamilton College, got into the act. Although local newspapers actually defended the community against the attacks, and not simply because of happy memories of the ice cream social, the larger cultural and political environment was uncongenial to peaceful coexistence. By 1879, a major convention of churches in Syracuse had taken direct moral aim at Oneida, urging official investigation of the community. As it turned out, the convention had the covert support of some members of the community. Sensing danger, the elder Noyes retreated in exile to Canada.[85]

Even from Canada, he was not without a modicum of influence. Recognizing that the Oneidans were fractured and weakening as a collective, he sent them a formal message: "I propose that we give up the practice of complex marriage not as renouncing belief in the principles and prospective finality of that institution, but in deference to the public sentiment which is evidently rising against it." He urged the community to embrace Pauline principles, which permitted conventional marriage but encouraged celibacy. To fail to do so, he worried, would mean the total ruin of the experiment in communism. If the group could eliminate the basis for moral commotion against the community, perhaps it could continue its experiment in economic communism, "to hold our property and business in common, as now." He argued that this "will be a good and graceful thing," not only to remove from Oneida's supportive neighbors "the burden of our unpopularity," but also to "show the world that Christian communism has self control and flexibility enough to live and flourish without Complex marriage." From a complex and conflicted set of motives, the community promptly ratified his proposal. But the move to conventional marriage ironically only exacerbated entropic tendencies, not only affecting internal social cohesion but also creating divisive disputes over the collective education of children. Two years later, the group dissolved itself as a community, converted all interests into joint stock, and re-created itself as Oneida Holding Company, Ltd. The radical communist experiment in social relations had become a corporation.[86]

As we've seen, Aristotle held that there were two constitutive functions of the familial household: production and reproduction. These functions were "natural" in the sense that they promoted survival. And when they were part of a polis, they might promote not merely survival but also human flourishing. The experiences of communal families in the eighteenth and nineteenth centuries are suggestive in light of Aristotle's view of the household.

Consider productivity. Certainly production mattered. The most stable and long-lived communities were those that organized themselves not merely for God but also for production. Put differently, it was not sufficient in the long term that a community might be intensely committed to a religious idea, no matter how commendable its pursuit might have been. What was also needed was a practical commitment to material sustenance and well-being. For reasons of both social control and ideological purity, Beissel at Ephrata came to believe that material pursuits were incompatible with those of the spirit. This belief permitted him to regain control of his community, and it may well have reinforced ideals that had animated its founding. But Beissel's success in this regard came at a price, for the life of the spirit may be important, but it cannot alone sustain a community over time. Compare the experience of the Shakers, who viewed a religious life as part and parcel of a way of life that included intense labor, a system of material production, and participation in commerce. Through diligence and sweat, as much as through prayer, the Shakers sustained their communities for generations.

Surprisingly, perhaps, they were able to sustain community despite forswearing the sexual means through which reproduction takes place. They could do so as long as they could draw new members from outside. Hence their liberal policy for entry into the community. But the commitment to freedom of movement was not one-sided. They permitted members freely to exit, too, from their Shaker family once they came of age. Many did, especially young adults who had grown up in the community but were aware of some of what existed outside. When they left, they usually did so with full appreciation of the benefits that the Shaker family had bestowed on them. But the allure of a society in which all things, including sex, are possible is seductive. In this regard, modernity was erosive of Shakers' communities.

But there were ways in which these primitive communities were more modern than the nation-state that surrounded them. One, importantly, involved the role and status of women. Among the Shakers, for example, not only was a woman the founder of the community, but woman was an essential element of the theological foundation for the group, and women enjoyed a formally equal role in governance and leadership. In fact, the Shakers came to look much like the communist Guardian class of Plato's *Republic*—the very form of family that Justice McReynolds would disparage in the following century in his opinion for the Court in *Meyer v. Nebraska*. They rejected marriage. They practiced sexual equality. Their property was held in common. Their children were raised in common. Despite all of these suspicious elements, they came to be tolerated. One reason was that they stuck to themselves, without massive amounts of proselytizing. Another was that they were hard working and productive, and people wanted their products. Still another, and probably crucial, was that no one was having sex.

The Oneida community resembled the Shakers in many substantial respects. But the Oneidans departed from the Shakers in one important way: they attempted to preserve an ideal of sexual equality without eliminating sexuality. Equal access to sex was an element of this approach. For the endeavor to succeed, however, Oneidans believed that two additional elements were crucial: abolishing monogamous marriage and assuring control over reproduction. Sex, nonmonogamous marriage, and control of reproduction, however, became targets of intense opposition in the larger society, subjecting the Oneida Community to constant threats to its survival. Perhaps surprisingly, these threats tended not to come from local neighbors, not at least after the Oneidans made their peace with neighbors through the magic of the ice-cream social. Proximate neighbors came to tolerate even the sexually unconventional community at Oneida, largely because its members were not socially disruptive (notwithstanding claims that nonmarital sex itself was socially disruptive) and the community's economic enterprises contributed to the material welfare of the area.

But local peace was not sufficient to protect the Oneida Community. By the late nineteenth century, forces for the eradication of sexual (and other forms of) immorality were not only organized but in the ascendency, especially on the national stage. Sexual morality—including marriage, sexual equality, and control of reproduction—was a substantial reason the Oneidans were badgered into abandoning their familial experiment, while the Shakers came to be tolerated as an eccentric but essentially harmless association. To put it simply, the dominant concern of opponents was over who was having sex with whom, and to what end. To be sure, the charge of communism was nontrivial to some opponents. For most, however, communism was of secondary concern. The fates of these two religious societies were not for reasons in the nature of things. They were instead a function of the operation of law imposed by the surrounding polity. Put differently, the ability of Oneida to promote its values was directly constrained by the moral values of the political society in which it grew and from which it could not completely separate.

This, of course, says something about the social uses of law, which the polity wielded as an instrument to kill new things. Officials used law to try to suppress or punish suspiciously strange religious practices—like a seventh-day Sabbath in the case of Ephrata, or wild and noisy worship in the case of the early Shakers. These attempts were not fully effective. More successfully, officials used law to kill off Oneidans' unconventional sexual practices. If officials used law for these ends, however, it is simplistic to allege that law was merely a (would-be) killer of novelty. For one thing, law's touch was sometimes relatively light. It was notable, for example that a court exempted the Brethren of the Community at Ephrata from the single-men's tax on the ground that the brothers were a family. It was notable, too, that the Supreme Court of Michigan treated an intergenerational household of Shakers as a family for the purpose of enforcing a policy of insurance. For another, law underwrote the religious liberty that permitted the very ideas that these communities (including the Oneidans) put into practice. Law allowed people to think as they would for the most part, though not always to write as they thought. In a sense, the freedom of conscience and belief constitutionalized Protestantism's priesthood of the believer. Law provided a space in which a group's associations and productive enterprises might flourish. It permitted groups the option of exit from more established religious institutions. Thus, far from being a source of social stability, religion was the engine for radical experimentation in the forms, functions, and values of family.

Tellingly, this sort of liberty was strongest in New England, where an ethos of liberal individualism was rooted most firmly. To be sure, as we've seen, the South had its own deviation from the nuclear model of the family. But, unlike in New England, southern families were not novel experiments but longstanding forms, rooted in traditionalist conservatism, and vigorously reinforced by law.

Still, it's plain that opposition to the Shakers' and the Oneidans' values and practices came largely from those who wielded the coercive sword of law. And, as time wore on, opposition was increasingly national. To some extent, this cut against the Madisonian intuition that, as you expand the geographic sphere and increase social complexity, you also expand the range of toleration. In fact, the cultural and political sources for suppressing familial experiments were increasingly nationalist by the end of the nineteenth century. The national template for family was bourgeois, nuclear, masculine, and (to a degree) anti-communist. We've already seen one institutional expression of this nationalization: the use of national power to Americanize the tribes, including tribal families and property. We'll see yet another in the chapter that follows.

8
Uncommon Families, Part 2
Polygamy

As we've already seen, the earliest examples of polygamy in North America were found in some of the native tribes, even before the coming of the Europeans. It's impossible to know with certainty when or how polygamy first appeared among whites. Doubtless, there was a version of it in North America that was similar to the English experience, in which (typically) husbands would leave their wives and children without benefit of divorce, and would nonetheless remarry. But polygamy as a formal practice is a different matter. It's easy enough to identify the group most popularly associated with the practice: Mormons. The story of Latter-day Saints in America is long and complex. It is also the source of much contention—theological, cultural, and political—both among Mormons and in the larger polity. It's not my point here to provide a comprehensive, much less definitive, rendition of the Mormon experience. Fine scholars have written ably on the larger history. What I want to do instead is to focus on Mormonism's roots, its doctrines and practices, and its importance in the story of the relation between families and the American constitutional order.

THE SOCIETY OF FREE BRETHREN AND SISTERS

Even before the Mormons, the earliest European-American practitioner of polygamy was reputed to be Jacob Cochran (sometimes spelled "Cochrane"), a charismatic preacher whose flock called themselves the Society of Free Brethren and Sisters but became known disparagingly as Cochranites. Cochran himself was born in 1782 in Enfield, New Hampshire, where the Shakers would eventually establish a community. Unsurprisingly, he gained influence in and around the "burned-out" section of New England.[1] He would eventually settle in Saco in what is now Maine, just inland from Saco Bay between the towns of Kennebunk and Portland. (Until 1820, Maine was a subdivision of the state of Massachusetts.) At one point, there may have been more than 2,000 Cochranites in or around Saco. This estimate comes from Ephraim Stinchfield, a Baptist preacher who sojourned briefly among the Cochranites as a kind of religious anthropologist. Like the Shakers, the group aimed to revive an apostolic, communitarian instantiation of the early Christian church. Like the Shakers, Cochranites' worship tended toward the ecstatic. After a jubilant session of singing, dancing, shouting, and speaking in tongues, came preaching, laying on hands (for healing and casting out demons), and an invitation to conversion. Like the Shakers, more than one Cochranite was jailed for this enthusiastic form of worship. Still, by all accounts, Cochran was supremely effective in drawing in converts.[2] And like the Shakers, at the heart of Cochranite doctrine was a repudiation of marriage. G. T. Ridlon, a historian from Maine, described the position this way:

> In the ideal state, inhabitants were neither married nor given in marriage: this should begin on earth, being God's standard for society, and be as nearly approximated as mortal conditions would admit of. The affinities were to be all spiritual. . . . [Cochran] admonished all who had been united in the bonds of matrimony according to the laws of the land to hold themselves in readiness to dissolve such union and renounce their vows.[3]

In these respects, the Cochranites look familiar. Unlike the Shakers, however, and even more than the Oneidans, Cochran's society was intensely sexual. It's difficult today to get a firm fix on the sexual practices of the group, partly because it was secretive about this aspect of its life and partly because critics were squeamish about reciting too explicitly details that they considered morally objectionable. Clearly, however, it was the group's sexual practices that most inflamed critics. Based on interviews with former members, Ridlon recited a few representative practices. One involved men's access to women. "All revelations to this end were to come through Cochran, of course, and in the allotment of the spoils the leader, by virtue of his rank, was sure to get the 'lion's share.'" Ridlon speculated that Cochran's women "were invariably the most robust and attractive women in the community." On at least one occasion, Cochran told a new brother that he (Cochran) had received a revelation direct from God that the two should swap wives. The brother consented, leaving his wife to Cochran, but on hastening to Mrs. Cochran he was surprised to find her angry and unyielding. "You go straight back and tell Jake Cochran his God is a liar," she is reported to have said. Cochran also sexualized worship. One way to do this was to use plays to illustrate biblical events. One such play depicted Adam and Eve, fully nude, in the Garden of Eden. He discontinued the plays when local authorities intervened.[4]

Stinchfield compared the group to an insanity-inducing disease: "religious hydrophobia." He was indignant, for example, when he visited the home of a member of Cochran's Society. "The Landlady, his Wife, met me as soon as I entered the room & wished to know whether I had the courage to kiss her."

Stinchfield said he "declined accepting her rude compliment . . . for which She called me a coward." More problematic than promiscuous kissing, for Stinchfield, was "spiritual wifery."[5] Both doctrinally and as a matter of practice, this resembled less polygamy than a kind of regulated predatory polyamory, in which certain men were allowed physical access to more than one woman.[6] Unlike the Oneida Community, women in Cochran's Society were not free to choose multiple partners, though some women did have more than one partner, as a matter of practice, because they were already married when chosen by another. As part of his investigation, Stinchfield interviewed former members, who described the group's quasi-Masonic rites. Among the ritual signs "was the male & female putting their thumbs & [forefingers] together in the form of a triangle and kissing thro [them]." Other members reported that "they Saw Cochran Take a young woman into a dark private room & Stay a considerable time. . . . He then took another Female into the Same room in the Same Manner & then another." It was also reported that Cochran imposed a solemn oath to hold secret "what took place in their private Meetings" and that anyone violating the oath would "Suffer eternal Damnation" and "be blotted out of the book of Life." Still another interviewee, a former member, reported that on one occasion Cochran "pointed to & named his Spiritual Wife & Said he was willing they should lodge together[,] which he did a number of Nights. . . . [The interviewee] testified that Jacob Cochran lodged two nights . . . with a woman not his wife & five couples more lodged in the Same house chamber not husband & wife."[7]

This sort of thing eventually put Cochran in the cross-hairs of the law. In 1819, he was indicted in the Supreme Judicial Court of York County, Massachusetts, for five offenses. The first trial was for "open and gross lewdness" and "lascivious behavior." It involved a young woman named Eliza Hill, who had lived in Cochran's household for about a month. She had been ill, and Cochran held himself out as a physician. Early one morning, she apparently awoke, bleeding from the nose and mouth. Cochran and the rest of the household woke, too. The prosecutor's chief witness, a former member of the Society, testified as follows:

> I saw him [Cochran] undress except his linen and go into bed, and he put his arm round Eliza Hill, and then told the others to pray. They laid in bed about an hour, then Eliza began to praize [sic] the Lord, and both got up and walked about almost naked. He took hold of her hand and led her into another room, and came out and said Eliza Hill had taken cold by sleeping alone, and some of the brethren must go in and lodge with her. Benjamin Andrews went in and laid with her, afterwards coming out, [and] said the dead had been raised.

She testified also that Cochran placed Ms. Hill on the bed between himself and another young woman, Sally Dennet. In closing argument, the prosecutor made much of this testimony: "Can any rational mind declare that it was not an act of lewdness, for a naked man to be in bed with two naked women, under pretense of curing one? Impossible!" Witnesses for the defendant contradicted this testimony, denying that Cochran ever got in bed with Ms. Hill but instead put her in bed with his wife.[8]

The prosecutor focused on evidence that Cochran had publicly condemned and preached against marriage. In his opening statement, the prosecutor had urged that marriage was "an institution of divine origin" and that doctrines repudiating it were a "contagion" on society. (In his closing argument, he would call the Cochranites' doctrines a "delusion" and an "infest[ation].") Evidence for the defendant tended to show that Cochran's position on marriage was simply a reflection of the Pauline admonition against marriage. Defense counsel urged that, if Cochran's positions on marriage were consistent with Christian doctrine, they were legally justified, not least because they were protected as part of the freedom of religion. The court itself, in instructing the jury, took pains to limit the legal effect of the defendant's claim in a way that anticipated later decisions of the Supreme Court of the United States in cases upholding the disenfranchisement and criminal punishment of Mormons: "The argument of counsel for the defendant, is conclusive, so far as relates to the right of a people to worship, in an orderly manner, in such form as will best coincide with their faith; but if any religious sect shall conduct in a disorderly or improper manner in open violation of the law, his religious profession ought not to protect him." In the end, despite some bullying by the judge, a single juror held out against conviction, saying he was unwilling to convict when the testimony of the prosecutor's sole witness was in doubt.[9]

Thus began Cochran's second trial, this time for "lying in bed with Abigail Clark, a married woman, and committing adultery, lewdness, &c." with her. (For reasons Blackstone's account of the common law explains, Cochran was not charged with committing adultery in the first trial, because his alleged paramour was not herself married. Sex between a married man and an unmarried woman might be lewd, but it was not, strictly speaking, adultery.[10]) The prosecution called two witnesses, both former members of the Society. One testified that she saw Cochran and Mrs. Clark in bed together at the Clarks' house one day, apparently naked, while Mr. Clark was out of town. Asked about the "posture" of the two, she said "Mr. Cochrane had Mrs. Clark in his arms, and one leg was thrown over her." The second witness said that she saw Cochran and Mrs. Clark lying together on the floor of her house a few nights later while Mr. Clark was present but sleeping. Each witness testified that Cochran insisted that she keep secret what she had seen.[11] Mrs. Clark took the stand and stated that she had long been ill, stemming from her having carried two stillborn children, and that "Mr. Cochrane attended her as a physician," but had "never conducted in an indecent manner, nor was in bed with her, to her knowledge." And she denied having lain with him on the floor, saying that she merely gave him a makeshift pallet on which to lie and then went to sleep with her husband. On cross-examination, however, she admitted that he lay in bed with her "and prayed with me." Mr. Clark testified that Cochran was present in his house both times by invitation and that he suspected nothing illicit.

Other witnesses denied having seen anything improper happen between Cochran and Mrs. Clark.[12]

In closing, counsel for the defendant challenged the credibility and motives of the prosecution's witnesses and argued that the jury should pause before convicting a man of crimes whose punishment included "solitary confinement and hard labor in the State prison." He also inveighed against the community's prejudice: "If any other than a Cochranite had been brought to the bar, and charges as faintly supported as in this case, he would have been acquitted." The prosecutor in turn used his closing as an exercise in preaching. He compared Cochran with Cain of Genesis. When a member of the audience noted that he was alluding to Ishmael, not Cain, the prosecutor quickly rejoined that "there was one of which I shall not mistake in the name, who will fully and completely compare with the defendant at the bar[:] Judas Iscarriot [sic]." He repeatedly argued as if the crimes charged included prostitution. He dismissed Mrs. Clark's testimony as the witless testimony of a woman incapable of forming independent judgment. And he ridiculed the notion that Cochran was tending to Mrs. Clark as a physician. "He knows nothing of medicine—No, not so much as the savages of Canada." The judge's instruction to the jury amounted to an addendum to the prosecutor's closing argument. "If you believe [the two principal witnesses for the prosecution], you must convict." Then the judge recited testimony in detail, and explained why the prosecutor's witnesses were credible and the witnesses for Cochran were not. The jury retired for lunch, then began deliberation. Within thirty minutes, the jury returned with a verdict of guilty. Apparently, Cochran anticipated this result. He absconded during lunch, and was nowhere to be found when the jury returned its verdict.[13]

What happened after that is unclear. Ridlon recited a report that Cochran "escaped from the officers on his way to prison and went to New Hampshire, where he continued to preach for many years."[14] In an account more likely to be accurate, D. M. Graham reported that Cochran was eventually apprehended, served four years in the state's prison, and died a few years after he was released.[15]

THE LATTER-DAY SAINTS—FROM NEW ENGLAND TO UTAH

If the Cochranites were not, strictly speaking, polygamous, many early Mormons came to be. The journey began with Joseph Smith, Jr. He was born in Sharon, Vermont, in 1805, just as the Second Great Awakening was catching fire in western New York. The movement was fully ablaze by the time Smith's family moved to Palmyra, New York, a few miles west of Oneida Lake, when he was ten years old. He grew up in this region amid wildly emotional evangelical revivals. His father, Joseph, Sr., was a spiritual man but suspicious of organized religion, who dabbled in arts of the occult that were popular among the folk of the day. He reported dreams and visions, and he used spells and chants to dig for money. Joseph,

Jr., was his father's son. He had a keen interest in religion and was schooled in various occult practices, including the use of "seer stones." The younger Joseph owned three such stones, and he insisted that if he placed them inside a hat and buried his face in the hat to block out the light, he could "see all things in and under the earth." Among the things he claimed to be able to see was buried treasure. This was both useful and dangerous. It was useful because it was a source of employment. It was dangerous because searches did not always go as searchers hoped. The danger was intensified by the fact that, even as a young man, Joseph possessed a personality that was both magnetic and repulsive. That is, he had an ability not only to draw people in but also to arouse intense anger among those who came in contact with him (even those who were initially drawn to him). He repeatedly found himself dealing with people who wanted to hurt him. In 1826, for example, after a bootless search for treasure, Smith was charged in a local court with being a "disorderly person and an imposter." It's not clear what the outcome of this prosecution was, but it was only the first of several prosecutions against him.[16]

Smith's search for treasure was an expression of a deeper, more spiritual search. Among the earliest questions he wrestled with was one involving true religion: Of all the faiths and creeds in the world, which one was true and right? Scripture alone did not answer the question, but it did, in his view, justify the quest: "If any of you lack wisdom, let him ask of God, that giveth to all liberally, and upbraideth not; and it shall be given him." (James 1:5 [KJV]) So he searched in solitary prayer in the forests of western New York, and at the age of fourteen experienced the first of his many visions and visitations from representatives of God. As he reported it twelve years later, two "personages" stood above him, divinely illuminated by a "pillar of light." They communicated a message of forgiveness and redemption. They also confirmed, he would report still later, Joseph's father's skepticism of established religion. The creeds of all sects, the visitors said, were "an abomination," and Joseph should "join none of them." He returned to his mother that evening and reported that Presbyterianism, the faith to which she had recently attached, "is not true." When Joseph told a local minister about the vision, the preacher responded with scorn. This reaction clarified Joseph's disconnection from organized faith.[17]

Three years later, at the age of seventeen, he was visited again, this time by a glorious angel named Moroni, who told Joseph about two divine forms of buried treasure. One was a set of golden plates containing symbols representing the story of God's dealings with "the ancient inhabitants" of North America. Second were two seer stones—the Urim and Thummim—which were specially designed for translating the plates into English. Moroni supplied a vision showing Joseph where the plates were buried. The angel also warned Joseph that he was prohibited from showing the plates to anyone else. A day or more later, Joseph passed out in the family's field. When he came to, he saw the angel again, who commanded him to tell his father, which he did. Unflinchingly, Joseph, Sr., told his son to obey the angel. The younger Smith went directly to the hillside he had seen in the vision and there found the plates and stones that the angel had described. He tried to take the golden plates, with a mind to selling them, but he received a severe shock, like electricity, to his hands. Again the angel appeared and warned Joseph that he could not retrieve the plates until he reached the age of twenty-one.[18]

In 1826, not long after his prosecution for being an imposter, Joseph met Emma Hale and resolved to marry her. She hesitated when he proposed. Her father passionately protested the proposal. In January of 1827, however, Joseph and Emma "eloped" to marriage. He had just turned twenty-one. The summer of that year, the couple moved in with Joseph's parents and soon after went to visit Emma's father. He raged against Joseph and the theft of his daughter. Joseph promised his father-in-law that he was done with using seer stones, and he agreed to go into a business that Emma's father proposed to set up for him in Pennsylvania. Joseph didn't keep either promise, though he did move to Pennsylvania. In the fall of 1827, he retrieved Moroni's plates. After an interlude and much agitation over the plates among townsfolk, Joseph and Emma moved to Harmony, Pennsylvania. There, in December of 1827, he began translating the plates using the Urim and Thummim.[19]

The path to translation was tortuous. For one thing, the characters were strange—unlike anything Smith had ever encountered. He called them "reformed Egyptian." He dictated his translation while speaking into his hat, to Emma. A couple of months into the effort, Martin Harris arrived from Palmyra, professing a vision inspired by God. Harris persuaded Smith to permit him to take some of the characters and translations to scholars, perhaps for confirmation of the validity of the texts. There's substantial dispute about what transpired during Harris's sojourn. What is not in dispute is that Harris visited a noted professor of classics, Charles Anthon of Columbia University. Anthon would later write that what he had seen was a mishmash of symbols, nothing like Egyptian hieroglyphics, and he had warned Harris that he was being duped. Harris reported that Anthon signed a certificate of the authenticity of the characters and of Smith's translation, but tore up the certificate when Harris told him that an angel had revealed the location of the plates from which the characters had been taken. Regardless of which account is accurate, Joseph took it as the fulfillment of a prophesy from the book of Isaiah.[20]

In the spring of 1828, after Harris's return from New York, he and Smith commenced translation with intensity, though Joseph refused to let Harris see the golden plates. Meanwhile Harris's wife was fretting aloud that Smith was making a fool of her husband. When they had prepared a manuscript of 116 pages, a persistent Harris persuaded Joseph to let him take the translation home to Palmyra to show it to his wife and four others, to prove to them that he was engaged in a real and substantial enterprise. In Palmyra, the manuscript was lost, stolen, or destroyed, perhaps by Harris's wife. Joseph was despondent for months after he found out about the manuscript's fate. For a time, Joseph lost use of his seer stones. In September, however, Moroni returned them to him, and he fitfully re-commenced the task of translating. At first, he dictated to Emma, then to Oliver Cowdery, who had heard about and become obsessed with the "Golden Bible" and moved from Vermont just to be near its owner. Joseph took on Oliver as his new scribe. But instead of attempting to retranslate the lost manuscript, they be-gan with new material, picking up where Smith and Harris had left off.[21]

As Joseph would later recount, he and Oliver received a visitation from John the Baptist in May of 1829, not long after they had commenced their work. John ordained them into the Priesthood of Aaron, with all priestly powers except for the laying on of hands for gifts of the Holy Ghost, designated Joseph as the first Elder and Oliver as the second Elder of a new church, and directed them to be baptized. Joseph and Oliver promptly went to the Susquehanna River and baptized each other. A few days later, they received a visitation from the Apostles Peter, James, and John, who ordained the two into the Priesthood of Melchizedek, with pow-ers that included the laying on of hands. With the help of David Whitmer, Smith and Cowdery eventually finished their translation in upstate New York, where an angel appeared, declaring the translation to have been achieved, in the words of Smith's introduction to his manuscript, "by the gift and power of God." Even Martin Harris belatedly saw the revelation, and he, Cowdery, and Whitmer signed a statement professing what they had witnessed. Within a week, Joseph showed the golden plates to his father, his brothers, and Whitmer's four sons, and they, too, signed statements attesting to what they had seen.[22]

In 1830, Smith published his manuscript as *The Book of Mormon: Another Testament of Jesus Christ*. *The Book of Mormon* claimed to fill out the Bible's story of God's presence in the world. It painted a vivid picture that affirmed Jo-hann Kelpius's speculation, more than a century earlier, that American Indians were descendants of the ancient Israelites. In doing so, it aimed to tie together the experience of Christians and Jews since the birth of Jesus and to locate that expe-rience in North America. Smith framed his book as the record of the historian and prophet Mormon, who, before his death in the fourth century A.D., transmitted his record on golden plates to his son Moroni. This record described two sets of mi-gration from the Middle East to North America. The first were the Jaredites, who migrated by ship at the time of the Tower of Babel, around 2500 B.C. Ultimately, the Jaredites were destroyed through internal conflict, but not before the prophet Ether predicted "that a New Jerusalem should be built up upon this land [in North America], unto the remnant of the seed of Joseph," and it would "become a holy city of the Lord; and it should be built unto the house of Israel." (Ether 13:1–10)[23]

The second migration, around 600 B.C. (just before the Babylonian captiv-ity), included the Hebrew prophet Lehi, his wife Sariah, and their sons. Among the sons was Nephi, who was faithful and obedient and was, directly or indirectly, the source of four books in *The Book of Mormon*. God instructed Lehi to leave Jerusalem, warning that the iniquity of the Jews would lead to the destruction of that holy city. Lehi departed with his family and sailed to North America, which was to become a "land of liberty," "a land of promise, a land which is choice above all other lands; a land which the Lord God hath covenanted with me [Lehi] should be a land for the inheritance of my seed." (2 Nephi 1:5, 7) As the chosen brother, Nephi incurred the jealousy and resentment of his less devout siblings. After Lehi died, his family fractured, with sons Laman and Lemuel setting themselves against Nephi. So Nephi, with his family and others, left his brothers. Known as Nephites, they lived faithful to God, and they prospered. Those who remained with his brothers came to be known as Lamanites. They lived in wickedness and were therefore "cut off from the presence of the Lord." Up to this time, the Lamanites had been "white, and exceedingly fair and delightsome." After they "hardened their hearts," however, God "did cause a skin of blackness to come upon them" so that they would "not be enticing to my people." (2 Nephi 5:1–23) American Indians, on this account, were descendants of the original Lamanites.[24]

The subsequent history was complex, involving periods of war, famine, and prosperity. In a clarifying moment after his crucifixion, however, Jesus appeared to the Nephites. He proclaimed the gospel of the beatitudes and the Lord's Prayer and he described himself as the fulfillment of Mosaic law: "Behold, I am the law and the light."(3 Nephi 15:9) After this appearance there were decades of communist peace and prosperity, and all the Lamanites who had been "converted unto the Lord" became Nephites, and, as had happened to Lamanites who had converted in previous years, "their curse was taken from them, and their skin became white like unto the Nephites. And their young men and their daughters became exceedingly fair." (4 Nephi 1; 3 Nephi 2:12–16) But, after two centuries of peace, there arose pride and selfishness and pursuit of wealth, and with them the division of society into classes, and with it wickedness and contention. (4 Nephi) Eventually, the Nephites themselves grew wicked, and by the time Mormon came to lead the Nephites in the fourth century A.D., the Nephite nation was in decline. In time, the Lamanites routed the Nephites and cut down Mormon. (Mormon 1–4, 8:5–7) As he lay wounded after the battle, with only twenty-four of his fellow Nephites surviving, Mormon handed the golden plates to his son Moroni. Eventually, the Lamanites would hunt down the remnant Nephites and kill them all, including Mormon. (Mormon 6) Moroni was the sole Nephite survivor, and he took up the task of his father, preserving the histories contained on the plates and even finding more plates. (Mormon 8) Moroni closed out *The Book of Mormon* by prescribing rites and doctrines of the church of Christ, including the condemnation of Pauline doctrines concerning infant baptism and the salvation of children. (Moroni 1–8)[25]

This story was extraordinary not only for its epic scope but also for its implicit claim that the Judeo-Christian Bible was incomplete and, in some respects, incorrect. Even before *The Book of Mormon* was released, Smith was taking steps to formally organize the Church of Christ, with branches in Fayette, Palmyra, and Colesville, New York. The new church provided an office and title for virtually every man, from the lowest to the highest: deacon, teacher, priest, elder. In this way the church combined elements of democracy with an emphatically hierarchical administrative structure. Ultimately, however, it was an autocracy, with Joseph at its head. He was its first seer, translator, elder, and eventually president. More simply, he was "the Prophet." Women were different. Unlike the Shakers or even the Oneidans but much like most of the rest of American institutions of the day, Mormons confined women to subordinate roles of domesticity. Men saw themselves as patriarchs. Thus, it was men who carried out the jobs of leading, teaching, and proselytizing. If the number of conversions over the next few years is any indication, they did their jobs with stunning success.[26]

Part of the reason for this success, of course, was Joseph Smith himself, who possessed mesmerizing "charisma, charm, and persuasiveness," as Remini puts it. Still another reason was the message, which sought to restore in North America the ancient Judaic-Christianity that had passed from the scene by the end of the first century A.D. A country of voluntary religion, widely based on revelation and emotion, provided a fruitful forum for Mormonism to flourish.[27] But the seeds of success were also sources of opposition. This opposition, which appeared almost everywhere the Mormons settled, was plainly a threat to the physical survival of the church, not to mention its members.

Mormons were chased from virtually every place they occupied, often because of a toxic combination of mobs and legal prosecutions. Soon after the formal founding of the Church, they fled upstate New York for Kirtland, Ohio. From Kirtland, they fled to Missouri, in the hope of establishing Zion. They tried to build stable communities in at least three locations in Missouri, each one provoking intense opposition from "Gentiles," as Joseph called non-Mormons. It was there that Smith changed the Church's name to the Church of Jesus Christ of Latter-day Saints. In Missouri in 1838, an anti-Mormon mob attacked the Saints, who resisted for a month in what came to be known as the Mormon War. There were deaths on both sides. At one point Governor Lilburn Boggs, declaring the Mormons "vermin," issued an executive order that they be "exterminated or driven from the state." In this milieu Missourians massacred the inhabitants of a Mormon settlement, including children, at Haun's Mill, and anti-Mormon militias numbering 2,500 surrounded the larger Mormon city of Far West, Missouri. Eventually, Smith surrendered and was charged with treason. While he awaited trial, property of the Latter-day Saints was confiscated, and the Saints fled eastward across the Mississippi River to western Illinois, near Quincy, where the locals cautiously embraced them. For reasons that remain mysterious, guards who were transporting Smith to stand trial in 1839 permitted him to escape.[28]

Soon after, he joined the Mormons in Illinois, purchased land along the Mississippi about forty miles north of Quincy, and christened the new settlement Nauvoo. Among his earliest ventures was to go to Washington to ask President Van Buren for federal reparations for the Mormons' loss of property in Missouri. The trip failed on that score, but Joseph succeeded in focusing national attention on the plight of the Latter-day Saints.[29] Mormons would soon find that national attention was a mixed blessing.

When first settled, Nauvoo was swampy and malarial, but within a couple of years the Saints made a life there and began to prosper. In fact, by the early 1840s, Nauvoo was the second largest city in Illinois (behind Chicago), with a chartered government and a city militia that was the largest armed force in the state. And, as Remini notes, the Prophet was the city's mayor, its chief justice, lieutenant general of the militia, trustee for the local university, real estate agent, publisher of a newspaper, owner of a store, and part owner of a steamboat.[30] Perhaps because his stature in Nauvoo bred a sense of security, Smith began to expand on the doctrines of the church. In 1842, he completed and published the *Book of Abraham*. In that work—combined with new ideas that were emerging in his preaching in the early 1840s and older ideas from the *Book of Moses,* published in the previous decade—Smith developed an impressively original set of theological positions: that God had originally been a corporeal (human) being, that in fact there were many gods, that there were many creations, and that it was possible (indeed desirable) to baptize the dead, which would permit the celestial reunion of extended family in the afterlife. The *Book of Abraham* also speculated about the cursed origins of the Negro race.[31]

Security proved fleeting. Relations with the Gentiles began to sour as early as 1842, and by 1844 anti-Mormon sentiment in the region had grown to a fevered pitch. In June of that year, Smith responded intemperately to a critical broadside in a local newspaper. He had the city council declare the paper a public nuisance, imposed martial law, and ordered the marshal to destroy the presses. Matters escalated rapidly. Illinois's governor mobilized the state's militia but promised legal protection to Smith if he would stand trial for the destruction of the press. Smith ordered the city's militia to disarm, but fled to Iowa, fearing for his safety. At Emma's urging, however, he returned to Illinois and surrendered. Within four days, he was dead, murdered by an armed mob while waiting for his trial.[32]

There's no single explanation for the antipathy that dogged the Saints wherever they settled. In New York, opposition was largely religious. The fact that the church was so aggressive, even imperialist, in its evangelizing was not a sufficient explanation, for proselytizing was part of the normal course of religious business in America, especially in upstate New York. But if proselytizing per se wasn't an issue, Smith's charismatic success in expanding membership was a source of irritation among leaders of mainstream flocks. Local opposition was also theological. Some dissent came from within his own flock, especially as other elders claimed gifts of revelation and prophesy. But most opposition came from without. One concern was Mormonism's unconventional and unyielding doctrines. Joseph's claim that other faiths were "false" religions and "abominations in the sight of God" made coexistence difficult. And many non-Mormons considered the notion that the Bible was incomplete—worse, that it was wrong in some respects—to be blasphemous. They thought Joseph arrogant, at the least, in presuming to offer a new "bible" to the world. And even if *The Book of Mormon* was an interestingly American version of Judeo-Protestantism, the themes and stories struck many as both contrived and dangerously nutty. Those objections, combined with the lingering suspicion that Joseph was a charlatan, made Mormonism an uncomfortable religious fit, even in the Burned-Over District.[33]

In Kirtland, suspicion about religious deviance was complemented by political concerns about the number of Mormons moving to the region. The concerns were twofold. First, Mormons' prosperity, combined with their almost tribal insularity—and commitment to taking care of their own—engendered jealousy and resentment. In addition, Mormon immigration threatened to alter the balance of local democratic power. This was apparently what agitated an anti-Mormon mob in 1832, as it dragged Joseph from his home and stripped, tarred, and beat him almost to death. But there were also stresses within the church. Perhaps the most substantial involved Joseph's decision to start a bank—despite Ohio's refusal to charter it—at precisely the time that the American banking system was collapsing. Smith's bank failed, leaving unpaid creditors, a mountain of worthless notes, and a large and vocal number of discontented Saints. They accused Joseph of being a liar and fraud, not to mention a blasphemer, imposter, and false prophet. Smith fled Kirtland out of fear for his safety even among his own people, though many of those who spoke against him eventually thought better and joined him in Zion.[34]

In Missouri, internal dissent was present. Some of it migrated from Kirtland over matters of finance. Some of it was linked to a secret society (Danites) that confronted and drove out dissenters, sometimes violently. And some of it was linked to an accusation that Oliver Cowdery, a respected elder of the church, had leveled against Joseph. The charge was adultery. Cowdery was excommunicated. Most of the troubles, however, came from outside the faith. As in Kirtland, non-Mormons worried about the balance of political power. That worry was intensified by the national dispute over slavery and Missouri's status as a slave state. The church was moderately antislavery (though not in the least sympathetic to blacks). The antislavery stance agitated proslavers, who were angry, reactionary, and in no mood to tolerate an odd and prosperous group that might challenge their political domination. Nor did it endear Mormons to the local community that they were theocratic, tended to be friendly with certain Indian tribes, and viewed their settlement in Missouri as a divine inheritance, based on rights superior to local (or national) law. When the church organized its own militia to meet and retaliate against threats and violence, the state had its pretext for proclaiming the Saints to be insurrectionary and driving them out of Missouri.[35]

Joseph's destruction of the newspaper in Nauvoo was emblematic of two substantial worries that provoked Gentiles in Illinois to follow Missouri's lead in expelling the Mormons. The first involved the potent combination of theocracy, political ambition, even arrogance, and arbitrary government. Political ambition was evident in Joseph's third-party bid for president of the United States in 1844, running against the Whig Henry Clay and the Democrat James K. Polk on a notably liberal platform. This in itself was harmless enough, at least in Illinois. But the move to theocratic authoritarianism—evidenced by Joseph's multiple public offices, his armed militia, his use of secret councils for control and governance, the destruction of the press, and the imposition of martial law—suggested to outsiders that Joseph's presidential foray was an expression of a power-hungry personality unconstrained by rational limitations.[36]

The second worry concerned an issue that underlay the crisis over Joseph's destruction of the press. It involved Mormon families. At first blush, this was a strange worry, for Mormon communities were largely communities of nuclear families, recognizable as such by even the most socially orthodox persons. If Jacob Cochran repudiated marriage, the Saints positively sanctified it. This fact alone made Mormons appear more conventional than some of the other religious experimenters of the eighteenth and nineteenth centuries. Beneath the surface, however, was an unconventional familial arrangement that combined Cochran's polyamory with the Mormon celebration of marriage.

The move to polygamy wasn't predictable in the beginning. *The Book of Mormon* contains not a single favorable doctrinal mention of plural marriage. There is, in fact, one passage that seems critical of the practice:

Behold, David and Solomon truly had many wives and concubines, which thing was abominable before me, saith the Lord. . . . Wherefore, I the Lord God will not suffer that this people shall do like unto them of old. Wherefore, my brethren, hear me and hearken to the word of the Lord: For there shall not any man among you have save it be one wife; and concubines he shall have none; For I, the Lord God, delight in the chastity of women. And whoredoms are an abomination before me; thus saith the Lord of Hosts. (Jacob 2:24–28)

Clouding the clarity of this passage, Joseph received a revelation on July 17, 1831, in which he was instructed on intermarriage with the tribes: "It is my will, that in time, ye should take unto you wives of the Lamanites and Nephites, that their posterity may become white, delightsome and Just, for even now their females are more virtuous than the gentiles." William W. Phelps committed this revelation to writing some time later, but he also cogitated over it: "I asked brother Joseph privately, how 'we,' that were mentioned in the revelation could take wives from the 'natives'—as we were all married men? He replied instantly[,] 'In the same manner that Abraham took Hagar and Katurah; and Jacob took Rachel[,] Bilhah and Zilpah: by revelation—the saints of the Lord are always directed by revelation.'"[37]

Perhaps coincidentally, beginning around 1832, Smith and Brigham Young began aggressively to seek converts from among the Cochranites in Maine. In fact, the church held two conferences in Saco in 1834. Calling Cochran "John the Baptist for the Mormon apostles," Ridlon dismissively observed that "a full-blooded Cochranite made a first-class Mormon saint." Ridlon attributed Mormon success in Saco to a shared commitment to emotional religiosity, prurience, and sexual predation, which rendered converts oblivious to mundane responsibilities toward their already existing families. Whether Ridlon's conflation of the two groups was justified, it was certainly the case that a number of early converts to Mormonism came from the remnants of Cochran's movement and joined the Saints first in New York, migrating eventually to Ohio, Missouri, Illinois, and Utah. And the term "spiritual wife," which would come to be embraced by Brigham Young and other Mormons, originated with Cochran.[38]

Joseph himself began to explore intimate relations outside his marriage to Emma around 1833 in Kirtland, though it's possible he did so even earlier. His initial foray in Kirtland didn't begin as a marriage, but was sealed roughly two years after the affair commenced. The object of his affection was Fanny Alger, who lived with the Smiths. She was sixteen at the time. Joseph tried to keep the relationship a secret, but when it nonetheless became public, Emma was livid, dismissing Fanny from the house. Some of the faithful were scandalized to the point of disaffection from the church. Indeed, Oliver Cowdery's objection to the affair was a ground for his charge that Joseph had committed adultery.[39] The explosive character of the relationship might have been one reason the church in 1835 adopted a declaration on marriage, which included the following: "Inasmuch as this Church of Christ has been reproached with the crime of fornication, and polygamy: we declare that we believe that one man should have one wife: and one woman but one husband, except in case of death, when either is at liberty to marry again. It is not right to persuade a woman to be baptized contrary to the will of her husband, neither is it lawful to influence her to leave her husband."[40]

Despite this declaration, Joseph began formally to enter into "celestial marriages" around 1838. Brodie calculates that he had at least forty-seven such unions — excluding Fanny Alger. She estimates that this number is understated, based partly on evidence discovered after the first printing of her book. Other historians contend the number is fewer than forty-eight, one suggesting that it was "at least twenty-seven." Still others estimate that it was much higher, as many as eighty-four. Because Brodie's is among the best documented accounts, I'll use her number as a rough estimate. There was no single pattern to Joseph's plural marriages. Often he was drawn to a woman who was a member of a household with whom he was boarding, or who was herself boarding in Joseph's household, or who was the child, wife, or relative of a close associate. Some women were older (six were in their fifties, and one might have been even older) and some younger (ten, including Fanny Alger, were in their teens, and five of those were sixteen or younger). Most were single at the time they were sealed to Joseph, one was widowed, and thirteen were married to living husbands.[41] This last circumstance suggests that Mormon polygamy was both polygynous and polyandrous. Polyandry was highly circumscribed, however, as only select women participated, and even those were strictly limited to two husbands at a time. Men, in contrast, at least those who participated in polygamy (and there were many), tended to enjoy more than two wives. Brigham Young had fifty-five, though some of these were not celestial ("for eternity") but "for time only" (including several who were widows of Joseph Smith), some were probably not conjugal, and several were widows. Six of his wives had living husbands at the time of their marriage to Young. In a few of those cases, he removed competing husbands by assigning them to missionary or diplomatic duties hundreds or thousands of miles from their wives.[42]

For Smith at least, the single thread running fairly continuously through his unions was his attempt to keep them secret. Each wife, of course, was aware of her new status, as was the man who performed the ceremonial sealing. The men who presided over plural marital ceremonies were those whom Smith had authorized to enter into plural marriages themselves (and who thus had their own reasons to maintain secrecy). Doubtless, Joseph wanted secrecy for protection— from physical assault by anti-Mormons, from legal prosecution, from the risk that fellow Mormons might object and thereby disrupt the community. He also tried to keep virtually all of his unions secret from his wife, Emma, who fiercely opposed the relationships she knew about during his life and emphatically denied they existed after his murder. But information was mobile, and, try as he might, Joseph could not confine it. Rumors leaked first to members of the Mormon community (many of whom did object, especially irate husbands of women chosen to be celestial brides), then to surrounding non-Mormon communities (almost all of whom objected), and eventually (most ominously) to the nation. In May 1842, just as the Mormons were suspected of attempting to assassinate Governor Boggs of Missouri (a suspicion never proven), the *New York Herald* ran an item on Nauvoo, reporting rumors of "promiscuous intercourse without regard to the holy bonds of matrimony."[43]

Perhaps recognizing that he needed formally to justify nonmonogamous relations, Smith recorded a revelation on July 12, 1843. This revelation did essentially three things. It proclaimed Joseph to be the single quasi-papal head of the true church. It commanded Emma, as Joseph's "handmaid," to "abide and cleave unto [him] and to none else," and to "forgive my servant Joseph his trespasses" so that her own sins might in turn be forgiven. And it declared that the Latter-day Saints, like Judaic patriarchs ("as the promise was made unto Abraham"), were permitted to have multiple wives and concubines. This renewed promise included several elements. Any marriage that is covenanted "not by me, nor by my word" does not endure eternally but lasts only for life in this world. Any marriage, however, that is properly covenanted "by my word, which is my law" and "sealed . . . by the Holy Spirit of promise" will endure forever and will bring the spouses honor and glory in the afterlife. "Then" he added, "shall they be Gods, because they have no end . . . [and] because they have all power, and [even] the angels are subject unto them." Even if they commit a "sin or transgression [against] the new and everlasting covenant," the eternal celestial marriage would survive the resurrection, as long as the sin falls short of murder.[44]

It was crucial to establishing and sustaining this regime that the Priesthood have exclusive power over marriage and its dissolution, notwithstanding the state's claimed monopoly over marriage and divorce. In this way, Mormon priests' authority over marriage revisited the conflict between ecclesiastic and secular authorities in England and Europe centuries before. But one aspect of priestly authority went beyond claims of even old English clerics. Any woman who has been pure in marriage while her husband has committed adultery may, "by the power of my Holy Priesthood," be removed from her husband and assigned to another who has been faithful. And if a man who is married to a virgin "desire[s] to espouse another," he is not guilty of adultery, "for they are given unto him." In fact, "if he have ten virgins given unto him by this law, he cannot commit adultery; for they belong to him." On the other hand, "if one, or either of the ten virgins, after she is espoused, shall be with another man, she has committed adultery, and shall be destroyed; for they are given unto him to multiply and replenish the earth, according to my commandment."[45] The preoccupation with virgins was puzzling, as Joseph and other Mormon patriarchs asserted the freedom to take wives who fell outside the ordinary definition of the word. The matter of virginity aside, Joseph stayed true to form in keeping the revelation secret, except among his inner group. Even so, he would be dead within a year.

Within two months after Joseph's death, his church fractured into at least four groups. The following year, all of Smith's killers were acquitted, and persecution of the Mormons resumed. In 1846, the largest of the remnant groups, led by Brigham Young, again migrated westward. To the Mormon mind, this trek reenacted the Mosaic exodus of the Old Testament, and it would prove similarly central to Mormon identity. Young's group settled in 1847 in the Salt Lake Valley, outside the United States and presumably beyond the violent reach of American law and culture.[46] As one of his wives later quoted him: "We are now out of reach of our enemies, away from civilization, and we will do as we please, with none to molest. The Gentiles cannot reach us now. If they try it they will find themselves in trouble."[47] Six months later, the United States acquired dominion over the Mexican Cession, which included the very land on which the Mormons had just settled.[48]

THE SAINTS IN UTAH

Notwithstanding Young's desire to be rid of the Gentiles, the Mexican Cession was both a problem and an opportunity for the Saints. It was a problem, obviously, because American political power had not been consistently kind to the Mormons nor to their faith. But it was an opportunity because, as a territory, the land was yet to be formed as a political entity. As we've already seen in Chapter 5, under the various national rules governing the settlement of territories, preparing a territory for statehood required, at bottom, people—free white people who could organize and extend political and legal authority over previously ungoverned lands. Mormons were willing and able to perform this role. Initially, at least, they had minimal competition in settling the starkly desolate tracts that made up much of the Mexican Cession, though that, too, would soon change, especially with the discovery of gold in northern California. So the Saints came, turning the Salt Lake Valley and environs into prosperous settlements of Mormon families, while still more families fanned out far beyond the Salt Lake.[49] Families, however, were precisely the problem for a new Mormon territory. For despite the Saints' experience in Illinois, and despite knowing how contentious polygamy was both within and outside the community, Young continued to practice the principle, to justify it in religious terms, and to promote it among the patriarchal faithful. In 1852, he would make public to the world Joseph's 1843 revelation on plural marriage.[50]

Before he did so, however, he devised a constitution for a territory he named Deseret. Ever ambitious, he mapped for the proposed territory a gigantic area that would have covered most of the Mexican Cession, including portions of what are now the states of Colorado, New Mexico, Arizona, California, Nevada, Wyoming, Oregon, Idaho, and Utah. (He carefully excluded portions of New Mexico and northern California, both of which had substantial Gentile populations.) In 1849, he petitioned Congress to admit Deseret as a state. Congress paused. Statehood in the West was caught up in fierce and eventually catastrophic debates surrounding slavery. In 1850, Congress enacted a complex compromise around territorial settlement that gave a partial loaf to several competing political factions. Among other things, it carved out Utah and New Mexico as territories and, under the principle of popular sovereignty, authorized them to develop their own domestic institutions.[51] The phrase "domestic institutions" was a partly descriptive and partly euphemistic way of referring to families — most notably slaveholding families. In short, if either territory wished to permit slavery, it could do so. Like many whites outside the South, Young had no affection for slavery, but neither did he care for blacks. As late as 1863, three months after the Emancipation Proclamation, he would affirm that interracial marriage was prohibited. "Shall I tell you the law of God in regard to the African race? If the white man who belongs to the chosen seed mixes his blood with the seed of Cain, the penalty, under the law of God, is death on the spot. This will always be so."[52] As early as 1849, he had barred blacks from becoming priests, a prohibition that persisted in the church for 130 years.[53] As a matter of local option, then, and as long as Young's preferences held in the territory, Utah would be free and white. Could it also be polygamous?

In 1851, President Millard Fillmore appointed Young to be governor of the Utah Territory. As Joseph Smith had done in Nauvoo, Brigham Young wasted no time building a theocracy in Utah, where religion, government, and economy were unified in the Church of Jesus Christ of Latter-day Saints. Also like Smith before, Young wielded power aggressively to promote the interests of the church and, even more, his own authority as head of the church. Within a year, federal officers in Utah began returning East, claiming they feared for their personal safety and were concerned that Mormons were on the verge of a rebellion against the United States. At least one of Utah's representatives (a Gentile) recommended an official investigation of conditions in the territory. By 1855, Young asserted that his power as governor derived from God and that even the president could not interfere with it. This, combined with his earlier publication of Joseph's revelation on plural marriage, put the territorial government on a collision course with the nation.[54]

It did not help the Mormon cause that Young had begun to preach that polygamy was a religious sacrament for men of faith, nor that he himself had forty-nine wives by 1856. This was the year of a presidential election, and while the nascent Republican Party was not dominant, it was certainly ascendant in the wake of the Whig Party's rapid disintegration. The Republican platform of 1856 assailed the Democrats' policy of popular sovereignty for the territories, insisting that it was merely a cover for "those twin relics of barbarism—Polygamy, and Slavery." The Democrat James Buchanan won the White House, but that fact protected neither the Mormons nor the practice of polygamy from national scrutiny. One reason was that Democrats began to worry that political conflict over polygamy would unsettle the compromises reached in 1850 and 1854 over slavery, which could make the party vulnerable in future elections. In the Democrats' coalition, the various elements touching on slavery were of far greater importance than those pertaining to the Mormon question. Besides, there were plenty of signs that most of the nation agreed that polygamy was wrong, while there was no consensus at all that slavery or slaveholding families were. Exacerbating tensions between Mormon Utahans and the nation was the fact that, from the beginning of Utah's territorial status, a large number of federal appointees, including judges, were non-Mormon, and a few were patently anti-Mormon. This chafed the Saints, who wanted comprehensive control of the territory's destiny. They made no pretense of hiding their irritation.[55]

In the spring of 1857, William W. Drummond, an associate justice on the supreme court of the Utah Territory (a Gentile and much despised among Mormons), resigned. In a report to the president, he complained that Governor Young had dispensed with the rule of law, that Mormons recognized only the authority of their religious leaders and not of secular (federal) officers, and that elements in the Mormon community had committed murder, destroyed official records, harassed federal officers, and slandered the national government. These claims were not baseless. Drummond urged President Buchanan to replace Young with a non-Mormon governor and to send enough troops, as he put it, to establish the rule of law.[56] The chief justice of Utah's high court sent a similar report to the president. Some of Buchanan's advisors pressed him to commence a crusade against the Mormons, one political advantage of which would be to distract the country from agitation over slavery. Stephen A. Douglas, the Democrat who had just defeated Abraham Lincoln for a Senate seat from Illinois, insinuated that Mormons might well be "outlaws and alien enemies" and that Mormonism might justly be purged from the polity. This move was a plain attempt to inoculate himself against the charge that his party's position on popular sovereignty permitted not just slavery in the territories but polygamy as well. Despite the counterfeit motive, the rhetorical move made its point: the Democrats were no more friends of the Mormons than the Republicans were.[57]

By mid-1857, more than 2,500 troops had gathered in Kansas for a march on Utah. In June, Buchanan declared that Utah was in rebellion against the United States. In July, he appointed Alfred Cumming, a non-Mormon, as governor, dispatched him westward under military escort, and ordered the first deployment of troops from Kansas to Utah. By August, Young began making overtures to the tribes for the purpose of jointly repelling U.S. troops, and he declared martial law in the territory. For a time, Capt. Van Vliet of the Army attempted to negotiate with Young over the terms on which the military might approach and enter the Salt Lake Valley, but Young made it clear that the Mormons would forcibly resist any entry. In fact, the Nauvoo Legion engaged federal troops quite effectively on several occasions—burning grassland, stampeding cattle, harassing the troops, and looting from them. In November, Cumming finally arrived in Utah and hunkered down with the army outside Salt Lake City.[58]

Lest there be any question that the nation had drawn a line in the sand where the Saints were concerned, Buchanan made it clear in his Address of December 8, 1857, on the State of the Union. He denied that he had any "right to interfere . . . [w]ith the religious opinions of the Mormons, as long as they remained mere opinions." But, he said, Brigham Young had taken actions that put him at odds with the interests, institutions, and values of the United States. In this regard, Buchanan made no explicit mention of polygamy, though he doubtless had it mind when he described Mormons' beliefs as "deplorable in themselves and revolting to the moral and religious sentiments of all Christendom" and when he referred to "institutions at war with the laws both of God and man." Technically, the latter claim was not entirely accurate, as there was no "law of man" prohibiting polygamy in Utah at the time. Polygamy aside, however, Buchanan saw a second problem in what he called the "despotic power" being employed in Young's government. Since Utah's establishment as a territory, Young had served simultaneously in three substantial offices, two secular and one religious. He was governor, he was superintendent of Indian affairs, and he was head of the Mormon Church. As to Young's religious role, Buchanan said that the church professed "to govern its members and dispose of their property by direct inspiration and authority from the Almighty. [Young's] power has been, therefore, absolute over both church and state." Plus, he was agitating the tribes against the United States and was himself "collecting and fabricating arms and munitions of war." On Buchanan's view, these were problems for at least two reasons. One was that the unity of secular and religious offices violated the American principle of separation of church and state. The other was that Young's power was inherently hostile to the authority of the United States. "The people of Utah almost exclusively belong to this church, and believing with a fanatical spirit that he is governor of the Territory by divine appointment, they obey his commands as if these were direct revelations from

Heaven." In a case of conflict between Young and the United States, therefore, the members of the church would doubtless yield "obedience to his will." For these reasons, Buchanan said he had appointed a new governor to replace Young, appointed other federal officers to replace the scores who had fled, and sent troops to support the new officials. "As Chief Executive Magistrate I was bound to restore the supremacy of the Constitution and laws" in Utah.[59]

Within a few months, Buchanan proclaimed a full pardon for treason and sedition to all Utahans who agreed to submit to the authority of the United States. And after intensive negotiations in the spring of 1858, Cumming peacefully arrived under armed escort and succeeded Young as governor. After marching through a deserted Salt Lake City, the army would encamp at Camp Floyd, roughly fifty miles from the city. As matters calmed, Saints who had fled the valley, anticipating violent calamity, returned to their homes.[60] If Buchanan's worries about polygamy were secondary to his interest in securing obedience to national authority in the territories, that hierarchy of values would soon change for the nation. In November, the Republican Party gained control of the House of Representatives. Within three years, Republicans would control both houses of Congress and the White House. In contrast with the preceding Democratic administration, Republican policy toward Utah would rely less on the military (which for five years was tied down fighting a brutal civil war to the east) than on the coercive power of law.[61]

And the Republicans would take dead aim at polygamy. In response, Mormons would revise their strategy for defending their way of life. In the mid-1850s, the strategy had been one of outright defiance, with Young sometimes flirting with the possibility of secession (even though Utah was not yet a "sovereign" state). Eventually, they would adopt a three-pronged strategy. The first involved what Sarah Barringer Gordon has characterized as evasion and obfuscation. Church leaders encouraged practitioners to hide evidence of polygamy from the outside world and, if necessary, to lie about the practice. The second was to invoke the value of local control under the constitutional banner of federalism. The third, and in some tension with the second, was to invoke the constitutional right to the free exercise of religion.[62] It is likely that these legal battles would have never occurred had the issues not been caught up in Utah's territorial status and aspiration for statehood. But territorial status, like the status of the tribes, gave Congress both the opportunity and the institutional authority to begin to nationalize the monogamous marital family. Once nationalized, the Supreme Court would eventually give it a constitutional blessing.

POLYGAMY AND THE CONSTITUTIONAL ORDER

As we've already seen, the Saints' defense of polygamy was primarily religious. The religious reasons were straightforward and familiar: the principle of polygamy was justified by revelation, it was consistent with the way of life of the earliest and revered Judaic patriarchs, its practice was essential to achieving the highest stations in the afterlife, and it complied with God's commands to be fruitful and multiply and to raise children in faith. Doubtless, most Mormons were sincere in believing the religious basis for the doctrine and in insisting that the Constitution protected its free exercise. And it's true that Mormon polygamy produced more children per father than did monogamy, even as the number of children per wife was lower than in monogamous marriages.[63]

But religion was not the only justification for the principle. Proponents sometimes offered moral justifications, rooted not in religion but in a kind of natural law. Put simply, monogamy was an unnatural form of social organization. As Orson Pratt urged in 1852, "Only about one-fifth of the population of the globe . . . believe in the one-wife system; the other four-fifths believe in the doctrine of a plurality of wives, . . . and are not so narrow and contracted in their minds as some of the nations of Europe and America." Numbers aside, the value of polygamy was also moral, on Pratt's view, because it helped reduce the social need for prostitution. This, he argued, was an unequivocal good. If so, it was inexplicitly rooted in a particular assumption about the character of male sexuality: that men would tend to seek multiple outlets for sex, regardless of whether men were in monogamous marriages. (This is an allegation that both Marx and Engels leveled against modern capitalist societies, which, in form at least, were monogamous.) The assumption would rest in uneasy tension, however, with the Saints' religious justification: that polygamy was a good in itself and its practice motivated by devotion to virtue and self-restraint. Given the assumption, moreover, the justification from religious virtue might seem suspicious in light of the fact that most wives in plural marriages entered marriage in their late teens, regardless of the age of the husband.[64]

Aside from the moral advantages derived from inhibiting prostitution, it's fair to ask what else might make polygamy socially advantageous or attractive. The answer to this question, according to polygamy's defenders, was rooted both in demographic considerations and in values of social care and status. Marriage, the argument went, was beneficial for women. Chiefly, it provided security, which was important to survival and, potentially, to flourishing. When men died, however, women were at risk of not being adequately supported. Life on the frontier in the nineteenth century could kill men. So might war. As to the latter, Mormon men did fight various native tribes (and sometimes paid with their lives), and in 1846 they participated in the Mexican War at the behest of the United States (although they did not see combat in that conflict). According to the demographic argument, these events made for an under-supply of men, which left widows and unmarried women vulnerable. Polygamy solved this social problem. There's no doubt that life was hard and that men (including husbands) died. This meant that a polygamous man might well end up marrying a widow—or an "older woman," as husbands sometimes put it. ("Older" in this context might refer to any widow at least eighteen years old.) Still, the difficulty with this argument, from a demographic standpoint, was that men were not in short supply in Utah. According to three censuses in at least one county in central Utah from 1860 to 1890, the numbers of men and women were strikingly equal.[65]

Thus, if polygamy had a sociological or demographic justification, especially from women's perspectives, it was for reasons other than the supply of men. Two reasons are plausible. One is that some women were able to gain social status when they were able to "marry up" through a polygamous marriage. This was a nontrivial social good for the women involved, at least according to some historical testimony. Another reason rests on the social potency of habit to reinforce a sense not only of normalcy but also of rightness. In short, women came to accept the principle because it was familiar (and was reinforced by social norms and rituals). This is not necessarily to suggest that women's beliefs in the value of polygamy were attributable to "false consciousness," to borrow Catharine MacKinnon's phrase, for women's testimony often spoke intelligently of polygamy's advantages, especially where domestic support and child rearing were concerned. Some of these advantages were also supported by evidence of the mortality, morbidity, and welfare of children in polygamous families, as compared with monogamous families around the same time. But it's true that women had a second-class status in the church, the community, and the family. "The man is the head and God of the woman," Brigham Young is reported to have said. During a minor challenge to his authority, he angrily lashed out: "Great God! Could women trammel me in this manner? NO! All their counsel and wisdom (although there are many good women) don't weigh as much as the weight of a fly turd. . . . It is not woman's place to counsel her husband." Thus, some women's views could be partly attributable to a less-than-reflective acceptance of the social milieu in which they found themselves.[66]

On their face, the justifications for polygamy suggested that the practice might not be irrational as a matter of social policy. But plural marriage plainly had plenty of detractors not only among the non-Mormon population but also among Mormons and, especially, ex-Mormons. One of the most famous was Ann Eliza Webb Young. There's some question about whether she was Brigham Young's twenty-seventh wife or his fifty-second. Regardless, she had grown up in the faith and knew well the principle to which she was attaching. Still, after five years of marriage, she filed for and received a divorce. As a parting gift to her former husband, she published a book about her experience and commenced a lecture tour that generated much attention. Her critique of Mormon polygamy was wide ranging. Wives, she said, led lives of jealousy, depression, humiliation, violence, and desperation. They competed with one another for their husband's attention and resources. Husbands were autocratic and controlling, not only in the household but also in dictating how their wives would vote. Women who were married to one but sealed to another were frequently uncertain about the paternity of their children. In contrast with the picture that women were cared for, Ann Eliza urged that wives had to be self-supporting, especially when their husbands were sent away for service as missionaries. And when missionary husbands returned from service, they frequently brought with them young women who were eager to be wives but unaware that they might be merely one among many in the same household. By Ann Eliza's report, Brigham could not consistently recognize his wives when he passed them on the street. More severely, some wives (though not Brigham's) died of starvation or exposure. Polygamy, she said, was "a system of bondage that is more cruel than African slavery ever was, since it claims body and soul alike."[67]

If the claim about African slavery was rhetorical exaggeration, it resonated among non-Mormons. Even before Ann Eliza's book appeared, Republicans accurately detected nativist advantage in taking on an institution that smacked more of Africa or Asia (or the native tribes) than of Europe. Polygamy, they urged, was morally unacceptable in a Christian society. And the territories should be reserved for white nuclear (Christian) families. To press the point in public policy, the Republican Congress enacted the Morrill Anti-Bigamy Act with President Lincoln's signature in July of 1862.[68] It made bigamy in any territory of the United States a crime, subject to fine or imprisonment up to five years. It nullified all enactments of the Territory of Utah or the provisional government of the State of Deseret that might imply approval of polygamy. And it limited the value of real property of any nonprofit entity (including a church) in any territory to $50,000; any real property acquired in violation of that limitation was subject to escheat to the United States.

Mere law on the books, however, was weak. Preoccupied with larger concerns, Lincoln was content to leave Brigham Young alone, if Young would leave him alone. Young complied, which meant that polygamy flourished despite the Morrill Act. If law was to be the nation's preferred method for social control, then the nation would have to control institutions of enforcement. The Poland Act of 1874 established that control, not in the territories generally but only in Utah.[69] The Act stripped lower territorial courts of considerable areas of jurisdiction, delegated jurisdiction in all substantial civil and criminal cases to district courts (appointed by the United States), and provided for a writ of error from the Supreme Court of the United States to the supreme court of the territory in criminal cases involving capital punishment or bigamy. The Act delegated to the U.S. marshal responsibility for serving and executing all process and writs. It delegated to the U.S. district attorney authority over the prosecution of all criminal cases in the territory, regardless of the court in which they were commenced. It stripped the territory of authority over marshals and prosecuting attorneys. It revised rules for empaneling grand juries and for striking petit juries. And it required that the judge, not the jury, pronounce punishment in criminal cases. Mormons were keenly aware of the stakes of this legislation and had lobbied intensively for its defeat when it was pending in the Congress. In the end, however, the political forces they faced—influenced in part by Ann Eliza Young's lectures back East—were too large.[70] The effect was a national takeover of the legal and administrative apparatus of a previously autonomous territory.

Within four months, George Reynolds, private secretary to Brigham Young, was indicted for violating the Morrill Act. After negotiating with the district attorney, church leaders had tapped Reynolds for the assignment, not only to test the constitutionality of the Act but also to influence the public face of polygamy. He was relatively young (thirty-two years old), had been a polygamist for only two months before the indictment, and had only two wives. He was devout. And, just as important to the Saints' leadership, he did not hold a prominent position in the Church.[71]

His counsel's primary strategy of defense was an old one: evasion and obfuscation. Every person on the witness list who was called to testify to the existence of a bigamous union denied all knowledge of the second marriage. In short, they lied. The case would have been lost to the prosecutor but for his inspired decision to find the second wife and summon her to testify, despite the fact that she was not on the witness list. Caught unaware, Reynolds could not coach her. Nor could he invoke a spousal testimonial privilege, because he denied the marriage on which a claim of privilege would be based. So she testified, with naive honesty, about her marriage. Within two hours of the close of testimony and argument, Reynolds was convicted. Although the supreme court of the territory reversed on a technicality, the district attorney secured a second indictment through process that was, to be kind, procedurally irregular. For the second trial, the second wife was nowhere to be found. Invoking her prior testimony, however, the prosecutor won a second conviction after a trial that was also procedurally irregular. The territorial supreme court affirmed, and Reynolds, via the Poland Act, obtained a writ of error from the Supreme Court of the United States.[72]

There Reynolds's counsel pressed his second strategy: to challenge the constitutionality of the Morrill Act. Specifically, they urged that Reynolds had a right under the free exercise clause to marry more than one woman at a time if he believed it to be his religious duty to do so. There was some support for the proposition in contemporary English law. *Regina v. Wagstaff* had held that parents who, for religious reasons, denied medical care to their children could not be convicted of manslaughter.[73] Reynolds's trial judge, however, had refused to charge the jury to this effect. Instead, he charged that "if the defendant, under the influence of a religious belief that it was right, . . . deliberately married a second time, having a first wife living, . . . the want of understanding on his part that he was committing a crime did not excuse him; but the law inexorably implies the criminal intent." Against Reynolds's objection, the trial judge offered yet another charge on the social cost of polygamy—especially the impact of the practice on children:

> I think it not improper, in the discharge of your duties in this case, that you
> should consider what are to be the consequences to the innocent victims
> of this delusion. As this contest goes on, they multiply, and there are pure-
> minded women and there are innocent children,—innocent in a sense even
> beyond the degree of the innocence of childhood itself. These are to be the

sufferers; and as jurors fail to do their duty, and as these cases come up in the Territory of Utah, just so do these victims multiply and spread themselves over the land.

The Supreme Court's opinion in *Reynolds v. U.S.* addressed challenges to both charges.[74]

Did the Morrill Act violate the Constitution's guarantee of the free exercise of religion? To answer that question, the Court investigated the history of the political meaning of "religion," especially in Virginia. The Court adopted Thomas Jefferson's view that the First Amendment erected a "wall of separation between church and state." But the Court concluded, as had President Buchanan before, that the wall barred only the regulation of opinion or belief; government was free to regulate "actions which [are] in violation of social duties or subversive of good order."

Was polygamy such an action? To answer this question, the Court investigated the history of laws prohibiting polygamy, initially in Europe and England, eventually in the United States, especially in Virginia. It's here that the Court first staked out a national commitment to monogamy as constitutive of life in civilized societies. "Polygamy has always been odious among the northern and western nations of Europe." Self-consciously or not, this identified the nation with predominately Protestant Europe. In fact, until the Mormons came along, the Court said, polygamy "was almost exclusively a feature of the life of Asiatic and of African people." The Court noted that, under English common law, simultaneous marriage to more than one person was "an offence against society," punishable in ecclesiastical courts. By statute during the reign of James I (1603–1625), the offense of bigamy was triable in civil courts and punishable by death. This statute, the Court recited, was "re-enacted, generally with some modifications, in all the colonies." Even Virginia, which had just enacted Jefferson's bill for religious freedom, adopted a version of the statute of James I, "death penalty included." The implication here was that, if Virginians were willing to kill polygamists, then surely the framers of the First Amendment did not intend for polygamy to be constitutionally protected. Since that time, the Court noted, polygamy was at all times punishable as a crime in all parts of the United States (until recently in Utah).

The upshot was that marriage was a fundamental institution, for reasons both "sacred" (the Court's term) and secular, without which the constitutional order itself was imperiled. "Upon [marriage] society may be said to be built, and out of its fruits spring social relations and social obligations and duties, with which government is necessarily required to deal." In fact, the very government a society enjoys, whether despotic or republican, grows out of the form of marriage a society permits. Polygamy promotes patriarchy, which, "when applied to large communities, fetters the people in stationary despotism." Monogamy is republican. Thus, Congress had authority to prohibit polygamy in the territories, and religious motive did not exempt Mr. Reynolds from an otherwise authoritative enactment.

As for the trial court's charge to the jury concerning the evils of polygamy, the Supreme Court said it was harmless and not erroneous. The judge had merely called attention "to the peculiar character of the crime." He did not attempt to incite passion or prejudice. He aimed only "to keep [the jurors] impartial."

There were several items of irony and interest here. One involved the Court's invocation of the sacred to limit religiously motivated action. Another was the Court's oddly incomplete account of political history, which ignored not only monogamous despotisms but also the long history of concubinage among the royalty and aristocracy even of northern and western Europe. Still another was the Court's hand wringing over patriarchy, essentially declaring it to be un-American, despite the fact that the United States practiced its own republican version of patriarchy. In fact, Mormon Utah was one of the few places in the United States where women could vote. To be sure, there were limits to women's freedom in exercising that right, supervised as they were by husbands and church fathers. But they did possess the formal right—for a time, at least.

In 1882, Congress enacted the Edmunds Act, which amended portions of the Morrill Act.[75] It redefined polygamy to include also Mormon ceremonies of celestial marriage, in which the husband would simultaneously (not merely *subsequently*) marry more than one person. And, for the first time in a federal statute, it criminalized cohabitation involving a man and more than one woman, so as to reach plural relations in which marriage could not be proved. But the Edmunds Act went still further, in an attempt to secure national, non-Mormon control over the territory. It barred from service on certain juries in Utah any person who was engaged or believed in bigamy, polygamy, or cohabitation. It barred bigamists, polygamists, or cohabitors—and women who cohabited with them—from voting or holding any office, appointed or elected, in the territory. And it transferred supervision and administrative control of elections to institutions responsible to the national government.

Three years later, the Supreme Court upheld the constitutionality of the Edmunds Act's provision for disenfranchisement.[76] Despite the theory of popular sovereignty that had animated the nation's territorial policy since before the Civil War, the Court said that Congress alone had authority to say whether the people of the territory (or any subset of the people) may vote or participate in the making of laws.[77] In fact, the United States could "declare that no one but a [monogamously] married person shall be entitled to vote."[78] All the more could Congress prohibit polygamists, bigamists, and cohabitors from voting.

> No legislation can be supposed more wholesome and necessary in the founding of a free, self-governing commonwealth, fit to take rank as one of the co-ordinate states of the Union, than that which seeks to establish it on the basis of the idea of the family, as consisting in a springing from the union for life of one man and one woman in the holy estate of matrimony; the sure foundation of all that is stable and noble in our civilization; the best guaranty

of that reverent morality which is the source of all beneficent progress in social and political improvement.[79]

In short, polygamists lacked attachment to a social institution—the monogamous family—that was essential to free government. Thus, Congress could prohibit nonmonogamists from asserting any sort of "political influence" in the polity.[80]

Two years later, Congress enacted the Edmunds-Tucker Act, which systematically and comprehensively seized control of the territory.[81] The Act contained substantive, evidentiary, procedural, and administrative provisions. Substantively, the Act made adultery a crime, broadened the definition of incest, and provided for punishment, including imprisonment in the penitentiary, for a new federal crime of fornication. Technically, these prohibitions applied to any territory of the United States, though, things being what they were, they had special resonance in Utah. Still other substantive provisions expressly applied only in Utah. For example, the Act nullified territorial laws that had permitted illegitimate children to inherit from their father, set forth detailed provisions regulating widows' rights to dower, disenfranchised all women in Utah (regardless of their marital or cohabitational status), and imposed new oaths for voting and holding office. These oaths went beyond the requirements of the old Edmunds Act, in that prospective voters or office-holders now had to attest to their marital status, that they would obey the Constitution and laws of the United States (including specifically the Edmunds Act and the Edmunds-Tucker Act), and that they would not "directly or indirectly, aid or abet, counsel or advise, any other person to commit any of [the] crimes" described in those statutes. The Act made it easier to prosecute crimes related to marriage by modifying the testimonial privilege between spouses and specifying standards for proving the existence of a marriage. The Act abolished local control of schools in Utah and prohibited the use of religious literature in schools. And the Act formally dissolved the Perpetual Emigrating Fund Company, which the Mormon Church had incorporated to provide financial assistance to persons who wished to emigrate to Utah, and dissolved the corporate entity that was the Church of Jesus Christ of Latter-day Saints.

As the Poland Act had done before, the Edmunds-Tucker Act also expanded national control over procedure, law making, and the administration of justice. This included a provision for procuring witnesses in crimes of sex or marriage, a new procedure for prosecuting adultery, a requirement that every ceremony of marriage be publically certified, a procedure for the escheat of property to the United States, and a procedure for compelling the production of records. These provisions and procedures applied in any territory. Others, however, pertained solely to Utah. The Act authorized new powers in U.S. commissioners and U.S. marshals there, stripped that territory's probate courts of their authority, prohibited popular election of judges (replacing elections with presidential appointment), enhanced national control of elections, imposed national control over redistricting and apportionment, and required congressional approval of any election officers.

And the Act annulled local laws regulating the militia in Utah and required national approval of all subsequent regulations of the territory's militia.

Such were the elements of free government as Congress conceived them. With respect to qualifications and oaths for voting and holding office, Idaho's territorial legislature enacted a statute that largely tracked the Edmunds-Tucker Act. It barred from voting and holding office practitioners of bigamy or polygamy and persons who teach, advise, counsel, or encourage others to engage in bigamy or polygamy. But the territorial act went one step further, barring anyone "who is a member of any order, organization, or association which teaches, advises, counsels, or encourages its members or devotees, or any other persons" to engage in bigamy or polygamy.[82]

In 1889, Samuel D. Davis and others were indicted and convicted in (the ironically named) Oneida County, in the Idaho Territory, for conspiring to "pervert and obstruct the due administration of the laws in the territory." Specifically, they took the oath to register to vote, despite the fact that they were Mormons. Davis challenged his conviction through a petition for a writ of habeas corpus, claiming that his imprisonment violated the First Amendment's prohibition of an establishment of religion. The district court granted the writ, then dismissed Davis's claim and remanded him to the sheriff to serve out his sentence. Davis appealed to the Supreme Court.[83]

The Court took up the claim as involving not establishment but the free exercise of religion. And it rejected the claim on grounds that closely resembled an establishment of religion.[84] "Bigamy and polygamy are crimes by the laws of all civilized and Christian countries. . . . They tend to destroy the purity of the marital relation, to disturb the peace of families, to degrade woman, and to debase man. . . . Few crimes are more pernicious to the best interests of society, and receive more general or more deserved punishment." As for Davis's claim that polygamy was protected as an aspect of the free exercise of religion, the Court made three moves. The first, and consistent with its earlier decision in *Reynolds,* was to narrowly define religion. For constitutional purposes, religion included beliefs or opinions and extended to modes of worship; but it did not encompass actions, especially actions that are "inimical to the peace, good order, and morals of society." Second, criminal laws that promote these ends were justified, even against a claim of religious liberty. Such claims "must be subordinate to the criminal laws of the country, passed with reference to actions regarded by general consent as properly the subjects of punitive legislation." Third, polygamy was such an action.

But why? One reason was that, if the free exercise of religion protected religiously motivated action, in contrast with mere belief, any number of heinous activities would be exempt from regulation. For example, "there have been sects which denied as a part of their religious tenets that there should be any marriage tie, and advocated promiscuous intercourse of the sexes, as prompted by the passions of its members." The court may have had in mind the Oneida Community, even if the Oneidans' actual practices didn't entirely conform with the Court's conjured vision of random acts of sex. "And history discloses . . . that the neces-sity of human sacrifices, on special occasions, has been a tenet of many sects." Surely, the Court reasoned, the Constitution did not impose a principle that would create a slippery slope to recognition of these practices. The second reason was that polygamy was universally condemned among modern Christians. "Probably never before in the history of this country has it been seriously contended that the whole punitive power of the government for acts, recognized by the general consent of the Christian world in modern times as proper matters for prohibitory legislation, must be suspended in order that the tenets of a religious sect encourag-ing crime may be carried out without hindrance." As suggested above, this move was ironic, in that it rejected a claim of free exercise by relying on a position that resembled an establishment, but irony is sometimes lost on judges, and it was in this case.

Three months after *Davis v. Beason* was announced, the Court rendered its decision in *Late Corporation of the Church of Jesus Christ of Latter-Day Saints v. U.S.*[85] The issue was essentially whether Congress had authority, under the Edmunds-Tucker Act, to repeal the charter of the Mormon Church and seize the church's property. In a divided decision, the Court held that Congress possessed plenary power over the territories and that the provisions in question, therefore, were not unconstitutional. This alone would have been an adequate ground for judgment, but the Court's majority did not resist the chance to take a swipe at the church's "nefarious doctrine" of polygamy, calling it "a crime against the laws, and abhorrent to the sentiments and feelings of the civilized world. . . . The orga-nization of a community for the spread and practice of polygamy is . . . a return to barbarism. It is contrary to the spirit of Christianity, and of the civilization which Christianity has produced in the western world." Just as the free exercise of reli-gion did not extend to religiously motivated political assassination or, as practiced "by our own ancestors in Britain," human sacrifice, the freedom of religion did not protect plural marriage. Led by Justice Fuller, three justices dissented, not be-cause Congress lacked "the power to extirpate polygamy in any of the territories," but because the Constitution prohibited Congress from confiscating the property of a corporation, even if the corporation were engaged in criminal activity.

The United States ended up seizing real property and personalty with a com-bined value of more than $1,000,000, much of which was frittered away by the court-appointed receiver. Four months after *Late Corporation* was announced, the president of the church received a revelation from Jesus that the Latter-day Saints should discontinue the practice of polygamy. He committed the revelation to writing, which he signed and published as "The Manifesto." This document repudiated the practice of polygamy, though it did not purport to alter existing plu-ral marriages. Within two weeks, the General Conference of the church officially adopted the Manifesto.[86] Three years later, Congress adopted a resolution releas-ing confiscated assets of the Church, justifying the release on the ground that the church had ceased practicing and advocating polygamy.[87] In 1894, President

Cleveland signed the Enabling Act permitting the people of Utah to ratify a constitution, form a government, and gain admission as a state "on an equal footing with the original States." Consistent with Congress's earlier disenfranchisement of women in Utah, the Enabling Act permitted only men to participate in the process leading to statehood. The Act also provided "that perfect toleration of religious sentiment shall be secured, and that no inhabitant of said State shall ever be molested in person or property on account of his or her mode of religious worship: Provided, that polygamous or plural marriages are forever prohibited."[88] In January 1896, eighteen years after Brigham Young's death, President Cleveland proclaimed Utah to be a state.[89] Two days later, officials for the newly formed government of the state were inaugurated in the Mormon Tabernacle.

The resolution of the Mormon Question completed a process through which the monogamous family was both nationalized and constitutionalized. This process had begun much earlier in the nineteenth century against discrete populations: the native tribes. By the end of that century, Congress had taken control of educating tribal children, suppressed familial arrangements that failed to conform with the common-law template, prescribed bourgeois nuclear families to take their place, and forced those families off of communal tribal lands onto single-family plots, from which thousands of Indians were eventually (sometimes ruthlessly) removed. If this result was perverse, many white Americans perceived it simply to be a price of civilization.

Mormons, too, formed insular communities, and they identified primally with Native Americans. Still, they weren't tribal in quite the same way the Indians were. They had certain advantages, also, from the standpoint of the constitutional order. They were bourgeois and enormously productive from a material standpoint. Their religious worldview combined familiar and obscure elements of patriarchal Judaism and Protestant Christianity. And they were white. Still, local communities from New York to Missouri responded violently toward the Saints. There were several reasons for this, most of which had nothing to do with polygamy or sex. By the time the Saints were forced from Nauvoo, however, the two central objections to the group involved its penchant for autocratic theocracy and its embrace of a nonconforming family. In the official American mind, these two elements were linked. Polygamy was barbarism. It debased women. It was inherently authoritarian. A regime grounded in values of liberty and equality required monogamy as its elemental social form.

9
Modern Times

Family in the Nation's Courts

NINETEENTH-CENTURY DEVELOPMENTS

If the Mormon cases were an indication that the Supreme Court was prepared to read a form of family into the Constitution, they were not the sole nor the first such indications. Many of the Court's early decisions involved applications of common law. Neither the existence nor the number of these cases is especially surprising, given the Court's function in the nineteenth century as the common-law court of last resort.[1] Still, if the Court was relying on the common law, this was common law with a difference. Although aspects of the Court's jurisprudence originated in England, the Court took pains to distinguish the American law from that of the mother country. A familiar trope was that the English law was the product of a feudal or aristocratic regime, which tended to concentrate wealth in a few families or in a few hands within families. This way of thinking about family, the court reasoned, was inappropriate in the United States, where norms and institutions were republican in character. (In this respect, the English law, though "common" and not civil, resembled the European model.)[2] As we've already seen, one arena in which republican norms did not hold in America was that of slavery; on this front, the Court occasionally took up cases involving the status of families as slave or free, though it rarely paused to consider potentially knotty questions about a difference of status between parents and children.[3]

In general, the Court's familial jurisprudence during the nineteenth century touched on three related themes. One was the doctrinal connection between economy and family. The second was a growing dissonance over the political status of family—whether it was an institution created and regulable by law or was a pre-political institution exempt from some sorts of regulation. The third, which rose to prominence in the cases on polygamy, was the importance of family in promoting and preserving a kind of moral order.

Unsurprisingly, most of the Court's decisions implicated matters of contract and property even when they also involved family. The contexts varied in which these matters arose. One involved the duty of a father to support his wife and family.[4] Another involved the privilege against adverse spousal testimony.[5] Still other cases addressed a range of issues, including the general status or contractual capacity of women,[6] the protection of a wife from liability for innocently promulgating fraudulent misrepresentations of her husband,[7] the insulation of property from access by creditors,[8] the permissibility of transfers of property between members of a family,[9] and the status of illegitimate children or heirs.[10] One case held that marriage was sufficient consideration to support a transfer of property;[11] but more typical were cases that considered marriage to be a distinct, noncommercial sort of contract, partaking of a kind of status specially governable under the civil law.[12]

Dissenting in an antebellum case, for example, Justice Daniel emphasized the sweeping power of states to regulate familial life. "This power [of regulation]," he said, "belongs to the particular communities of which those families form parts, and is essential to the order and to the very existence of such communities."[13] At the same time, however, he could talk about families in libertarian terms that seemed to anticipate the notion of a private sphere for familial life, though he confined this doctrine to denying regulatory authority to the national government:

> It is not in accordance with the design and operation of a Government having its origin in causes and necessities, political, general, and external, that it should assume to regulate the domestic relations of society; should, with a kind of inquisitorial authority, enter the habitations and even into the chambers and nurseries of private families, and inquire into and pronounce upon the morals and habits and affections or antipathies of the members of every household.[14]

As we've seen, the states' control of at least one aspect of domestic relations was abolished after the Civil War. The abolition of slavery and the Fourteenth Amendment's concomitant reconfiguration of liberty and governmental power might have suggested a couple of innovations. One possibility, against Justice Daniel, was an expansive new national power over domestic relations, even beyond dismantling the relations entailed in slavery. The Court, however, held that the states' antebellum authority over the marital family persisted after the War.[15] The second possibility, exploiting Daniel's libertarian trope, might have imagined family either as a repository of privilege or immunity against certain sorts of regulation by states or as a contractual relation whose obligations states were constitutionally prohibited from impairing. Typically, though not consistently, the Court resisted this reading.

In *Maynard v. Hill,* for example, the Court held that marriage was "not . . . a contract within the meaning of the clause of the constitution which prohibits impairing the obligation of contracts," but was "the creation of law itself."[16] This implied that the marital relation "cannot be dissolved by the parties when con-summated, nor released with or without consideration. The relation is always regulated by government."[17] Thus, "the relation once formed, the law steps in and holds the parties to various obligations and liabilities." To hearken back to Chapter 1, marriage "is an institution, in the maintenance of which in its purity the public is deeply interested, for it is the foundation of the family and of society, without which there would be neither civilization nor progress."[18]

If marriage was a subject for intensive scrutiny and regulation by states, however, there was evidence by the last half of the nineteenth century that the marital family was emerging as an institution partially autonomous from govern-ment. Challenging the view of *Maynard,* the Court in *Meister v. Moore* declared that although "marriage is everywhere regarded as a civil contract" whose formal prerequisites are regulated by statutes, those statutes "do not confer the right." Marriage, the Court maintained "is a thing of common right," and may be created through means other than those permitted by statute.[19]

Another line of cases suggested that family might actually constrain the exercise of governmental power. These cases concerned the ostensible right of livelihood, and they linked livelihood to the support not only of self but also of family. Justices (not always the Court) frequently traced it to common law, but the Fourteenth Amendment expanded opportunities for applying the right.[20] Some of the earliest of the Court's decisions in this vein, though not grounded in the Fourteenth Amendment, involved disbarments of attorneys.[21] Most cases in which the Court linked family to livelihood, however, involved allegations of monopoly or restraint of trade.[22] The point of the justices' reasoning in this context was that some forms of capital threatened one of the polity's fundamental social units—the family. This logic could be converted from a shield against government to a jus-tification for the exercise of governmental power against family-threatening mo-nopolies and corporations.[23] It might also justify, on one justice's account, treating corporate and individual incomes differently, for purposes of a national income tax.[24]

Three features of the Court's treatment of the relationship between family and the right to livelihood stand out. First, a conventional rights-oriented view of livelihood—that it might impose limits on governmental action—was not the predominant theme of the Court's general jurisprudence of the family. Even when that theme was present in particular opinions, its reach was quite constrained. It did not (yet) support a view of family as partially autonomous from governmental control, a view that would emerge in the next century.

Second, when justices linked the right of livelihood to family, they consis-tently did so with the pregnant presumption that the right was a concomitant of the common-law duty to support one's family. In short, it was a right (and obligation) of men, not women, and white men at that. Hence, despite the Court's exquisite sensitivity to the value of practicing law in other contexts, the Court upheld the power of a state to deny categorically to women licenses to practice law.[25] Justice Bradley's concurrence invoked the domestic function of women to justify this result: "The paramount destiny and mission of woman are to fulfil the noble and benign offices of wife and mother. This is the law of the Creator. And the rules of civil society must be adapted to the general constitution of things, and cannot be based upon exceptional cases."[26] Implicit in Bradley's conception was the role of woman as moral guardian and educator. It's also worth noting that the Court was willing to permit discrimination on the basis of race, nationality, and/or marital status where the right of livelihood was concerned. Thus, the Court justified legal restrictions on Chinese laborers on the ground of family: "Not being accompanied by families, except in rare instances, their expenses were small; and . . . [t]he competition between them and our people was for this reason altogether in their favor."[27]

Third, as we saw in Chapter 8, preserving a "special" place for women was one reason the Court acknowledged—even cheered—a power in Congress, the territories, and the states to prohibit polygamy on the frontier:

> Bigamy and polygamy are crimes by the laws of all civilized and Christian countries. They are crimes by the laws of the United States, and they are crimes by the laws of Idaho. They tend to destroy the purity of the marriage relation, to disturb the peace of families, to degrade woman, and to debase man. . . . To extend exemption from punishment for such crimes would be to shock the moral judgment of the community.[28]

Plainly, protecting women was only part of the Court's calculus. Also integral was an express desire to reinforce a particular moral view of the relation between spouses. Coupled with this moral view was a political notion: family—specifically, the monogamous nuclear family—was essential to the well-constituted society. "Polygamy," said the Court with no apparent sense of irony, "leads to the patriarchal principle, . . . which, when applied to large communities, fetters the people in stationary despotism, while that principle [of despotism] cannot long exist in connection with monogamy."[29]

We've already seen that sentiments celebrating the political virtues of the monogamous family were not confined to cases involving plural marriage. The thrust of the Court's reasoning in *Maynard v. Hill,* for example, was that marriage "is not so much the result of private agreement as of public ordination. In every enlightened government it is pre-eminently the basis of civil institutions, and thus an object of the deepest public concern. In this light, marriage is more than a contract. . . . It is a great public institution, giving character to our whole civil polity."[30] Nor, of course, was such reasoning confined to the Court. Kent's *Commentaries* affirmed that the nuclear family was the best instrument for the transmission of social values to succeeding generations.[31] But the constitutional significance of family was intensified by the radical challenge polygamy posed to social convention and by Congress's perception that a particular form of social order must underwrite the establishment of constitutional order in the territories. Family, properly conceived, helped generate those "natural sentiments and affections" that tie people to home and country.[32]

The Court's unabashed embrace of monogamy and a monogamous version of patriarchy reinforced traditional notions of familial relations long embedded in common law, as we saw in detail in Chapter 2. It also confirmed family's moral function in at least two respects: (1) forms of family that deviated from the Court's model were considered dangerous to social morality and political order and therefore were punishable as crimes; and (2) restrictions on women's economic capacity fortified a conception of their role as moral guardian and educator. As we saw in Chapter 5, this latter consideration supplied a jurisprudential bridge between ancient common-law tropes and an emerging bourgeois sense of both family and women. One element of this transition played out in the doctrine of separate spheres, a popular iteration of which was the Cult of True Womanhood. Another involved the place (and innocence) of children who needed nurturing to come to their full capacity as persons.

A third element was the rise of the cultural appeal of companionate marriage: marriage based not only on "affection and mutual respect" but also on choice. Over the course of the nineteenth century, this view of marriage increasingly implied the legal freedom to leave the marriage.[33] To be sure, the expansion of access to exit was gradual and, given states' control of marriage and divorce, uneven. In the early nineteenth century, many states, especially in the South, permitted only legislative divorce. Even before the constitutional founding, however, some states, especially in the North, were revising their laws to provide a judicial process for obtaining a legal dissolution of marriage. The availability of judicial forums had the potential to make divorce available to a far larger number of couples. Still, states restricted access to the process by specifying fault-based grounds—including adultery, desertion, cruelty, or habitual drunkenness—and by requiring that the petitioning spouse be free of wrong-doing. Even so, some states imposed a heavier evidentiary burden on a petitioning wife than on a petitioning husband. Gendered discrimination aside, the imposition of restrictions on access to divorce produced at least three consequences: some couples stayed in loveless (or worse) marriages; others produced fabricated evidence to obtain a divorce; and still others simply went separate ways outside the law. Despite restrictions, the number of divorces increased steadily across the nineteenth century. By the end of the century, courts were granting more than 55,000 divorces per year. (Legislatures had astutely gotten out of the divorcing business.) Perhaps unsurprisingly, this trend incited a moral reaction, with some critics predicting that society—there was special worry about the lower classes—would be "demoralized and corrupted" by the too-ready availability of divorce. Despite dire predictions, the trend intensified into and through the twentieth century.[34]

These three developments occurred simultaneously in social practices, popular culture, and law. As to the last, they plainly pushed against the English law's constructed family. There was one additional development in the nineteenth century that's worthy of mention, because it, too, cut against the traditional common law: adoption. The first statutes to permit adoption were enacted in the South before the Civil War. These statutes had less to do with liberty than with a pragmatic desire to cure the legal defect of illegitimacy and thus to permit biological children full privileges of inheritance.[35] Louisiana was the first state to permit "private statutes" of adoption—essentially legislative adoptions—in 1837. The first state to provide a general regularized procedure for adoption was Mississippi in 1846. It not only covered illegitimate children but also permitted making an heir of any other person. This was significant, not only because it was an innovation on the common law but also because it provided legal authorization to form an intergenerational family of persons who were biologically unrelated, authorization that cut against not only common law but a version of natural law as well. Alabama followed suit in 1850. The first recognizably modern scheme for adoption, which included a procedure for terminating antecedent parental privileges, was adopted in Massachusetts in 1851, revised in 1871, and refined again in 1876.

THE CONSTITUTIONAL FAMILY IN THE EARLY TWENTIETH CENTURY

Despite the states' innovations on this last front, a version of the common law (and nature, too) persisted as elements of the Court's jurisprudence. Two cases in point were *Meyer v. Nebraska* (1923)[36] and *Pierce v. Society of Sisters* (1925).[37] Both cases involved state policies regulating the education of children. In *Meyer,* the state of Nebraska had prohibited teaching in or the teaching of a modern language other than English to students who had not yet completed the eighth grade. Mr. Meyer, a teacher in a parochial school, taught German to a ten-year-old student, for which he was convicted of violating the statute. In *Pierce,* the state of Oregon required that parents of children between the ages of eight and sixteen educate their children in public schools. A parochial school and a private military academy challenged Oregon's statute. Both states justified their policies not only generally as rational regulations of education, which was traditionally within the province of the states, but also specifically to promote the formation of American citizens, by requiring education either in a common language or in common schools. Plainly, however, both policies grew out of the sort of xenophobia that is a persistent strain of American political culture. As it had demonstrated in the nineteenth and early twentieth centuries, the Court itself was not immune to this strain. Still, the Court struck down the policies.

Its reasons rested on a form of liberalism that explicitly incorporated common law into the concept of liberty in the Fourteenth Amendment:

> Without doubt, [liberty] denotes not merely freedom from bodily restraint but also the right of the individual to contract, to engage in any of the

common occupations of life, to acquire useful knowledge, to marry, establish a home and bring up children, to worship God according to the dictates of his own conscience, and generally to enjoy those privileges long recognized at common law as essential to the orderly pursuit of happiness by free men.[38]

If this was common law, however, it was a peculiarly American version of common law, rooted in an American tradition of liberalism (extending to John Locke), a tradition that the Reconstruction Amendments had revised (or elevated). In some of its late nineteenth-century decisions, as we saw in the previous section, the Court had been able to talk of the economic right to livelihood and the familial right of parenthood as if they were cut from the same cloth. In *Meyer* and *Pierce,* however, the identity of the petitioners made it more difficult for the Court to do so. Mr. Meyer's livelihood was at stake, but not his parental privileges. And the Society of Sisters and the Hill Military Academy were corporations, not families. The Court acknowledged the analytic difficulty in *Pierce.* "Appellees are corporations, and therefore, it is said, they cannot claim for themselves the liberty which the Fourteenth Amendment guarantees." Nonetheless, the Court held that "they have business and property" that are "threatened with destruction" by the state's policy. These material interests, the Court held, were protected within the concept of liberty in the due process clause of the Fourteenth Amendment.[39] The Court spoke of Mr. Meyer's liberty, too, as distinct from that of family. "The calling [to teach] always has been regarded as useful and honorable, essential, indeed, to the public welfare."[40]

If distinct, the petitioners' claims to liberty in these contexts were adjacent to claims of the children's parents, who the Court held had a right to engage a teacher or to contract with a corporation to provide educational services. But the Court made clear that the parents' claims were not merely matters of contract. They also involved a different sort of liberty. "Corresponding to the right of [parental] control, it is the natural duty of the parent to give his children education suitable to their station in life." Perhaps in other societies government could insert a heavy hand between a parent and child, or even assume primary authority for raising children, as in ancient Sparta or Plato's ideal commonwealth, but not in America. "Although such measures have been deliberately approved by men of great genius, their ideas touching the relation between individual and State were wholly different from those upon which our institutions rest."[41] Thus, in the United States, parents are at liberty "to direct the upbringing and education of children under their control. . . . The fundamental theory of liberty upon which all governments in this Union repose excludes any general power of the State to standardize its children. . . . The child is not the mere creature of the State; those who nurture him and direct his destiny have the right, coupled with the high duty, to recognize and prepare him for additional obligations."[42]

At the same time that the Court was insisting that parenthood was noble and constitutionally protected, it was also holding there were circumstances in which—or persons for whom—a state could constitutionally intrude into aspects of the parental domain. The Court's reasoning married the ethic of ancient Sparta and Plato's *Republic* with the evolutionary biology of Charles Darwin. The social question was how to restrain the proliferation of persons who were perceived to be undesirable? We've already seen one answer to that question, adopted by the nation: restricting immigration. By the early years of the twentieth century, a different sort of policy was gaining traction in the culture and approval among scientific communities. The policy was eugenics—the self-conscious attempt to improve the genetic constitution of society through prescribed selective breeding. The principal proposal wasn't to encourage breeding by the "better sort" of persons but to inhibit breeding by the "lesser sort." There were several ways to describe the lesser sort in the parlance of the day: unfit, feeble-minded, socially inadequate, defective. The concern was not only about individual persons, but also about class. How to prevent their propagation? The answer—originating with Francis Galton in Britain but positively taking flight in the United States— was sterilization. In short, if we can't exterminate undesirables already in our midst, we can prevent their transmitting their decadent traits to future generations. Proponents of this view included some of society's best and brightest—Alexander Graham Bell and the presidents of Stanford University and the University of Wisconsin—and some surprising allies, like Margaret Sanger (the founder of Planned Parenthood), Emma Goldman, and the American Association of University Women.[43]

Legislatures in several states adopted the policy, though governors in five states vetoed the legislation. Courts in seven other states struck down enactments, not for substantive reasons but because of procedural inadequacies. To cure these defects, Harry Laughlin crafted a model statute for sterilization. Laughlin was a biologist who migrated eastward from Iowa to Missouri to Long Island, New York. To pursue his interest in the genetic transmission of defective traits, he established the Eugenics Record Office in New York, with financial underwriting by Mary Harriman (wife of railroad magnate E. H. Harriman and mother of Averell), the Rockefeller family, and the Carnegie Institution. Eighteen states enacted Laughlin's model statute, including Virginia, which (along with California) was in the vanguard of the eugenics movement. By the 1930s, two-thirds of the states had enacted compulsory sterilization laws. On the ground in various jurisdictions, the model statute provided procedural cover for an emerging regulatory apparatus. Aggressive administrators went after a range of undesirables. Notably, African Americans were not the primary objects of the policy, though blacks were certainly not exempt from its reach. Instead, administrators had three favored targets: lower-class persons with large numbers of children (not only those from disfavored ethnic backgrounds), defective persons (including not only those with mental disabilities but also alcoholics, drug addicts, even the deaf and blind), and persons (overwhelmingly women) accused of sexual immorality. This last target may seem strange, as the criminal law punished prostitution as a voluntary act, not a genetic fate. In many cases, however, proponents did not justify sterilization for the purpose of punishment, at least not solely so. Instead, or in addition, there was a widespread belief—even among the healing professions and scientific community—that female sexual promiscuity was a manifestation of an inheritable mental defect that should be nipped in the bud, as it were.[44]

Such was the state of Virginia's view of Emma Buck, who, after conviction for prostitution, was committed to the State Colony for Epileptics and Feeble-Minded in Lynchburg. Her daughter Carrie, then thirteen, was placed with a foster family. Three years later, she gave birth to her own daughter (Vivian) after she was raped by her foster mother's nephew. Whether from outrage or fear of social disapproval or some other motive, the foster parents had Carrie committed to the same State Colony. Administrators at the Colony administered the Binet-Simon intelligence test, devised under the auspices of Stanford University, to both women. They scored Emma as having a mental age of nine, and Carrie a mental age of seven. They did not test Vivian, because she was too young, but a nurse did visit her when she was seven months old, and reported her to be "slow"; she had a "look" about her that was "not quite right." On the basis of that testimony, expert administrators concluded that Vivian, too, was feeble-minded. In fact, she wasn't. By the time she got to school, her teachers described her as "bright." (Nor, it turned out, was Carrie herself, in the parlance of a later day, retarded. Nor, for that matter, was Carrie's mother.) But administrators didn't scrutinize or wait for evidence that might challenge their deeply held belief. They were keen to establish the validity of the model statute, and Carrie Buck provided their test case.[45]

Pursuant to Virginia's version of the model act, the superintendent of the colony, Dr. Albert S. Priddy, petitioned a specially appointed three-person board for permission to sterilize Carrie Buck as a "moral delinquent . . . of the moron class." A guardian was appointed to represent Carrie in the proceedings. It turns out the guardianship was largely a sham, as pro-eugenic agents directed strategy and argument for both sides in the case. In short, *Buck v. Bell,* as the case would come to be called after Priddy died of Hodgkin's and was succeeded by Dr. J. H. Bell, was a "friendly" dispute, contrived to give legal blessing to the administrative process and decision. Hence, after the board granted permission to sever her Fallopian tubes, Carrie's guardian appealed first to the Circuit Court for the county, then to the Supreme Court of Appeals for the state. In the hearings in these forums, he offered precious little on her behalf. By the time the case reached the Supreme Court of the United States, then, the record included uncontradicted evidence that Carrie, her mother, and her daughter were of substantially inferior mental capacity. It included Laughlin's written report, which stated that "these people belong to the shiftless, ignorant, and worthless class of anti-social whites of the South." And it included Laughlin's deposition. Although he had never laid eyes on any of the Bucks and lacked any genealogical data, he testified that Carrie was "sexually very immoral." He concluded that sterilizing her would be "a force for the mitigation of degeneracy."[46]

In the Supreme Court, Carrie's guardian offered two constitutional arguments against coercive state sterilization. Perhaps tellingly, he did not argue that the procedures themselves were inadequate, for the purpose of due process. The omission hardly mattered, however, in light of the summary conclusion in Justice Oliver Wendell Holmes's Opinion of the Court that the procedures were adequate. The guardian argued instead that the policy violated a substantive liberty (including, in his words, "bodily integrity," a common-law privilege) instantiated in the due process clause of the Fourteenth Amendment; and that it violated equal protection, because it carved out a class of persons—the feeble-minded—and subjected them to differential treatment simply because of their membership in the class. These were not the sorts of trivial arguments one might have expected in light of the guardian's performance in state judicial forums. But they found an unreceptive Court.[47]

Holmes described Carrie as "a feeble minded white woman" who was "the daughter of a feeble minded mother . . . , and the mother of an illegitimate feeble minded child." He recited Virginia's claims that "heredity plays an important part in the transmission of insanity, imbecility, &c.," that "the sterilization of mental defectives" could be carried out without medical risk to the patient, that it would permit the State to discharge "defective persons" from their mental institution because they would no longer pose a genetic threat to society, and that the State would therefore be relieved of the financial burden of supporting them.[48] But did coercive sterilization violate constitutionally protected liberty as expressed in the due process clause? Deferring to the findings of the legislature and to the specific evidence in judicial proceedings below, Holmes held that it did not.

> We have seen more than once that the public welfare may call upon the best citizens for their lives. It would be strange if it could not call upon those who already sap the strength of the State for these lesser sacrifices, often not felt to be such by those concerned, in order to prevent our being swamped with incompetence. It is better for all the world, if instead of waiting to execute degenerate offspring for crime, or to let them starve for their imbecility, society can prevent those who are manifestly unfit from continuing their kind. . . . Three generations of imbeciles are enough.[49]

With his own judicial scalpel, then, Holmes severed the reproductive capacity of persons who, for reasons of genuine disability or merely familial embarrassment, came to be labeled inherently defective. Pierce Butler dissented without opinion.[50]

REPRODUCTION AND THE CONSTITUTIONAL FAMILY

By the late 1920s, a genotype of family was born as a jurisprudentially recognized institution possessing a constitutional status. The institutional and ethical DNA of this institution was complex and even conflictual. One strand included respect for an image of tradition; another acknowledged the formative facts of social change and legal innovations. One strand included affection and even veneration of the familiar; another expressed anxiety, aversion, and fear of unconventional forms or persons. One strand grew from the need for a social institution that was both a product and a producer of coercive power, another from a commitment to values of liberty and equality that were viewed as both elements of and limitations on that power. Relatedly, one strand emphasized the role of democratic or administrative regulation, another the need for a protected sphere autonomous from regulation.

These conflicted strands continued to influence the development of the constitutional aspects of the institution after its birth, whose ontogeny, to borrow from Holmes in a different context, "could not have been foreseen completely by the most gifted of its begetters."[51] For example, one could detect two possible sources for Pierce Butler's opposition to coerced sterilization. One was a kind of liberalism, grounded in his libertarian suspicion of governmental power of almost any sort. Although he typically applied his analytic powers to attacking governmental regulation of enterprise, he also sometimes wrote on behalf of the rights of criminal defendants, and it is not a stretch to imagine that some such liberal concern animated his dissent in *Buck v. Bell.* The other source was that he was Roman Catholic. Even before the 1920s, some theologians in the American Church had begun writing about the morality of forced sterilization specifically and eugenics generally. But as late as 1927, there was not yet a definitive canonical Catholic position on the practice, though one was slowly emerging. It appeared fully in the 1930s, when Pope Pius XI issued an encyclical, *On Christian Marriage,* which not only articulated the Church's doctrine on birth control—criticizing it as an attempt to "deliberately frustrate" reproduction—but also attacked sterilization. Soon after, leaders in the American Church began to incorporate concern for ostensible "defectives" into an ethic of social liberalism (in contrast with libertarian liberalism) that was not inconsistent with some of the aims and principles of Franklin Roosevelt's New Deal.[52]

Roosevelt's presidency famously produced a fundamental change in the makeup and jurisprudential orientation of the federal judiciary. It was not clear in the beginning whether or how this change might affect constitutional doctrines related to family. It was possible, for example, to imagine that the deferential approach of *Buck v. Bell* would become entrenched and that *Meyer* and *Pierce* would be abandoned as artifacts of the newly repudiated *Lochner* era. But the constitutional jurisprudence of family took a turn in 1942, in *Skinner v. Oklahoma.* The case addressed the constitutionality of Oklahoma's Habitual Criminals Sterilization Act. Adopted in 1935, the statute provided a procedure for sterilizing any person convicted two or more times of "felonies involving moral turpitude." Jack Skinner was convicted once for stealing chickens and twice for armed robbery, each crime falling within the statutory definition of moral turpitude. After the third conviction he was adjudicated a habitual criminal and was sentenced to be sterilized. The Supreme Court overturned the sentence. Writing for the Court,

Justice Douglas noted that, although one might be sterilized for stealing chickens, the Act exempted from this punishment certain white-collar crimes, including tax evasion, embezzlement, corruption in political office, bribery of a public official, and "offenses arising out of the violation of the prohibitory laws." The Court held that unequal punishment for what was "intrinsically the same quality of offense" violated the Fourteenth Amendment's equal protection clause. This, however, was equal protection with a twist, for it involved differential treatment with respect to what Douglas called "a right which is basic to the perpetuation of a race—the right to have offspring," a right linked to marriage, which the Court in *Meyer* had recognized as an element of liberty at common law. Distinguishing *Buck v. Bell* without overruling it, the Court in *Skinner* held: "Marriage and procreation are fundamental to the very existence and survival of the race. The power to sterilize, if exercised, may have subtle, far-reaching and devastating effects. In evil or reckless hands it can cause races or types which are inimical to the dominant group to wither and disappear. There is no redemption for the individual whom the law touches. Any experiment which the State conducts is to his irreparable injury. He is forever deprived of a basic liberty."[53]

The libertarian and social strands of liberalism and official Roman Catholic teaching all could celebrate *Skinner,* but the Court's emphasis on reproduction would eventually follow a path that separated the camps. The wedge involved not procreation per se but contraception. Since 1879, the state of Connecticut had had on the books a statute that prohibited both using any drug or device for preventing conception and aiding, abetting, or counseling another in the use of contraceptives. At the time of enactment, the statute had the support of a Protestant majority, egged on by the same Anthony Comstock whose war on vice had bullied the Oneida community into conformity. By the mid-twentieth century, as Walter Murphy reports, "it was the large Catholic population who were, at least according to their bishops, in favor of the statute."[54] In 1961, two justices, dissenting from the denial of a writ of certiorari in a case that raised a challenge to the statute, signaled that they were ready to sustain the challenge. Though each was born in the upper Midwest, the justices were in some respects unlikely allies. John Marshall Harlan II was a traditionalist conservative, and William O. Douglas was a modernist liberal. Each drew a conceptual map for counsel to follow in future challenges to the statute. Although the two maps bore a family resemblance to each other, they differed in tenor and in implication. Douglas's dissent invoked constitutional text and an expansive reading of precedents in the service of a libertarian philosophy that distinguished law from morality. Harlan's dissent, in contrast, drew on a reading of liberty that was rooted in traditional institutions and values and that preserved morality as a legitimate basis for legal regulation.[55]

Four years later, the Court struck down Connecticut's statute in *Griswold v. Connecticut.* As noted above in Chapter 1, Justice Douglas wrote the Opinion of the Court, locating the right to contraception within a zone of privacy implicit in various textual provisions of the Bill of Rights and amplified in decisions of the

Court. Privacy, he wrote, was an element of substantive liberty in the due process clause of the Fourteenth Amendment. Justice Harlan concurred separately,
incorporating by reference his prior dissent in *Poe v. Ullman*. Perhaps in a nod to
Harlan, Douglas moderated the individualist implications of the Court's opinion
by situating the right in the marital family.[56]

Given this move, it was not a foregone conclusion that the Court would recognize the right as belonging to individuals per se, as opposed to married couples.
But the Court reached this conclusion in 1972 in a 6–1 decision in *Eisenstadt v.
Baird*. One justification the state of Massachusetts had offered for its own anticon-
traceptive statute was moral: that the prevention of procreation by artificial means
was itself immoral and thus that contraceptives may be "forbidden to unmarried
persons who will nevertheless persist in having intercourse." The Court of Appeals below had rejected this justification outright, holding that the state's "view
of morality is not only the very mirror image of sensible legislation; we consider
that it conflicts with fundamental human rights. In the absence of demonstrated
harm, we hold it is beyond the competency of the state."[57] Writing for the Supreme Court, Justice Brennan flirted with this move, but ultimately pulled back,
concluding that "we need not and do not . . . decide that important question in this
case." Instead, in a quick and simple assertion, Justice Brennan wrote that,

> whatever the rights of the individual to access to contraceptives may be, the
> rights must be the same for the unmarried and the married alike. . . . It is
> true that in *Griswold* the right of privacy in question inhered in the mari-
> tal relationship. Yet the marital couple is not an independent entity with a
> mind and heart of its own, but an association of two individuals each with
> a separate intellectual and emotional makeup. If the right of privacy means
> anything it is the right of individual, married or single, to be free from un-
> warranted governmental intrusion into matters so fundamentally affecting a
> person as the decision whether to bear or beget a child.[58]

Justice Harlan had died two months before *Eisenstadt* was handed down. His replacement on the Court, William Rehnquist, took no part in the decision. Warren
Burger, the new chief justice, was the sole dissenter.

In law schools today, it's common to treat *Griswold* as the critical juncture
in the development of a "personal" sphere of constitutional rights, distinct from
strictly economic matters. There's no denying its significance in this respect,
though the seeds for that move had been planted in decisions decades before. If
contraception wasn't a logically necessary extension of the previously recognized
rights of parenthood and procreation, neither was it illogical nor even radical. It's
likely that the more fateful jurisprudential step was *Eisenstadt*'s move to extend
ownership of *Griswold*'s liberty to individuals. Even in discussing marriage, it
was telling that the Court in *Eisenstadt* talked about the couple not as a unity but
as an association of two individuals. This individualist way of thinking about
rights—and family—had long roots in American history, extending back to the

Revolutionary period. And liberal individualism had always been a prominent element of American law and culture. Still, from a jurisprudential perspective, *Eisenstadt*'s small but significant step would have substantial implications for constitutional doctrines concerning not only control of reproduction but also sexual liberty and the proper role of morality in justifying governmental action.

These three elements would coalesce in the Court's jurisprudence involving one of the two most divisive social issues of our day: the right to terminate a pregnancy. Despite the holdings in *Griswold* and *Eisenstadt,* it was not logically necessary for the Court in *Roe v. Wade* to hold that the Constitution protected a right of abortion—and this was not merely because abortion, as Justice Rehnquist pointed out in dissent, "is not 'private' in the ordinary usage of that word." After all, the ethical and medical dimensions of preventing a pregnancy are distinguishable from those of terminating a pregnancy. If protecting the latter wasn't logically required by the former, however, neither was it logically barred. Much depended on how the principle or value underwriting the prior decisions was articulated. The Court in *Roe* did not offer much on this front. Speaking through Justice Blackmun, the Court recited the provisions of the Bill of Rights that Douglas had invoked in *Griswold,* cited the other prior familial decisions of *Meyer, Pierce, Skinner,* and *Eisenstadt,* and concluded tersely that the "right of privacy . . . is broad enough to encompass a woman's decision whether or not to terminate her pregnancy."[59]

To be sure, the court noted that pregnancy and an unwanted child could produce "specific and direct harm"—physical, psychological, familial, and social—especially when the mother was not married, but also even if she were. But the Court stopped short of holding that the right was grounded in women's special status with respect to childbearing. For that matter, the Court stopped short of holding that the right belonged exclusively to the mother, holding that, "in all its aspects, [abortion] is inherently, and primarily, a medical decision, and basic responsibility for it must rest with the physician." This approach, said the Court, "vindicates the right of the physician to administer medical treatment according to his professional judgment up to the points where important state interests provide compelling justifications for intervention." Those justifications included both "protecting the health of the pregnant woman" and "protecting the potentiality of human life." The latter interest, the Court emphasized, did not mean that the fetus was a rights holder. But the state was permitted to regulate and even prohibit abortion during the third trimester of pregnancy, "except where it is necessary, in appropriate medical judgment, for the preservation of the life or health of the mother."

Roe's thin justification persisted in more than a dozen cases in which the Court took on the job of assessing the constitutionality of myriad policies that states enacted to regulate abortion. The Court upheld some policies but struck down others, including two that implicated familial structure and relations. One required that an unmarried minor obtain the consent of a parent before she could undergo an abortion. Doubtless, this policy rested on the Lockean assumption that minors lacked full capacity to make some important decisions. They needed guidance, in the words of *Pierce v. Society of Sisters,* from "those who nurture" them. The Court held that the requirement was impermissible unless the state provided an alternative avenue for minors who might fear their parents' reaction: the consent of a judge.[60] In later decisions, the Court upheld the power of states to require that an unmarried minor *notify* her parents, but only if the state also provided a judicial bypass.[61] Another policy the Court struck down required that a married woman of any age obtain the consent of her husband before an abortion.[62] This policy probably rested on an ancient notion of the legal unity of husband and wife, a notion that was moribund, if not dead, by this time. The Court later also struck down a requirement that a married woman notify her husband before terminating a pregnancy, even though the policy might have rested on a more liberal view of the partnership that is companionate marriage.[63]

One problem for the trimester framework that the Court had deployed for evaluating the weightiness of states' interests in women's health and in potential life was that the principles underwriting the framework were eroding. In *Roe,* the Court had marked the end of the first trimester as the point at which a state could begin to regulate on behalf of the woman's health, because this was the point at which mortality in abortion became greater than mortality from childbirth. The Court had marked the end of the second trimester as the point at which a state could substantially restrict or prohibit abortion, because this was the point at which the fetus was viable—i.e., had the capacity for "meaningful life outside the mother's womb."[64] Advances in medical technology posed a problem for these markers, as abortion became increasingly safer later in the pregnancy, and it became possible to sustain "meaningful life" earlier in the pregnancy. As Justice O'Connor put it, dissenting in a decision in 1983, *Roe's* trimester framework was "on a collision course with itself."[65]

Three years later, in *Planned Parenthood of Southeastern Pennsylvania v. Casey,* a divided Court salvaged the right but made two changes in the doctrine. An indication of the depth of the division was that the key opinion in the case was a joint opinion of three (sometimes four) justices. The joint opinion became the lodestar for discussing the right to abortion. One change, embraced only by a plurality, was to abandon the trimester framework in favor of a new standard in which the Court asked whether a state's regulation imposed an undue burden on the right to obtain an abortion before viability. After viability, a state could prohibit the procedure outright, "except where it is necessary, in appropriate medical judgment, for the preservation of the life or health of the mother."[66] (Nonetheless, the Court would later uphold a Congressional enactment prohibiting the use of a particular procedure—partial birth abortion—despite the absence of statutory language providing an exception for the life or health of the mother and regardless of the judgment of the presiding physician.[67])

Casey's second change was to provide a new foundation for the right. On this front, the joint opinion commanded a majority. The Court redefined the substantive liberty in terms of principles that had emerged in several prior constitutional decisions: the right to make "basic decisions about family and parenthood," the right to bodily integrity, and the right to make choices concerning marriage, procreation, contraception, family relationships, child rearing, and education. These choices, the Court held, were protected because they involve "the most intimate and personal choices a person may make in a lifetime" and because they are "central to personal dignity and autonomy." Addressing the question evaded in *Eisenstadt*, the question of the location of moral judgment, the Court held that "at the heart of liberty is the right to define one's own concept of existence, of meaning, of the universe, and of the mystery of human life. Beliefs about these matters could not define the attributes of personhood were they formed under the compulsion of the State."[68] In *Casey*, to a degree not seen in *Roe*, the Court emphasized that the owner of this right was the mother.

> The liberty of the woman is at stake in a sense unique to the human condition and so unique to the law. The mother who carries a child to full term is subject to anxieties, to physical constraints, to pain that only she must bear. That these sacrifices have from the beginning of the human race been endured by woman with a pride that ennobles her in the eyes of others and gives to the infant a bond of love cannot alone be grounds for the State to insist she make the sacrifice. . . . The destiny of the woman must be shaped to a large extent on her own conception of her spiritual imperatives and her place in society.[69]

Griswold, Eisenstadt, and *Roe,* the Court concluded, remained part of a common constellation of constitutional liberty.

Justice Scalia filed a muscular dissent. He mocked the Court's attempt to rehabilitate the definition of the right. Unenumerated rights, he urged, may be judicially protected only at the most specific, concrete level discernible from a "relevant tradition." (By "relevant," he had in mind Anglo-American.) In short, text and tradition are the sole sources for defining constitutional liberty. And the right to abortion finds no home in either source. Dissenting in a later case, he would ridicule what he called the "sweet mystery of life" as a basis for constitutional right. He also criticized the Court's attempt to locate moral judgment in the individual. Where a claimed right is not detectable in either text or an identifiable tradition, moral questions—like "homosexual sodomy, polygamy, adult incest, . . . suicide," and abortion—should be decided by democratic means, through competition in the political marketplace. "Value judgments should be voted on [by the polity], not dictated [by the Court]." Finally, he argued, *Roe* should be overturned. As a matter of constitutional law, he said, it was wrong when it was decided, and it remains wrong. "We should get out of this area, where we have no right to be, and where we do neither ourselves nor the country any good by remaining."[70]

WOMEN'S STATUS

By the time *Casey* was decided, it was clear that the Court viewed control of reproduction not only as a value in itself, related to autonomy and bodily integrity, but also as an instrumental element of women's access to productive labor and to other social goods. If women could control reproduction, they could mitigate one barrier to their full participation in economic life, not to mention other aspects of the life of the country. Because the joint opinion in *Casey* focused so strongly on the existential dimensions of pregnancy, as compared with lost opportunity for work, the opinion disguised somewhat the productive and participatory dimensions of the reproductive right. But those dimensions were much more visible in two other areas of American law.

One was statutory. In 1963, Congress enacted the Equal Pay Act.[71] This statute, amending the Fair Labor Standards Act, prohibited designated classes of employers from providing lower wages to women who were engaged in work that "requires . . . skill, effort, and responsibility" that are equal to work performed by men. (Notably, executive, administrative, and sales jobs were excluded from the Act's coverage.) The mantra, in short, was equal pay for equal work. The Act carved out exceptions for seniority, merit, differences in the quality or quantity of productivity, and "any other factor other than sex."

Even more far reaching than the Equal Pay Act was Title VII of the Civil Rights Act of 1964, which prohibited discrimination on the basis of sex with respect to hiring, firing, classifying, and segregation in employment practices.[72] (Title VII applied also to unions, many of which intensely opposed sexual equality in the workplace.) An employer could justify an otherwise prohibited practice by demonstrating that there was a necessary and bona fide business-related reason for the practice. An early question about the reach of Title VII involved health insurance coverage for pregnancy. If an employer's health insurance policy provided a range of benefits for non-employment-related sickness, accidental injury, and other medical conditions, but excluded coverage for pregnancy, did the employer discriminate on the basis of sex? In *General Electric Co. v. Gilbert,* the Supreme Court held that it did not, reasoning that the health plan merely excluded "one physical condition—pregnancy—from the list of compensable disabilities."[73] Congress responded by enacting the Pregnancy Discrimination Act of 1978, amending Title VII. The PDA redefined the statutory language "because of sex" and "on the basis of sex" to include "pregnancy, childbirth, or related medical conditions," and it required that women affected by those conditions "be treated the same for all employment-related purposes . . . as other persons not so affected but similar in their ability or inability to work."[74]

The second area in which women's access to material goods and social roles was visible was constitutional law. The Court's earliest forays into the constitutional law of gender elevated traditional roles above the value of liberal equality that the Court had celebrated in the Mormon cases. We saw in the first section of this chapter that the Court in *Bradwell v. Illinois* had affirmed a state's authority to exclude women from the practice of law. Concurring with exceptional forthrightness, Justice Bradley relied on the "historical fact" that women were not permitted to engage in every possible gainful pursuit in civil society.

> The natural and proper timidity and delicacy which belongs to the female sex evidently unfits it for many of the occupations of civil life. The constitution of the family organization, which is founded on divine ordinance, as well as in the nature of things, indicates the domestic sphere as that which properly belongs to the domain and functions of womanhood. The harmony . . . of interest and views which belong . . . to the family institution is repugnant to the idea of a woman adopting a distinct and independent career from that of her husband. So firmly fixed was this sentiment in the founders of the common law that it became a maxim of that system of jurisprudence that a woman had no legal existence separate from her husband.[75]

Justice Bradley conceded that the old rules of common law in these regards were changing, even in the nineteenth century. As a constitutional matter, however, "the general rule" persisted in his view.

Although it arose seventy-five years later, *Goesaert v. Cleary* followed suit, upholding a Michigan statute that prohibited any woman from obtaining a bartender's license unless she was "the wife or daughter of the male owner" of an existing establishment. Writing for the Court, Justice Frankfurter conceded "the vast changes in the social and legal position of women." Still, states were permitted to draw hard lines between the sexes, especially in the sale of liquor. "The oversight assured through ownership of a bar by a barmaid's husband or father minimizes hazards that may confront a barmaid without such protecting oversight."[76]

Not until 1971 did the Court strike down a sex-based restriction on access to civil roles. The case was *Reed v. Reed,* involving an Idaho law that gave men an automatic preference over women in the granting of letters of administration for the probate of decedents' estates. The state had claimed that men were presumptively more capable than women in matters of business and that permitting women to serve as administrators would require a hearing to determine who was better qualified to serve. Better and cheaper, the state urged, to simply assume that men were better qualified. In an opinion by Chief Justice Burger, the Court rejected Idaho's interest in administrative efficiency and held that the policy was simply irrational and therefore unconstitutional.[77] Participating in writing the Brief of Appellant was a young New York lawyer, Ruth Bader Ginsburg.[78]

Two years later, the Court struck down a federal statute that automatically provided an allowance for housing and health care to wives of male members of the armed forces, but provided benefits to husbands of female members only if they could prove that their husbands were in fact dependent on their wives for more than half of their support. Lt. Sharron Frontiero challenged the policy.[79] She earned almost 75 percent of the couple's income. But because her husband's expenses were quite small, she could not demonstrate that he relied on her for half of his support. Like Idaho in *Reed,* the United States in *Frontiero v. Richardson* argued that its policy was justified by administrative convenience. Ginsburg, who was the founder of the new ACLU's Women's Rights Project, filed a brief on behalf of the ACLU as amicus curiae, and this time she participated in oral argument.[80] She argued that sex-based classifications should be subjected to strict scrutiny, like classifications on the basis of race.[81] Although eight justices agreed that the United States' policy was unconstitutional, only four endorsed strict scrutiny. The other four concurred on the ground that the policy was irrational or invidious and therefore unconstitutional on the reasoning of *Reed v. Reed.* Only Justice Rehnquist dissented.

Ginsburg's strategy as chief litigator for the Project was to identify and participate in cases in which the interests of both men and women were promoted by a norm of sexual equality. Her reflective intuition was that the gentlemen on the Court would be less likely to uphold policies in which men were put to disadvantage. The intuition seems generally to have been well founded. One case in which it was not successful, however, was *Kahn v. Shevin,* involving a challenge to a Florida law that gave a special exemption on property taxes to widows. A young ACLU attorney in Miami had initiated the challenge on behalf of a widower who was denied the exemption because of his sex. He lost at trial, and, without notifying the national office, pressed for review in the Supreme Court. Because the national office of the ACLU was uncomfortable having an unknown lawyer from south Florida handling the brief and argument before the Court, Ginsburg took responsibility for a case she would have preferred to avoid. She disliked her chances in the case from the beginning. For one thing, she did not believe the policy was plainly irrational. For another, she knew that Justice Douglas's widowed mother was financially stressed, and that he was sensitive to the economic vulnerability of widows. For another, the case simply didn't fit the lesson plan she had charted for educating the Court in dealing with sex-based inequalities.[82] She lost. It was her only loss before the Court. Justice Douglas wrote the opinion of the Court.[83]

Her next case, however, possessed traits more closely aligned with her lesson plan. Stephen Wiesenfeld was a young widower whose wife had died giving birth to the couple's son. He filed for survivor's benefits through his wife's Social Security, but he was denied because he could not prove he had been dependent on his wife's earnings. Widows automatically received the benefit, the assumptions being that wives were dependent and that men could rely on others to raise their children. These stereotypes, Ginsburg urged, injured men as well as women. The loss in *Kahn* was more than a tactical setback. It compromised Ginsburg's ability to push for strict scrutiny. So, instead of pushing for that rigorous standard, she decided to offer an intermediate standard of review—a standard resting between rational basis and strict scrutiny.[84] Although the Court didn't embrace overtly her proposed heightened standard, it did unanimously strike down the Social Security Act's differential treatment of widows and widowers.[85]

Finally, in 1976, she was able to persuade a majority on the Court to adopt heightened (but not strict) scrutiny. The case involved an Oklahoma statute that permitted women between the ages of eighteen and twenty-one to buy beer with an alcoholic content of 3.2 percent ("near beer"), but denied the privilege (if "privilege" is the way to describe it) to males in the same age cohort. The policy itself was neither important nor poignant, but the differential treatment did illustrate a pervasive social stereotype: that boys were aggressive and hard to control, while girls were docile and obedient. In fact, there was statistical evidence suggesting that young men in this cohort were more than ten times as likely to be arrested for driving under the influence than were young women. This statistical difference made Oklahoma's policy seem perfectly rational. But the Court struck it down, employing Ginsburg's recommended heightened scrutiny. Only Justice Rehnquist and Chief Justice Burger dissented.[86]

Successful as it was, Ginsburg's strategy was not without detractors. Some feminists—Catharine MacKinnon chief among them—argued that a liberal, legalistic approach to equality was incapable of dealing directly and effectively with deeply embedded values, doctrines, and practices that reinforced the subordination of women as a distinct social class. Only a radical form of feminism— "unmodified" by liberal legalism—could promote genuine equality and erode the foundations of masculine supremacy. In fact, MacKinnon argued at one point, it was impossible to point to a single case using Ginsburg's approach from which a woman genuinely benefitted as against a man.[87] On the other side of the ideological spectrum, the executive director of Eagle Forum derided Ginsburg as an "embittered feminist," whose jurisprudence was an "extremist" and "radical" assault on traditional values and an attempt to "convert America into a 'gender-free' society." Her aim, according to this critique, was not "to redress any legitimate grievances women might have, but . . . to change human nature, social mores, and relationships between men and women." Her method was to undermine laws that not only reinforced human nature but also, in many cases, protected women.[88] In short, if MacKinnon claimed that Ginsburg's strategy was largely ineffectual, the head of Eagle Forum attacked it as a revolutionary transformation of American society and values.

In fact, although Ginsburg's legal strategy did not reflect MacKinnon's methods nor even some of her goals, it did mark a change in the manner in which governmental policy operated differentially on the basis of gender. The strategy would have implications for a range of policies involving differential access to education, employment, and civic life. Thus, the Court would strike down policies making jury service optional for women but mandatory for men,[89] excluding men from a nursing program at a state-supported university,[90] and, eventually, excluding women from the opportunity to attend an elite state-supported military academy.[91] In this last case, now-Justice Ginsburg wrote the opinion of the Court, and even Chief Justice Rehnquist concurred, with only Justice Scalia dissenting. Even so, the Court was unwilling to strike down a policy authorizing the president to register men but not women for service in the armed forces.[92] And the Court upheld a state law that punished as statutory rape sexual intercourse with a girl (but not a boy) younger than eighteen years old.[93]

If measured and uneven, the Court's jurisprudence took decisive steps toward checking governmental policies (and, under statute, some private practices) that tended to confine women to traditional occupations and social roles. Indeed, the principle animating the new constitutional law of gender was that women were no longer expected to find their place and status solely in home and family. If they wished to find fulfillment in the familial sphere, they were free to do so. But they were not obliged. Nor, for that matter, were men directed exclusively to spheres outside the home. The Family and Medical Leave Act of 1994—which provided "eligible employees" of either sex a guarantee of twelve weeks' unpaid leave for purposes related to familial care—pushed even further in this direction.[94] The Court affirmed the authority of Congress to enact FMLA, pursuant to section 5 of the Fourteenth Amendment, in 2003.[95] *Pace* Catharine MacKinnon, these changes weren't trivial. On the contrary, they were momentous. To be sure, the lived experience of many persons and families had long reflected the give-and-take required when, with limited resources, they navigated the vicissitudes of life. We saw this from the time of the founding and extending through westward expansion. From the standpoint of the nation's law and Constitution, however, the changes were substantial. If so, oddly enough, they were not revolutionary. The fully formed seed for change had been implanted in American thought more than a century before by Margaret Fuller and cultivated in the Mormon decisions of the late nineteenth century. What's more, its ethical DNA, consisting of versions of liberty and equality, had been a constitutive element of American ethos even before the formal founding of the constitutional order. Having said this, it was not inevitable that Fuller's seed would bear fruit, much less grow to maturity. Things could have been different, and may yet be again. If so, that different world, too, might be the recognizable progeny of American constitutional thought.

THE SUPREME COURT AND SOCIAL CHANGE

If cases related to gender were the most significant of the Court's decisions touching on family, they were not the only ones. It's impossible to consider every possible case and issue. But it's worthwhile to consider a few that are salient to the theme of constitutional change.

In general, the American law of domestic relations was adapting to social developments on the ground. Adaptation had characterized the American law from the founding of the nation, of course. But economic and social change escalated in the twentieth century, as the nation moved from a predominately agricultural to an increasingly industrial and commercial economy. The consequences of this transformation were many. One was that the heart of material economy was no longer in the countryside but in cities. Demographic and geographic mobility had always been a conspicuous American characteristic, but innovations in communication and transportation, combined with economic change, intensified the trend. As people gathered in cities, the nation saw a relative decline in the number and importance of discrete communities in which residents knew one another—sometimes all too well. There was a decline also in the frequency with which persons live most of their lives near extended families and their childhood home. As many of these insular communities stalled or declined, cities rose, populated with people who were strangers to one another. And the economy was, in many ways, producing a society of individuals.[96] Unsurprisingly, law reflected these new modes of production, social organization, and demographic distribution. States were sometimes in the vanguard of adaptation, and other times playing catch-up as social change outpaced states' ability or willingness to adapt. Either way, state policies became the locus for and subjects of contestation, in which not only individuals but also families were implicated. And, for reasons that Tocqueville sagely anticipated, legal contestation inexorably gravitated upward to the Supreme Court. This was not necessarily a power-grab by the Court. It was simply part of the institutional logic of the system of law that emerged under the post–Civil War Constitution.

Thus, several of the Court's forays into family were largely in areas in which states had long been present and sometimes over which they had a monopoly. For example, states regulated not only access to marriage, but also the terms of and conditions for exit from marriage. In contrast with the nineteenth century, the twentieth-century Court never attempted to devise or enforce substantive grounds for divorce, much less a general federal common law of domestic relations. In fact, the Court abjured even the possibility of diversity jurisdiction in matters of family law—whether related to divorce or to other issues.[97] But a host of constitutional issues surrounded the manner in which states administered their laws of divorce. When did a state properly have jurisdiction over a marriage or over the parties, such that it possessed authority to grant a divorce? What kind of notice was due to a respondent in a proceeding for divorce? Was a state obliged to make its domestic relations courts available even to persons who lacked the means to pay a filing fee? To what extent was an adjudication of divorce in one state binding in another? If "competing" courts in different states adjudicated the dissolution of marriage, which court's judgment was binding?[98]

Divorce was only one area of family in which constitutional questions presented themselves. When children ran afoul of the criminal law, states had long made it clear that the parent was not the sole source of discipline and authority. But when the state stepped in, what process was owed to children? Were they entitled to their own representation, distinct from both parent and state? Were they to be treated like adults, subject to adult standards and discipline, or was a special system appropriate (or even required) for them? If a special system was called for, what were the constitutional standards and procedures for conviction and punishment within that system? And what sort of confinement, punishment, or supervision was appropriate or permissible?[99]

How should the state consider children born to parents who were not married to each other? This was not a novel question, but it gained special attention in the twentieth century, as social developments unfolded, and as the administrative apparatus of governments (both national and state) expanded into issues related to support for and welfare of children. As we saw in Chapter 2, the old English law treated bastardy harshly, imposing legal disabilities of substantial consequence. So did much of American law for quite some time, projecting onto illegitimate children a second-class status for many purposes.[100] Slowly, illegitimacy lost some but not all of its stigma, in some but not all places. Still, some stigma and no small amount of differential treatment remained in states' policies. For example, at least one state barred illegitimate children from recovering damages for the wrongful death of their mother and barred the mother from recovering damages for the wrongful death of her child.[101] And many states denied illegitimate children the right to inherit from their father's intestate estate, even if the father had publicly acknowledged his children.[102]

States sometimes justified these policies as incentives for (prospective) parents to produce legitimate offspring—in short to get married and to have sex only within marriage. Such justifications collided with two problems. The first was that the incentives that laws produced in this direction seemed to be weak, especially among the poor or outcast, who had little to lose by way of status or property. The rich could find ways to take care of their own—or not, if they chose. To the extent that the law created an effective incentive it was frequently for an unwed parent to forsake the bastard child. The second problem, which grew from the first, was that the policy ran afoul of a principle so basic that it formed part of the rhetorical logic of the American separation from Britain: it punished children for the sin of their parents. Such punishment was inconsistent with norms of fairness and equity. It penalized the innocent. And in many cases it left children with little means of support aside from the kindness of extended family or, failing that, the intercession of the state. Through doctrines developed in the twentieth century, the Supreme Court extended heightened scrutiny to governmental policies that imposed differential burdens on illegitimates. In doing so, it mitigated the moral perversity and social harshness of punitive policies and lifted the children of unwed parents above the ancient common law's doctrine of *filius nullius*.[103]

On the flip side of the coin of illegitimacy was the father. Paternity raised issues of constitutional significance on at least two fronts. One involved the identity and obligations of the putative father. Frequently enough, there were questions about who the biological father was. Still more frequently, illegitimate children received no support from their father, even when his identity was known (or assumed). Whatever the purpose for establishing paternity, the burden of proving it rested on the child or the mother. But how long might they take to assert a claim? Some states adopted fairly brief statutes of limitations. Pennsylvania, for example, at one time had a six-year limitation. This might have been sensible enough for the mother, though some mothers for a number of reasons—including fear of or disdain for the father or worries about the cost and uncertainty of the judicial process—did not press to establish paternity even when doing so might provide material support for the child. But what of the interests the children themselves might have in establishing paternity? Was cutting off a claim for relief at age six sufficiently protective of their interests? States had argued that problems of proof, and attendant problems of fairness to putative fathers, were substantial enough to justify a short limitation. The Court itself acknowledged the legitimacy of such concerns, especially in the context of support.[104] But eventually the Court struck down the short limitation, and Congress soon followed suit, imposing nationwide an eighteen-year statute of limitations on actions for paternity and support.[105] The justification included the undeniable social problems (and public burden) resulting from unsupported children, not to mention considerations of equity and fairness for the unsupported child. Recall Thomas Paine's critique of the English Crown: what sort of sovereign devours her own children?

Paternity's second front involved the father's access to his children. To what extent might a state deny a biological father access to his child born out of wedlock, deny him custody of the child after the mother's death, or deny him a right to block the child's adoption by another? In a series of decisions, the Court imposed limits on a state's authority to enforce such policies against a biological father who, though not married to the mother, had established a relationship with his child.[106] These limitations could find support in the Court's earlier twentieth-century decisions involving parenthood: *Meyer v. Nebraska, Pierce v. Society of Sisters,* and *Skinner v. Oklahoma.* To be sure, those decisions linked procreation and parenthood to marriage, but doctrinal developments after *Skinner,* including especially the Court's move to make the stigma of illegitimacy quasi-suspect, logically implied that a biological connection itself could be significant, even if not created within a marriage.

Still, in *Michael H. v. Gerald D.,* the Court confined the reach of doctrines respecting the constitutional significance of paternity per se.[107] The case involved a child (Victoria) born to a woman (Carole) who was married to one man (Gerald) but having an affair with a second (Michael), with whom she and Victoria also lived off and on for the first three years of Victoria's life. A blood test showed to a virtual certainty that Michael was the father, and during their time together, Michael established a paternal (and, by accounts, a caring) relationship with Victoria. When Carole and Gerald reunited, Michael petitioned a court of proper jurisdiction in California for an order allowing him visitation. (He did not seek custody.) California's law, however, provided that a child born in wedlock was presumptively the child of the husband, and the presumption was irrebuttable in this circumstance. Michael challenged the presumption as a violation of his parental liberty under the Constitution. Writing partly for a plurality of four justices and partly for only two (including himself), Justice Scalia sought to cabin the concept of liberty across the board. Familial liberty, he argued, was limited to those rights that are both "fundamental" and "traditionally protected by our society." Moreover, he urged, constitutional liberty was confined to "the most specific level at which a relevant tradition protecting, or denying protection to, the asserted right can be identified." In this case, he said, the most specific way to define the right was the right of "an adulterous natural father in Michael's situation" to assert a parental interest as against the husband of the mother. Justice Scalia concluded that there was no such tradition.[108]

To support this conclusion, Justice Scalia relied on two sources of common law. One—Bracton's *De Legibus et Consuetudinibus Angliae*—was (literally) Medieval, having been written in the mid-thirteenth century. The second—Sir Harris Nicolas's *Treatise on the Law of Adulterine Bastardy*—was published in 1836 as an attack on *Banbury's Case,* an English decision from the seventeenth century.[109] Notably, *Banbury's Case* had softened the evidentiary burden for proving that a wife's child was actually the progeny of a man not her husband. Looking back across more than a century, Sir Harris crankily complained that the decision had altered the formerly rigid rule of the English common law, most recently compiled by Sir Edward Coke in the late sixteenth century. Put differently, Nicolas, like Justice Scalia, wanted the "original" English common law, not a version dating only to the 1600s. While Nicolas was asserting in the mid-nineteenth century that *Banbury's Case* was a deviant decision, an American commentator recognized around the same time that the case's liberalizing rule—permitting parties to challenge the parental presumption arising from the marital relationship—was considered authoritative by English courts.[110]

In this light, Justice Scalia's invocation of Bracton and Nicolas is interesting for several reasons. For one, in propping up the traditions of "our society," he relies not on American but on English sources. Second, those sources were not only ancient but had been repudiated by an authoritative decision of an English court. Third, therefore, neither Bracton nor Nicolas expressed the English common law as it stood at the time of the American founding. This is the very period that Justice Scalia (in other contexts) says is significant, even (he sometimes insists) binding. Fourth, his citations neglect the extent to which the colonies, not to mention the states of the independent nation, repudiated outmoded concepts from the ancient common law. Fifth, and related to the fourth, reliance on those ancient sources overlooks (or simply rejects) the ways in which the common law has not been a static entity but a dynamic and adaptive source of law, both in North America and even in England. In short, Justice Scalia's citations appear to be illegitimate.

Another related area of the changing law of domestic relations involved the administrative regulation and oversight of parents generally. After uncounted years of virtually unfettered deference to parental discretion in child rearing and discipline, states began to realize that the mere fact of parenthood—whether biological or legal—did not always produce a caring or attentive relationship. In fact, relations between some parents and children could be degrading or dangerous to the child, sometimes even fatal. States had always stood in theory as *parens patriae* to vulnerable members of the population. But only as states refined and enhanced their administrative capacity did they acquire the practical ability to intercede to prevent or deter neglect or abuse. In some circumstances, states might attempt to remove children from their homes or even in extreme cases move to terminate parental rights. These governmental actions raised nontrivial constitutional questions, paralleling those raised by the appearance of the juvenile-justice system. What process was appropriate, not only for protecting the interests of children but also for respecting the privileges of parenthood? What circumstances might justify a state's intercession into the life of the family? What degree of intercession was appropriate? And what process was due to a parent whose relationship with his/her children was to be suspended or severed? Was the parent entitled to notice, representation, and a hearing? What standard of proof of parental misfeasance did the state have to meet? More than once, the Supreme Court was asked to address such questions.[111]

These are all issues involving nuclear families. The Court was also invited to weigh in on constitutional aspects of governmental policies involving non-nuclear familial arrangements. Again, these were cases that grew out of the logic of the twentieth-century constitutional world as it emerged after the Civil War and Reconstruction. Aside from the biological relation between parent and child, are there relations outside of marriage that are entitled to constitutional protection? The freedom of association, as it has come to be called, supplies a baseline for a generic right to associate with persons for any number of purposes (though certainly not all purposes). Are there associations outside of marriage that are entitled to be designated "familial," with whatever constitutional status and protection such a designation might suggest?

The Court signaled one avenue for expanding the constitutionally protected family in *U.S. Department of Agriculture v. Moreno*.[112] The Food Stamp Act of 1964 provided financial support for eligible households to purchase food. The Act defined a "household" as "a group of related or non-related individuals, who . . . are living as one economic unit sharing common cooking facilities and for whom food is customarily purchased in common." In 1971, Congress redefined "household," and the secretary of agriculture adopted conforming regulations authorizing benefits only to households consisting of persons all of whom "are related to one another." The Supreme Court struck down the amendment as a violation of the equal protection clause, holding that the new restrictive definition was irrational in light of the Act's purpose: to stimulate the agricultural economy by supporting the purchase of food to meet the nutritional needs of poor households. The new policy, the Court said, was motivated by "a bare congressional desire to harm a politically unpopular group," and such a motive was not a legitimate interest. (The unpopular group consisted of "hippies" who had gathered as quasi-families in communal households, much like some of the communal families of the nineteenth century.) The Court also rejected as irrational the government's claim that the program was justified as an attempt to promote sexual morality. Justice Douglas, concurring, went further, claiming that the amendment trammeled the freedom of association and fell hardest on the poor. "Taking a person into one's home because he is poor or needs help or brings happiness to the household is of the same dignity," he said, as are the relations that the Court had previously recognized as being protected.

If Justice Douglas's gloss on the Opinion of the Court had legs, however, they did not travel far. One year later, the Court upheld a zoning ordinance of the Village of Belle Terre prohibiting occupancy of any single-family dwelling by more than two persons who are unrelated to one another "by blood, adoption, or marriage." Owners of a house in the Village rented to six students from SUNY Stony Brook, none of whom was related to the others. Following Justice Douglas's lead in *Moreno,* the owners challenged the ordinance as a violation of the right to privacy. Indeed, Justice Marshall urged that the ordinance ran afoul of the right to choose one's personal companions, which was relevant to the kind and quality of intimate relations within the home. "The selection of one's living companions involves . . . choices as to the emotional, social, or economic benefits," benefits which may derive not only from traditional forms of family but also from "alternative living arrangements." The ordinance, said Marshall, discriminated "on the basis of . . . a personal lifestyle choice as to household companions." Marshall's opinion, however, was a dissent. The Court, through Justice Douglas, upheld the zoning ordinance as economic or social legislation that evinced no animosity toward unmarried persons, but promoted legitimate local interests in overcrowding, traffic, parking, and noise.[113]

Although the Court deferred to restrictive zoning in the white, well-to-do Village of Belle Terre on Long Island, it was skeptical of a similar ordinance in East Cleveland, a predominately African American city in Ohio. The latter ordinance restricted occupancy in a single-family zone to persons who were lineally related to one another by blood or marriage. This permitted multigenerational households other than nuclear families, but only if all of the occupants were lineally related to one another. Inez Moore lived in a single-family home with two grandsons who were cousins to each other, not brothers. Although the city provided a procedure for requesting a variance, Ms. Moore directly challenged the ordinance after she was convicted of violating it. The city was thoroughly middle class, and the city council wanted to preserve its middle-class character by reinforcing nuclear families, which were not consistently characteristic of households of the urban poor. Like Belle Terre, East Cleveland also asserted governmental interests in controlling overcrowding and regulating parking. The Court, however, struck down the ordinance as defining "family" too narrowly. In doing so, Justice Powell's plurality opinion acknowledged that "the institution of the family is deeply rooted in this Nation's history and tradition" and that it is an important institution for "inculcat[ing] and pass[ing] down many of our most cherished values, moral and cultural." Still, Justice Powell said, "ours is by no means a tradition limited to respect for the bonds uniting the members of the nuclear family. The tradition of uncles, aunts, cousins, and especially grandparents sharing a household along with parents and children has roots equally venerable and equally deserving of constitutional recognition." Implicitly hearkening to the Court's earlier celebration of parenthood in *Pierce v. Society of Sisters,* Powell closed by insisting that "the Constitution prevents East Cleveland from standardizing its children—and its adults—by forcing all to live in certain narrowly defined family patterns."[114]

A generation later, the Court was less inclined to celebrate extended family in *Troxel v. Granville.*[115] The context was less than happy. Tommie Granville and Brad Troxel had had an extended intimate nonmarital relationship that produced two daughters. When the relationship ended, Brad moved back to his parents' home, where he and his parents enjoyed visitation with the (grand)children on weekends. After two years apart from Tommie, Brad committed suicide. For several months, his parents continued to see their grandchildren regularly, until Tommie notified them that she wanted to limit them to one brief visit per month. The Troxels filed a petition in the Superior Court of Washington, pursuant to a state statute permitting any person to petition for visitation at any time. The standard for adjudicating the petition was the best interest of the child. The Troxels sought semi-monthly visitation, along with two weeks in the summer. They offered the girls a continuing, loving relationship, not only with grandparents but also with cousins who lived in the vicinity. And they offered exposure to music. For themselves, no doubt, the Troxels wanted to maintain a relationship with two young girls who were the last living link to their son.

Finding that visitation was in the best interest of the girls, the trial court issued an opinion that could trace a direct line to Justice Powell's opinion in *Moore v. East Cleveland.* "I look back on some personal experiences. . . . We always spen[t] as kids a week with one set of grandparents and another set of grandparents, [and] it happened to work out in our family that [it] turned out to be an enjoyable experience. Maybe that can, in this family, if that is how it works out." A deeply divided Supreme Court reversed. Justice O'Connor's plurality noted that, as a demographic matter, is was "difficult to speak of an average American family." She observed that in 1996, 28 percent of children under the age of eighteen lived with a single parent. And in 1998, 5.8 percent of children under eighteen "lived in the household of their grandparents." Thus, "the nationwide enactment of nonparental visitation statutes is assuredly due, in some part, to the States' recognition of these changing realities of the American family." Nonetheless, Justice O'Connor held that parents had a fundamental right to make "childrearing decisions." As long as the parent is "fit" and "cares for his or her children," there is "normally no reason for the State to inject itself into the private realm of the family," especially when the intervention is "simply because a state judge believes a 'better' decision could be made," and even when the intervention promotes connection with extended family.[116]

By the dawn of the twenty-first century, the Court had woven family broadly into the constitutional jurisprudence of the nation. Whether this development has been desirable, I offer no judgment. But desirable or not, it is real. Even justices who sometimes (though inconsistently) forswear invocation of family as a fundamental interest, right, or tradition can find the lure of family a seductive ground for constitutional decision. In *McDonald v. Chicago*, for example, Justice Alito, joined by Chief Justice Roberts and Justices Scalia, Kennedy, and Thomas, held that the Second Amendment's right to keep and bear arms was based on an individual's right of self-defense. This right was not for self alone, however. It existed also for family. Thus, abjuring the militia clause, the Court insisted that handguns are constitutionally protected "because they are 'the most preferred firearm in the nation to 'keep' and use for protection of one's home and family.' . . . [T]his right is 'deeply rooted in this Nation's history and tradition.'"[117]

Conclusion

The Meanings of Marriage

I've married two hundred couples in my day. Do I believe in it? I don't know. I suppose I do. M marries N. Millions of them. The cottage, the go-cart, the Sunday afternoon drives in the Ford—the first rheumatism—the grandchildren—the second rheumatism—the death-bed—the reading of the will. Once in a thousand times it's interesting.[1]

Thornton Wilder, *Our Town*

Guns, not for militias but instead for the sake of hearth and home and family? Even if it's textually jarring, the grafting of guns onto family isn't impossible in light of American experience, both old and more recent, and of the values and practices for which experience has provided a home. Experience has always supplied much of the impetus for and the content and direction of American constitutional law. By the first decade of the twenty-first century, a slightly different doctrinal connection has grown also from experience, both old and more recent. It has involved two jurisprudential strands. The first strand grew from doctrines developed in the nineteenth century. By the twentieth century, it became known as the right to marry. The second strand was newer, at least as a matter of constitutional law. It has involved certain sorts of rights or immunities surrounding sexual orientation. Initially, it might have appeared unlikely that the two would connect. But given a constitutionally supported social milieu that encouraged impressive amounts of associational liberty, and given the fact that the bramble bush of law permits sometimes disparate limbs and branches and shoots to converge and even intertwine, it's not inconceivable that these two branches of doctrine would approach each other. Even so and even now, it's impossible to know what, if anything, may come of the convergence.

THE RIGHT TO MARRY

From the inception of the American constitutional order, people have sensibly assumed that adults—and children under some circumstances—may marry. Law, religious doctrine, and social habit have underwritten this assumption. Thus, it's fair to say that there has been a long-standing social consensus that marriage is a privilege, in the sense of its being an entitlement. If there has been agreement on this point, there was, from the inception, disagreement on others. Was marriage a sacred institution, or was it secular (or both)? Was marriage for life, or was it (properly) terminable (and, if so, how and why)? Was marriage essential to an orderly or decent society, or was it (or was its form at least) socially contingent? Was marriage necessarily between two people, or did it permit more than two? Was it desirable, or not? And, if desirable, what were the goods of or reasons for marriage—as a social (or spiritual) institution and as a relationship?

If marriage was an entitlement, it was also a domain for governmental regulation. In the United States, as we've seen, regulation has been the province of states in the first instance and for most purposes. States have regulated marriage and policed its bounds in at least three ways. First, they have set conditions on who may marry whom, when, and how. They have prohibited marriage where one of the parties is already married, is too young, is insane, has procured the marriage through fraud or duress, or is of a different putative race from the other party. They have treated marriage as voidable (or terminable) where the parties are too closely related by consanguinity or affinity or, in a few states, where the husband is incurably impotent. Second, many states have, at one time or another, subjected to criminal punishment or civil liability certain sexual behavior outside of marriage. Among the acts made criminal have been fornication, adultery, incest, bestiality, sodomy, rape, statutory rape, and pederasty. Among the acts giving rise to civil liability have been criminal conversation (sexual intercourse between a married person and one to whom s/he is not married), alienation of affections (interference with the conjugal affection and society of the marital relationship), and loss of consortium (to similar effect). Not all of the prohibitions and conditions of either the first or second type have survived.

Third, states have prescribed privileges and duties within the marriage. Among the privileges that persist in law and policy today are a right to spousal visitation in forums restricted to "immediate family," coverage in health insurance policies and pensions, participation in medical decisions involving a spouse, advantages and benefits related to taxation, the ability to qualify as a beneficiary or dependent in life insurance policies, entitlement to bereavement leave on the death of a spouse, the ability to live in areas zoned single-family, a presumption to inheritance in the absence of (or in lieu of) a will, exemptions from levy and execution, unemployment benefits in certain circumstances, a right against compelled adverse testimony of a spouse in certain circumstances, and causes of action for injury to a spouse. States have also enforced privileges arising from the dissolution of a marriage. These include a right to the division of marital property, consideration for custody of and/or visitation with children, and consideration for periodic payments either as spousal support or child support.

As we've seen, however, marriage has not been the domain of states exclusively. For more than two centuries, the national government, too, has involved itself in matters of family.[2] In the westward migrations, the nation used families to extend authority of the nation across the continent. In its policies toward American Indians, the nation promoted bourgeois nuclear families as the linchpin of its ambition to break up the tribes and assimilate their members. In the name of sexual decency, the United States took the lead in trying to stamp out communal families—and, at the beginning of the twentieth century, enacted a prohibition on the transportation of women across state lines "for immoral purposes." Even more emphatically, when Mormons moved west in search of Zion, the nation (including its judiciary and its army) invoked its authority over the territories to prohibit polygamy and deny rights of citizenship to persons who espoused it. In one case, at least, the nation even conditioned statehood on the repudiation of polygamy. With the rise of an extensive apparatus for administrative regulation of large aspects of human endeavor, Congress enacted policies concerning women and children in the workplace—including statutes providing for equal opportunities on the basis of sex with respect to employment and education, the Pregnancy Discrimination Act of 1978, and the Family and Medical Leave Act. Congress has also made special provision for spouses and marital families for purposes of income taxation, estate and gift taxation, Social Security, and entitlements. And recently, the Congress enacted the Defense of Marriage Act, more about which below.

If marriage has been a site for regulation, American law has also recognized it as a domain for the exercise of individual choice. Indeed, as we saw in Chapter 1, the Supreme Court implicitly recognized in *Maynard v. Hill* a freedom to choose even to divorce.[3] Even before *Maynard,* the Court in *Meister v. Moore* held that there was a right to marry at common law, under which the parties might enter into a marriage simply by choosing to be and by holding themselves out to the world as married, without the forms and formalities of the civil law.[4] This was a distinctly non-English way of doing things, where family was concerned. To be sure, the Court recognized, states might abolish this "common-law" liberty by express statute, but the Court suggested that the formative history and tradition of America provided a right antecedent to the civil law. Still, the polygamy cases indicated that the constitutional domain of the freedom to choose was not unlimited. Just as Congress imposed monogamy on the tribes, the Court held that the Constitution imposed a similar norm on the rest of us. This was not merely for the sake of Christian civilization, the Court reasoned, but also to promote "liberty and equality" and to reinforce "the moral judgment of the community."[5] Without the religious moralism, but with a nod to a liberal version of liberty, the Court affirmed the constitutional status of marriage in several early twentieth-century decisions, including *Meyer v. Nebraska, Pierce v. Society of Sisters,* and *Skinner v. Oklahoma.*

Not until the latter half of the twentieth century, however, did the Court pick up the doctrinal suggestion of *Meister v. Moore,* to hold that there was per se a constitutional right to marry, a right that constrained government's authority to regulate. The first decision extended a portion of the logic of *Skinner v. Oklahoma,* concerning race. In the aptly titled case of *Loving v. Virginia,* the Court held that states were constitutionally barred from using their criminal law not only to obliterate certain races, but also to prohibit persons of putatively different races from marrying each other.[6] As we saw in Chapter 4, this holding was not obvious, given the nation's racialist policies in the nineteenth and early twentieth centuries, policies which the Court itself had ratified. Indeed, the Court in 1883 upheld a criminal statute, much like Virginia's, prohibiting interracial marriage.[7] In 1954 in fact, the Court denied certiorari to a black woman in Alabama who was convicted of marrying a white man.[8] And in 1956, the Court ducked the chance to consider the constitutionality of Virginia's law.[9]

Eleven years later, the Court's jurisprudential orientation, not to mention a portion of the public's ethos, had shifted. The Court struck down Virginia's prohibition on two partially distinct theories. One was that, as an explicit racial classification, the prohibition was an invidious discrimination, subject to "the most rigid scrutiny." Under this standard, the classification "must be shown to be necessary to the accomplishment of some permissible state objective, independent of . . . racial discrimination." The second, drawing from *Skinner,* was that "marriage is one of the 'basic civil rights of man,' fundamental to our very existence and survival." On either theory, Virginia's arguments—that it was not discriminating because it punished both parties equally and that the state had a legitimate interest in preserving the racial integrity, vigor, and pride of its citizens (both of which borrowed from the Court's own reasoning in *Pace v. Alabama*)—were invalid. "The Fourteenth Amendment requires that the freedom of choice to marry not be restricted by invidious racial discriminations. Under our Constitution, the freedom to marry, or not marry, a person of another race resides with the individual and cannot be infringed by the State."[10]

What about a restriction based not on race but on the inability to support one's children? In *Zablocki v. Redhail,*[11] the law of the state of Wisconsin provided that any noncustodial parent who was subject to a judicial order to support his child was prohibited from marrying (or remarrying) unless he first obtained permission of a state court. The court was prohibited from granting permission unless the petitioner could demonstrate that he was meeting his child-support obligation and that the child was not likely to become a "public charge." Roger Redhail was denied a license to marry because he was delinquent in paying support to his daughter, whom he had fathered when he was in high school, and because she had been receiving public assistance since she was born. Wisconsin offered sensible reasons for its policy: protecting the welfare of noncustodial children, ensuring the financial stability of the noncustodial parent, and ensuring that that parent's decision to marry was an intelligent choice. The state might also have offered protecting the public fisc.

Writing for the Court, however, Justice Marshall struck down the state's policy, invoking not strict scrutiny but an intermediate standard of review. In *Loving,* the Court had kept equal protection and the substantive liberty to marry partially segregated from each other. In *Zablocki,* the Court's theory combined these two doctrinal branches: "When a statutory classification significantly interferes with the exercise of a fundamental right, it cannot be upheld unless it is supported by sufficiently important state interests and is closely tailored to effectuate only those interests." (This was one of several precursors to the undue burden test of *Planned Parenthood v. Casey.*) Although this particular liberty involved access to a quasi-public institution, the Court located the right under the umbrella of the right of privacy, announced in *Griswold v. Connecticut.* "It is not surprising that the decision to marry has been placed on the same level of importance as decisions relating to procreation, childbirth, child rearing, and family relationships," the Court reasoned in *Zablocki.* "It would make little sense to recognize a right of privacy with respect to other matters of family life and not with respect to the decision to enter the relationship that is the foundation of the family in our society." Thus, if Mr. Redhail's "right to procreate means anything at all, it must imply some right to enter the only relationship in which the state of Wisconsin allows sexual relations to take place."

This last reference, to Wisconsin's prohibition on fornication, is interesting. On one way of reading, it might have signaled that the Court still viewed marriage as the official institution in which sexual relations may legally occur. In short, marriage is essentially—or at least importantly—about procreation. More crudely, marriage is a license to have sex. There are reasons to believe that this was not Justice Marshall's intended meaning. For one thing, the Court had acknowledged in other decisions—like *Eisenstadt v. Baird,* the abortion decisions, and various decisions destigmatizing illegitimacy—that marriage was no longer the sole province in which sex may occur. For another, Justice Marshall hinted elsewhere in *Zablocki* that if the threshold for entering into marriage were too high, illegitimate babies would be the consequence. But if he was agnostic about the moral necessity of sex within marriage, the logic of his reference to Wisconsin's law against fornication might suggest that he did not consider access to marriage to be fundamental. Put differently, if Wisconsin law had not prescribed that marriage was the locus for legal sex, would the Court have been less inclined to hold that the institution is constitutionally fundamental? Within a decade, the Court would hold that any legal link between marriage and procreation—or simply between marriage and sex—was no longer essential to the constitutional status of marriage.

The case was *Turner v. Safley.*[12] The context was prison. If ever there were domains in which government might possess authority to restrict access to marriage, they would surely include penal institutions. Regulations of Missouri's Division of Corrections prohibited an inmate from marrying unless the superintendent of the inmate's prison granted permission. The superintendent's authorization was restricted solely to circumstances in which "there are compelling reasons to do so." Testimony at trial indicated that "only a pregnancy or the birth of an illegitimate child" would count as compelling. Although the Court rehearsed the doctrine that "the decision to marry is a fundamental right," it resisted the logical step of raising the standard of review. Thus, instead of employing either *Loving*'s strict scrutiny or *Zablocki*'s "critical examination," the Court in *Turner* applied—or purported to apply—the rational-basis test. So structured, the state's reasons for its policy seemed solid. One justification involved the internal security of prisons. A concrete concern here was that love triangles "might lead to violent confrontations between inmates." The second justification was rehabilitation. Here, the testimony suggested a concern that "female prisoners often were subject to abuse at home or were overly dependent on male figures," conditions which had often led to the inmates' involvement in criminal activity in the first place. One superintendent expressed the view that such prisoners "needed to concentrate on developing skills of self-reliance," an interest which the prohibition on marriage promoted.

The Court, through Justice O'Connor, rejected both justifications and struck down the policy. Justice O'Connor second-guessed the prison's interest in security. For one thing, she said, it was not the actual motivating reason for the policy. For another, because love triangles can develop even without a formal marriage, the state's rationale defied logic and "common sense." She also rejected the argument from rehabilitation, holding that it was based on a sexist stereotype and that the policy "sweeps much more broadly than can be explained by [the state's] penological objectives."

Of greater significance than the Court's analytical slipperiness was its lucid account of the reasons marriage retains its fundamentality even behind prison walls.

Many important attributes of marriage remain . . . after taking into account the limitations imposed by prison life. First, inmate marriages, like others, are expressions of emotional support and public commitment. These elements are an important and significant aspect of the marital relationship. In addition, many religions recognize marriage as having spiritual significance; for some inmates and their spouses, therefore, the commitment of a marriage may be an exercise of religious faith as well as an expression of personal dedication. Third, most inmates eventually will be released by parole or commutation, and therefore most inmate marriages are formed in the expectation that they ultimately will be fully consummated. Finally, marital status often is a precondition to the receipt of government benefits . . . , property rights . . . , and other less tangible benefits (e.g., legitimation of children born out of wedlock). These incidents of marriage, like the religious and personal aspects of the marriage commitment, are unaffected by the fact of confinement or the pursuit of legitimate corrections goals.

As often happens, the Court distinguished without overruling a prior conflicting decision—*Butler v. Wilson*—which had held that a state may prohibit marriage of an inmate who is incarcerated under a life sentence.[13] Precedent aside, the Court in *Turner* clearly committed itself to a companionate, as opposed to a reproductive, understanding of the constitutional significance of marriage.

SEXUAL ORIENTATION

Historically, the Court's decisions were devoid of any mention of "homosexual" or "homosexuality" until well into the twentieth century. This is understandable, if we note that the terminology didn't appear at all in the English language until the final decade of the nineteenth century, and even then it appeared mainly in scientific and psychiatric literature. Around the same time, one might read or hear the term "invert" or "sexual invert" to refer to a person who, according to the OED, "exhibits instincts or behaviour characteristic of the opposite sex." To a lesser degree than "homosexual," the latter term clearly connoted a normative presumption of heterosexuality. To depart from that presumed orientation was a kind of defect. It "inverted" what was normal. This judgment clearly had ancient—and religious—roots, which even ostensibly scientific psychiatric studies of the day retained. It was not until the latter half of the twentieth century that the status of same-sex orientation and the terms to describe it began to lose their presumptive judgment in much ordinary conversation, and in psychiatry, too. Thus, many people today understand that gender is less bimodal, and sexuality more fluid or dynamic, than even our current conventional terminology might suggest.

Interestingly, some of the native tribes came to this view long before "white" America did, though, as one might expect, they came to it through a different route. As we saw in Chapter 1, diverse cultures have produced a variety of systems of belief to which stories of creation are foundational. These creation myths are important cultural keys to believers' understanding of the world—including the purpose(s) and value(s) of human existence, including sexuality and family. Western stories of creation tended to be sexually bimodal in ways that were congenial to masculine supremacy. In contrast, one Hindu myth was notably androgynous, though it did not inhibit the emergence and persistence of a patriarchal culture. American Indians, too, had their stories of creation. The stories varied greatly, and to diverse effect, across tribes. But one thematic thread that has run through the myths of several tribes—including the Zuni, Navajo, Lakota (Sioux), Arapaho, Mohave, Papago, Omaha, and Kamia—gave rise to a sexual status that anthropologists came to call the "berdache," or Man-Woman. As Walter Williams defines the term, berdache refers to "a morphological male who does not fill a society's standard man's role, who has a nonmasculine character. This type of person is often stereo-typed as effeminate, but a more accurate characterization is androgyny." In American Indian usage, the term can refer to two types of person. One is the hermaphrodite, who possesses physical characteristics that cross the line between genders. The other is one who is physically unambiguous but takes on a social role or character that crosses the standard gendered line.[14] It's worth noting that this way of putting it presupposes a baseline understanding of roles and physical traits that count as normally male and female. In that respect, it is similar to the European-American dualist presumption. The Native American account parts company with the Western, however, in its understanding of what counts as "natural" and in its willingness to carve out acceptable, sometimes integral, social roles for the berdache.

The diversity of creation myths among the tribes makes it impossible to describe them all here. In general, however, a common element of these stories includes one or more sexually ambiguous beings who were present around the time the world came to be and who were important to the primordial formation, form, and functions of human societies. The Navajo myth is among the most elaborate, involving the gradual elevation of people into and through five distinct worlds. As Williams recites it, "the first people were First Man and First Woman, who were created equally and at the same time." They were unhappy in the first world and in the second, so they escaped into a third world, where they met twin beings—Turquoise Boy and White Shell Girl—who were the first berdaches. In the language of the Navajo, each was a *nadle,* or "one who is transformed." In the third world, with the help of the twins, First Man and First Woman began farming. Then one of the twins invented pottery. The other invented basketry. Together they made axes and hoes. These were the foundations of civilization. As the story unfolds, a great flood arose and threatened the survival of the people. Turquoise Boy helped the people climb to safety from the third world to the fourth, and White Shell Girl helped them climb yet further into the fifth world, which is the one the Navajo people presently inhabit. Navajo culture reflects this myth, holding the *nadle* in high regard as not only socially significant but even as a spiritual being, integral to Navajo society.[15]

To be sure, not all tribes raised berdaches to the level of spiritual leaders. Some tribes merely tolerated them. Others did not. But in a nontrivial number of Indian cultures, the berdaches' role is even ceremonial, almost shaman-like. They also have important practical functions. For the tribe, they serve as mediators, "not just between women and men, but also between the physical and the spiritual." For their families, they perform significant productive, largely feminine, labor. Because of their spiritual, social, and familial functions, berdaches may elevate the status of their family within the tribe. The berdaches' role may also be erotic, in which they "generally (but not always) take a nonmasculine role, either being asexual or becoming the passive partner in sex with men. In some cultures the berdache might become a wife to a man." Predictably, this mode of social organization did not sit well with the waves of Europeans who came across the continent—"from the Spanish conquistadors to the Western frontiersmen and Christian missionaries and [governmental] officials"—who viewed it as not only puzzling but morally offensive.[16]

Well into the twentieth century, American law tended to reflect this European view. The constitutional sign of this tendency was *Bowers v. Hardwick,* involving a challenge to a Georgia statute that made oral or anal sex a crime, punishable by as much as twenty years in prison for a single violation.[17] Technically, the statute didn't distinguish between same-sex and heterosexual acts. The Supreme Court, however, treated the case as involving strictly the question of whether the Constitution "confers a fundamental right upon homosexuals to engage in sodomy." Justice White, writing for the Court, narrowly read the precedents—from *Meyer v. Nebraska* to the abortion decisions as they then stood—and concluded that the right of privacy did not cover this case, because the case did not involve marriage and procreation. Nor, said the Court, was the right to same-sex sodomy "implicit in ordered liberty" or "deeply rooted in this Nation's history and tradition." The Court held that it was obliged to read those standards strictly, so as to prevent judge-made law. Nor did it make a difference that the triggering encounter in *Bowers* occurred between consenting adults within the privacy of the home. The Constitution, the Court held, does not insulate the home as a haven for criminal acts, even if the crimes are victimless.

Beyond (or beneath) the claim of right, the challenger had argued also that the statute was simply irrational, because it rested solely on "the presumed belief of a majority of the electorate in Georgia that homosexual sodomy is immoral and unacceptable." The Court rejected this argument, holding that "the law . . . is constantly based on notions of morality, and if all laws representing essentially moral choices are to be invalidated . . . , the courts will be very busy indeed." It mattered, said the Court, that twenty-five states criminalized sodomy. And for Chief Justice Burger, who concurred in the Court's opinion, it mattered that ancient Roman law treated homosexual sodomy as a capital crime, that England by statute (during the Reformation) and at common law (at the time of the American Revolution) had made it a crime, and that "Judeao-Christian [*sic*] moral and ethical standards" condemned the practice.

Justice Blackmun, writing for four justices, dissented on the ground that the Court had defined the right too narrowly. "This case is about 'the most comprehensive of rights and the right most valued by civilized men,' namely, 'the right to be let alone.'" Justice Stevens, writing for three justices, filed a separate dissent. He noted first, that Georgia's statute, like most statutes forbidding sodomy—at the founding, at the time the Fourteenth Amendment was ratified, and by the latter half of the twentieth century—did not distinguish between same-sex and heterosexual acts. Thus, the initial question for Justice Stevens was not whether a state may proscribe homosexual sodomy, but whether it may "totally prohibit the described conduct by means of a neutral law applying without exception to all persons subject to its jurisdiction." He concluded that the answer was no, and that "the fact that a governing majority in a State has traditionally viewed a particular practice as immoral is not a sufficient reason for upholding a law prohibiting the practice; neither history nor tradition could save a law prohibiting miscegenation from constitutional attack." In short, choices by persons, married or not, "concerning the intimacies of their physical relationship, even when not intended to produce offspring," fall within the concept of liberty in the Fourteenth Amendment, as applied by the Court in *Griswold, Eisenstadt,* and the abortion decisions. Given this, Justice Stevens's second question was whether the state could save the statute "by announcing that it will only enforce the law against homosexuals." Again, he answered no. For one thing, the assumption underwriting a policy of selective enforcement is that homosexuals do not possess the same liberty that others possess. That assumption is fallacious, he said, for in a polity of free and equal citizens, all have "the same interest in liberty that the members of the majority share." For another, "a policy of selective enforcement must be supported by a neutral and legitimate interest—something more substantial than a habitual dislike for, or ignorance about, the disfavored group." He concluded that there was no such interest supporting enforcement of the statute in *Bowers.*

Within a decade, social ferment over homosexuality would produce a flurry of public debate, governmental policy, and judicial decisions, just as *Roe v. Wade* had done before (and continues to do). One of those decisions, from the Supreme Court, involved neither sodomy nor sexual behavior at all, but a question of status. The central question of *Romer v. Evans* arose from a constitutional referendum (Amendment 2) in which the people of the state of Colorado prohibited the state—including its officers, agencies, schools, and political subdivisions—from adopting or enforcing any policy "whereby homosexual, lesbian or bisexual orientation, conduct, practices or relationships shall constitute or otherwise be the basis of or entitle any person or class of persons to have or claim any minority status, quota preferences, protected status or claim of discrimination." The impetus for the measure was to negate some local ordinances listing sexual orientation as an impermissible ground for discrimination with respect to a variety of transactions and public accommodations, and to reverse an executive order from the governor directing agencies not to discriminate in hiring or promotion with respect to sexual orientation (among other traits). The state asserted interests in respecting citizens' freedom of association, placing homosexuals on a par with everyone else, and conserving resources to fight discrimination against other groups.[18]

Justice Kennedy wrote for the Court. His threshold question was whether Amendment 2 imposed special disabilities on homosexuals, or simply prohibited special treatment. He concluded that the first interpretation was the accurate one. On his reading, Amendment 2 carved out homosexuals as a class, not only excluding them from the protection of antidiscrimination laws, but also potentially excluding them from general laws, and, in the process, imposing a special burden on them in seeking political change. How to think about this, as a constitutional matter? Justice Kennedy declined to find that sexual orientation per se was a constitutionally suspect basis for differential treatment. Hence, the ostensible standard of review was rational basis. Did Colorado's justification satisfy the standard? Under a deferential application of the standard, one might think so, especially as this was an amendment to the state's constitution. But the Court, applying a distinctly nondeferential standard, struck down Amendment 2. The Court offered two bases for this conclusion. One was that it imposed a special, sweeping disability on a single named group, disqualifying them "from the right to seek specific protection from the law." This disqualification was simultaneously "too narrow and too broad" to be justified by Colorado's asserted interests. Second, the Court held that the only plausible explanation for Amendment 2 is that it was born of animosity toward the class of persons affected. Citing *U.S.D.A. v. Moreno,* the Court held that "a bare desire to harm a politically unpopular group cannot constitute a legitimate governmental interest." Colorado, the Court said, has made a class of persons "a stranger to its laws."

Justice Scalia dissented. His opening salvo placed squarely on the table a governmental interest that Colorado had not itself offered: preserving traditional sexual mores. This, he said, was a legitimate interest. Its enforcement, moreover, did not convert "seemingly tolerant Coloradans" into bigots. The battle over sexual morality is a cultural struggle ("a Kulturkampf"), he said, properly waged through democratic processes, and not by "the elite class from which the Members of this institution are selected."

How does Amendment 2 attempt to preserve sexual mores? It merely "puts gays and lesbians in the same position as all other persons" and goes no further than to deny homosexuals special treatment under the law. The only disability imposed is that they must first amend the state's constitution before securing the special rights that Amendment 2 prohibits. This disability, said Justice Scalia, is not a constitutionally cognizable injury. "The world has never heard of such a principle." In fact, even the Supreme Court had heard of—had even announced—such a principle, albeit in the context of race, in *Reitman v. Mulkey* (1967),[19] though Justice Scalia didn't cite it.

But was it a special case when Amendment 2 singled out homosexuals—called them by name, perhaps with animus—and subjected them to this heightened procedural requirement for seeking political change? Justice Scalia said no. For one thing, there have been plenty of examples of groups who've been required to resort to a constitutional amendment to achieve their aims. Proponents of the sale of alcohol, for example, had to do so, and succeeded. Persons who want an established religion or a monarchy have also been put to this inconvenience. So, too, have been polygamists. The constitutions of five states "to this day contain provisions stating that polygamy is 'forever prohibited.' Polygamists, and those who have a polygamous 'orientation,' have been 'singled out' by these provisions for much more severe treatment than merely denial of favored status; and that treatment can only be changed by [amending] the state constitutions." In fact, he noted (citing *Davis v. Beason* and *Murphy v. Ramsey*) that the Court has held not only that polygamy may be made a crime, but also that polygamists (and, he might have added, those who are members of an organization that "encourages" polygamy) could be denied the right to vote. Was this—is this—"animosity?" Of course it is, he said. But that is okay. Or at least it is permitted in the democratic system that the Constitution established. Animosity toward homosexuality is not "Unamerican," any more than is animosity toward "murder, . . . or polygamy, or cruelty to animals."

Justice Scalia's concern about the doctrinal status of *Bowers* in the wake of *Romer* was well placed. Within a decade, the Court revisited *Bowers* and over-ruled it. The case was *Lawrence v. Texas*.[20] The statute at issue called out homosexuals—or homosexual sex—by name, labeling it "deviate sexual intercourse." But the Court, again through Justice Kennedy, did not base its decision on that aspect of the case. Instead, the Court held that *Bowers* had framed the right too narrowly. "Liberty presumes an autonomy of self that includes freedom of thought, belief, expression, and certain intimate conduct." This includes a "liberty of the person both in its spatial and more transcendent dimensions." Both dimensions are implicated in sexual conduct between consenting adults, in private, and not for money. "The right to make certain decisions regarding sexual conduct" is a right owned by all persons. It "extends beyond the marital relationship." It is an interest in liberty in "the most private human conduct, sexual behavior, in the most private of places, the home." It is fundamental not merely because it is private but also because it is connected with the "dignity [of] free persons."

Bowers was wrong about more than simply the definition of the right, said Justice Kennedy. It was wrong also about tradition. There was no long-standing history of laws directed at homosexual conduct per se, he said. Typically, antisodomy laws were framed as general laws that applied equally to everyone. Historically, they performed two functions. First, they were part of a general condemnation of nonprocreative sex, even between heterosexuals. Second, they were used to provide coverage for legal prosecution where sexual acts were nonconsensual, but the absence of consent was difficult to prove. Laws targeting homosexuals per se did not arise in the United States until the last third of the twentieth century. Sure, lots of people condemned homosexuality as immoral. But a moral majority may not enforce its views via the criminal law. Justice Kennedy also invoked more recent history—"our laws and traditions in the past half century" which have signaled "an emerging awareness" of the scope of liberty—to shed light on whether homosexual sexual acts may be proper objects of punishment. Justice Kennedy noted liberalizing trends on the question, beginning midcentury. In its Model Penal Code in 1955, the American Law Institute recommended against "criminal penalties for consensual sexual relations conducted in private." Some states began to follow this recommendation. Similar developments occurred in Britain and Europe. After *Bowers,* nearly half of the twenty-five states that had maintained criminal penalties against sodomy abandoned them. One of those states was Georgia, whose supreme court ruled in 1998 that the state's sodomy statute violated the right to privacy in the Georgia constitution.²¹ Moreover, there was a general "pattern of nonenforcement with respect to consenting adults in private." Finally, the constitutional law of the United States had undermined *Bowers*'s restrictive view of liberty. The two most salient new decisions were *Planned Parenthood v. Casey* (with Justice Kennedy in the joint opinion) and *Romer v. Evans* (with Justice Kennedy writing the Opinion of the Court). Ostensibly applying a rational-basis standard of review, the Court concluded in *Lawrence* that Texas's statute "furthers no legitimate . . . interest which can justify its intrusion into the personal and private life of the individual."

In dissent, Justice Scalia mocked the Court's decision. First, he noted, morality has long been a proper basis for the criminal law. He recited prohibitions on "bigamy, same-sex marriage, adult incest, prostitution, masturbation, adultery, fornication, bestiality, and obscenity." Second, liberty includes only those rights that are both fundamental and "deeply rooted in this Nation's history and tradition." Homosexual sodomy is not such a right, he said. For one thing, the history of the United States shows a sustained practice of prosecutions for sodomy. For another, the traditions of other countries are not relevant to the constitutional status of rights. It is "this Nation's" traditions alone that matter. The United States is not a prisoner to "foreign moods, fads, or fashions." For another, an "emerging awareness" of the content of liberty "in matters pertaining to sex" is not sufficient to establish the content of liberty as a matter of constitutional law. Only "tradition"—by which he had in mind a tradition older than the last fifty years—may do so. What's more, said Justice Scalia, there is no such awareness emerging in America, for states continue to prosecute crimes for such matters, including for prostitution, adult incest, adultery, obscenity, child pornography, and even homosexual sodomy. Finally, he insisted it was hypocritical for the Court to overrule *Bowers v. Hardwick* for the reasons proffered, but not to strike down *Roe v. Wade*. Thus, Justice Scalia, too, found it hard to resist enlistment in the culture war.

He closed with the observation that Justice Kennedy's opinion in *Lawrence* was "the product of a Court, which is the product of a law-profession culture, that has largely signed on to the so-called homosexual agenda." That agenda aims to eliminate "the moral opprobrium that has traditionally attached to homosexual conduct." This, he said, may be the view of law professors, but it is not the "mainstream" view of most Americans. In fact, Congress has refused to include discrimination against homosexuals within the prohibitions of the Civil Rights Act, Congress has mandated such discrimination with respect to service in the armed forces, and the Court itself has held that discrimination against homosexuals is a constitutional right for an organization like the Boy Scouts. Still, "I have nothing against homosexuals, or any other group, promoting their agenda through normal democratic means. Social perceptions of sexual and other morality change over time, and every group has the right to persuade its fellow citizens that its view of such matters is the best." But, he concluded, he would leave change in the hands of citizens, as opposed to "imposing [the Court's] views in the absence of democratic majority will."

SAME-SEX MARRIAGE

Justice Kennedy obliquely distinguished the right at stake in *Lawrence* from any putative right to enter into same-sex marriage: "[The case] does not involve whether the government must give formal recognition to any relationship that homosexual persons seek to enter."[22] The distinction was not insensible, given the difference between criminally punishing private conduct and restricting access to a quasi-public institution. This was cold comfort to Justice Scalia, however, who has a keen eye for the logical implications of precedent and for the lurking risk of constitutional change. Taking direct aim at the Court's distinction in *Lawrence,* he tersely wrote, "Don't believe it." In his view, the principles that supported the Court's opinion were sufficiently broad and substantial to cover same-sex marriage. "What justification could there possibly be for denying the benefits of marriage to homosexual couples . . . ? Surely not the encouragement of procreation, since the sterile and the elderly are allowed to marry. This case 'does not involve' the issue of homosexual marriage only if one entertains the belief that principle and logic have nothing to do with the decisions of this Court."[23]

Justice Scalia was writing with one eye to the future and another to the recent past. For even before *Lawrence,* same-sex marriage was emerging as an issue in states and in the nation. To be sure, the Court itself in 1972 had dismissed an appeal from a decision of Minnesota's supreme court, holding that exclusion of same-sex couples from marriage did not violate the Constitution.[24] Technically, the dismissal, based on the absence of a "substantial federal question," operated as a decision on the merits. However, because the Court provided no reasoned decision supporting its dismissal, and because it has frequently been unfaithful to its own precedents, there was reason to question the strength of a curt dismissal dating back to 1972. Besides, at its strongest, the dismissal signaled merely that recognition of same-sex marriage was not constitutionally required, not that it was constitutionally prohibited.

Concerns about the vitality of the Supreme Court's precedent aside, by 2003 only two states had even flirted with same-sex marriage (or with its kissing cousins, domestic partnership and civil union), and one of those states reversed itself. In 1993, Hawaii's supreme court held that a state statute limiting marriage to opposite-sex couples was a form of sex-based discrimination, which triggered strict scrutiny under the state's constitution.[25] On remand, the trial court held there was no compelling reason to exclude same-sex couples from the benefits of marriage. This sparked a prompt response from voters, who amended Hawaii's constitution to authorize the legislature to reserve marriage to heterosexual couples. The state supreme court retreated.[26] In Vermont, the state's supreme court held that excluding same-sex couples from the privileges and benefits of marriage violated the common-benefits provision of Vermont's constitution. The court ruled, however, that the state could reserve the title of "marriage" for opposite-sex couples, as long as some equivalent institution was provided for same-sex couples.[27]

Compare these uneven results with referenda in several other states approving amendments to the states' constitutions, defining marriage exclusively as a relation between one man and one woman. What's more, Congress weighed in with a statute in 1996 whose aim was to limit the spread of legal recognition for gay marriage. That enactment—the Defense of Marriage Act (DOMA)[28]—contains two substantive provisions. One specifies that, for the purpose of interpreting federal law, the term "marriage" refers only to "the legal union between one man and one woman as husband and wife," and the term "spouse" refers "only to a person of the opposite sex who is a husband or a wife." The other provision is a grammatical labyrinth. It provides essentially that no state (or other legal jurisdiction) in the United States "shall be required to give effect to any public act, record, or judicial proceeding" of any other jurisdiction "respecting a relationship between persons of the same sex that is treated as a marriage under the laws of" the other jurisdiction or respecting "a right or claim arising from such relationship." This latter provision attempts, in short, to make Article IV's full faith and credit clause unavailable to proponents of same-sex marriage (or to married same-sex couples who might migrate to a jurisdiction that doesn't recognize their union).

Events, of course, have not stood still. Beginning with Massachusetts in 2003–2004, ten jurisdictions—Connecticut, the District of Columbia, Iowa, Maine, Maryland, Massachusetts, New Hampshire, New York, Vermont, and Washington—have adopted same-sex marriage. They have done so by statute, by judicial decision applying the state's constitution, or by statewide referendum. Two Indian tribes—the Coquille (in Oregon) and the Squamish (in Washington) —have also approved same-sex marriage. Ten states—California, Colorado, Delaware, Hawaii, Illinois, Nevada, New Jersey, Oregon, Rhode Island, and Wisconsin—recognize some version of civil union or domestic partnership for same-sex couples. The Obama Administration's Justice Department has announced that it will no longer defend the Defense of Marriage Act in court. And in 2012, a Gallup Poll showed for the first time that a majority of Americans (53 percent) support legal recognition of same-sex marriage. This figure is almost double the percentage of Americans who supported legal recognition as recently as 1996. Against these developments, thirty jurisdictions prohibit any sort of same-sex union—whether marriage, civil union, or domestic partnership. Most of these jurisdictions have entrenched their prohibitions in state constitutions. Only one state—New Mexico—lacks any law that speaks expressly to same-sex unions. *Pace* Thornton Wilder, marriage has indeed become interesting.

California has taken a winding path on the question of marriage. In brief, although the state since 1999 has recognized domestic partnerships for same-sex couples, and although the state since 2003 has treated domestic partnerships as endowed with all the benefits and responsibilities of marriage, the people of California approved by initiative (Proposition 8) an amendment to the state's constitution confining marriage to unions "between a man and a woman." Parties challenged the amendment in federal court, alleging that Proposition 8 violated the Constitution of the United States. In an oddly narrow decision in *Perry v. Brown*, the U.S. Court of Appeals for the Ninth Circuit struck down the amendment.[29] The circuit court stayed its decision, pending possible review by the Supreme Court. The Court did grant certiorari, not only in *Perry* (now named *Hollingsworth v. Perry*) but also in *United States v. Windsor*, in which parties have challenged the constitutionality of DOMA's restrictive definition of marriage for purposes of federal law.

In the Epilogue following this chapter, we'll take up the Supreme Court's disposition of each of these cases. For now, let's consider a world in which the Court rejects both challenges and in so doing maintains the status quo. This is a world in which the legality of same-sex unions is decided state-by-state, under state laws and state constitutions. We may call it a world of democratic federalism. Even William Eskridge, who is a strong proponent of same-sex marriage, has argued for an incremental strategy of democratic federalism for pursuing that goal.[30] And although some opponents of same-sex marriage might fantasize about the possibility of ratifying a prohibition amendment to the Constitution of the United States, most opponents have pragmatically adopted a strategy of democratic federalism. Why? Why might parties who disagree about the desirability of legal protection for same-sex marriage nonetheless agree about the institutional process for achieving their political and legal goals?

There might be several reasons to like democratic federalism as a method for resolving substantive disagreement. Democracy may be valuable because it permits people, as a collective (or as an aggregation of individuals), to reach enforceable judgments about values and institutions—usually without bloodshed. It is an ancient liberty and an elemental part of the ways of the American order. Federalism may be useful for several reasons. It may promote normative pluralism, consistent with local needs and preferences. This provides outlets for political and institutional experimentation, even as to policies or values that remain controversial at the national level. It can arrange a set of institutions whose authority and accountability are distinct from the nation as a whole. Finally, and relatedly, it can provide an institutional structure that both reinforces and checks political power in useful ways. To be sure, federalism is usually not an end in itself, even if politicians and judges frequently talk as if it were. Sometimes it's destabilizing. And not infrequently it provides institutional cover for the operation of local prejudice and the violation of rights. Still, it can be useful.[31]

DOMA, of course, plainly tilts the playing field of federalism against proponents of same-sex marriage. To that extent, DOMA is a thin attempt to nationalize an antimarriage policy. Even so, it's worth speculating what the future might hold in a world of federalism, even a federalism that's partially constituted by DOMA.

Knotty legal questions will still arise from the presence of same-sex unions in some jurisdictions, especially when marriages or partnerships fray. What to do with jointly held (or separately owned but shared) property? How to handle questions involving custody of or visitation with children in a same-sex family? And what about provision for or enforcement of obligations of support, for either a child or a spouse? Even in intact or happy unions, questions may arise that will call upon state courts to make choices concerning the privilege of a spouse to visit a spouse or a child who is hospitalized, the enforcement of intra-marital powers of attorney, the recognition of the evidentiary privilege against adverse spousal testimony in courts of law, and the recognition and enforcement of a host of other possible administrative rights or institutional entitlements. These are merely a few of the issues that could arise. It's likely that a body of law — or multiple partially overlapping bodies of law — will grow to deal with aspects and consequences of same-sex unions. This tendency will be intensified in courts of equity, including courts that possess primary authority over domestic matters, but it will not be confined to equity. The tendency will be unavoidable if DOMA is rescinded or declared unconstitutional, either because it exceeds Congress's enumerated and implied powers or because it constitutes the sort of class-based legislation that the Court struck down in *Romer v. Evans*. But even if DOMA remains, courts will have to sort out many of the legal, technical, and even existential issues that arise from shared lives. Under the scenario of the status quo of democratic federalism, change will come through the gradual accretion of law. Its content may be unpredictable. And its pace may be slow and fitful. But it will happen, welcome or not.

Still, there might be reasons to dislike or distrust the present status-quo process of democratic federalism in this context. One might dislike it, for example, if the process produces results that are incompatible with preferences, or if the wheels of change are turning either too slowly or too quickly. Both proponents and opponents of same-sex marriage may dislike the process of democratic federalism for one or both of these reasons. Proponents of same-sex marriage may want a faster, more decisive, more national commitment to marriage than the current, slower, fractured process provides. In light of political realities in many parts of the country, amending the Constitution to secure same-sex marriage is presently impossible. Proponents' institutional solution of choice, therefore, is a rights-based decision of the Supreme Court, declaring prohibitions against same-sex marriage to be unconstitutional. *Hollingsworth v. Perry* provides their first substantial vehicle for such a ruling. There are risks in this strategy, even if it's successful, for it may unleash forces that are unforeseen and not easily controlled. Even a decision of the Court may not be able to forestall those forces. For many who support marriage, however, the potential gains may be worth the possible dangers.

Under a process of democratic federalism, opponents may well fear a scenario in which same-sex marriage has the potential to gradually expand, not only through the operation of local democratic decisions but also through the judicial decisions that, by adjudicating familial disputes, normalize aspects of marriage even in jurisdictions that prohibit it. This fear may be enhanced by concerns that currents of public opinion—not only on toleration for gays and lesbians but also on the question of marriage itself—will soon become so strong that opposition is futile. In this context, the Supreme Court cannot decisively aid opponents' cause, because the Court cannot command the abolition of same-sex marriage. It might well rule emphatically that prohibitions on same-sex marriage do not violate the Constitution, and such a decision would not be trivial. But the Court cannot nationalize prohibition, and in fact the Court has the potential to do mischief from opponents' perspective. In light of this, opponents have reason to be attracted to an abolitionist amendment to the Constitution, akin to the various amendments that states have ratified for their constitutions. Even if it were feasible (which it seems no longer to be), there are risks in a strategy of amendment. Like a judicial decision constitutionalizing a right to same-sex marriage, the process of attempting to amend may unleash forces that are unforeseen and not easily controlled. Besides, as we've seen before, even constitutional text cannot forestall change forever.

VALUES AND SAME-SEX MARRIAGE

Given these political, legal, and cultural dynamics, it's likely that the trajectory of change (or the dynamics of conservation) will eventually be in the hands of the Court, for better or worse. As Justice Scalia stated in dissent in *Lawrence,* the logical props for a constitutional decision striking down prohibitions on same-sex marriage have been in place since at least 2003, perhaps even earlier. Why then is the outcome of a case like *Hollingsworth v. Perry* (assuming that the Court reaches the merits of that conflict) uncertain? Why, especially, is it uncertain when even Justice Scalia acknowledges that the logic and principle of precedent support constitutional recognition of same-sex marriage? One reason, of course, is that Justice Scalia is not constrained by precedent when it conflicts with beliefs that are sufficiently deep-seated. But he is merely an overt (though not the most overt) personification of a fact that the Supreme Court rarely acknowledges but frequently embodies: it is an institution whose decisions are laden with (and driven by) values. In saying this, I don't intend to embrace the crude "attitudinalist" position found in some scholarship in political science.[32] For one thing, values may explain many aspects of the Court's jurisprudence, but they do not explain everything. For another, justices' values are not simplistic and certainly not unidimensional. They are layered. They can be complex. They include a sense of institutional role and responsibility, including a commitment to the rule of law. Some values may conflict with others. And they may even admit to a justice's concern about how opinions will go down in conversation with European judges in Salzburg during the summer recess. But justices' values are real. And they are motivating, even if not always controlling.

In light of this, instead of considering the sometimes arid legalistic analysis of the weight of governmental interests and the proximity of governmental policy to those interests, we might do well to approach the close of this chapter with a rehearsal of some of the reasons most frequently heard for a prohibition on same-sex marriage. I do not presume that the sketch that follows is comprehensive or exhaustive. But I believe it is representative.

The Definition of Marriage. One reason some opponents offer for their opposition is that same-sex marriage violates the very definition of marriage, which is a relation between a man and a woman. This, of course, is circular, for it assumes the very question at issue: What is the meaning (or what are the meanings) of marriage?

Tradition. To finesse this difficulty, some opponents urge that the definition is supported by tradition. Indeed it is. But there have been many definitions of marriage supported by tradition at one time or another: that it was patriarchal; that it could be regulated internally through violence; that this mode of regulation was largely insulated from legal restraint; that one could not marry outside of one's class without penalty; that one could not marry outside of one's race without prosecution; that material production or the transmission of wealth was the primary legal function of the marital family; that procreation was the primary social function of marriage; that marriage was strictly a spiritual institution, ordained by God, to whom civil authorities were subordinate. Each of these traditions has weakened or fallen by the wayside. Perhaps, then, the most enduring tradition where marriage is concerned is a tradition of change. We saw the birth of this tradition at the inception of the constitutional order. In light of these dynamics, two questions arise. One is whether tradition is the best lens for viewing the meaning of marriage. The other is, assuming that tradition may support a cogent justification, to which tradition(s) shall we adhere, and why?

Divine Law. A third argument is that same-sex marriage violates divine law. This is the position of Robert George and others in "The Manhattan Declaration," a document that speaks from a sincere desire for "obedience to the one true God, the triune God of holiness and love."[33] In that voice, the Declaration condemns both homosexual intimacy and same-sex marriage. It is difficult to know what to do with an argument so framed, in a religiously pluralist society with a Constitution that prohibits the establishment of religion. (By "religiously pluralistic" in this context, I include persons on whom religion has no hold.) Arguments that are animated by devotion to religion are permissible—and may even be beneficial—in such a society. But the overt imposition of a particular sectarian view of sex, sexuality, and marriage skirts the boundary of the constitutionally permissible. To be sure, those who profess and promote such views may attempt to alter the Constitution, by amending or replacing it with one that is more theocratic. If the Constitution is changed in this way, arguments could properly be framed in terms of who best understands the inscrutable will of God. As history has shown, such disagreements can be ferocious—even deadly. In the meantime, governmental and constitutional justifications require at least the semblance of secular garb.

Homosexuality as Immoral. One way of providing such clothing is to argue that homosexuality is immoral and therefore may be regulated, and *a fortiori* may be excluded from marriage. There's much to say about this claim—more than I can begin to offer here—but I might venture a few thoughts. Justice Scalia and then-Justice Rehnquist have argued that, in a democracy, questions of morality are essentially the province of the individual. From that premise, they have not concluded that individual moral preferences are to be constitutionally protected. Instead they have urged that such preferences become part of the democratic marketplace, and in the struggle for supremacy in that marketplace, the winner "takes on a generalized moral rightness or goodness." This aura is not acquired from "the intrinsic worth of the value," nor from the fact that it comports with "someone's idea of natural justice." The value prevails because the people (or their representatives) have ratified it.[34] We need not embrace these justices' subjectivist utilitarianism to appreciate that, within the constitutional bounds of collective decision, a democratic polity tends to be agnostic about many values. Still, there are constitutional limits to democracy's ability to authorize policy for moral (or other) reasons. In *Lawrence v. Texas,* the Court held that moral offense alone was an insufficient basis for putting people in jail for sexually intimate conduct in private quarters. The question is whether this reasoning, if valid, extends to the prohibition of same-sex marriage. In dissent, Justice Scalia said that it does. There are reasons to believe he will not hold himself to that judgment in *Hollingsworth v. Perry.* Even so, it's a fact that a substantial and growing part of American society no longer believes that homosexuality is per se immoral. If this trend continues, then even democracy will not forever hold back acceptance of homosexual intimacy and also same-sex marriage, regardless of what the Court decides.

Homosexuality as Unnatural. A similar argument is that homosexuality is unnatural. The key here is to understand what nature requires or permits or prohibits. There is an obvious way in which homosexuality is not unnatural. In fact, it is as natural to the species as being left-handed. (To be sure, there was a time when left-handers were morally suspect. Hence the terms *sinister* in Latin and Italian, and *gauche* in French.) Many of the native tribes recognized this fact, made accommodations for it, and found ways to thoroughly integrate it into their cultures (though this and other practices brought them into conflict with the Europeans). Still, it's possible to think about nature, not as simply something that exists in the species, but as something that carries a moral connotation. If it is a proxy for divine law, then it may be subject to a set of criticisms and concerns similar to those I mentioned above. If it is merely a restatement of subjective moral preference, as Justice Rehnquist argued, then it is entitled to no special status in a democracy, and could well be barred by the logic of *Lawrence v. Texas.* If, however, it's framed in terms of what human beings must (not) be or do in order for human beings to flourish in a good society, then nature takes on a different hue. In fact, it may be attractive. The challenges on this front are twofold: (1) to demonstrate that nature (or human flourishing or the common good or human dignity) prohibits intimacy between persons of the same sex, even in a sustained relationship, and (2) to persuade one's fellow citizens that this is what nature or the common good requires. It seems increasingly unlikely that these challenges can be met in today's United States. On the contrary, through lived experience, we're witness to a growing body of evidence that gays and lesbians are fully capable of living dignified, productive, ethically responsible lives, both in society and as couples in sustained relationships.[35]

Procreative Marriage. There is another way in which we might think of same-sex relations as being unnatural, however, though this way connects with an additional concern: the basic purpose for marriage. Here again, "The Manhattan Declaration" supplies the position with unflinching forthrightness: marriage is "intrinsically" tied to "procreation and the unique character and value of acts and relationships whose meaning is shaped by their aptness for the generation, promotion and protection of life. In spousal communion and the rearing of children (who, as gifts of God, are the fruit of their parents' marital love), we discover the profound reasons for and benefits of the marriage covenant." This is a noble, if idealistic, view of marriage. But, as I've suggested above, it is not the only noble view. It is not the view that American culture has insisted upon, practiced, or aspired to for more than two centuries. Nor is it the view of the common law, in either its ancient form or its form in modernity. Nor is it the view presupposed by a host of state laws and policies. Nor, as the Court summarized in *Turner v. Safley,* is it the view that constitutional doctrine has embraced. A more realistic view of marriage might note that the world can be a puzzling place, even forbidding or hostile. It can therefore be difficult—even, for many people, psychologically disabling—to navigate alone in the world, without companionship. If two persons choose to commit to stay with each other to survive in the world, to love and comfort each other, perhaps even to flourish, that, too, can be a noble partnership, even if it doesn't presuppose or entail the production of children.

Harm to Children. Even so, perhaps it is nonetheless a mistake, a socially harmful error, to weaken or sever the links among marriage, sexual love, procreation, and care for children. Note that the premise—that same-sex marriage (not to mention a host of other social practices) will weaken or sever these links—may be inaccurate. But let's assume that the premise is correct. Does it follow that marriage that is not linked to procreation will be harmful to the welfare of children? The United States, indeed much of the Western world, is in the midst of an experiment in whether societies that protect a large domain for associational liberty and choice can sustain themselves demographically, economically, and ethically. Children's welfare is plainly part of this experiment. But it's doubtful that same-sex marriage undermines children's welfare. To the extent that such unions do not produce children, despite the technological means to do so, then children's welfare is barely implicated, except in indirect ways that presuppose the immorality of same-sex relations. If children are part of same-sex households, one question is whether those households are less able to provide for those children, to nurture them, and to give them the means to flourish. I confess I do not have an answer that's robustly informed by contemporary sociological scholarship. Based on experiential observation, however, I would predict that, in aggregate, same-sex households will do as well as—and no worse than—heterosexual households. In terms of providing materially for children, in fact, same-sex households may well do better (again in aggregate). Of course individual children might care little about an aggregated world, and in any event material welfare is not their sole concern. Here again, experiential observation suggests that children in same-sex households do well, especially in a social environment that embraces them and their families.[36]

A Weakening Marital Family. There is another possible critique, however, that the general weakening of the marital family—especially through divorce or the creation of children out of wedlock—puts children at risk. In material terms, the risk is that many children in single-parent households are supported less well than are children in two-parent households. Consequently, they are more likely to receive public assistance, which is demeaning to the children and a drain on social resources. This is a nontrivial concern, especially if one disapproves of public programs of social welfare (even when those programs are justified by reference to "the common good"). But it is difficult to put this cost at the feet of gays and lesbians who wish to enter into stable and productive relationships. Nonmaterially, the critique is that children are at risk because the breakup of families threatens their emotional well-being. Sometimes this is accurate. In an ideal world, for both logistical and emotional reasons, children often benefit from having support from two parents instead of one. But millions of children do not live in an ideal world. In fact, their single parent may well be superior, emotionally and otherwise, to an intact two-parent family. But even if there's harm in familial dissolution or in bastardy, it is difficult to lay these harms at the feet of same-sex couples.

Other Social Harms. Children's welfare aside, might same-sex marriage be socially destructive in other ways? "The Manhattan Declaration" suggests three sorts of harms that flow from same-sex marriage. First, its presence in the polity jeopardizes the religious liberty of those who conscientiously object to it.[37] Second, "the rights of parents are abused" when programs in "family life and sex education" in public schools teach children "that an enlightened understanding recognizes as 'marriages' sexual partnerships that . . . parents believe are intrinsically non-marital and immoral." Third, same-sex marriage damages the common good "when the law itself, in its critical pedagogical function, becomes a tool for eroding a sound understanding of marriage." Given what I've said above, it is difficult to credit these criticisms.

The Slippery Slope. Finally, there is a concern that, if same-sex marriage is validated through the granting of a civil status, so too in principle must other forms of sexual relations: "polyamorous partnerships, polygamous households, even adult brothers, sisters, or brothers and sisters living in incestuous relationships."[38] As a matter of legal toleration, as opposed to official recognition, these relations may already reside beneath the radar of law, simply through private ordering. This is one risk (if that is the right word) of living in a society with a substantial degree of associational liberty. But does recognition of same-sex marriage logically require recognition of these other relationships? Quite frankly, this is a genuine possibility. After all, if Justice Scalia acknowledges that the principles of *Romer* and *Lawrence* permit same-sex marriage, then it is possible that the principles underlying same-sex marriage might extend as well to other private choices with respect to marital relations, at least if same-sex marriage is made legal through a constitutional decision of a court, unless there's a persuasive case that the social costs of polygamy, polyamory, and adult incest are in principle distinguishable from same-sex marriage. There might well be.

Even the possibility of incest, for example, has the potential to affect the way that people see themselves as members of a family. Its practice, moreover, raises a nontrivial and widespread risk of acute and concrete harms to particular families. If families remain an important social institution, whether with or without a constitutional status, these risks are legally salient. Polygamy and polyamory are more difficult cases, but are qualitatively distinguishable from two-person same-sex relationships in at least four ways. The first is that, on their face, they are not monogamous, which is significant from the standpoint of the American history of the regulation of and autonomy within the family. The second is that they are structurally incapable of replicating the intense emotional connections that not only produce psycho-social benefits but also evade the genuine social risks of jealousy.[39] Third, these relations tend by their nature to be less stable—less enduring—than are two-person relations, though this may be truer of polyamory than of polygamy. Fourth, therefore, they are less readily able to perform the civilizing functions—from both a social and a psycho-emotional standpoint—that nuclear relations involving two persons may perform. That said, I can't deny the possibility, in a polity possessing a robust constitutional role for courts, that some version of principle might entail recognition of one or more of these relations. I can say, however, that this risk is *de minimis* if recognition of same-sex marriage comes, not through judicial pronouncement of a constitutional right, but through democratic decision. For those who may be worried about the logical extension of principle, and for others who want to support same-sex marriage without the baggage of polyamory, polygamy, or incest, this may be one reason for preferring democratic over judicial solutions.

None of these arguments and observations makes a decisive affirmative case for a constitutional right to same-sex marriage. But they do demonstrate that the arguments against same-sex marriage have crumbled, almost to oblivion. Whether a court—whether the Supreme Court—decides to take the step to recognize a constitutional right to same-sex marriage, however, depends not merely on logic, but on willed choice. It also depends, of course, on whether the justices believe the issue is better decided through processes of representative democracy than through the judicial process. The former process would permit public opinion to percolate.

It would allow democratic institutions to do their work and thus permit the political experimentation that's now occurring to continue. And it would achieve a form of "democratic legitimacy" without risking the sort of popular backlash that may result from a decision that strikes down the policies of a considerable number of states. Despite these considerations, a conscientious justice might well calculate that the risk of backlash is a risk worth taking, for the sake of social welfare, of existential goods, or (not least) of constitutional principle. We may be fairly sure of one lesson from our history: a justice who acts on that calculation will not have departed from the fundamentals of the American order, even as s/he has changed it.

AMERICAN CONSTITUTIONAL FAMILIES

I recently was privileged to join a Roundtable on Marriage, Morality, and the Law, in conjunction with the annual Walter Murphy Memorial Lecture at Princeton University. One of the questions posed to the members of the Roundtable was this: "Is there a constitutional ideal of marriage?" This question provides a thematic opportunity for closing out this chapter.

In the beginning in British North America, the colonies' account of and commitment to family were more fluid than one might have expected in light of claims today that family was stable and unchanged for centuries. The fluidity in early America reflected demographic, social, and economic conditions in the colonies, not to mention the relatively thin institutions of law at that time. These conditions contributed to the loosening and even the repudiation of aspects of the English common law in North America. Things were different here than in England. As a social matter, families in North America looked different from the English legal model. There was relatively greater equality between the sexes and across generations. There was more negotiation of familial roles. And these were reinforced in part by the capacity for exit. The ability to exit was not necessarily "legal," but people simply left. These institutional characteristics were congenial to the emergence and vitality of three values in the colonies: liberty (associational and other), relative equality, and self-government. The combination of social innovation and shifts in values became relevant to tensions that led to the secession of the colonies from Britain. The colonies simply left.

When the Constitution appeared on the scene, neither it nor its proponents said much about family, other than to worry about potential problems of familial self-dealing within government and the need to inhibit the rise of familial dynasties. Still, assumptions about the forms and functions of families were in the background. But no single type of family provided an exclusive form for nor fit with the polity. In fact, there were three prominent types for which one might have found support. One, the Jeffersonian model, was an agrarian family of independent farmers residing on land that was owned fee simple, free from bondage to lords, and congenial to the organic localist production of democratic virtue. The second, Hamiltonian, model was linked to commercial capitalist modes of production and to nationalist, liberal, and individualist virtues. The third was the slaveholding family, apology for which could be traced to the Bible, to sociology, and to a form of Aristotelian natural law. It was not strictly nuclear in form, nor consistently monogamous in practice. But, among the three forms, the slaveholding family came closest to enjoying explicit constitutional sanction. Eventually, of course, there was trouble in the house divided, in part because of a fourth type: the frontier family. In fact, it's more accurate to use the plural "families" in this context, as there were several versions of family on the frontier, linked to distinct modes of production, from farming, to ranching, to mining, to bourgeois trades and occupations that grew in and around settlements that dotted the West. For the most part, however, at least in the Northwest and Far West, they were white. These families tended to strongly exhibit the colonial characteristics of negotiated roles, equality (especially of gender), and exit. As in the colonies, these practices and values could thrive because of an environment in which law was relatively weak.

These four types aside, from the beginning and even before the Constitution, there were deviations from the nuclear model. These deviations were animated largely by religious devotion. They included communal families (some sexual, some asexual), polygamous families (very sexual), and the native tribes. Their experiences were varied. Before the American Revolution, a crop of communal families grew mainly in wilderness. Despite their relative isolation, they were suspect in the eyes of the proto-legal society that was emerging, mainly along the Atlantic coast. They rejected marriage. They were theologically unconventional. And many of them spoke German. Still, they came to be tolerated, in part because they were fairly harmless. If they survived, they tended to keep moving away from English-speaking settlements. And, to anyone's knowledge, no one was having sex.

After the constitutional founding, the experience of two enduring communal families diverged. The Shakers were initially suspect, because they rejected marriage, practiced sexual equality, held property in common, and raised children in common. Despite their structural resemblance to Plato's Guardians, they came to be tolerated. They stuck to themselves. They were hard-working and productive. "Outsiders" wanted their products. And, to anyone's knowledge, no one was having sex. The Oneida Community was initially suspect but came to be embraced by surrounding local communities. The Oneidans stuck to themselves. They were hard-working and productive, contributing to the local economy. And outsiders wanted their products. Still, the state and nation hounded them out of existence as a social formation, because they rejected monogamous marriage in favor of group marriage, and they were having sex (albeit thoroughly regulated sex). Among the Oneidans, the one institutional form that survived by the end of the nineteenth century was the industrial corporation.

Polygamists—at least the Mormons, less so the Cochranites—would seem to have been candidates for toleration. They were productive. For most purposes, they stuck largely to themselves. And they tended to move ever westward, to avoid conflict. Still, they were driven from the United States and eventually out of legal existence, at least as practitioners of polygamy. Why? They were too productive. They stuck too much to themselves. When they didn't stick to themselves they were proselytizing, which was problematic because they were theologically unconventional and wildly successful in attracting converts. It's also the case that they liked marriage too much (and too frequently). And the men at least (and sometimes the women) were having sex with more than one person.

The native tribes, of course, were pushed out of existence and came close to being exterminated. They lacked "true religion." They were communist, lacking any notion of bourgeois property. Socially, too, they weren't organized into bourgeois nuclear families. Their ethical systems—including the ethics of sex and sexuality—were strange to Europeans. And they were living on land the United States wanted for white settlement.

By the end of the nineteenth century, then, the nation had dug in against these deviating forms—to suppress communalists, to excommunicate polygamists, and to destroy the tribes without killing all the Indians. It was in opposition to them that the nation committed publicly, and as a matter of policy, to the monogamous nuclear family. In general terms, opposition was for the sake of preserving civilization and progress. (Hence, civilization was not a static thing, but evolving.) When the Supreme Court bestowed its blessing on the national policy, however, it did so by insisting that the nuclear family promoted two abstract values central to the American order: liberty and equality. At the time, there was reason to think that the Court's commitment to these values was more rhetorical than real. Racially restrictive familial policies persisted, for example, at both national and state levels. And gendered hierarchy lingered. But, values being what they are, these two had lives of their own.

In the twentieth century, the Court began to adapt them to cultural, economic, and technological changes in American society, applying them to a number of problems and issues, in a variety of contexts, concerning various families. By the middle of the century, the Court recognized a right that wasn't a right to marry per se, but an equal right of access to marriage. This way of putting it implied that a state was under no obligation to secure marriage itself, and perhaps could get rid of the institution altogether as a matter of public licensure, though interests in liberty would continue to require respect for forms of intimate association. But whether marriage was required or not, the Court's articulated justification for the right acknowledged several marital goods—emotional, social, spiritual, and sexual—that applied even to persons in prison. It is, moreover, an institution that has been the locus for public recognition and public benefits. Thus, if marriage (or family generally) has a constitutional status, it is not because it is a political institution, but because it houses a constitutionally salient set of interests. This plurality of goods has underscored the multiple meanings of marriage and family in the American constitutional order.

The history of family in the United States—and of how it came to be in the Constitution—has been a story of change and contestation. The issues we see today in debates over divorce, gender, work, and even same-sex marriage are simply manifestations of that history. There has always been a plurality of views about the point of and reasons for marriage. If there's anything that comes close to a "constitutional model"—as an officially sanctioned institution—it's monogamy, though even that has been contested, and its form and function have altered through the years. Aside from this, there is no constitutional ideal of marriage, nor of family. There are merely constitutional parameters within which debates over marriage and family have played out. America has always been a place for experiments and for diverse ways of life.

Epilogue

The American landscape of marriage and family continues to change, even as I write. In just the six months since the previous chapter was written, we witnessed change on at least three notable fronts.

The first was demographic. In a report released in May 2013, the Pew Research Center announced that "a record 40% of all households with children under the age of 18 include mothers who are either the sole or primary source of income for the family." This figure was 11 percent as recently as 1960. Among these households with "breadwinner moms," 37 percent are married mothers with incomes higher than their husbands'. The substantial majority of 63 percent are unmarried mothers (divorced, widowed, or never married). Predictably, the median income of households with married breadwinner moms (almost $80,000) is substantially larger than that of households in which the female breadwinner is unmarried ($23,000). But the data show a significant difference, too, in the median *personal* income of married breadwinner moms ($50,000), as compared with their unmarried counterparts ($20,000). Unmarried female heads of household tend to be younger, more likely to be black or Hispanic, and less likely to have earned a college degree than married women who are primary breadwinners.[1] Plainly, these findings reflect underlying changes in women's access to the workforce and to higher education. They also reflect widespread changes in attitudes toward — or in some cases opportunities for — marriage, not to mention attitudes toward sex outside of marriage.

The second front was political. Legislatures in three states — Rhode Island (effective August 1, 2013), Delaware (effective July 1), and Minnesota (effective August 1) — authorized same-sex marriage. The Little Traverse Bay Bands of Odawa Indians also approved same-sex marriage, as long as at least one of the prospective spouses is a member of the tribe. These changes are part of a continuing political dynamic propelled by seismic shifts in public acceptance of gays and lesbians and in public approval of same-sex marriage. In March 2013, a Washington Post–ABC News poll showed that a substantial majority of Americans (58 percent) believe "it should be legal . . . for gay and lesbian couples to get married."[2]

The third front of change was constitutional. On June 26, 2013, the Supreme Court of the United States handed down decisions in two cases in which litigants challenged the constitutionality of governmental prohibitions or differential treatment of same-sex marriage. In only one of those cases did the Court reach the merits. In the other, the Court held that the parties lacked standing to press an appeal; even so, the Court's disposition had the effect of adding one more state to the ranks of states permitting marriage between persons of the same sex.

The case decided on the merits was *United States v. Windsor*.[3] Edith Windsor and Thea Spyer were domiciled in New York City. In 1993, after the city of New York commenced recognizing same-sex domestic partnerships, the couple registered as domestic partners. In 2007, the couple sojourned to Canada, where they were married. After their wedding, they continued to reside in New York City. Ms. Spyer died in 2009, leaving all of her estate to Ms. Windsor. Ordinarily, a surviving spouse may claim a marital exemption from the federal estate tax. Section 3 of the Defense of Marriage Act, however, barred the exemption in Windsor's case because she and Spyer were of the same sex. The bar applied even though the state of New York recognized their marriage as legal. Ms. Windsor paid the tax, then asked for a refund, which the Internal Revenue Service denied. She sued in federal district court, claiming that §3 of DOMA violated the principle of equal protection as applied to the federal government through the Fifth Amendment's due process clause. The district court held that §3 was unconstitutional. The U.S. Court of Appeals for the Second Circuit affirmed. In a 5–4 decision, the Supreme Court struck down §3.

To understand how and why, it's useful to start with Justice Alito's dissent in the case. He divided his analysis into two parts: liberty and equality. First, did §3 violate a substantive liberty, protected by the due process clause? To answer this question, Justice Alito made two analytic moves. The first adhered to the Court's method in *Bowers v. Hardwick*: to frame the claim to liberty narrowly and concretely. Framed this way, the question was not whether there's a general right to marry, but whether there's a right of persons of the same sex to marry. The second move was to insist that any claim to substantive liberty must meet three tests: it must be "fundamental," must be "deeply rooted in this nation's history and tradition," and must be "implicit in ordered liberty." Same-sex marriage, he said, failed these criteria, for same-sex marriage was not traditional but was a brand new thing under the sun.

Here Justice Alito channeled arguments of the family values movement, which we saw at the beginning of this book. "The family is an ancient and universal institution. Family structure reflects the characteristics of a civilization, and changes in family structure and in the popular understanding of marriage and the family can have profound effects." He argued that we have already seen one such change, in the historic shift from a procreative view of marriage to a companionate view, built on the notion that "romantic love is a prerequisite to marriage." The consequences of this shift alone have been subtle and substantial. We have no idea what the additional "long-term ramifications of widespread acceptance of same-sex marriage will be." Better, he urged, to leave the issue in the hands of democratic institutions. "The people have a right to control their own destiny."

Justice Alito's second question was whether §3 violated equal protection of the laws. Counsel for Ms. Windsor (and the United States) argued that heightened scrutiny was appropriate and that, under this standard of review, DOMA did indeed violate the principle of equal protection. Justice Alito called this position "misguided." Why? His chief reason was that, because the case did not involve a suspect classification, like race or gender, the proper standard of review was not heightened scrutiny but rational basis, and DOMA's defense of traditional marriage clearly met this lower standard.

What Ms. Windsor was actually arguing for, said Justice Alito, was a hybrid claim that essentially asked the Court to resolve the question of "what marriage is." As he had suggested in his discussion of substantive liberty, there are in the United States two contested views of marriage. "The 'traditional' or 'conjugal' view sees marriage as an intrinsically opposite-sex institution," because it was "created for the purpose of channeling heterosexual intercourse into a structure that supports child rearing." Thus, borrowing from Robert George, marriage is "a comprehensive, exclusive, permanent union that is intrinsically ordered to producing new life, even if it does not always do so."[4] The "newer" view of marriage, which Justice Alito called the "consent-based" view, sees marriage as "mutual commitment—marked by strong emotional attachment and sexual attraction." He acknowledged that this view "now plays a very prominent role in the popular understanding" of marriage. And it was crucial to Ms. Windsor's claim: "because gender differentiation is not relevant to this [consent-based] vision, the exclusion of same-sex couples is [argued to be] rank discrimination."

Although he asserted that an original understanding of the Constitution would likely support the traditional view, Justice Alito concluded that "the Constitution does not codify either of these views of marriage." Therefore, legislatures may choose one or the other.

There are at least four problems with Justice Alito's positions in *Windsor*. The first is his reduction of views of marriage into two general types. In fact, there is, and has long been in the United States, a wide range of views of the point and purpose of marriage, perhaps as many views as there have been marriages. The second is his conflation of companionate marriage with romance and sexual attraction. Certainly romance and attraction may be part of a companionate marriage. But they aren't essential. Better, perhaps, to say "mutual affection" or simply "attachment." A third problem is his narrow and simplistic approach to equal protection. Even if we confine our focus to suspect classifications, Justice Alito flattens the doctrinal picture. But equal protection has long included substantive components. In fact, as we saw in the preceding chapter, one substantive component is marriage. Thus, his claim that equal protection is "ill suited for use in evaluating the constitutionality of laws based on the traditional understanding of marriage" ignores the Court's equal protection cases that speak directly to marriage. As we've seen, *Loving v. Virginia* relies on both equal protection and substantive liberty; and *Zablocki v. Redhail* and *Turner v. Safley* integrate equal protection with the substantive right to marry. The fourth problem, which grows out of the third, is that *Zablocki* and *Turner* positively embrace a companionate view of marriage as a constitutional commitment. Like them or not, any articulate view of the scope of the right to marry must come to terms with those decisions. Justice Alito mentioned none of them.

Justice Kennedy wrote the Opinion of the Court. He acknowledged that, "until recent years, many citizens had not even considered the possibility that two persons of the same sex might aspire to . . . lawful marriage. For marriage between a man and a woman no doubt had been thought of by most people as essential to the very definition of [marriage] and to its role and function throughout the history of civilization." But change came, he said, and with it "the beginnings of a new perspective, a new insight." Along with this perspective came change in the public policy of several states, including New York, to permit same-sex couples to enjoy the same "status and dignity" in marriage that heterosexual couples had long enjoyed.

Historically, the Court noted, the regulation of marriage in the United States has been the province of states. Indeed, "the definition of marriage is the foundation of the State's broader authority to regulate the subject of domestic relations with respect to the '[p]rotection of offspring, property interests, and the enforcement of marital responsibilities.'" The Constitution, moreover, delegates no power over domestic relations to the federal government. For these reasons, the national government, "through our history, has deferred to state-law policy decisions with respect to domestic relations." This is not to say, however, that the national government lacks any authority in the realm of marriage and family. Congress has authority to enact regulations that are rationally related to the federal government's delegated powers, even though the regulations define or otherwise regulate marriage or other aspects of domestic life. And Congress has enacted hundreds of statutes that touch on marriage and the family.

Justice Kennedy held that DOMA is different from these other, permissible regulations. For one thing, DOMA's reach is far greater than that of other ordinary statutes, applicable to "over 1,000 federal statutes and the whole realm of federal regulations." Second, DOMA is directed to—and treats differentially—a class of persons whom states have sought to protect. Third, and related to the second, DOMA violates a basic principle that all married persons within each state be treated consistently. Fourth, DOMA is a "discrimination of unusual character." As I read the Court's opinion, two characteristics make DOMA unusual. It carves out a class of persons for "injury and indignity." And it treats differentially persons who are similarly situated under the laws of their respective states; that is, it treats differentially same-sex and opposite-sex couples, though state law treats them identically. Either way, the Court held that it is obliged to give "careful consideration" to whether DOMA violates the Constitution. (Here the Court cited *Romer v. Evans*.)

What, then, does "careful consideration" tell us about DOMA's constitutionality? The Court provided a twofold answer. First, DOMA is not a "routine classification," for it impinges on marriage, which is a special relationship that implicates constitutionally salient considerations of "status and dignity." These considerations include "private, consensual sexual intimacy between two persons." This form of intimacy is "but one element in a personal bond that is more enduring." (Here the Court cited *Lawrence v. Texas*.) Marriage is the archetype of this enduring bond. And the state of New York has sought to extend "the protection and dignity" of that bond to same-sex couples who wish to enter it. "This status is a far-reaching legal acknowledgment of the intimate relationship between two people, a relationship deemed by the State worthy of dignity in the community equal with all other marriages. It reflects both the community's considered perspective on the historical roots of the institution of marriage and its evolving understanding of the meaning of equality."

Second, DOMA is constitutionally infirm because of the *manner* in which it impinges on marriage. It does so in two ways. One is that "DOMA seeks to injure the very class New York seeks to protect. By doing so, it violates basic due process and equal protection principles applicable to the Federal Government." The other is that the purpose and effect of DOMA evince "a bare congressional desire to harm a politically unpopular group." In short, DOMA is "motivated by an improper animus or purpose." (Here again, the Court cited *Romer v. Evans*.) How do we know DOMA's purpose is illicit? One indication is its "unusual character," noted above. Another is its very text, including its title ("Defense of Marriage") and its legislative history. Still another can be found in the arguments offered by DOMA's defenders—that the point of the statute is "to discourage enactment of same-sex marriage laws and to restrict the freedom and choice of couples married under those laws if they are enacted." If DOMA imposes a broad set of burdens on same-sex couples, it also permits these couples to evade certain "duties and responsibilities"; this evasion itself violates principles of equality. Finally, DOMA's harms are not merely material but also expressive, touching the lives of not only the marital couple but also their children. "The differentiation demeans the couple, whose moral and sexual choices the Constitution protects, and whose relationship the State has sought to dignify. And it humiliates tens of thousands of children now being raised by same-sex couples, . . . [making] it even more difficult for the children to understand the integrity and closeness of their own family and its concord with other families in their community and in their daily lives."

Perhaps ironically, perhaps understandably, if Justice Alito's dissent squarely (but incompletely) addressed the constitutional right to marry, Justice Kennedy's Opinion of the Court partially evaded it and cautiously confined its holding with considerations of federalism. The Court's caution incites questions. For example, what happens to federal recognition when a couple, lawfully married in one state, moves to a different state in which marriage between persons of the same sex is neither permitted nor recognized? Aspects of the Court's opinion seem to suggest that the federal government is not obliged to extend recognition or benefits to a validly married same-sex couple living in a prohibitionist state. Indeed, on a narrow reading of *Windsor,* the federal government may be obliged *not* to extend recognition or benefits to such a couple. This result would give rise to enormous administrative complexity and inconsistency. For this reason (and others), the current president has a motive not to enforce federal law differentially according to the state in which the couple happens to reside.[5] Perhaps this structural political solution is sufficient to avoid the jurisprudential problem, at least for the short term. Or perhaps the Court, if later asked, would hold that it did not intend in *Windsor* that married same-sex couples in prohibitionist states be treated differently from identical couples in states providing what has come to be known as "marriage equality." For now, however, there remains an administrative question about the scope of the Court's reasoning.

This specific question aside, there's a larger question of whether, and how far, *Windsor* will travel outside the context of DOMA. To put a finer point on it, do the logic and holding of *Windsor* mean that states' prohibitions of same-sex marriage are unconstitutional? As the preceding chapter noted, the Court had an opportunity in *Hollingsworth v. Perry* to strike down California's prohibition and (potentially) to strike down prohibitions in every state. In the end, the Court declined the opportunity, dismissing the appeal in *Hollingsworth,* and vacating the decision of the Ninth Circuit.[6] This had the effect of reinstating the decision of the U.S. District Court for the Northern District of California, which had struck down California's prohibition on broad constitutional grounds.[7] The district court's decision has no precedential effect outside California, but it does make that state the fourteenth jurisdiction (including the District of Columbia, but excluding Indian tribes) to permit same-sex marriage. What, though, of the reach of *Windsor* in states besides California?

The Court was careful to confine its holding in *Windsor* to "lawful marriages." Moreover, the Court provided a potential doctrinal device to distinguish DOMA from the policies of states: "While the Fifth Amendment itself withdraws from Government the power to degrade or demean in the way this law does, the equal protection guarantee of the Fourteenth Amendment makes that Fifth Amendment right all the more specific and all the better understood and preserved." As Justice Scalia pointed out in dissent, this doctrinal move is puzzling. Still, *Windsor* for now leaves in place the regime of democratic federalism discussed in the preceding chapter. As noted in that chapter, and as Michael Klarman has argued, there may be good reasons to permit the political process to continue to percolate.[8] Notwithstanding these considerations, might the logic of *Windsor* extend to states' prohibitions as well as to DOMA?

Dissenting in *Windsor*, Chief Justice Roberts insisted that the Court's reasoning does not apply to the policies of states. Justice Scalia disagreed. In a separate vigorous dissent, he belittled the Court's claim that its decision in *Windsor* is confined to DOMA. As he put it, citing his previous dissent in *Lawrence v. Texas*, "I have heard such 'bald, unreasoned disclaimer[s]' before." While noting that there are reasons to distinguish *Windsor* from future cases in which the Court considers on the merits the constitutionality of prohibitions against same-sex marriage, he said he is skeptical that the principle of *Windsor* will in fact be confined. "The only thing that will 'confine' the Court's holding is its sense of what it can get away with." Justice Scalia went so far as to rewrite three paragraphs, drawn directly from the Court's opinion in *Windsor*, to show "how inevitable" it is that the Court will "reach the same conclusion with regard to state laws denying same-sex couples marital status." "As far as this Court is concerned, no one should be fooled; it is just a matter of listening and waiting for the other shoe."[9]

Unless and until the other shoe drops, democratic federalism still holds. Even so, change may yet come. One reason is that democratic federalism in this context may provide incentives for married same-sex couples to avoid prohibitionist states—as places to live, to work, and (for the truly principled or risk averse) even to sojourn. As a social and political matter, many people in prohibitionist states might be content with this dynamic, content to keep out undesirable elements. The difficulty for these states is that perceived social and political gain may mean genuine economic loss, as prohibitionist states lose access to the money, the talents, and the productive energy of gay and lesbian citizens. Businesses who want to attract and hold the talents and productive energy of gay and lesbian employees may find that they, too, have reasons to avoid establishing or maintaining enterprises in prohibitionist states. It will be difficult to measure capital avoidance or flight of this sort. But the risk is not imaginary.

This is the way of the American order. Influencing the shape and direction of law and the Constitution are the push and pull of people and institutions; of preferences, interests, and values; and of habits, events, and practices. They have always done so. To be sure, law and Constitution in turn do shape the various elements of human experience, both subtly and profoundly. But, for good or ill, the Constitution's meaning is not firmly fixed, and the relations between law and humanity are reliably complex and contingent.

Notes

INTRODUCTION: FAMILY VALUES

1. Mary Ann Glendon, *The Transformation of Family Law: State, Law, and Family in the United States and Western Europe* (Chicago: University of Chicago Press, 1989), 1.
2. http://www.winst.org.
3. Robert P. George and Jean Bethke Elshtain, eds., *The Meaning of Marriage: Family State, Market, and Morals* (Dallas: Spence Publishing, 2006), viii.
4. Robert P. George, "What's Sex Got to Do with It? Marriage, Morality, and Rationality," in George and Elshtain, eds., *The Meaning of Marriage,* 151.
5. Roger Scruton, "Sacrilege and Sacrament," in George and Elshtain, eds., *The Meaning of Marriage,* 7–21.
6. See Jennifer Roback Morse, "Why Unilateral Divorce Has No Place in a Free Society," in George and Elshtain, eds., *The Meaning of Marriage,* 74 et seq.
7. Ibid., 77.
8. Laura Sanchez, "Covenant Marriage," in *Encyclopedia of Human Relationships,* Harry T. Reis and Susan Sprecher, eds. (Thousand Oaks, CA: Sage, 2009), 364–366.
9. Morse, "Unilateral Divorce," 94–97.
10. See W. Bradford Wilcox, "Suffer the Little Children: Marriage, the Poor, and the Commonweal," in George and Elshtain, eds., *The Meaning of Marriage,* 245–249.
11. Harold James, "Changing Dynamics of the Family in Recent European History," in George and Elshtain, eds., *The Meaning of Marriage,* 66–67 (quoting Malthus's *Essay on the Principle of Population*).
12. Ibid., 67–69.
13. Maggie Gallagher, "(How) Does Marriage Protect Child Well-Being?" in George and Elshtain, eds., *The Meaning of Marriage,* 198–200, 204–208.
14. See David F. Forte, "The Framers' Idea of Marriage and Family," in George and Elshtain, eds., *The Meaning of Marriage,* 100–115. "What Americans of the late eighteenth century did was to synthesize the notion of marriage as a freely entered political institution, being an organic part of the larger political society, with a Christian notion of its interior life." Ibid., 106.

15. Lynn D. Wardle, "The Attack on Marriage as the Union of a Man and a Woman," 83 *North Dakota Law Review* 1365 (2007).

16. Elie Wiesel, *Night,* Marion Wiesel, trans. (New York: Hill and Wang, 2006), 3.

17. John C. Calhoun, "Speech on the Reception of the Abolition Petitions" (February 6, 1837).

18. Alexander H. Stephens, "Cornerstone Speech" (Savannah, Georgia, March 21, 1861).

CHAPTER ONE: FAMILY AND CIVILIZATION

1. *Maynard v. Hill,* 125 U.S. 190, 211–212 (1888) (quoting from *Adams v. Palmer,* 51 Me. 481, 483).

2. *Griswold v. Connecticut,* 381 U.S. 479, 486 (1965).

3. Possible exceptions include the prohibition of titles of nobility (Art. I, §§9, 10) and the indirect recognition of slavery (Art. I, §§2, 9; Art. IV, §2; Art. V).

4. See *Poe v. Ullman,* 367 U.S. 497 (1961) (Harlan, J., dissenting), at 539, 549.

5. *Griswold,* 482–486 (Douglas, J., for the Court).

6. Compare *Meyer v. Nebraska,* 262 U.S. 390, 399 (1923), with *Michael H. v. Gerald D.,* 491 U.S. 110, 124–126 (1989) (Scalia, J., announcing the judgment of the Court).

7. See, again, Justice Antonin Scalia's plurality in *Michael H.* For a general defense of tradition as an interpretive source, see Anthony Kronman, "Precedent and Tradition," 99 *Yale Law Journal* 1029 (1990). Justice Douglas's final paragraph in *Griswold* nods subtly to traditions of the sort that Kronman extols. Recall, for example, Douglas's claims that marriage is old and promotes "a way of life" that is "noble." *Griswold v. Connecticut.*

8. An example is Justice Benjamin Cardozo's opinion for the Court in *Palko v. Connecticut,* 302 U.S. 319 (1937). See also Walter F. Murphy, "An Ordering of Constitutional Values," 53 *Southern California Law Review* 703 (1980).

9. Charles L. Black, Jr., *Structure and Relationship in Constitutional Law* (Baton Rouge: Louisiana State University Press, 1969); John Hart Ely, *Democracy and Distrust: A Theory of Judicial Review* (Cambridge, MA: Harvard University Press, 1980).

10. *Griswold v. Connecticut* (Douglas, J., for the Court) (invoking "penumbras" and "emanations" for purposes behind particular guarantees of rights). Cf. *Jacobson v. Massachusetts,* 197 U.S. 11 (1905) (Harlan, J., for the Court) (asserting that "the spirit is to be collected chiefly from [the] words" (quoting from *Sturges v. Crowninshield* [1819]). For a comparative view, see Aharon Barak, *Purposive Interpretation in Law,* Sari Bashi, trans. (Princeton, NJ: Princeton University Press, 2005).

11. William J. Brennan, Jr., "The Constitution of the United States: Contemporary Ratification," 27 *South Texas Law Review* 433 (1986). See also Justice Brennan's dissent in *Michael H. v. Gerald D.*

12. *U.S. v. La Jeune Eugenie,* 26 F. Cas. 832 (D. Mass. 1822) (Story, J.); *Rochin v. California,* 342 U.S. 165 (1952) (Frankfurter, J., for the Court) (specifying the values of "English-speaking peoples"); *Trop v. Dulles,* 356 U.S. 86 (1958) (Warren, C.J., announcing the judgment of the Court) (invoking "civilized standards" of "decency" and "the dignity of man").

13. *Calder v. Bull,* 3 U.S. (Dall.) 386 (1798) (Chase, J., for the Court); *Bradwell v. Illinois,* 83 U.S. 130 (1872) (Bradley, J., concurring). See also Thomas C. Grey, "Do We

Have an Unwritten Constitution?" 27 *Stanford Law Review* 703 (1975) (discussing natural right as a source for higher law); Michael S. Moore, "A Natural Law Theory of Interpretation," 58 *Southern California Law Review* 277 (1985); Robert P. George, *Making Men Moral: Civil Liberties and Public Morality* (New York: Oxford University Press, 1993). Compare *U.S. v. Marshall*, 908 F. 2d 1312 (7th Cir. 1990) (Posner, J., dissenting) (noting similarities between natural law and pragmatism).

14. Fourth Brāhmaṇa: 1–3, Bṛhad-āraṇyaka Upaniṣad, S. Radhakrishnan, ed., *The Principal Upaniṣads* (New Delhi: Harper Collins Publishers India, 1994).

15. Genesis 1:26–28, *New Revised Standard Version* (Nashville: Thomas Nelson Publishers, 1989).

16. Ibid., 2:4, 7, 18, 21–25.

17. Exodus 20:1, 12, 14, 17.

18. Leviticus 18.

19. See generally, Friedrich (Frederick) Engels, *The Origin of the Family, Private Property and the State, in Light of the Researches of Lewis H. Morgan* [1877] (New York: International Publishers, 1972).

20. Matthew 5:27–31. Compare Matthew 19:9; Mark 10:11–12; Luke 16:18.

21. John 8:2–9.

22. 1 Corinthians 7:1–10.

23. Ibid., 7:4.

24. Ephesians 5:22–24, 6:1, 6:5.

25. Qur'ān 4:23–25, Maulana Muhammad Ali, ed. (Columbus, OH: Ahmadiyyah Anjuman Isha'at Islam, Lahore, Inc., 1994).

26. Ibid., 24:30–33.

27. Ibid., 4:34.

28. Ibid., 2:226–228.

29. Although I did not discuss it above, this solicitude is suggested in a passage quoting Jesus: "Let the children come unto me, and do not stop them; for it is to such as these that the kingdom of heaven belongs. Truly I tell you, whoever does not receive the kingdom of God as a little child will never enter it." Luke 18:15. Compare Matthew 18:1–5, 19:13–15.

30. See Translator's Introduction to G. W. F. Hegel, *The Philosophy of History*, J. Sibree, trans. (Kitchener, Ontario: Batoche Books, 2001), 5.

31. Hegel, *The Philosophy of History*.

32. G. W. F. Hegel, *Philosophy of Right*, T. M. Knox, trans. (New York: Oxford University Press, 1952, 1967), 110 et seq.

33. Ibid., 155 et seq.

34. Hegel, *The Philosophy of History*, 48–49. See also Leo Strauss and Joseph Cropsey, eds., *History of Political Philosophy*, 3rd edition (Chicago: University of Chicago Press, 1987), at 733.

35. Hegel, *Philosophy of Right;* Hegel, *The Philosophy of History*. For a useful discussion of Hegel's account of the movement of history, see Charles Taylor, *Hegel and Modern Society* (Cambridge: Cambridge University Press, 1979), at 95–100.

36. For canonical volumes on Darwin's theory of natural selection, see Charles Darwin, *On the Origin of Species by Means of Natural Selection, or, The Preservation of Favoured Races in the Struggle for Life* [1859] (New York: New York University Press, 1987); Darwin, *The Descent of Man, and Selection Related to Sex* [1871] (New York: New York University Press, 1989).

37. Compare Karl Marx and Friedrich Engels, *The Communist Manifesto* [1848, 1888], A. J. P. Taylor, ed. (New York: Penguin Books, 1967), with Engels, *Origin of the Family, Private Property and the State*.

38. Many practitioners in the academic discipline of sociology have reversed the causal arrow, claiming that social change, often subtle and sometimes invisible, drives change in the political economy.

39. See, for example, Gary S. Becker, *A Treatise on the Family* (Cambridge, MA: Harvard University Press, 1981); Richard A. Posner, *Sex and Reason* (Cambridge, MA: Harvard University Press, 1992); Joseph A. Schumpeter, *Capitalism, Socialism, and Democracy* (New York: Harper & Row, 1976).

40. Marx and Engels, *Communist Manifesto*, 100–101.

41. Engels, *Origin of the Family, Private Property and the State*, 94–146, 217–237.

42. Ibid., 139–142.

43. Ibid., 142–144. On the transition from status to contract, see Henry Maine, *Ancient Law: Its Connection with the Early History of Society and Its Relation to Modern Ideas* [1861] (New York: E. P. Dutton, 1954), ch. 5.

44. Engels, *Origin of the Family, Private Property and the State*, 139, 144, 146.

45. Schumpeter, *Capitalism, Socialism, and Democracy*.

46. Ibid., 156–160.

47. Ibid., 160–162.

48. See, e.g., Owen D. Jones, "Brains, Evolution, and Law: Applications and Open Questions," in *Law and the Brain*, S. Zeki and O. Goodenough, eds. (New York: Oxford University Press, 2006); Owen D. Jones, "Evolutionary Analysis in Law: An Introduction and Application to Child Abuse," 75 *North Carolina Law Review* 1117 (1997).

49. *Goodridge v. Department of Public Health*, 798 N.E.2d 941 (Supreme Judicial Court of Mass. 2003), Cordy, J., dissenting.

50. Dan Cere, *The Future of Family Law: Law and the Marriage Crisis in North America* (2005), http://www.marriagedebate.com/pdf/future_of_family_law.pdf. Heading up this report were Mary Ann Glendon, from Harvard Law School, and Dan Cere, from McGill University in Montreal.

51. *The Bhagavadgītā in the Mahābhārata*, J. A. B. van Buitenen, trans. (Chicago: University of Chicago Press, 1981).

52. One early example is the conflict between Cain and Abel. Genesis 4:1–16. Another is the competing inheritance of two sons of Abraham, Ishmael and Isaac. Genesis, chs. 16–18. These are just two of many examples.

53. See Mark 3:31–35. Compare Matthew 12:46–50.

54. Matthew 10:34–37. Compare Luke 12:49–53, 14:27–28. See also Jesus's depiction of the consequences of his death: "Brother will betray brother to death, and a father his child, and children will rise against parents and have them put to death; and you will be hated by all because of my name. But the one who endures to the end will be saved." Mark 13:12–13. Compare Luke 21:16–19.

55. See Friedrich Nietzsche, *On the Genealogy of Morals* [1887], Walter Kaufmann, trans. (New York: Vintage Books, 1967).

56. Ibid. See also Friedrich Nietzsche, *Human, All Too Human* [1878], Marion Faber, trans. (Lincoln: University of Nebraska Press, 1984), sec. 45.

57. To be sure, Marx and Engels had a robust and substantial account of the subjugation and objectification of women. Against MacKinnon's view, however, they claimed that the source of women's status was economic, not sex itself.

58. Catharine A. MacKinnon, "Feminism, Marxism, Method, and the State: Toward Feminist Jurisprudence," *Signs: Journal of Women in Culture and Society* 8 (1983): 635. MacKinnon's is not the sole feminist theory, of course. For my purposes here, however, it is useful—for its themes, for its coherence, for its theoretical sensibility, and for its intellectual power.

59. Catharine A. MacKinnon, *Toward a Feminist Theory of the State* (Cambridge, MA: Harvard University Press, 1989), 237 et seq.

60. Engels anticipated something like this claim. See *Origin of the Family, Private Property and the State* 135–138.

61. MacKinnon, "Feminism, Marxism, Method, and the State." For an implicit critique of MacKinnon's critique of privacy, see Don Herzog, *Household Politics: Conflict in Early Modern England* (New Haven, CT: Yale University Press, prepublication version dated 2012), http://deepblue.lib.umich.edu/bitstream/2027.42/90021/12/Herzog.pdf.

62. Sigmund Freud, *Civilization and Its Discontents* [1930], James Strachey, trans. (New York: W. W. Norton, 1961), chaps. 3, 5, and 6.

63. Ibid., 48–49.

64. Ibid., 71–72.

65. See Sophocles, "Oedipus the King," in *The Three Theban Plays,* Robert Fagles, trans. (New York: Penguin Books, 1984).

66. For Freud, the psychological mechanism for the emergence of superego is linked to the relation between the male child and his parents: Out of affection for his mother, the child develops a jealous hatred for his father. This jealousy incites a desire to kill the father. This desire provokes guilt, because the child also loves (and depends upon the protection of) his father. This guilt engenders remorse, in the form of an internalized need for punishment. This need becomes the conscience, which makes possible anticipatory self-regulation. Freud, *Civilization,* chap. 8.

67. Freud, *Civilization.*

68. Ibid., 20–21, 30–32.

69. Ibid., 49.

70. Bertrand Russell, *Marriage and Morals* (New York: Horace Liveright, 1929).

71. Ibid., 118–129, 143–144, 288 et seq.

72. Ibid., chap. 20. See also Bertrand Russell, *Why I Am Not a Christian, and Other Essays on Religion and Related Subjects,* Paul Edwards, ed. (New York: Simon and Schuster, 1957).

73. Christopher Lasch, *Haven in a Heartless World: The Family Beseiged* (New York: W. W. Norton, 1979), at xix–xxiv, 3–21, 167–189. Compare Schumpeter, *Capitalism, Socialism, and Democracy* (tracing family's decline to the institutional structure and behavioral motives of capitalism), and Daniel Bell, *The Cultural Contradictions of Capitalism* [1976] (New York: Basic Books, 1996) (tracing the decline to culture).

CHAPTER TWO: THE ENGLISH ANCESTRY OF THE AMERICAN LAW OF FAMILY

1. Matthew Hale, *The History and Analysis of the Common Law of England: Written by a Learned Hand* (Stafford: J. Nutt, 1713), chap. 1; William Blackstone, *Commentaries on the Laws of England,* 4 vols., 1765–1769 (Chicago: University of Chicago Press, 1979), hereafter cited as "Blackstone."

2. Blackstone 4: 208.

3. Blackstone 3: 139.

4. Blackstone 3: 140–141.

5. Blackstone 1: 206.

6. See, e.g., James R. Stoner, Jr., *Common Law and Liberal Theory: Coke, Hobbes, and the Origins of American Constitutionalism* (Lawrence: University Press of Kansas, 1992); John C. P. Goldberg, "The Constitutional Status of Tort Law: Due Process and the Right to a Law for the Redress of Wrongs," 115 *Yale Law Journal* 524 (2005).

7. Blackstone 3: 86–87 (emphasis in original).

8. For an account of how law functioned in this way in the United States, see Hendrik Hartog, *Man and Wife in America: A History* (Cambridge, MA: Harvard University Press, 2000).

9. For a discussion of the *Commentaries'* influence in the United States, before and after independence, see Dennis R. Nolan, "Sir William Blackstone and the New American Republic: A Study of Intellectual Impact," 51 *N.Y.U. Law Review* 731 (1976).

10. Blackstone 1: 410.

11. Ibid., 410 et seq.

12. Ibid., 411–413.

13. Ibid., 416.

14. Ibid., 413–414.

15. Ibid., 410.

16. The term "menial" refers not simply to the lowliness of the labor, but also to the fact that the work was performed (and the servant lived) *intra moenia*, or within the walls of the household. Ibid., 414.

17. The third type of servitude consisted of "*labourers*, who are only hired by the day of the week, and do not live *intra moenia*, as part of the family." The fourth class were distinguished by their "superior . . . ministerial" responsibilities: stewards, factors, and bailiffs. Ibid., 414–415.

18. Ibid., 413–414.

19. Ibid., ch. 14.

20. Ibid., 416.

21. Ibid., 418–419.

22. Homer H. Clark, Jr., *The Law of Domestic Relations in the United States*, 2nd ed. (St. Paul, MN: West Publishing, 1988), 286. Unmarried women, however, could not be jurors, could not vote or hold public office, and had a restricted privilege to inherit. Ibid.

23. Blackstone 1: 430.

24. Frederick Pollock and Frederic William Maitland, *The History of English Law before the Time of Edward I*, 2nd ed., 2 vols. (Cambridge: Cambridge University Press, 1898), 2: 399, 400, 406, 414 (hereafter cited as "Pollock and Maitland").

25. Blackstone 1: 433.

26. Pollock and Maitland 2: 403.

27. Blackstone 1: 430.

28. Pollock and Maitland 2: 405.

29. Blackstone 1: 430–431.

30. Pollock and Maitland 2: 405.

31. Blackstone 1: 430.

32. Ibid. Blackstone noted that a wife might "*purchase* an estate without the consent of her husband, and the conveyance is good during the coverture, till he avoids it by some act declaring his dissent." Blackstone 2: 292.

33. Blackstone 1: 432.
34. Pollock and Maitland 2: 403–404; Blackstone 2: 126–128.
35. Pollock and Maitland 2: 404–405.
36. Ibid., 405.
37. Blackstone 2: 129–130; Blackstone 4: 416–417.
38. Pollock and Maitland 2: 404.
39. Blackstone 2: 135–136.
40. Blackstone 2: 136.
41. See Susan Staves, *Married Women's Separate Property in England, 1660–1833* (Cambridge, MA: Harvard University Press, 1990), 29, 37.
42. Blackstone 2: 137.
43. Blackstone 4: 423; Blackstone 2: 137–138.
44. Blackstone 2: 138–139.
45. Staves, *Married Women's Separate Property,* 35.
46. Blackstone 1: 431–432.
47. Ibid., 432.
48. Ibid.
49. Ibid., 433.
50. Ibid., 431.
51. *Semayne's Case* (K.B., 1604), reported in Sir Edward Coke, *The Selected Writings and Speeches of Sir Edward Coke,* Steve Sheppard, ed. (Indianapolis: Liberty Fund, 2003), vol. 1, 135–141.
52. Blackstone 4: 75, 203–204. A servant who killed the master was guilty of the same crime. See generally, Edward Coke, *The Third Part of the Institutes of the Laws of England* [1644], ch. 2, in Coke, *Selected Writings,* vol. 2, 992–1027.
53. Blackstone 1: 434–435.
54. Ibid., 434, 442–443, 444–445.
55. Ibid., 443.
56. Ibid., 436–437.
57. Ibid., 437.
58. Ibid., 438–439.
59. Ibid., 439–440.
60. The process of "Catholic emancipation" in British law began in the eighteenth century.
61. Blackstone 1: 440–441.
62. Ibid., 440–441.
63. Ibid.
64. Blackstone 1: 441–442.
65. Ibid., 444–445.
66. Ibid., 446.
67. Ibid., 447. Blackstone noted that the English rule, harsh as it was, was still more moderate than the civil, which prohibited even gifts from parents to their illegitimate children and any sort of maintenance.
68. Ivy Pinchbeck, *Women Workers and the Industrial Revolution, 1750–1850* (London: Frank Cass, 1977); Bridget Hill, *Women, Work, and Sexual Politics in Eighteenth-Century England* (Oxford: Basil Blackwell, 1989).
69. 43 Eliz. I, cap. 2.

70. Joan Lane, *Apprenticeship in England, 1600–1914* (London: University College of London Press, 1996), 14; Steve Hindle, "'Waste' Children? Pauper Apprenticeship under the Elizabethan Poor Laws, c. 1598–1697," in *Women, Work, and Wages in England, 1600–1850*, Penelope Lane, Neil Raven, and K. D. M. Snell, eds. (Suffolk: The Boydell Press, 2004), 1–46.

71. 14 Charles II, cap. 12.

72. Blackstone 1: 447.

73. See generally, Steve Hindle, *On the Parish? The Micro-Politics of Poor Relief in Rural England, c. 1550–1750* (New York: Oxford University Press, 2004), 306–325. Hindle notes that zealous overseers would often "risk the wrath" of judges by "removing the impotent [i.e., the deserving poor] as well as the vagrant" from their parishes. Ibid., 310. Compare Lorie Charlesworth, *Welfare's Forgotten Past: A Socio-Legal History of the Poor Law* (New York: Routledge, 2010), 52–57, arguing that aspects of the Poor Laws "favoured the poor."

74. See Hill, *Women, Work and Sexual Politics*, 238. Hill argues, in fact, that a destitute woman might get herself pregnant in order to better her chance of locating a husband on whom she could rely for maintenance. Doubtless this did happen, though it is impossible to know how frequently.

75. Ibid., 239; Blackstone 1: 446.

76. Antonio Buti, "The Early History of the Law of Guardianship of Children: From Rome to the Tenures Abolition Act 1660," *University of Western Sydney Law Review* 5 (2003); Blackstone 1: 449–450.

77. Ibid. Before the Tenures Abolition Act, the designation of guardian was dictated by rules of law, not by the testamentary preference of the father. In some cases, this earlier rule benefitted the mother, who was legally designated to serve in certain guardianships under most circumstances. Under the Act of 1660, the father might designate as guardian someone other than the surviving mother.

78. Blackstone 1: 449–450. Blackstone noted that the English rule of choosing a guardian from outside the line of inheritance departed from the ancient Roman rule, which designated as guardian the person next in line to inherit. This rule, of course, produced many dead wards. As Blackstone put it, the Roman rule was like handing over the lamb to the wolf, to be devoured (*"quasi agnum committere lupo, ad devorandum"*). Ibid., 450.

79. Blackstone 1: 451–453.

80. Statute of Marlborough 1267, cap. 17. As explained below, "socage" was a feudal tenure in land that did not include military obligations. The guardian in chivalry, who governed a child whose father had been a tenant of land held under knight-service, was distinctly not a fiduciary to his ward. The Tenures Abolition Act abolished the guardianship in chivalry.

81. See, e.g., Richard L. Greaves, *Society and Religion in Elizabethan England* (Minneapolis: University of Minnesota Press, 1981), 146–149. Some guardians pursued advantage in a different way—by marrying their wards. For a fictitious nineteenth-century rendering of such a marriage, see Charles Dickens, *Bleak House* (1853).

82. Buti, "Early History"; Blackstone 2: 70.

83. Blackstone 1: 450–451.

84. Blackstone 2: 246–247. "This is a very antient rule in the law of England; and it's reason is too obvious, and too shocking, to bear a minute discussion." Ibid.

85. Blackstone 1: 293–295, 426, 439, 451; Blackstone 2: 291–292; Blackstone 3: 427; Blackstone 4: 24–25.

86. Thomas Hobbes made memorable use of the trope in his critique of the breakdown of political order in mid-seventeenth-century England. Hobbes, *Leviathan, or The Matter, Forme and Power of a Commonwealth Ecclesiasticall and Civil* (London: Printed for Andrew Crooke, 1651).

87. Don Herzog, *Happy Slaves: A Critique of Consent Theory* (Chicago: University of Chicago Press, 1989), 45.

88. Ibid., 39–51. See also Frank Aydelotte, *Elizabethan Rogues and Vagabonds* (Oxford: Clarendon Press, 1913).

89. Proclamation of the Queene (1579), from *A Booke Containing All Such Proclamations, as Were Published during the Raigne of the Late Queene Elizabeth* (1618). Tabling houses were places for gambling and wagering. Tipling houses were establishments whose primary purposes were the sale and consumption of alcoholic drink. Gaming was a crime. Blackstone 4: 171–174. Tipling, or drunkenness, was a minor crime, for which the drunk was summarily placed in stocks for five hours. Other statutes regulated the licenses of ale houses and provided for punishment of both drunks and the owners who accommodated them. Blackstone 4: 64.

90. Blackstone 4: 170.

91. Blackstone 4: 165.

92. Blackstone 1: 421.

93. Blackstone 3: 92–93.

94. Blackstone 1: 421.

95. On seventeenth-century motives and practices concerning marriage, see Herzog, *Happy Slaves*, 59–63.

96. Blackstone 1: 422–423.

97. Ibid., 422, 424–426; 26 Geo. II, cap. 33 (1753).

98. Ibid., 426.

99. For a useful discussion of the purposes for the Marriage Act, see Erica Harth, "The Virtue of Love: Lord Hardwicke's Marriage Act," *Cultural Critique* 9 (1988): 123.

100. Ibid., 125.

101. Ibid., 126–127, citing the Lords' decision in *Cochrane alias Kennedy v. Campbell* (involving a conflict between two surviving widows over entitlement to a widow's pension).

102. Blackstone 1: 427–428; Blackstone 4: 163. Pollock and Maitland argued that requiring either a license or the publication of banns was designed to prohibit what they called a "death-bed marriage" in which a dying sinner, facing a priest and the threat of eternal damnation, agreed "to 'make an honest woman' of his mistress." Pollock and Maitland 2: 375. As noted above, the reasons for the requirement were more complex than this explanation indicates.

103. Pollock and Maitland 2: 375–377.

104. Blackstone 1: 429.

105. Blackstone 3: 139.

106. Blackstone 4: 64.

107. Ibid., 65.

108. John Locke, *Second Treatise of Government* [1690], C. B. Macpherson, ed. (Indianapolis: Hackett, 1980), §26.

109. The claim of "un-Englishness" is only partly accurate. Certain ancient (pre-English) inhabitants of Britain held land by allodial title (i.e., not subject to a limiting claim by any superior) and in common.

110. Evelyn Cecil, *Primogeniture: A Short History of Its Development in Various Countries and Its Practical Effects* (London: John Murray, 1895), 29–30. One county in England that retained the custom of gavelkind, for the benefit of male children, was Kent. Outside England, Wales also kept this custom.

111. Ibid., 30–32; Blackstone 2: 214–216.

112. Cecil, *Primogeniture,* 33–36; Blackstone 2: 215–216.

113. Cecil, *Primogeniture,* 40–41.

114. Blackstone 2: 84; Cecil, *Primogeniture,* 42–43.

115. Blackstone 1: 437–438.

116. Blackstone 2: ch. 7.

117. Ibid., 116–117; Arthur W. Blakemore, *Law of Real Property* (Chicago: Blackstone Institute, 1914), 75–78; Charles D. Spinoza, "The Legal Reasoning behind the Common, Collusive Recovery: *Taltarum's Case* (1472)," 36 *American Journal of Legal History* 70 (1992).

118. Cecil, *Primogeniture,* 47–49; Lloyd Bonfield, "Property Settlements on Marriage in England from the Anglo-Saxons to the Mid-Eighteenth Century," in *Marriage, Property, and Succession,* Lloyd Bonfield, ed. (Berlin: Duncker & Humblot, 1992), 287 et seq.

CHAPTER THREE: FAMILY AT THE BIRTH OF THE AMERICAN ORDER

1. Gordon J. Schochet, *The Authoritarian Family and Political Attitudes in 17th-Century England: Patriarchalism in Political Thought,* 2nd ed. (New Brunswick, NJ: Transaction Books, 1988), 86–98.

2. Ibid., 115–158.

3. Robert Filmer, *Patriarcha* [1648], in *Patriarcha and Other Writings,* Johann P. Sommerville, ed. (New York: Cambridge University Press: 1991), 1, 4–6, 12.

4. Ibid., 2, 10.

5. Ibid., 10–11.

6. Ibid., 34, 35, 42.

7. In his *First Treatise of Government* (1690), Locke pressed a systematic critique of Filmer's patriarchy. I am more concerned with Locke's own positive accounts of political authority and of family, which appear in his *Second Treatise of Government* (1699). See John Locke, *Second Treatise of Government* [1690], C. B. Macpherson, ed. (Indianapolis: Hackett, 1980).

8. Locke, *Second Treatise,* §§4–15. Locke left open the possibility that the state of nature was not hypothetical but real. As evidence for its reality, he cited relations among nations (§14), the writings of Richard Hooker (§15), and the indigenous peoples of North America (§49). The state of nature was even evident in civil societies living under absolute monarchs who claimed to be above the law (§§93–94).

9. Ibid., §§6–8, 87. The notions of reason and limits are present also in Locke's discussion of property. §§25–51.

10. Ibid., §§4, 87.

11. Ibid., §§7–8, 123, 128.

12. Ibid., §124.

13. Ibid., §§91, 125–126.

14. Ibid., §§13, 125.

15. Ibid., §§123, 126.

16. Ibid., §§87–90, 92–93, 95, 127–131.

17. Ibid., §28.

18. Ibid., §§53, 64.

19. Ibid., §52. Despite this position, Locke (like Blackstone later) persisted in referring to "paternal" authority. Ibid., §§65, 69, 71.

20. Ibid., §52. He observed, moreover, that when mother and father disagree, the ultimate decision "naturally falls to the man's share, as the abler and the stronger." Ibid., §82. He also borrowed a familial hierarchy from Aristotle: "Let us consider a *master of a family* with all these subordinate relations of *wife, children, servants,* and *slaves,* united under the Domestic rule of a family." Ibid., §86 (emphases in original).

21. Ibid., §3 (emphases in original).

22. Ibid., §§56, 58, 65. The use of the masculine gender is intentional. Despite his differences with Filmer over patriarchy, Locke's model for personhood was usually masculine.

23. Ibid., §§55–65. See also §§87–90, 92–93, 95, 127–131. This notion cut against that of Thomas Hobbes, an absolutist for whom liberty resided in "the absence of externall Impediments" and in "the Silence of the Law." Thomas Hobbes, *Leviathan* [1651], Richard Tuck, ed. (New York: Cambridge University Press, 1991), 91, 152.

24. Locke, *Second Treatise,* §§55, 57–63.

25. Ibid., §71.

26. Holly Brewer, *By Birth or Consent: Children, Law, and the Anglo-American Revolution in Authority* (Chapel Hill: University of North Carolina Press, 2005), 1–5.

27. See Hobbes, *Leviathan,* chap. 14, where it's apparent that it is logically impossible for persons to consent in the way that Hobbes presents.

28. Locke, *Second Treatise,* §§77–78, 80.

29. Ibid., §§79–80.

30. Ibid., §81.

31. On the emergence of the contractual conception of marriage, see Mary Lyndon Shanley, "Marriage Contract and Social Contract in Seventeenth Century English Political Thought," *Western Political Quarterly* 32 (1979): 79.

32. Locke, *Second Treatise,* §§123, 131.

33. Ibid., §§96–98, 124–125, 131.

34. By "property" in this context, I have in mind those things, both real and personal, that persons can, on Locke's terms, come to own. Ibid., §§25–51. For Locke's treatment of family generally, see §§52–95.

35. Ibid., §§89, 120, 131. For Locke's account of the mutation of limits as one moves from the state of nature to civil society to civil government, see §§25–51.

36. Ibid., §83.

37. Ibid., §§81–82.

38. Ibid., §§77–80.

39. Ibid., §§240–243.

40. Ibid., §§211–220.

41. Ibid., §§221–222.

42. Ibid., §230.

43. Ibid., §225.

44. Edward S. Corwin, "The 'Higher Law' Background of American Constitutional Law" [1955], in *Corwin on the Constitution*, vol. 1, Richard Loss, ed. (Ithaca, NY: Cornell University Press, 1981).

45. Gordon S. Wood, *The Radicalism of the American Revolution* (New York: Random House, 1991), 98. Among those who referred to the English Constitution as mixed, see William Blackstone, *Commentaries on the Laws of England*, 4 vols., 1765–1769 (Chicago: University of Chicago Press, 1979), 1: 50–51 (hereafter cited as "Blackstone"); Bernard Bailyn, *The Ideological Origins of the American Revolution* (Cambridge, MA: Belknap Press of Harvard University Press, 1967), 67–76; Corinne Comstock Weston, *English Constitutional Theory and the House of Lords, 1556–1832* (New York: Columbia University Press, 1965), 87–141. Compare Christopher Hill, *The World Turned Upside Down: Radical Ideas during the English Revolution* (Harmondsworth, UK: Penguin Books, 1975), 14 (describing the English political settlement as "parliamentary sovereignty, limited monarchy, imperialist foreign policy, a world safe for businessmen to make profits in").

46. For an account of some of the constitutional changes presaged by the Glorious Revolution, see generally J. R. Tanner, *English Constitutional Conflicts of the Seventeenth Century, 1603–1689* (Cambridge, UK: Cambridge University Press, 1928).

47. Wood, *Radicalism*, 95–99.

48. Baron de Montesquieu, *The Spirit of the Laws* [1748], Franz Neumann, ed. (New York: Hafner Press, 1949), 68.

49. Wood, *Radicalism*, 124.

50. Ibid., 132. See also Wilson H. Grabill et al., *The Fertility of American Women* (NY: John Wiley, 1958), 5–12; Daniel Scott Smith, "The Demographic History of Colonial New England," *Journal of Economic History* 32 (1972): 174–179.

51. Wood, *Radicalism*, 125.

52. Ibid., 125–128.

53. Locke, *Second Treatise*, §§25–51 (where, by my count, Locke invoked variants of the words "use" and "useful" seventeen times).

54. Vernon Louis Parrington, *Main Currents in American Thought: The Colonial Mind, 1620–1800*, vol. 1 (New York: Harcourt Brace, 1927), 143–147. In the words of Crèvecoeur, "Go thou, and work and till; thou shalt prosper, provided thou be just, grateful and industrious." Ibid., 145.

55. See, e.g., Pauline Meier, *American Scripture: Making the Declaration of Independence* (New York: Vintage Books, 1997), 165–167. Maier may place too much emphasis on property. In fact the sources for Jefferson's invocation of happiness were more complex than Meier allows. See, e.g., Garry Wills, *Inventing America: Jefferson's Declaration of Independence* (New York: Doubleday, 1978), 248–255. Maier's observation, however, does support the claim that, by the time of the Revolution, the political idea of happiness was linked to material concerns, at least in *some* colonial quarters. See generally Jeffrey Barnouw, "American Independence: Revolution of the Republican Ideal; A Response to Pocock's Construction of 'The Atlantic Republican Tradition,'" in *The American Revolution and Eighteenth-Century Culture*, Paul J. Korshin, ed. (New York: AMS Press, 1986), 31.

56. See Corwin, "The 'Higher Law' Background," 80; Michael Kammen, *A Machine That Would Go of Itself: The Constitution in American Culture* (New York: Knopf, 1986), 14–16.

57. Wood, *Radicalism,* 124–134.

58. Ibid., 112–117.

59. Ibid., 122.

60. Ibid., 112–124, 134–145; Bernard Bailyn, *The Origins of American Politics* (New York: Random House, 1968), 131–132.

61. Gordon S. Wood, *The Creation of the American Republic, 1776–1787* (Chapel Hill: University of North Carolina Press, 1998), 488–489. Even so, many Americans felt that there were noticeable class divisions.

62. Wood, *Radicalism,* 114–115, 174–176. Compare Bailyn, *Origins of American Politics,* 28–30, 72–80. Bailyn focuses on the political origins of the demise of the English system of patronage in the colonies. His focus, however, doesn't negate the importance of social or economic sources of political change.

63. See Nancy F. Cott, "Divorce and the Changing Status of Women in Eighteenth-Century Massachusetts," *William & Mary Quarterly* 33 (1976): 588–589.

64. See Daniel Scott Smith, "Parental Power and Marriage Patterns: An Analysis of Historical Trends in Hingham, Massachusetts," *Journal of Marriage & Family* 35 (1973): 425.

65. Daniel Blake Smith, *Inside the Great House: Planter Family Life in Eighteenth-Century Chesapeake Society* (Ithaca, NY: Cornell University Press, 1980), 52–53, 111–113; Wood, *Radicalism,* 145–150.

66. Philippe Aries, *Centuries of Childhood: A Social History of Family Life* (New York: Vintage Books, 1962), 402–404, 412–413 (claiming that affectionate care for children was the basic indicator of the emergence of the "modern" family).

67. See Carl N. Degler, *At Odds: Women and the Family in America from the Revolution to the Present* (New York: Oxford University Press, 1980), 8–20.

68. Jay Fliegelman, *Prodigals and Pilgrims: The American Revolution against Patriarchal Authority, 1750–1800* (New York: Cambridge University Press, 1982), 267.

69. Blackstone 4: 27. See also Jerrilyn Greene Marston, *King and Congress: The Transfer of Political Legitimacy, 1774–1776* (Princeton, NJ: Princeton University Press, 1987), 20–31.

70. Wood, *Radicalism,* 165–167.

71. Peter Shaw, *American Patriots and the Rituals of Revolution* (Cambridge, MA: Harvard University Press, 1981), 39.

72. See Edwin G. Burrows and Michael Wallace, "The American Revolution: The Ideology and Psychology of National Liberation," 6 *Perspectives in American History* 167 (1972), 186–189.

73. See Ian R. Christie, "British Response to American Reaction to the Townshend Acts, 1767–1775," in *Resistance, Politics, and the American Struggle for Independence, 1765–1775,* Walter H. Conser, Jr., et al., eds. (Boulder, CO: Lynne Rienner Publishers, 1986), 193, 198 ("'I heartily wished to repeal the whole law [imposing a duty on tea] . . . if there had been a possibility of repealing it without giving up that just right which I shall ever wish the mother country to possess, the right of taxing the Americans'" [quoting statement of Lord North, in 1770]); ibid., at 207 ("All measures for the support of the constitutional Authority of this Kingdom in Massachusetts Bay will be ineffectual and delusive, until the Government of that Province, upon just Principles of dependency on the Mother Country, can be restored to its proper vigour and activity" [quoting Letter from the Colonial Secretary to General Thomas Gage (June 12, 1770)]); Soame Jenyns, "The Objections

to the Taxation of our American Colonies, Briefly Considered" (1765), reprinted in *The American Revolution through British Eyes,* Martin Kallich and Andrew MacLeish, eds. (New York: Harper & Row, 1962), 6, 8 ("Can there be a more proper time for this mother country to leave off feeding out of her own vitals, these children whom she has nursed up . . . ?"). See also Wood, *Radicalism,* 165–167. Even John Dickinson, a colonist and eventually a revolutionary, implored, "Let us behave like dutiful children who have received unmerited blows [in the form of the Townshend Acts] from a beloved parent. Let us complain to our parent; but let our complaints speak at the same time the language of affliction and veneration." John Dickinson, "Letter III" (December 14, 1768), *Letters from a Farmer in Pennsylvania to the Inhabitants of the British Colonies,* reprinted in *Empire and Nation,* William E. Leuchtenberg and Bernard Wishy, eds. (Englewood Cliffs, NJ: Prentice Hall, 1962), 15, 20.

74. Debate on the Declaratory Act and the Repeal of the Stamp Act, in Kallich and MacLeish, *American Revolution,* 24, 28 (statement of Lord Camden, February 24, 1766: "The forefathers of the Americans . . . looked for protection, and not for chains, from their mother country"); Petitions of the London Merchants against the Stamp Act (January 17, 1766), in Kallich and MacLeish, *American Revolution,* 16, 18 (urging repeal of the Stamp Act in order to promote among the colonies a "firm attach[ment] to the mother country"); William Pitt, Addressing the House of Lords in Opposition to the Quartering Act (May 26, 1774), in Kallich and MacLeish, *American Revolution,* 41, 42 ("The Americans had almost forgot, in their excess of gratitude for the repeal of the stamp act, any interest but that of the mother country"); William Pitt, Speech on the Stamp Act (January 14, 1766), in Kallich and MacLeish, *American Revolution,* 10, 11 ("The Americans are the sons, not the bastards of England"); Richard Price, *Observations on the Nature of Civil Liberty, the Principles of Government, and Justice and Policy of the War with America,* 8th ed. (1778), 37, 104–105.

75. Paine was not the first to wage a pitched battle against even the maternal metaphor. For a discussion regarding his predecessors, see Edwin G. Burrows and Michael Wallace, "The American Revolution: The Ideology and Psychology of National Liberation," *Perspectives in American History* 6 (1972): 167, 186–189.

76. Thomas Paine, *Common Sense* (1776), reprinted in *Thomas Paine: Collected Writings,* Eric Foner, ed. (Des Moines, IA: Library of America, 1995), 5, 22–23 (emphasis in original).

77. Thomas Paine, *The Crisis, Number VII* (1778), in Foner, *Collected Writings,* 191, 207.

78. Ibid., 206–207.

79. Ibid., 207.

80. Paine, *Common Sense,* 48.

81. Ibid., 15–16.

82. Ibid., 17.

83. Thomas Paine, "Common Sense, on the King of England's Speech" (1782), in Foner, *Collected Writings,* 287, 293–295.

84. Paine, *Common Sense,* 19.

85. Thomas Paine, *Rights of Man Part One* (1791), in Foner, *Collected Writings,* 433, 476.

86. Ibid., 474–476. This claim resonated among Americans, who, in Whiggish fashion, tended to claim that English liberty had originated among the Anglo-Saxons but was lost with the imposition of "the Norman yoke." See Forrest McDonald, *Novus Ordo*

Seclorum: The Intellectual Origin of the Constitution (Lawrence: University Press of Kansas, 1985), 76–77.

87. Paine, *Rights of Man Part One*, 478–479.

88. Paine, *Common Sense*, 16 (emphasis in original). The phrase "ass for a lion" trades on Aesop's fable of the ass in the lion's skin. The lion was a symbol of the English monarchy.

89. Thomas Paine, *Rights of Man Part Two* (1792), in Foner, *Collected Writings*, 541, 562–563.

90. Ibid., 562–564.

91. See Locke, *Second Treatise*, §§106–107.

92. Paine, *Rights of Man Part One*, 517.

93. Ibid., 518.

94. Ibid.

95. Ibid., 536–537.

96. Paine, *Rights of Man Part Two*, 562.

97. On primogeniture generally, see Allison Reppy and Leslie J. Tompkins, *Historical and Statutory Background of the Law of Wills* (Washington, DC: Library of Congress, 1929), 68–78.

98. Paine, *Rights of Man Part One*, 478.

99. On the relations between republicanism and virtue in eighteenth-century American thought, see Joyce Appleby, *Liberalism and Republicanism in the Historical Imagination* (Cambridge, MA: Harvard University Press, 1992), 161–187; Patrice Higonnet, *Sister Republics: The Origins of French and American Republicanism* (Cambridge, MA: Harvard University Press, 1988), 107–120; McDonald, *Novus Ordo Seclorum*, 70; Thomas L. Pangle, *The Spirit of Modern Republicanism: The Moral Vision of the American Founders and the Philosophy of John Locke* (Chicago: University of Chicago Press, 1988), 112–127; J. G. A. Pocock, *The Machiavellian Moment: Florentine Political Thought and the Atlantic Republican Tradition* (Princeton, NJ: Princeton University Press, 1975), 519–529; Paul A. Rahe, *Republics Ancient and Modern: Classical Republicanism and the American Revolution* (Chapel Hill, NC: University of North Carolina Press, 1992), 600–605; M. N. S. Sellers, *American Republicanism: Roman Ideology in the United States Constitution* (New York: New York University Press, 1994), 235–236.

100. McDonald, *Novus Ordo Seclorum*, 74. This strand, which traced its intellectual pedigree to James Harrington's *The Commonwealth of Oceana* (London: John Streater, 1656), was especially strong in the southern colonies. Ibid.

101. McDonald, *Novus Ordo Seclorum*, 73–5. This strand of republicanism made sense of Paine's critique of "the state of the currency," in which he was concerned that a man be able to "support his family as long again as before [the crisis]." Thomas Paine, *The American Crisis III* (1777), in Foner, *Collected Writings*, 116, 143. Agrarian republicanism was antagonistic to republican thought in Puritan New England, which held that public virtue could be sustained not through social and political structure, but only through the presence of privately virtuous individuals. Ibid., 144–146. This different conception would become useful in New England's transition from an agrarian to a commercial and industrial capitalist economy. Agrarians critiqued this conception for permitting an "unnatural" accumulation of wealth. See generally Daniel Bell, *The Cultural Contradictions of Capitalism* (New York: Basic Books, 1996), 21; Joseph A. Schumpeter, *Capitalism, Socialism, and Democracy* (New York: Harper & Row, 1976), 156–163; Max Weber, *The Protestant*

Ethic and the Spirit of Capitalism, Talcott Parsons, trans. (New York: C. Scribner's Sons, 1930), 153–183.

102. Paine, *Rights of Man Part Two*, 624–641, 639.

103. Ibid., 636, 639.

104. Ibid., 624–631.

105. See Lawrence M. Friedman, *A History of American Law*, 2nd edition (New York: Touchstone, 1985), 234.

106. Ibid., 66.

107. Ibid., 239; McDonald, *Novus Ordo Seclorum*, 12.

108. McDonald, *Novus Ordo Seclorum*, 20–21.

109. Bailyn, *Ideological Origins*, 274–275.

110. Paine, *Rights of Man Part One*, 537–538.

111. Aristotle, *Politics*, in *The Complete Works of Aristotle*, vol. 2, Jonathan Barnes, ed. (Princeton, NJ: Princeton University Press), III.7.1279a30–1279a35.

112. Ibid., III.7.1279b4–1279b5.

113. Ibid., III.9.1280a8–10.1289a39.

114. Ibid., III.11.1281a40–1282a41.

115. Polybius, *The Histories*, VI.3. Aristotle was attracted less to a mixed form per se than to a single form that combined social elements. See, e.g., Aristotle, *Politics*, IV.7.1293b15–1293b20.

116. Polybius, *Histories*, VI.3.

117. Ibid., VI.11.

118. Ibid., VI.3–4.

119. Montesquieu, *Spirit of the Laws*, 151–162.

120. Blackstone 1: 50–52.

121. Bailyn, *Ideological Origins*, 273–274.

122. Blackstone 1: 50–52; Montesquieu, *Spirit of the Laws*, 151; Bailyn, *Ideological Origins*, 20–23. Bailyn says Blackstone's account was "misleading" as an explanation of "the actual working of English government." Ibid., 23. Even if Bailyn is right, Blackstone's account might still have informed colonial conceptions of the proper structure and function of government.

123. Bailyn, *Ideological Origins*, 274–281.

124. McDonald, *Novus Ordo Seclorum*, 160–161.

125. On Jefferson's views of the relation between natural aristocracy and human progress, see Letter from Thomas Jefferson to John Adams (October 28, 1813), in *Thomas Jefferson: Writings*, Merrill D. Peterson, ed. (New York: Library of America, 1984), 1304, 1306.

126. Richard K. Matthews, *The Radical Politics of Thomas Jefferson: A Revisionist View* (Lawrence: University Press of Kansas, 1984), 122.

127. As noted above, Blackstone located the three forms of rule (or social classes) within Crown and Parliament. One notable aspect of this arrangement was the absence of a constitutional place for the judiciary. The upshot of the arrangement was parliamentary supremacy, which Blackstone explicitly embraced. See Blackstone 1: 91. Montesquieu, in contrast, emphasized the need to keep the three governmental functions—legislative, executive, and (especially) judicial—distinct and separate, each with its own domain of power. See Montesquieu, *Spirit of the Laws*, 151–162.

128. Even Alexander Hamilton tended to disavow a monarchic character in the executive. See Hamilton, *The Federalist*, No. 70 (1788), in *The Federalist Papers*, Clinton

Rossiter, ed. (New York: New American Library, 1961). Still, he praised the judiciary in terms evocative of Jefferson's natural aristocracy. See Hamilton, *The Federalist*, No. 78 (1788).

129. See George Clinton, "Letters of Cato," No. 6 (December 16, 1787), in *The Antifederalists*, Cecelia M. Kenyon, ed. (New York: Bobbs-Merrill, 1966), 312, 316–317 (predicting that the president and the Senate would combine against the representatives to strangle liberty in the United States); Richard Henry Lee, "Letters from the Federal Farmer," No. 3 (October 10, 1787), in *The Antifederalists*, 215–220 ("When we examine the powers . . . of the executive, we shall perceive that the general government . . . will have a strong tendency to aristocracy"); George Mason, "Objections of the Proposed Federal Constitution" (October 7, 1787), in *The Antifederalists*, 192–195 ("It is at present impossible to foresee whether [the Constitution] will, in its operation, produce a monarchy, or a corrupt oppressive aristocracy; it will most probably vibrate some years between the two, and then terminate in one or the other"); "Letters of Centinel," No. 1 (October 5, 1787), in *The Antifederalists*, 3, 7, 12–14 (arguing against equal representation of states in the Senate and the presidential power to pardon); "Letters of Centinel," No. 3 (November 5, 1787), in *The Antifederalists*, 15, 17–19 (contending that the national government would be constructed "on the most unequal principles, destitute of accountability to its constituents"); "Letters of John DeWitt," No. 3 (November 5, 1787), in *The Antifederalists*, 102–106 (noting that the Senate would be the "Aristocratical" branch and the executive the "monarchical" branch of the proposed government); "Letter of Montezuma" (October 17, 1787), in *The Antifederalists*, 61–67 ("This constitution is calculated to restrain the influence and the power of the LOWER CLASS" [emphasis in original]).

130. Michael Kammen traces this phrase to James Russell Lowell's address to the Reform Club of New York in 1888, but emphasizes that the metaphor of Constitution as a machine had roots extending back to the founding. See Kammen, *Machine That Would Go of Itself*, 17–19.

131. See James Madison, *The Federalist*, No. 10 (1787) (explaining the roots of "faction" in, among other things, "the various and unequal distribution of property") and No. 39 (1788) (defining an essential characteristic of a republic to be that the members of the government "be derived from the great body of society, not from an inconsiderable proportion or favored class of it").

132. James Madison, *The Federalist*, No. 52.

133. Brewer, *By Birth or Consent*, 34.

134. James Madison, *The Federalist*, No. 14 (1787).

135. John Jay, *The Federalist*, No. 4 (1787).

136. But see John Jay, *The Federalist*, No. 64 (1788); Alexander Hamilton, *The Federalist*, No. 76 (1788).

137. John Jay, *The Federalist*, No. 64 (1788).

138. For a claim that, if Louis XIV never made the statement, he might as well have done so, see Crane Brinton et al., *A History of Civilization: Prehistory to 1715*, 5th edition (New York: St. Martin's Press, 1976), 399. Louis's successor, Louis XV, would insist (not apocryphally): "It is in my sole person that sovereign authority resides." R. C. van Caenegem, *An Historical Introduction to Western Constitutional Law* (Cambridge: Cambridge University Press, 1995), 98.

139. See Alexander Hamilton, *The Federalist*, No. 76.

140. Alexander Hamilton, *The Federalist*, No. 77.

292 NOTES TO PAGES 77–78

141. James Madison, *The Federalist*, No. 57.

142. U.S. Const., art. I, §9, cl. 8. and §10, cl. 1.

143. U.S. Const., art. IV, §4.

144. See McDonald, *Novus Ordo Seclorum*, 5.

145. For Madison's understanding of the normative and institutional requirements of republican government, see *The Federalist*, Nos. 10, 14, 37, 39, 43, 49, 51, 52, 55, 57, 62. For Hamilton's contributions, see Nos. 9, 22, 28, 34, 68, 70, 71, 77, 78, 83.

146. U.S. Const., art. II, §1, cl. 5. This provision contains an exemption for persons who were citizens of the United States "at the time of the Adoption of this Constitution."

147. For textual references to the status of slavery, see U.S. Const., art. I, §2 (counting slaves—"all other Persons"—as three-fifths of persons for the purpose of allocating representation in Congress); art. I, §9 (denying Congress the power to interfere with "the Migration or Importation of such Persons" before 1808); art. IV, §2 (providing for the return of fugitives from slavery: "Person[s] held to Service or Labour"); art. V (barring for twenty years any constitutional amendment concerning the importation of slaves).

148. See "Letter from Philadelphiensis to His Fellow Citizens" (February 7, 1788), in Kenyon, ed., *The Antifederalists*, 69, 71; The Pennsylvania Minority, "The Address and Reason of Dissent of the Minority of the Convention of the State of Pennsylvania to Their Constituents" (December 12, 1787), in ibid., 27, 45.

149. See Cecelia Kenyon, "The Political Thought of the Antifederalists," in Kenyon, ed., *The Antifederalists*, xxxix–xli; Herbert J. Storing, *What the Anti-Federalists Were For* (Chicago: University of Chicago Press, 1981), 15–17, 69. Compare Wood, *Creation*, 519–524, 563–564 (noting the Antifederalists' worry that the Constitution of 1787 marked a sharp break with revolutionary ideology, especially in its delegation of executive powers to a single president and in its aggrandizement of national power).

150. Alexander Hamilton, *The Federalist*, No. 17 (1787).

151. James Madison, *The Federalist*, No. 46 (1788).

152. Aristotle famously claimed that the state is the natural extension and highest form of human sociability. In this hierarchy, human association begins with the procreative relation between man and woman and the economic relation between master and slave. Those pairs (with their progeny) are the household. The coalition of a number of households, in turn, forms the village. And "the final association, formed of several villages, is the state." Aristotle, *Politics,* I.1.1252a1–1253a4; I.2.1252b1–1252b18; I.2.1252b28–1252b30.

153. See Cicero, *De Officiis*, Walter Miller, trans. (London: W. M. Heinemann, 1956), at I.xvii.58, I.xlv.160. Cicero set out the hierarchy in two ways. The first was this: "Now, if a contrast and comparison were to be made to find out where most of our moral obligation is due, country would come first, and parents; . . . next come children and the whole family, who look to us alone for support and can have no other protection; finally, our kinsmen, with whom we live on good terms and with whom, for the most part, our lot is one." The second was this: "Our first duty is to the immortal gods; our second, to country; our third, to parents; and so on, in a descending scale, to the rest."

154. Compare Aristotle, *Politics,* I.7.1255b18–1255b39 (describing familial authority as akin to a monarchy). See also Aristotle, *Nicomachean Ethics,* Martin Ostwald, ed. and trans. (New York: MacMillan, 1986), V.6.1134b10–1134b11: "What is just for the master of a slave and just for a father is similar to, but not identical with, the politically just."

155. Aristotle, *Politics,* II.2.1261a17–1261a22.

156. Ibid., II.2.1261a16–1262b36. Suggestively, Aristotle's discussion of a separate space for family introduced his treatment of private ownership of property. Ibid., II.1–5.1264a1–.1264b25.

157. Cicero, *De Officiis*, I.xvii.53–58.

158. See Locke, *Second Treatise*, §§123–131.

CHAPTER FOUR: SLAVES, THE SLAVEHOLDING HOUSEHOLD, AND THE RACIAL FAMILY

1. Thomas Wiedemann, *Greek and Roman Slavery* (Florence, KY: Routledge, 1980), 1–12.

2. See generally Gary B. Nash, *Red, White, and Black: The Peoples of Early North America*, 3rd ed. (Englewood Cliffs, NJ: Prentice-Hall, 1992), 144–161; Benjamin Quarles, *The Negro in the Making of America*, 3rd ed. (New York: MacMillan, 1987), 15–61.

3. Lawrence M. Friedman, *A History of American Law*, 2nd ed. (New York: Simon & Schuster, 1985), 85–87, 218–229.

4. See *U.S. v. Boisdore*, 52 U.S. 63, 95 (1850).

5. William Blackstone, *Commentaries on the Laws of England*, 4 vols., 1765–1769 (Chicago: University of Chicago Press, 1979), 1: 411–413.

6. John Locke, *Second Treatise of Government* [1690], C. B. Macpherson, ed. (Indianapolis: Hackett, 1980), §27.

7. See, e.g., Thornton Stringfellow, "The Bible Argument: or, Slavery in Light of Divine Revelation," in *Cotton Is King, and Pro-Slavery Arguments*, E. N. Elliott, ed. (Augusta, GA: Pritchard, Abbott & Loomis, 1860), 461 et seq. An earlier version of this monograph was published as Thornton Stringfellow, *Scriptural and Statistical Views in Favor of Slavery* (Richmond: J. W. Randolph, 1856). See also Thornton Stringfellow, *Slavery: Its Origin, Nature, and History, Considered in Light of Bible Teachings, Moral Justice, and Political Wisdom* (New York: John F. Trow, 1861).

8. Stringfellow, "The Bible Argument," 462–472.

9. Ibid., 473–478. Stringfellow distinguished *involuntary* slavery, which God permitted, from voluntary slavery, which God had prohibited, at least for the Israelites.

10. Ibid., 478–480.

11. In this chapter, biblical references are to the King James Version because of its widespread use (at least among Protestants) in nineteenth-century America.

12. Rev. Richard Fuller and Rev. Francis Wayland, *Domestic Slavery Considered as a Scriptural Institution*, revised and corrected ed. (New York: Lewis Colby, 1845).

13. Ibid., 210–211.

14. "Speech on the Admission of Kansas," U.S. Senate, *Congressional Globe, 35 Cong., 1 Sess.*, 961–962 (March 4, 1858).

15. James P. Holcombe, "Is Slavery Consistent with Natural Law?" *Southern Literary Messenger* (December 1858).

16. George Fitzhugh, *Sociology for the South, or the Failure of Free Society* (Richmond, VA: A. Morris, 1854), 30.

17. C. Vann Woodward, "George Fitzhugh, *Sui Generis*," in George Fitzhugh, *Cannibals All! or, Slaves without Masters* (1857), C. Vann Woodward, ed. (Cambridge, MA: Harvard University Press, 1960), xxxvi–xxxvii.

18. Fitzhugh, *Cannibals All!*, 16–17.

19. Ibid., 20. Fitzhugh, *Sociology for the South*, 46.

20. Fitzhugh, "Slavery Justified," in *Sociology for the South*, 226.

21. Fitzhugh, *Cannibals All!*, 190–198.

22. Eugene Genovese, *Roll, Jordan, Roll: The World the Slaves Made* (New York: Random House, 1974), 73–75.

23. Ibid., 58–63. But see Genovese's discussion of whipping as punishment. Ibid., 63–68.

24. But see Nash, *Red, White, and Black*, 172–200.

25. Kenneth M. Stampp, *The Peculiar Institution: Slavery in the Ante-Bellum South* (New York: Vintage Books, 1956), 340.

26. Ibid., 198, 340–347.

27. Genovese, *Roll, Jordan, Roll*, 459–462, 465–472.

28. Ibid., 464, 472–475.

29. Ibid., 475–480.

30. Ibid., 482–492.

31. Philippe Ariès, *Centuries of Childhood* (New York: Knopf, 1962), 125.

32. Genovese, *Roll, Jordan, Roll*, 502–503, 505, 508–509.

33. Ibid., 505–506, 515–518.

34. Ibid., 509–514.

35. Ibid., 519–521.

36. Stampp, *The Peculiar Institution*, 352–354; Genovese, *Roll, Jordan, Roll*, 421.

37. Stampp, *The Peculiar Institution*, 355; C. Vann Woodward, ed., *Mary Chesnut's Civil War* (New Haven, CT: Yale University Press, 1981), 29; Genovese, *Roll, Jordan, Roll*, 414, 422. Genovese's use of the term "miscegenation" to describe cross-racial sex might be open to question. For one thing, the term seems not to have appeared in the United States until 1863. *Oxford English Dictionary*. For another, *Black's Law Dictionary* (incorrectly) confines the term to interracial marriage only, not to sex. Regardless, I'll keep the term to refer to sex or marriage between persons of different designated races, whether before or after the Civil War.

38. Genovese, *Roll, Jordan, Roll*, 415–419, 422–423.

39. Helen Catterall, ed., *Judicial Cases Concerning American Slavery and the Negro*, vol. 1 (Washington, DC: The Carnegie Institution of Washington, 1926), 318.

40. *Mosser v. Mosser*, 29 Ala. 313 (1856).

41. Genovese, *Roll, Jordan Roll*, 418–422, 428–429.

42. Stampp, *The Peculiar Institution*, 172, 199–200; *Cannon v. Jenkins* (Supreme Court of North Carolina, 1830), cited in Catterall, *Judicial Cases Concerning American Slavery and the Negro*, vol. 2 (Washington, DC: Carnegie Institute, 1929), 58–59.

43. Robert William Fogel and Stanley L. Engerman, *Time on the Cross: The Economics of American Negro Slavery* (Boston: Little, Brown, 1974), 5, 52; Genovese, *Roll, Jordan, Roll*, 455–457; Stampp, *The Peculiar Institution*, 252, 257.

44. Stampp, *The Peculiar Institution*, 229–231; Genovese, *Roll, Jordan, Roll*, 453–454.

45. Ordinance for the Government of the Territory of the United States, North-west of the River Ohio (July 13, 1787), in *Federal and State Constitutions, Colonial Charters, and Other Organic Laws*, Francis Newton Thorpe, ed., vol. 2 (Washington, DC: Government Printing Office, 1909), 957. The Ordinance required, however, that fugitives from slavery be "lawfully reclaimed, and conveyed" to their owners.

46. Missouri Enabling Act, *U.S. Statutes at Large*, vol. 3, p. 545 (March 6, 1820).

47. For a general discussion of these events, see Mark E. Brandon, *Free in the World: American Slavery and Constitutional Failure* (Princeton, NJ: Princeton University Press, 1998), 69–74, 80–84.

48. 60 U.S. (19 How.) 393 (1857).

49. For a more complete account of the debates between Lincoln and Douglas, see Brandon, *Free in the World,* 116–138.

50. Abraham Lincoln, Speech at Springfield, Illinois (June 16, 1858), in Roy P. Basler, ed., *The Collected Works of Abraham Lincoln* (New Brunswick, NJ: Rutgers University Press, 1953), vol. 2, 461–462.

51. Fitzhugh, *Sociology for the South,* 94. Hofstadter notes that Lincoln, who followed Fitzhugh's writings attentively, had read the passage "with mounting anger and loathing." Richard Hofstadter, *The American Political Tradition and the Men Who Made It* (New York: Random House, 1973), 151–152.

52. Lincoln, Speech at Springfield, Illinois (July 17, 1858); First Debate, at Ottawa, Illinois (August 21, 1858); Second Debate, at Freeport, Illinois (August 27, 1858); Third Debate, at Jonesboro, Illinois (September 15, 1858); Sixth Debate, at Quincy, Illinois (October 13, 1858); Seventh Debate, at Alton, Illinois (October 15, 1858); in Basler, ed., *Collected Works of Abraham Lincoln,* vol. 2, at 507–508; vol. 3, at 18–19, 40–42, 116, 277, 311–312.

53. Lincoln, Speech at Chicago (July 10, 1858), in Basler, ed., *Collected Works of Abraham Lincoln,* vol. 2, 498.

54. Brandon, *Free in the World*, 130.

55. Lawrence M. Friedman quotes Alabama's law of 1868 as an example of this type of postwar statute: "freedmen and women . . . living together as man and wife, shall be regarded in law as man and wife;" and the children of those relations are "declared . . . [to be] entitled to all the rights, benefits and immunities of children of any other class." Friedman, *History of American Law,* 496–497.

56. Peggy Pascoe, *What Comes Naturally: Miscegenation Law and the Making of Race in America* (New York: Oxford University Press, 2009), 31.

57. Pascoe, *What Comes Naturally,* 20–25; Rachel F. Moran, *Interracial Intimacy: The Regulation of Race and Romance* (Chicago: University of Chicago Press, 2001), 19–20, 24–25, 40; Daniel J. Sharfstein, *The Invisible Line: Three American Families and the Secret Journey from Black to White* (New York: Penguin Press, 2011). Jurisdictions that enacted laws after Independence prohibiting interracial marriage included Massachusetts, Delaware, Rhode Island, the District of Columbia, Indiana, Maine, Illinois, Michigan, Iowa, California, Kansas, Nebraska, Washington, New Mexico, Ohio, and Utah. Alabama and Georgia came late to legal prohibition, enacting statutes only on the eve of the Civil War. See Pascoe, *What Comes Naturally*, 21.

58. Pascoe, *What Comes Naturally,* 40–45; Moran, *Interracial Intimacy,* 26–27.

59. Pascoe, *What Comes Naturally,* 56–63.

60. Pascoe, *What Comes Naturally,* 139–150.

61. Ibid., 136–137. For examples of persons who were willing to brave the courts despite charges of miscegenation, see Sharfstein, *Invisible Line.*

62. Pascoe, *What Comes Naturally,* 135–136.

63. Cited in *Pace v. State of Alabama,* 106 U.S. 583 (1883).

64. *Pace v. State of Alabama.*

65. Moran, *Interracial Intimacy,* 17, 40.

66. See, e.g., Kerry Abrams, "The Hidden Dimension of Nineteenth-Century Immigration Law," 62 *Vanderbilt Law Review* 1353 (2009).

67. 1 Stat. 103 (March 26, 1790).

68. 16 Stat. 254 (July 14, 1870).

69. 22 Stat. 58 (May 6, 1882).

70. Rogers M. Smith, *Civic Ideals: Conflicting Visions of Citizenship in U.S. History* (New Haven, CT: Yale University Press, 1997), 360–361. For a nice description of rhetorical attempts to connect race, family, and immorality, see Nancy F. Cott, *Public Vows: A History of Marriage and the Nation* (Cambridge, MA: Harvard University Press, 2000), 132–146.

71. Smith, 362–364, 441–443.

72. For a general discussion of the exclusion cases, see Smith, 365–369, 443–448.

73. 34 Stat. 1228 (March 2, 1907). That Act was amended in 1922 and again in 1931, to make the woman's loss of citizenship contingent upon whether her foreign husband was ineligible for naturalization. If a woman lost her citizenship by marriage but her husband later naturalized, the wife regained her citizenship, and the timing related back to the date of her original loss of citizenship.

74. Annette Gordon Reed, *The Hemingses of Monticello: An American Family* (New York: W. W. Norton, 2008).

75. Edward Ball, *Slaves in the Family* (New York: Farrar, Straus and Giroux, 1998); Sharfstein, *Invisible Line,* 321–330.

CHAPTER FIVE: HOME ON THE RANGE

1. James Madison, *The Federalist,* No. 10 (1787), in *The Federalist Papers,* Clinton Rossiter, ed. (NY: New American Library, 1961).

2. See Frederick C. Prescott, ed., *Alexander Hamilton and Thomas Jefferson* (New York: American Book Company, 1934), lxii.

3. Thomas Jefferson, "Summary View of the Rights of British America" (1774), in *Thomas Jefferson: Writings,* Merrill D. Peterson, ed. (New York: Library of America, 1984), 105–106.

4. Ibid., 118–119.

5. Ibid., 106. The phrase "at the expense of" connotes something like "through the energy of," not, as modern usage would imply, "to the disadvantage of."

6. Ibid., 119.

7. See, e.g., Jefferson, "Autobiography" (1821), in Peterson, ed., *Writings,* 32–33, 38–39, 44. "In the earlier times of the colony when lands were to be obtained for little or nothing, some provident individuals procured large grants, and, desirous of founding great families for themselves, settled them on their descendants in fee-tail. The transmission of this property from generation to generation in the same name raised up a distinct set of families who, being privileged by law in the perpetuation of their wealth were thus formed into a Patrician order, distinguished by the splendor and luxury of their establishments. . . . To annul this privilege, and . . . to make an opening for the aristocracy of virtue and talent . . . was deemed essential to a well ordered republic." Ibid., 32.

8. Thomas Paine, *Rights of Man, Part One* (1791), in *Thomas Paine: Collected Writings,* Eric Foner, ed. (New York: Library of America, 1995).

9. See Dumas Malone, *Jefferson the Virginian* (Boston: Little, Brown, 1948), 247–260.

10. Jefferson, "Letter to John Jay" (August 23, 1785), in Peterson, ed., *Writings,* 818. He recapitulated this position in Query XXII of his "Notes on the State of Virginia" (1787), in ibid., 301.

11. Jefferson, "Letter to John Jay," in Peterson, ed., *Writings,* 818–89. See also "Notes on the State of Virginia," ibid., 300–301.

12. Jefferson, "Letter to James Madison" (December 20, 1787), in Peterson, ed., *Writings,* 918.

13. Jefferson, "Letter to George Mason" (February 4, 1791), in Peterson, ed., *Writings,* 972: "The only corrective of what is corrupt in our present form of government will be the augmentation of the numbers in the lower house, so as to get a more agricultural representation, which may put that interest above that of the stock-jobbers."

14. Jefferson, "First Inaugural Address" (March 4, 1801), in Peterson, ed., *Writings,* 494–495.

15. See, e.g., Jefferson, "Letter to P. S. Dupont de Nemours" (April 24, 1816), in Peterson, ed., *Writings,* 1384–1387. For a useful overview of Jefferson's agrarianism, see Vernon L. Parrington, *The Romantic Revolution in America, 1800–1860* (New York: Harcourt, Brace & World, 1927, 1954), 9–19.

16. Prescott, *Alexander Hamilton,* xvii–xxvi, xxxix.

17. See Alexander Hamilton, *The Continentalist No. I* (July 12, 1781), *The Continentalist No. IV* (August 30, 1781), and "Letter to James Duane" (September 3, 1780), in *The Papers of Alexander Hamilton,* Harold C. Syrett, ed. (New York: Columbia University Press, 1961), vol. 2, 649–652, 669–674, 400–418.

18. See, e.g., Alexander Hamilton, "Letter to John Jay" (April 26, 1775), in Syrett, ed., *Papers,* vol. 2, 176–178.

19. See Hamilton's remarks in the Constitutional Convention, as recorded in James Madison, *Notes of Debates in the Federal Convention of 1787,* Adrienne Koch, ed. (New York: W. W. Norton, 1987), 129–139.

20. Alexander Hamilton, "Report Relative to a Provision for the Support of Public Credit" (January 9, 1790), in Syrett, ed., *Papers,* vol. 6, 51 et seq. (1962). See also the letters and papers on the national bank that are collected in *The Works of Alexander Hamilton,* Henry Cabot Lodge, ed. (New York: Knickerbocker Press, 1904), vol. 3, 319 et seq.

21. Alexander Hamilton, "Report on the Subject of Manufactures" (December 5, 1791), in Syrett, ed., *Papers,* vol. 10, 230 et seq. (1966).

22. Ibid., 232.

23. Prescott, *Alexander Hamilton,* xxxii–xxxiii.

24. Alexander Hamilton, *The Federalist,* No. 17 (1787).

25. See, e.g., his qualified embrace of agriculture in Alexander Hamilton, "Report on the Subject of Manufactures," in Syrett, ed., *Papers,* 231, 235.

26. Civil Code of the State of Louisiana (1825), sec. VII, art. 305–311; Revised Civil Code of the State of Louisiana (1870), sec. 7, art. 281–291. See also E. D. Saunders, *Saunders' Lectures on the Civil Code of Louisiana* (New Orleans: E. S. Upton Printing, 1925), 59–60; Theo W. Bauer, "Private Sales of Minors' Property in Louisiana," 12 *Loyola Law Journal [New Orleans]* 20 (1931); Leon Sarpy and Adrian G. Duplantier, "Minor's Investment in Louisiana—A Legal Anachronism," 33 *Tulane Law Review* 803, 804 (1958–1959);

Nathan Greenberg, "The Family Meeting and Its Successor in Louisiana," 25 *Tulane Law Review* 237 (1950–1951); W. O. Hart, "Rights of Women in Louisiana," 1 *Loyola Law Journal [New Orleans]* 14 (1920); W. R. Irby, "The Basic Elements of Tutorship in Louisiana," 44 *Tulane Law Review* 452 (1970).

27. Carl N. Degler, *At Odds: Women and the Family in America from the Revolution to the Present* (Oxford: Oxford University Press, 1980), 8.

28. Ibid., 8–15, 168.

29. See Alexis de Tocqueville, *Democracy in America*, vol. 2, part 3, ch. 12. See also chs. 10–11.

30. Degler, *At Odds*, 8, 28.

31. Ibid., 9, 66, 144.

32. See William Blackstone, *Commentaries on the Laws of England*, 4 vols., 1765–1769 (Chicago: University of Chicago Press, 1979), 1: 434–441, 453. One more ancient notion was sacrificed. Upon dissolution of a marriage, the father was traditionally presumed to be the fit custodian of his children. In the early-to-mid-nineteenth century, however, this presumption began gradually to give way to a countervailing presumption—that the mother by nature was the fitter parent, at least with respect to children of tender years. See *Helms v. Franciscus*, 2 Bland Ch. 544 (Md. 1830).

33. Barbara Welter, "The Cult of True Womanhood: 1820–1860," 18 *American Quarterly* 151 (1966). For a discussion that extends the notion of women's domestic and civilizing mission westward, see Dee Brown, *The Gentle Tamers: Women of the Old Wild West* (Lincoln: University of Nebraska Press, 1958), 207.

34. Welter, "Cult of True Womanhood," 151–152.

35. Margaret Fuller Ossoli, *Woman in the Nineteenth Century, and Kindred Papers Relating to the Sphere, Condition and Duties, of Woman* (Boston: John P. Jewett, 1855), 5–9.

36. Ibid., 169–176.

37. Ibid., 14.

38. See generally, for example, George M. Stephenson, *The Political History of the Public Lands: From 1840 to 1862* (New York: Russell & Russell, 1917, 1967); Paul W. Gates, *Landlords and Tenants on the Prairie Frontier* (Ithaca: Cornell University Press, 1973); Parrington, *Romantic Revolution*, 28.

39. See, e.g., John A. Garraty, *The American Nation: A History of the United States*, 2nd edition (New York: Harper & Row, 1971), 111–114.

40. Resolution of Continental Congress on Public Lands (October 10, 1780), *Journals of the Continental Congress*, G. Hunt, ed., vol. 18 (Washington, DC: U.S. Government Printing Office, 1910), 915.

41. Virginia's Cession of Western Lands to the United States (December 20, 1783), in *Federal and State Constitutions, Colonial Charters, and Other Organic Laws*, Francis Newton Thorpe, ed., vol. 2 (Washington, DC: Government Printing Office, 1909), 955–956.

42. Garraty, *The American Nation*, 177–179, 202–204.

43. Report of Government for the Western Territory (April 23, 1784), in *Journals of the Continental Congress*, J. C. Fitzpatrick, ed., vol. 26, 275 et seq.

44. Land Ordinance of 1785 (May 20, 1785), in *Journals of the Continental Congress*, J. C. Fitzpatrick, ed., vol. 28, 375 et seq.

45. Gates, *Landlords and Tenants*, 141.

46. Act of the Congress of the Confederation for the Government of the Territory of the United States, North-West of the River Ohio (July 13, 1787), in *Federal and State Constitutions,* F. N. Thorpe, ed., vol. 2, 957 et seq. The Ordinance was reenacted after the Constitution was ratified. Ordinance for the Government of the Territory North-West of the River Ohio (August 7, 1789), 1 *Stat.* 50–53.

47. See Eric Foner and John A. Garraty, eds., *The Reader's Companion to American History* (Boston: Houghton Mifflin, 1991), 877.

48. This policy ended with the Pre-Emption Act of 1841. See Hildegard Binder Johnson, *Order upon the Land: The U.S. Rectangular Land Survey and the Upper Mississippi* (New York: Oxford University Press, 1976), 64.

49. Daniel Feller, *The Public Lands in Jacksonian Politics* (Madison: University of Wisconsin Press, 1984), 126.

50. Land Act of 1800 (May 10, 1800), 2 *U.S. Statutes at Large* 73 et seq.

51. Land Act of 1820 (April 24, 1820), 3 *U.S. Statutes at Large* 566–567 et seq.

52. Feller, *Public Lands,* 35.

53. On the Jeffersonian origins of the policy of cheap land, see Gates, *Landlords and Tenants,* 140.

54. Frederick Jackson Turner, *The Frontier in American History* (New York: Dover Publications, 1953, 1996), 20.

55. Stephenson, *Political History,* 25.

56. Ibid., 40–42.

57. Ibid., 43.

58. Ibid., 45–62. Tyler had been elected vice president in 1840. He became president when William Henry Harrison ("Old Tippecanoe") died one month after taking office.

59. Pre-Emption Act of 1841 (September 4, 1841), 5 *U.S. Statutes at Large* 453 et seq.

60. Feller, *Public Lands,* 29–30.

61. Ibid., 29–31, 196.

62. Ibid., 81.

63. See Gates, *Landlords and Tenants,* 6–22.

64. Feller acknowledges this, *Public Lands,* 31.

65. See *Fletcher v. Peck,* 10 U.S. (6 Cranch) 87 (1810). For a narrative recounting of *Fletcher,* see C. Peter McGrath, *Yazoo: Law and Politics in the New Republic* (Providence: Brown University Press, 1966).

66. Circular from the Treasury That Gold and Silver Only Be Received in Payment for the Public Lands (July 11, 1836), in *American State Papers, Public Lands,* vol. 8, (Washington, DC: Gales & Seaton, 1861), 910. See also Andrew Jackson, Eighth Annual Message to Congress (December 5, 1836), in *Messages and Papers,* James D. Richardson, ed., vol. 4 (Washington, DC: Bureau of National Literature, 1897), 1455.

67. See Gates, *Landlords and Tenants,* 14–15.

68. This theme is an important element of the accounts of Frederick Jackson Turner and his intellectual heirs. See Turner, *The Frontier in American History;* Stephenson, *Political History;* Raynor G. Wellington, *The Political and Sectional Influence of the Public Lands, 1828–1842* (Cambridge, MA: Riverside Press, 1914).

69. See Wellington, *Political and Sectional Influence,* 12–48.

70. For accounts of the roles of regional division and national policy toward public lands in the election of 1840 and the Pre-Emption Act, see Stephenson, *Political History,* 19–37; Wellington, *Political and Sectional Influence,* 75–113.

71. For a discussion of some of the ways in which conflicts over slavery were implicated in policies of territorial expansion, see Mark E. Brandon, *Free in the World: American Slavery and Constitutional Failure* (Princeton, NJ: Princeton University Press, 1998), 66–74.

72. Treaty of Guadalupe Hidalgo (signed February 2, 1848; ratified May 30, 1848), in William M. Malloy, ed., *Treaties, Conventions, International Acts, Protocols, and Agreements between the United States of America and Other Powers,* vol. 1, (Washington, DC: Government Printing Office, 1910), 1107 et seq.

73. For a brief discussion, see Brandon, *Free in the World,* 80–81.

74. See Stephenson, *Political History,* 122–124.

75. Ibid., 118–122.

76. Ibid., 186–188.

77. Ibid., 126–130.

78. For a full account of the homestead bills in 1860, see ibid., 190–220.

79. Compare Democratic Platform of 1860 (June 18, 1860) with Democratic (Breckenridge Faction) Platform of 1860 (June 1860), in Kirk Harold Porter and Donald Bruce Johnson, eds., *National Party Platforms, 1840–1968* (Urbana: University of Illinois Press, 1970), 30–31.

80. Republican Platform (May 16, 1860), in Porter and Johnson, eds., *National Party Platforms,* 31–33.

81. Act to Secure Homesteads to Actual Settlers on the Public Domain (May 20, 1862), 12 *U.S. Statutes at Large* 392 et seq.

82. Act to Aid in the Construction of a Railroad and Telegraph Line (July 1, 1862), 12 *U.S. Statutes at Large* 489 et seq.

83. George Washington Julian, *Political Recollections, 1840–1872* (Chicago: Jansen, McClurg, 1884), 216–218.

84. Johnson, *Order upon the Land,* 66 (citing H. N. Smith, *Virgin Land: The American West as Symbol and Myth* [Cambridge, MA: Harvard University Press, 1950], 90, and J. F. Hart, "The Middle West," *Annals of the Association of American Geographers* 62 [1972], 258).

85. See Lewis Atherton, *The Cattle Kings* (Bloomington: Indiana University Press, 1961); David Montejano, *Anglos and Mexicans in the Making of Texas, 1836–1986* (Austin: University of Texas Press, 1987).

86. See, for example, the Timber Culture Act of 1873, the Desert Land Act of 1877, and the Timber and Stone Act of 1878.

87. Specie Payments Act (January 14, 1875), 28 *U.S. Statutes at Large* 296.

88. See Johnson, *Order upon the Land,* 64.

89. Ibid., 38.

90. Feller, *Public Lands,* 198.

91. Lawrence M. Friedman, *A History of American Law* (New York: Simon & Schuster, 1973, 1985), 363–364. The notion that settlers carried law with them originated with John Phillip Reid, *Law for the Elephant: Property and Social Behavior on the Overland Trail* (San Marino, CA: Huntington Library, 1980), 362.

92. Friedman, *History of American Law,* 364. This claim is problematic on three fronts: Its assumption that the land was "empty" overlooks the presence of Indians and others who inhabited much of the territory; the claim that migrants were "Americans" overlooks the sometimes complex allegiances and identities that many settlers brought

with them; and the claim that they carried the common law may assume too much about the precise content of the norms they adhered to.

93. U.S. Const., art. IV, sec. 3. Congress exercised such authority, even before the Constitution's adoption, through the Northwest Ordinance.

94. Friedman, *History of American Law,* 163–165, 365.

95. In this section, I'm interested primarily in agrarian settlement in what we now think of as the greater Midwest. Hence, I do not attend to urban settlement, mining communities, the "fur frontier," or the explorers' frontier.

96. John Mack Faragher, *Women and Men on the Overland Trail* (New Haven, CT: Yale University Press, 1979), 16.

97. Julie Roy Jeffrey, *Frontier Women: "Civilizing" the West? 1840–1880* (New York: Hill and Wang, 1979, 1998), 40–47.

98. Degler, *At Odds,* 47.

99. Jeffrey, *Frontier Women,* 40–42.

100. Glenda Riley, *Female Frontier: The Comparative View of Women on the Prairie and the Plains* (Lawrence: University Press of Kansas, 1988), 18 (quoting from John B. Newhall, *Glimpse of Iowa in 1846* [Iowa City: State Historical Society, 1957]).

101. Jeffrey, *Frontier Women,* 39; Glenda Riley, *The Origins of the Feminist Movement in America* (St. Louis: Forum Press, 1973).

102. Ibid., 51–52.

103. Ibid., 54, 56; Glenda Riley, *Women on the American Frontier* (St. Louis: Forum Press, 1977), part iii.

104. Jeffrey, *Frontier Women,* 57. There were other changes *en route,* with respect to both the mundane and the sublime. For example, most women eventually modified or abandoned eastern standards of feminine dress; some took to wearing bloomers. Ibid., 50–51, 55–56. And many families were forced to sacrifice ritual and leisure on the Sabbath, which Jeffrey argues "had become by mid-century a symbol of women's religious and moral authority." Ibid., 54–55.

105. Ibid., 78; Sandra L. Myres, *Westering Women and the Frontier Experience, 1800–1915* (Albuquerque: University of New Mexico Press, 1982), 171.

106. Elizabeth Jameson, "Women as Workers, Women as Civilizers: True Womanhood in the American West," in *The Women's West,* Susan Armitage and Elizabeth Jameson, eds. (Norman: University of Oklahoma Press, 1987). John Mack Faragher argues that, with few exceptions, labor on the frontier was strictly segregated by sex. "Midwestern society," he says, "had a developed sense of gender distinction. The existence of a strict division of labor and separate cultural character models for men and women suggests that significant portions of men's and women's time were spent in the company of their own sex." Faragher, *Women and Men,* 110. While there is no denying the sexual segregation of much labor on the frontier, Faragher overstates its strictness. Moreover, as I try to show below, he claims too much (or too little) when he asserts that "women played no part in public life." Ibid.

107. Riley, *Female Frontier,* 53.

108. Jeffrey, *Frontier Women,* 78.

109. Ibid., 78–80.

110. Deborah Fink, *Agrarian Women: Wives and Mothers in Rural Nebraska, 1880–1940* (Chapel Hill: University of North Carolina Press, 1992), 60; Mary Ellen Jones, *Daily Life on the Nineteenth-Century American Frontier* (Westport, CT: Greenwood Press, 1998), 193.

111. Compare Jeffrey, *Frontier Women,* 81–84, 90–93, with Riley, *Female Frontier,* 53.

112. See Katherine Harris, "Homesteading in Northeastern Colorado, 1873–1920: Sex Roles and Women's Experience," in Armitage and Jameson, eds., *Women's West,* 165–167. Harris recites three classic "pre-industrial" familial forms: evangelical (rigidly hierarchical and male-dominated), genteel (hierarchical, but with a functional role for women), and moderate (less hierarchical, with greater sharing of roles). She claims that familial variation was even more complex in nineteenth-century America, but suggests that eastern families (at least of certain classes) tended toward the model of gentility, while families on the frontier tended toward the moderate model. Ibid., 175–176. Harris may exaggerate the level of sexual equality in homesteading families, but the tendencies she observes seem accurate. See also Joann Vanek, "Work, Leisure, and Family Roles in Farm Households in the United States, 1920–1955," *Journal of Family History* 5 (1980): 422.

113. Myres, *Westering Women,* 182–185; Jeffrey, *Frontier Women,* 87–90.

114. There were both commonalities and differences between western agrarianism and the variety of agrarian republicanism that had traditionally resided in the South. One common element was a distrust of capital. In southern agrarianism, this distrust was connected to Locke's notion of property: a property in one's person was primary; abstract or artificial forms of property were secondary. See Anne Norton, *Alternative Americas: A Reading of Antebellum Political Culture* (Chicago: University of Chicago Press, 1986), 124–127. Slaves, of course, were notable exceptions to the principle of property in one's person.

115. Fink, *Agrarian Women,* 60–61 (extrapolating from an earlier study of agrarian households, by Sarah Elbert, "The Farmer Takes a Wife: Women in America's Farming Families," in *Women, Households, and the Economy,* Lourdes Beneria and Catharine R. Stimpson, eds. [(New Brunswick, NJ: Rutgers University Press, 1987), 173, 191–195]).

116. Harris, *Women's West,* 167.

117. Jeffrey, *Frontier Women,* 107–108.

118. Myres, *Westering Women,* 182–185.

119. Jeffrey, *Frontier Women,* 98.

120. Jones, *Daily Life,* 204.

121. Jeffrey, *Frontier Women,* 98, 107–123.

122. Jameson, "Women as Workers," *Women's West,* 157.

123. Jones, *Daily Life,* 209.

124. Jameson, "Women as Workers," *Women's West,* 157.

125. Michael Lewis Goldberg, *An Army of Women: Gender and Politics in Gilded-Age Kansas* (Baltimore: Johns-Hopkins University Press, 1997), 130.

126. Ibid., 131–132 (citing the *Kansas Farmer,* 4 September 1889).

127. Ibid., 142, 160–163.

128. Ibid., 168.

129. Ibid., 165.

130. This proposition had been thrown into question by the Kansas-Nebraska Act of 1854 and by *Dred Scott v. Sandford.* The former enacted Stephen A. Douglas's theory that the people of each territory were sovereign and should be permitted to legislate (with respect to slavery, for example) free from Congressional interference. The logic of *Dred Scott,* in contrast, implied that neither Congress nor the territories could interfere with a slaveholder's right to take his property wherever he pleased. Union victory in the Civil War implicitly but effectively overturned both notions.

131. Populist Party Platform (July 4, 1892), in *Documents of American History,* vol. 1,

Henry Steele Commager and Milton Cantor, eds. (Englewood Cliffs, NJ: Prentice-Hall, 1988), 593–594.

132. Ibid., 594–595.

133. Certain tenets of the movement were later revived in two forms. Socialist parties and organizations, which were a presence in parts of the Midwest in the first forty years of the twentieth century, picked up part of the Populist mantle. And New-Deal liberalism pursued and enacted some policies that the Populists had originally embraced.

134. Jeffrey, *Frontier Women*, 227, 234–236.

135. Women acquired suffrage first in Wyoming (1869), then in Utah (1870). By 1914, women had acquired the right to vote in ten of eleven western states, but in only one state in the East. See Myres, *Westering Women*, 213–237.

136. Jameson, "Women as Workers," *Women's West*, 157. She points out, for example, that the Populists in the 1890s successfully promoted suffrage in Colorado and Idaho but failed in California and Kansas where "the countryside voted for suffrage, but urban voters defeated it." Ibid.

137. Myres, *Westering Women*, 220–221.

138. Ibid., 221–223.

139. Susan Lee Johnson, *Roaring Camp: The Social World of the California Gold Rush* (New York: W. W. Norton, 2000), 172–174.

140. Johnson, *Roaring Camp*, 127, 174; Walter L. Williams, *The Spirit and the Flesh: Sexual Diversity in American Indian Culture* (Boston: Beacon Press, 1986), 159; Peter Boag, *Same-Sex Affairs: Constructing and Controlling Homosexuality in the Pacific Northwest* (Berkeley: University of California Press, 2003), 22, 30–33, 41, 44.

141. Dee Garceau, "Nomads, Bunkies, Cross-Dressers, and Family Men: Cowboy Identity and the Gendering of Ranch Work," in *Across the Great Divide: Cultures of Manhood in the American West*, Matthew Basso et al., eds. (New York: Routledge, 2001), 154.

142. Williams, *The Spirit*, 157–159. See also Michael Bronski, *A Queer History of the United States* (Boston: Beacon Press, 2011), 44–45.

143. Garceau, in Basso et al., eds., *Across the Great Divide*, 154–157, 160–162.

144. Ibid., 159–160.

145. Peter Boag, *Re-Dressing American's Frontier Past* (Berkeley: University of California Press, 2011), 17–58.

146. Ibid., 33–38, 100; Evelyn A. Schlatter, "Drag's a Life: Women, Gender, and Cross-Dressing in the Nineteenth Century West," in *Writing the Range: Race, Class, and Culture in the Women's West*, Elizabeth Jameson and Susan Armitage, eds. (Norman: University of Oklahoma Press, 1997), 335–336, 342–344; San Francisco Lesbian and Gay History Project, "'She Even Chewed Tobacco': A Pictorial Narrative of Passing Women in America," in *Hidden from History: Reclaiming the Gay and Lesbian Past*, Martin Bauml Duberman, Martha Vicinus, and George Chauncey, Jr., eds. (New York: New American Library, 1989), 185–186, 190.

147. Boag, *Redressing America's Frontier*, 26, 48–50. In the parlance of the day, to "make love" was merely to carry on a romance, including holding hands and petting and such.

148. Ibid., 25–26, 32–33, 43–48, 53–58, 109; Schlatter, "Drag's a Life," Jameson and Armitage, eds., *Writing the Range*, 334–345.

149. Boag, *Redressing America's Frontier*, 74, 83, 89–91, 130–158.

150. Turner, *Frontier American History*, 35.

CHAPTER SIX: TRIBAL FAMILIES AND THE AMERICAN NATION

1. See Stephen Macedo, *Diversity and Distrust: Civic Education in a Multicultural Democracy* (Cambridge, MA: Harvard University Press, 2000), 45–94.

2. Macedo, *Diversity and Distrust,* 74–103.

3. *Pierce v. Society of Sisters,* 208 U.S. 510 (1925).

4. For a description and vigorous defense of the project of making citizens in the image of the regime, see Amy Gutmann, *Democratic Education* (Princeton, NJ: Princeton University Press, 1987). See also Macedo, *Diversity and Distrust.* For a thoughtful and moderated account of this project, see Linda C. McClain, "The Domain of Civic Virtue in a Good Society: Families, Schools, and Sex Equality," 69 *Fordham Law Review* 1617 (2001).

5. Howard Munford Jones, *O Strange New World—American Culture: The Formative Years* (New York: Viking Press, 1964), 1–34.

6. John Locke, *Second Treatise of Government* [1690], C. B. Macpherson, ed. (Indianapolis: Hackett, 1980), § 49.

7. See Jones, *O Strange New World,* 40–70.

8. Ronald Howard, "Native Americans (1600–1754)," in *American Eras,* 8 vols. (Farmington Hills, MI: Gale Group, 1997–1998), http://galenet.galegroup.com/servlet/HistRC/; Jones, *O Strange New World,* 15–19, 50–56.

9. Howard, "Native Americans."

10. Theodore Fischbacher, *A Study of the Role of the Federal Government in the Education of the American Indian* (Ph.D. dissertation, Arizona State University, 1967), 66.

11. Howard, "Native Americans;" Fischbacher, *Role of the Federal Government,* 64–66.

12. See Constitution of the United States, art. I, sec. 8 (delegating to Congress the power to regulate commerce with the Indian tribes); Fischbacher, *Role of the Federal Government,* 99.

13. Fischbacher, *Role of the Federal Government,* 69–73.

14. Ibid., 43–45.

15. See Constitution, art. I, sec. 2 (excluding from representation "Indians not taxed"); Fourteenth Amendment (also excluding from representation "Indians not taxed").

16. *Elk v. Wilkins,* 112 U.S. 94 (1884).

17. H.R. 6355, 43 Stat. 253, 68th Congr., 1st sess. (June 2, 1924).

18. See Testimony of Robert Odawi Porter, President of the Seneca Nation of Indians, before the Committee on Indian Affairs, U.S. Senate (February 9, 2011), http://www.indian.senate.gov/hearings/upload/RobertPortertestimony020912.pdf.

19. Fischbacher, *Role of the Federal Government,* 102–103.

20. 3 Stat. 516 (March 3, 1819).

21. James Monroe, Second Annual Message to Congress (November 17, 1818), in *A Compilation of the Messages and Papers of the Presidents,* James D. Richardson, ed., vol. 2 (New York: Bureau of National Literature, 1897), 608, 615.

22. Fischbacher, *Role of the Federal Government,* 111–114.

23. Indian Removal Act, 4 Stat. 411–412 (May 28, 1830).

24. Lucille Griffith, *Alabama: A Documentary History to 1900,* rev. ed. (University: University of Alabama Press, 1972), 118.

25. Andrew Jackson, Seventh Annual Message to Congress (December 7, 1835), in

Richardson, ed., *A Compilation of Messages and Papers of the Presidents*, vol. 3, 1366, 1390–1392; Fischbacher, *Role of the Federal Government*, 119–120.

26. Fischbacher, *Role of the Federal Government*, 121, 137.

27. Ibid., 128.

28. Congress formally recognized in 1871 the demise of treaties as instruments for dealing with the tribes. 16 Stat. 544 (March 3, 1871).

29. Ulysses S. Grant, First Inaugural Address (March 4, 1869), in *Inaugural Addresses of the Presidents of the United States* (Washington, DC: U.S. Government Printing Office, 1989), 145–148.

30. Fischbacher, *Role of the Federal Government*, 153–158; 17 Stat. 461 (February 14, 1873).

31. 24 Stat. 388–391 (February 8, 1887); 25 Stat. 890 (March 2, 1889).

32. Fischbacher, *Role of the Federal Government*, 235–238.

33. Report of the Commissioner of Indian Affairs Hiram Price (October 24, 1881), in Wilcomb E. Washburn, ed., *The American Indian and the United States, a Documentary History*, vol. 1 (New York: Random House, 1973), 299–300.

34. Ibid., 311.

35. Fischbacher, *Role of the Federal Government*, 241.

36. Merrill Edwards Gates, "Land and Law as Agents in Educating Indians" (Address to the American Social Science Association, Saratoga, NY, September 11, 1885), 16–17 (emphasis in original).

37. Ibid., 17 (quoting Henry Sumner Maine, *Lectures on the Early History of Institutions* [London: John Murray, Ltd., 1875]).

38. Ibid., 17–19.

39. Ibid., 21 (emphasis in original).

40. Martha Elizabeth Layman, *A History of Indian Education in the United States* (Ph.D. dissertation, University of Minnesota, 1942), 439.

41. Fischbacher, *Role of the Federal Government*, 12, 250.

42. Ibid., 276–281.

43. Ibid., 199–203.

44. G. Stanley Hall, *Adolescence: Its Psychology and Its Relations to Physiology, Anthropology, Sociology, Sex, Crime, Religion, and Education*, vol. 2 (New York: D. Appleton, 1916), at 696. Although the Commissioner of Indian Affairs was eventually delegated authority to force Indian children to attend schools on the reservation, he did not possess authority to force them to attend off-reservation schools. Charles Martin Scanlon, *The Law of Church and Grave: The Clergyman's Handbook of Law* (New York: Benziger Brothers, 1909), 200–201.

45. David Wallace Adams, *Education for Extinction: American Indians and the Boarding School Experience, 1875–1928* (Lawrence: University Press of Kansas, 1995), 31, 53.

46. Fischbacher, *Role of the Federal Government*, 203–208.

47. Quoted in Clyde Ellis, *To Change Them Forever: Indian Education at the Rainy Mountain Boarding School, 1893–1920* (Norman: Univ. of Oklahoma Press, 1996), 11.

48. For a quasi-autobiographical account of the school, see Richard Henry Pratt, *Battlefield and Classroom: Four Decades with the American Indian, 1867–1904*, Robert M. Utley, ed. (New Haven, CT: Yale University Press, 1964).

49. Adams, *Education for Extinction*, 51–55.

50. Quoted in Gates, "Land and Law," 14–15 (emphases in original).

51. Adams, *Education for Extinction*, 51–55.

52. Ibid., 117–124. In some off-reservation schools, marching drills were a daily, lengthy, and punitive ritual.

53. Ibid., 142–156.

54. Ibid., 52–54.

55. Ibid., 156–163.

56. Ibid., 57.

57. Fischbacher, *Role of the Federal Government*, 128–129.

58. See, e.g., the report of C. C. Painter, *The Condition of Affairs in Indian Territory and California* (Philadelphia: Office of the Indian Rights Association, 1888).

59. Adams, *Education for Extinction*, 162–163. Pratt had insisted that outing could not work on the frontier, where the amenities, institutions, and ethos of civilization were scarce.

60. There is reason to believe, however, that Carlisle was more successful in this regard than were most of the other schools. Ibid., 288–289, 298.

61. Ibid., 55.

62. Ibid., 273–306; Pratt, *Battlefield and Classroom*, xvi.

63. All of these changes became official policy by the 1930s.

64. Friedrich Engels, *The Origin of the Family, Private Property, and the State, in the Light of the Researches of Lewis H. Morgan* (New York: International Publishers, 1972), 128–129.

CHAPTER SEVEN: UNCOMMON FAMILIES, PART 1

1. Yaacov Oved, *Two Hundred Years of American Communes* (New Brunswick, NJ: Transaction Books, 1988), 20.

2. Revelation 12:1–6 (KJV).

3. Oved, *Two Hundred Years*, 21–22; Corliss Fitz Randolph, "The German Seventh Day Baptists," in *Seventh Day Baptists in Europe and America*, vol. 2, Albert N. Rogers, ed. (Plainfield, NJ: American Sabbath Tract Society, 1910), 946–954.

4. Fitz Randolph, "German Seventh Day Baptists," 968–978.

5. Ibid., 979–989; Oved, *Two Hundred Years*, 23–24.

6. Fitz Randolph, "German Seventh Day Baptists," 983–991. Oved spells the name "Eckerling." Oved, *Two Hundred Years*, 28 et seq.

7. Fitz Randolph, "German Seventh Day Baptists," 992–1003.

8. Ibid., 1002–1006, 1016–1018, 1076–1083; Oved, *Two Hundred Years*, 24–27.

9. Fitz Randolph, "German Seventh Day Baptists," 1006–1007.

10. Ibid., 1036–1038.

11. Ibid., 1047–1050, 1052–1053, 1099–1102; Oved, *Two Hundred Years*, 28–29.

12. Fitz Randolph, "German Seventh Day Baptists," 1040, 1051–1054, 1102–1105; Oved, *Two Hundred Years*, 28.

13. Oved, *Two Hundred Years*, 30–33.

14. Ibid., 39–40.

15. Edward Deming Andrews and Faith Andrews, *Work and Worship among the Shakers: Their Craftsmanship and Economic Order* (New York: Dover Publications,

1982), 12–13; Priscilla J. Brewer, "The Shakers of Mother Ann Lee," in *America's Communal Utopias*, Donald E. Pitzer, ed. (Chapel Hill: University of North Carolina Press, 1997), 39–40.

16. Andrews and Andrews, *Work and Worship*, 13; Brewer, "The Shakers," 40.

17. Andrews and Andrews, *Work and Worship*, 14; Oved, *Two Hundred Years*, 41.

18. Andrews and Andrews, *Work and Worship*, 17–18; Brewer, "The Shakers," 41; Oved, *Two Hundred Years*, 41–42.

19. Andrews and Andrews, *Work and Worship*, 18–20; Oved, *Two Hundred Years*, 41.

20. Andrews and Andrews, *Work and Worship*, 20; Oved, *Two Hundred Years*, 41–43; Brewer, "The Shakers," 40–41.

21. Brewer, "The Shakers," 42; Oved, *Two Hundred Years*, 43–44.

22. Benjamin Seth Youngs, *The Testimony of Christ's Second Appearing*, 2nd ed. (Albany: E. and E. Hosford, 1810), 7–8.

23. Ibid., xxv–xxvi.

24. Quoted in Marianne Finch, *An Englishwoman's Experience in America* (London: Richard Bentley, 1853), 126–128. According to Shaker doctrine, father and mother in the New Covenant were Christ and Ann Lee, "the two first visible parents in the work of redemption," and "the two first foundation pillars of the Church of Christ." Youngs, *The Testimony*, 440.

25. Joseph Meacham, *A Concise Statement of the Principles of the Only True Church* (Benningtion: Haswell & Russell, 1790), 8, 9, 14–16.

26. *A Brief Exposition of the Established Principles and Regulations of the United Society of Believers, Called Shakers*, Improved Ed. (Hartford: Elihu Geer, 1850), 20–21 (quoting from Matthew 10:34–38).

27. Meacham, *Concise Statement*, 12.

28. *Brief Exposition*, 21.

29. *A Summary View of the Millennial Church, or United Society of Believers, Commonly Called Shakers*, 2nd ed. (Albany: C. Van Benthuysen, 1848), reproduced in edited form at http://www.passtheword.org/SHAKER-MANUSCRIPTS/Millennial-Church/millndex.htm.

30. Finch, *Englishwoman's Experience*, 128.

31. John Dunlavy, *The Manifesto, or A Declaration of the Doctrine and Practice of the Church of Christ* (New York: Edward O. Jenkins, 1847), 297–299.

32. The quoted phrases come from *A Summary View of the Millennial Church*, 2nd ed.

33. Andrews and Andrews, *Work and Worship*, 24–27, 29; Finch, *Englishwoman's Experience*, 147–148.

34. See the First Article of the Covenant for the Church at New Lebanon (1795), in Andrews and Andrews, *Work and Worship*, 21–22.

35. Dunlavy, *The Manifesto*, 299.

36. Andrews and Andrews, *Work and Worship*, 22.

37. Finch, *Englishwoman's Experience*, 122, 124–125.

38. Ibid., 125.

39. Andrews and Andrews, *Work and Worship*, 22–23.

40. Ibid., 30, 170–173.

41. Ibid., 30–31.

42. *Brief Exposition*, 10–11, 6.

43. Andrews and Andrews, *Work and Worship*, 166–169.

44. Mary Dyer, *A Brief Statement of the Sufferings of Mary Dyer, Occasioned by the Society Called Shakers* (Boston: William S. Spear, 1816), 3–15.

45. *Dyer v. Dyer*, 5 N.H. 271 (1830), 272–273; Elizabeth A. DeWolfe, *Shaking the Faith: Women, Family, and Mary Marshall Dyer's Anti-Shaker Campaign, 1815–1867* (New York: Palgrave Macmillan, 2002), 55–57.

46. DeWolfe, *Shaking the Faith*, 57–83.

47. Dyer, *A Brief Statement*, 10.

48. Calvin Green and Seth Y. Wells, *A Summary View of the Millennial Church, or United Society of Believers (Commonly Called Shakers)* (Albany: Packard & Benthuysen, 1823), 63–65.

49. Ibid., 65, 67.

50. Ibid., 67.

51. Charles Dickens, *American Notes for General Circulation* [1842], New Century Ed. (Boston: Dana Estes, n.d.), 311–315; Dyer, *A Brief Statement*, 8.

52. Ibid., 315–316.

53. Oved, *Two Hundred Years*, 54–55.

54. Friedrich Engels, "Description of Recently Founded Communist Colonies Still in Existence" (first published in *Deutsches Bürgerbuch für 1845*), Marx/Engels Collected Works, vol. 4, at http://www.marxists.org/archive/marx/works/cw/index.htm.

55. Henry B. Brown, "The Distribution of Property," 27 *American Law Review* 656 (1893), 671. Even if doctrines of socialism were eventually to wane in America, Justice Brown would soon indelibly mark his tenure on the Supreme Court by writing the Opinion of the Court in *Plessy v. Ferguson*, 163 U.S. 537 (1896).

56. DeWolfe, *Shaking the Faith*, 124–125, 151, 180.

57. *Carmichael v. North-western Mutual Benefit Association* (Mich. 1888), cited in 29 *Albany Law Journal* 25 (1894).

58. Oved, *Two Hundred Years*, 59–64, Brewer, "The Shakers," 48–50.

59. Oved, *Two Hundred Years*, 167–168; Robert S. Fogarty, ed., *Special Love / Special Sex: An Oneida Community Diary* (Syracuse, NY: Syracuse University Press, 1994), 4–5; Lawrence Foster, "Free Love and Community: John Humphrey Noyes and the Oneida Perfectionists," in Pitzer, ed., *America's Communal Utopias*, 254–255. On Noyes's depression, shame, and insecurity, see Robert David Thomas, *The Man Who Would Be Perfect: John Humphrey Noyes and the Utopian Impulse* (Philadelphia: University of Pennsylvania Press, 1977), 10–12.

60. Oved, *Two Hundred Years*, 168–169; Fogarty, *Special Love*, 5–6; Thomas, *The Man*, 20–28; Constance Noyes Robertson, *Oneida Community Profiles* (Syracuse: Syracuse University Press, 1977), 20–21.

61. *Battle-Axe and Weapons of War* 1, no. 2 (Philadelphia: August 1837), 1.

62. Robertson, *Oneida Community Profiles*, 21–22.

63. Oved, *Two Hundred Years*, 169–170; Thomas, *The Man*, 93–95. See also Spencer Klaw, *Without Sin: The Life and Death of the Oneida Community* (New York: Penguin Press, 1993), 44–45.

64. Klaw, *Without Sin*, 46–50; Thomas, *The Man*, 95–97; Oved, *Two Hundred Years*, 170.

65. Thomas, *The Man*, 96–97.

66. Ibid., 97–98; Fogarty, *Special Love*, 6–9; Constance Noyes Robertson, ed.,

Oneida Community: An Autobiography, 1851–1876 (Syracuse, NY: Syracuse University Press, 1970), 268.

67. Oved, *Two Hundred Years*, 172.

68. Thomas, *The Man*, 97–104; Fogarty, *Special Love*, 6–8.

69. Robertson, *Oneida Community Profiles*, 25–36.

70. Thomas, *The Man*, 105–109; Klaw, *Without Sin*, 59–61; Robertson, *Oneida Community: An Autobiography*, 268–269.

71. Klaw, *Without Sin*, 65–70.

72. Ibid., 72–81; Oved, *Two Hundred Years*, 174–175, 177.

73. Lawrence Foster, "Free Love in Utopia: How Complex Marriage Was Introduced in the Oneida Community," CESNUR Center for Studies on New Religions, 2002 International Conference on *Minority Religions, Social Change, and Freedom of Conscience*, at http://www.cesnur.org/2002/slc/foster.htm; Oved, *Two Hundred Years*, 175.

74. Foster, "Free Love in Utopia."

75. Klaw, *Without Sin*, 77–88; Robertson, *Oneida Community: An Autobiography*, 294.

76. Robertson, *Oneida Community: An Autobiography*, 311–315.

77. Oved, *Two Hundred Years*, 179–180.

78. *Bible Communism: A Compilation from the Annual Reports and Other Publications of the Oneida Association and Its Branches; Presenting, in Connection with Their History, a Summary View of Their Religious and Social Theories* (Brooklyn, NY: Office of the Circular, 1853), 51–52 (emphases in original).

79. Oved, *Two Hundred Years*, 179; Robertson, *Oneida Community: An Autobiography*, 335.

80. Robertson, *Oneida Community: An Autobiography*, 335, 337–339.

81. Ibid., 340.

82. Pierrepont Noyes, *My Father's House: An Oneida Boyhood* (Gloucester, MA: Peter Smith, 1966), 147–157.

83. Oved, *Two Hundred Years*, 180–181; Noyes, *My Father's House*, 159–160.

84. Noyes, *My Father's House*, 160–161.

85. Oved, *Two Hundred Years*, 183–184; Klaw, *Without Sin*, 243–247.

86. Oved, *Two Hundred Years*, 184–188; Noyes, My Father's House, 162–164, 174–176, 180–181.

CHAPTER EIGHT: UNCOMMON FAMILIES, PART 2

1. For a useful and thorough depiction of what he called "the Cochran delusion," see G. T. Ridlon, Sr., *Saco Valley Settlements and Families, Historical, Biographical, Genealogical, Traditional, and Legendary* (Portland, ME: by the author, 1895), 269–280.

2. Ephraim Stinchfield, *Cochranism Delineated: A Description of & Specific for a Religious Hydrophobia* (1819). A faithful transcription of Stinchfield's original manuscript is accessible at www.MaineMemory.net/media/pdf/13109.pdf (copyright 2004 by www.MaineMemory.net).

3. Ridlon, *Saco Valley*, 272.

4. Ibid., 272–273.

5. Stinchfield, *Cochranism*.

6. According to the *Oxford English Dictionary*, the term "polyamory" originated in the 1990s. Hence it is not one that either Cochran or his followers would have employed. But, in light of Cochranite practice, the term is descriptive. Richard Price disagrees. He claims not only that the Cochranites practiced polygamy (which is debatable), but also that Joseph Smith repudiated the practice (which is dubious). In short, according to Price, Smith was framed by self-interested and libidinous Mormon Restorationists. This claim lacks convincing evidence. See Richard Price, "Joseph Smith: Innocent of Polygamy" (2006), at http://restorationbookstore.org/articles/doctrine/js-notpoligamist.htm.

7. Stinchfield, *Cochranism*.

8. Gamaliel E. Smith, *Report of the Trial of Jacob Cochrane, on Sundry Charges of Adultery, and Lewd and Lascivious Conduct* (Kennebunk, ME: James K. Remich, 1819), 5–16, 21.

9. Smith, *Report of the Trial*, 5–25.

10. At common law, adultery was sex with another man's wife. William Blackstone, *Commentaries on the Laws of England*, 4 vols., 1765–1769 (Chicago: University of Chicago Press, 1979), 3: 139.

11. Smith, *Report of the Trial*, 26–27, 32–33.

12. Ibid., 28–31.

13. Ibid., 33–40.

14. Ridlon, *Saco Valley*, 278.

15. D. M. Graham, *The Life of Clement Phinney* (Dover, NH: William Burr, 1851), 86–90. Graham urged that public humiliation, jail, and an early death were the usual "inglorious" end of Protestant "fanatics." In Catholicism, in contrast, he argued that secrecy often permitted "delusion" to persist. As he put it, "the sacredness of the confessional, or the gloomy walls of a nunnery, have screened . . . crimes from the penalties of law and justice." Ibid., 90.

16. Robert V. Remini, *Joseph Smith* (New York: Penguin, 2002), 1–17, 28–36, 49–50; Richard L. Bushman, *Joseph Smith and the Beginnings of Mormonism* (Urbana: University of Illinois Press, 1984), 31, 37–39, 49–53; Richard Lyman Bushman, *Joseph Smith: Rough Stone Rolling* (New York: Alfred A. Knopf, 2005), 24–27, 36–37.

17. Remini, *Joseph Smith*, 37–40; Bushman, *Rough Stone Rolling*, 37–41; Richard Lyman Bushman, *Mormonism: A Very Short Introduction* (New York: Oxford University Press, 2008), 16–18.

18. Remini, *Joseph Smith*, 43–47; Bushman, *Rough Stone Rolling*, 41–45.

19. Remini, *Joseph Smith*, 50–56; Bushman, *Rough Stone Rolling*, 52–54, 58–63.

20. Remini, *Joseph Smith*, 57–58; Bushman, *Rough Stone Rolling*, 63–66.

21. Remini, *Joseph Smith*, 59–61; Bushman, *Rough Stone Rolling*, 66–74.

22. Remini, *Joseph Smith*, 62–68; Bushman, *Rough Stone Rolling*, 74–79.

23. Remini, *Joseph Smith*, 70.

24. Bushman, *Joseph Smith and the Beginnings of Mormonism*, 115–116; Remini, *Joseph Smith*, 69.

25. Bushman, *Joseph Smith and the Beginnings of Mormonism*, 115–119.

26. Remini, *Joseph Smith*, 79–82, 84–86.

27. Ibid., 84–87, 90–91.

28. By far the best detailed account of the Mormons' exodus from each of their various settlements is Bushman, *Rough Stone Rolling*. On the treks from New York to Kirtland to Missouri to Illinois, see also Remini, *Joseph Smith*, 89–138; Bushman, *Mormonism*, 10–12, 36–38, 42–44.

29. Bushman, *Rough Stone Rolling*, 391–398.

30. Remini, *Joseph Smith*, 144–150, 162–163.

31. Bushman, *Rough Stone Rolling*, 421–423, 452–458; Fawn M. Brodie, *No Man Knows My History: The Life of Joseph Smith, the Mormon Prophet*, 2nd ed. (New York: Alfred A. Knopf, 1971), 173–174.

32. Remini, *Joseph Smith*, 166–175.

33. Bushman, *Rough Stone Rolling*, 116–126; Remini, *Joseph Smith*, 74, 89–94.

34. Bushman, *Rough Stone Rolling*, 328–338; Remini, *Joseph Smith*, 122–126.

35. Bushman, *Rough Stone Rolling*, 327–332, 346–368; Remini, *Joseph Smith*, 132–139.

36. Remini, *Joseph Smith*, 160–178.

37. H. Michael Marquardt, *The Joseph Smith Revelations: Text and Commentary* (Salt Lake City: Signature Books, 1999), 374–375.

38. Ridlon, *Saco Valley*, 281–284. Brigham Young's fourth wife, Augusta Adams Cobb, was a former Cochranite who was married at the time Young took her as his wife. On Mormon usage of "spiritual wife," see Richard S. Van Wagoner, "Mormon Polyandry in Nauvoo," *Dialogue: A Journal of Mormon Thought* 18 (1985): 67, 75 n. 9.

39. Some reports indicate that Fanny was living there as a housekeeper. Ann Eliza Young states that she was Emma's "adopted daughter." Ann Eliza Young, *Wife No. 19* [c. 1875] (New York: Arno Press, 1972), 66. See also Bushman, *Rough Stone Rolling*, 323–327, 347–348; Brodie, *No Man Knows*, 181–183.

40. *Book of Doctrine and Covenants*, Section 111 (Independence, MO: Herald Publishing House, 1970). This volume was published by the Reorganized Church of Jesus Christ of Latter Day Saints, which is not the dominant denomination within the Mormon Church. But there is no reason to doubt the authenticity of the declaration in Section 111. Brodie notes that Cowdery penned the resolution, that Joseph was in Michigan when it was adopted, and therefore that he might not have approved of it. Brodie, *No Man Knows*, 185.

41. Brodie, *No Man Knows*, 457–488; Remini, *Joseph Smith*, 153–154.

42. For an insider's critical account of Young's marriages, see Young, *Wife No. 19*.

43. Brodie, *No Man Knows*, 269, 399, 420–421; Remini, *Joseph Smith*, 151–156.

44. Revelation received at Nauvoo, Illinois, on 12 July 1843, in Marquardt, *The Joseph Smith Revelations*, 323–328.

45. Ibid.

46. Ray B. West, *Kingdom of the Saints: The Story of Brigham Young and the Mormons* (New York: Viking Press, 1957), 144–157, 160–190; Leonard J. Arrington, *Brigham Young: American Moses* (New York: Alfred A. Knopf, 1985), 113–166.

47. Young, *Wife No. 19*, 127.

48. West, *Kingdom of the Saints*, 190.

49. Arrington, *Brigham Young*, 167–191; West, *Kingdom of the Saints*, 191–203, 210–211.

50. West, *Kingdom of the Saints*, 178–180, 225–228.

51. Arrington, *Brigham Young*, 174–176, 223–227; West, *Kingdom of the Saints*, 205; Ernest S. Taves, *This Is the Place: Brigham Young and the New Zion* (Buffalo, NY: Prometheus Books, 1991), 99–110.

52. Brigham Young, "The Persecution of the Saints. Their Loyalty to the Constitution. The Mormon Battalion. The Law of God Relative to the African Race" (March 8, 1863), *Journal of Discourses*, vol. 10 (Liverpool: Daniel H. Wells, 1865), 104, 110, at http://www.journalofdiscourses.org/volume10/.

53. Lester E. Bush, Jr., "Mormonism's Negro Doctrine: An Historical Overview," *Dialogue: A Journal of Mormon Thought* 8 (1973): 71. See generally Lester E. Bush, Jr., and Armand L. Mauss, eds., *Neither White nor Black: Mormon Scholars Confront the Race Issue in a Universal Church* (Midvale, UT: Signature Books, 1984).

54. Arrington, *Brigham Young,* 227–235, 244–246; West, *Kingdom of the Saints,* 227–228.

55. Arrington, *Brigham Young,* 210–212; West, *Kingdom of the Saints,* 228–229.

56. See Everett L. Cooley, ed., *Diary of Brigham Young, 1857* (Salt Lake City: University of Utah Tanner Trust Fund, 1980), 53–54 n. 53; James B. Allen and Glen M. Leonard, *The Story of the Latter-day Saints* (Salt Lake City: Deseret Book, 1976), 298–299; West, *Kingdom of the Saints,* 249–250.

57. Gary Vitale, "Abraham Lincoln and the Mormons: Another Legacy of Limited Freedom," *Journal of the Illinois State Historical Society* 101 (2008): 265–266.

58. West, *Kingdom of the Saints,* 253–263; Allen and Leonard, *The Story,* 299–303.

59. James Buchanan, "First Annual Message to Congress on the State of the Union" (December 8, 1857), http://www.presidency.ucsb.edu/ws/index.php?pid=29498.

60. Leonard J. Arrington, *Great Basin Kingdom: An Economic History of the Latter-day Saints, 1830–1900* (Urbana: University of Illinois Press, 1958), 175–194; Allen and Leonard, *The Story,* 305–310.

61. Allen and Leonard, *The Story,* 310–314.

62. Sarah Barringer Gordon, *The Mormon Question: Polygamy and Constitutional Conflict in Nineteenth-Century America* (Chapel Hill: University of North Carolina Press, 2002), 6–10, 85–89.

63. Jessie L. Embry, *Mormon Polygamous Families: Life in the Principle,* vol. 1 (Salt Lake City: University of Utah Press, 1987), 39–45. One obvious reason for the larger number of children per father was that a polygamous husband of a pregnant wife could immediately turn his attention to a sister wife.

64. Embry, *Mormon Polygamous Families,* 45–47; Arrington, *Brigham Young,* 323.

65. Embry, *Mormon Polygamous Families,* 47–49; Ernest H. Taves, *This Is the Place,* 56, 80.

66. Embry, *Mormon Polygamous Families,* 45–49.

67. Young, *Wife No. 19,* 94–180.

68. 37th Congress, Sess. II, Ch. 126, 501–502 (July 1, 1862).

69. 43rd Congress, Sess. I, Ch. 469, 253–256 (June 23, 1874).

70. Gordon, *The Mormon Question,* 112–113.

71. Allen and Leonard, *The Story,* 358; Gordon, *The Mormon Question,* 114.

72. Gordon, *The Mormon Question,* 114–116.

73. 10 Cox Crim. Cases 531 (1868). See also Donald L. Drakeman, *Church, State, and Original Intent* (New York: Cambridge University Press, 2010), 30.

74. 98 U.S. 145 (1878).

75. 47th Congress, Sess. I, Ch. 47, 30–32 (March 22, 1882).

76. *Murphy v. Ramsey,* 114 U.S. 15 (1885).

77. Ibid., 44.

78. Ibid., 43.

79. Ibid., 45.

80. Ibid.

81. 49th Congress, Sess. II, Ch. 397, 635–641 (March 3, 1887).

82. Section 501, Revised Statutes of Idaho, quoted in *Davis v. Beason*, 133 U.S. 333 (1890).

83. Gordon, *The Mormon Question*, 226–228.

84. *Davis v. Beason*, 133 U.S. 333 (1890).

85. 136 U.S. 1 (1890).

86. Arrington, *Great Basin Kingdom*, 365–378; Allen and Leonard, *The Story*, 413–415.

87. Joint Resolution 11, 28 Stat. 980, 53rd Cong., 1st session (October 25, 1893).

88. Act of July 16, 1894, ch. 138, 28 Stat. 107.

89. Allen and Leonard, *The Story*, 417–418.

CHAPTER NINE: MODERN TIMES

1. See, e.g., *Fletcher v. Peck*, 10 U.S. 87 (1810), in which Chief Justice Marshall applied the common-law doctrine protecting bona fide purchasers for value who had no notice of a defect in title. On the constitutional status of the common law, see John C. P. Goldberg, "Rights and Wrongs," 97 *Michigan Law Review* 1828, 1846 (1999).

2. See *Gardner v. Collins*, 27 U.S. 58, 93 (1829); *Bosley v. Wyatt*, 390, 397–398 (1852); *McDonogh's Executors v. Murdoch*, 56 U.S. 367, 408 (1853); *Croxall v. Shererd*, 72 U.S. 268, 284–286 (1866); *Bates v. Brown*, 72 U.S. 710, 714–716 (1866). In two cases — one involving a right to livelihood, the other involving the protection of families against creditors — justices cited English common law approvingly. See *Slaughter-House Cases*, 83 U.S. 36, 103–106 (1872) (Field, J., dissenting); *Central Nat'l Bank of Washington v. Hume*, 128 U.S. 195, 211–212 (1888).

3. See, e.g., *Menard v. Aspasia*, 30 U.S. 505 (1831); *Prigg v. Commonwealth of Pennsylvania*, 41 U.S. 539 (1842); *Dred Scott v. Sandford*, 60 U.S. 393 (1857).

4. See *Thurlow v. Commonwealth of Massachusetts*, 46 U.S. 504, 507 (1847) (upholding state statute regulating the liberty of "any person [who] shall, by excessive drinking of spiritous liquors, so misspend, waste, or lessen his estate as thereby either to expose himself or his family to want or indigent circumstances, or the town to which he belongs to expense for the maintenance of him or his family"); *Williamson v. Berry*, 49 U.S. 495, 555–556, 560 (1850) (observing that "if the father is not able to maintain his children, the court will order maintenance out of their own estate" [Nelson, J., dissenting]); *Hoyt v. Hammekin*, 55 U.S. 346, 350 (1852) (holding that, under civil law, property purchased for a minor daughter by her mother could not be conveyed away by the father, even with the mother's consent); *Central Nat'l Bank of Washington v. Hume*, 128 U.S. 195, 211 (1888) (extending the duty to support after death, to insulate against claims of creditors the estate of a deceased father).

5. *Stein v. Bowman*, 38 U.S. 209, 220–223 (1839) ("This rule [forbidding testimony of a wife against her husband] is founded upon the deepest and soundest principles of our nature. Principles which have grown out of those domestic relations, that constitute the basis of civil society; and which are essential to the enjoyment of that confidence which should subsist between those who are connected by the nearest and dearest relations of life. To break down or impair the great principles which protect the sanctities of husband and wife, would be to destroy the best solace of human existence").

6. See *Wallingsford v. Allen*, 35 U.S. 583 (1836) (concerning wife's authority to

manumit a slave transferred to her for her use by her husband); *Silver v. Ladd*, 74 U.S. 219, 224, 227–228 (1868) (holding that a widow with children was a "head of family" for purposes of congressional statute concerning disposition of lands in the territories); *Bradwell v. State of Illinois*, 83 U.S. 130 (1872) (upholding state's prohibition against licensing women to practice law); *Jackson v. Jackson*, 91 U.S. 122 (1875) (action for divorce, raising question about title to property purchased with money wife had prior to the marriage); *Stringfellow v. Cain*, 99 U.S. 610 (1878) (concerning widow's capacity, as head of family, to continue an adverse possession commenced by her husband); *Brodnax v. Aetna Ins. Co.*, 128 U.S. 236 (1888) (concerning wife's capacity to pledge her separate property to cover husband's debt); *Marchand v. Griffon*, 140 U.S. 516 (1891) (concerning wife's capacity to enter into contracts); *Ankeney v. Hannon*, 147 U.S. 118 (1893) (wife's contract with creditor can not bind her separate property acquired after the contract); *Hamilton v. Rathbone*, 175 U.S. 414 (1899) (involving effect of married women's property act on wife's capacity to dispose of property).

7. *Sexton v. Wheaton*, 21 U.S. 229, 239 (1823) ("All know and feel . . . the sacredness of the connexion between husband and wife. All know, that the sweetness of social intercourse, the harmony of society, the happiness of families, depend on the mutual partiality which they feel, that delicate forbearance which they manifest toward each other").

8. See *Ogden v. Saunders*, 25 U.S. 213, 283, 289–290 (1827) ("society has an interest in preserving every member of the community from despondency—in relieving him from a hopeless state of prostration, in which he would be useless to himself, his family, and the community"); *Drury v. Foster*, 69 U.S. 24 (1864) (holding a mortgage not binding on the estate of a *feme covert*); *P.H. Allen & Co. v. Ferguson*, 85 U.S. 1 (1873) ("Neither the supreme will, so far as we can ascertain it, nor the laws of the land, require that a debtor whose family is in need . . . should prefer a creditor to his family"); *Fink v. O'Neil*, 106 U.S. 272, 275–276 (1882) (upholding the power of a state to exempt homesteads from levy and execution: "These laws are founded in a humane regard to the women and children of families"); *Huntington v. Saunders*, 120 U.S. 78 (1887) (conveyance from husband to wife not reachable by creditors to satisfy husband's debt); *Central Nat'l Bank of Washington v. Hume*, 128 U.S. 195 (1888) (payment under life insurance policy to widow not reachable by creditors of husband: the "public policy which . . . recognizes the support of wife and children as a positive obligation in law as well as morals, should be extended to protect them from destitution after the debtor's death"); *Shauer v. Alterton*, 151 U.S. 607 (1894) (involving intra-familial transfers that made creditors vulnerable).

9. See *Wallingsford v. Allen*, 35 U.S. 583 (1836) ("Agreements between husband and wife, during coverture, for the transfer from him of property directly to the latter, . . . [though] void at law, [may be sustained] when a clear and satisfactory case is made out, that the property is to be applied to the separate use of the wife"); *Taylor v. Taylor*, 49 U.S. 183, 199–201 (1850) (intra-familial transfers of property, as for example between parent and child, are subject to a fiduciary obligation); *Garner v. Second Nat'l Bank of Providence*, 151 U.S. 420 (1894) ("husband and wife could treat each other as lender and borrower, and . . . such a contract would carry with it the usual incident of interest, the same as with other parties").

10. See *Stevenson's Heirs v. Sullivant*, 18 U.S. 207 (1820) (on the question of whether illegitimate children are entitled to property that their mother held through the father of her legitimate children); *Blackburn v. Crawford's Lessee*, 70 U.S. 175 (1865) (involving descent of intestate property to illegitimate heirs); *Gay v. Parpart*, 106 U.S. 679 (1883)

(conveyance by father of illegitimate children to the children's mother permissible as against the father's marital family: "in executing and delivering . . . that assignment he did a meritorious act, honorable and just, as the only atonement he could make for the deception he practiced upon her, and as placing in her hands the means of supporting the children of whom he was the father"); *Conley v. Nailor*, 118 U.S. 127 (1886) (involving a challenge to deeds executed by an elderly man to his mistress, for whom he had abandoned his marital family: "It is not now open to question that a deed made by a father for the benefit of his illegitimate child is upon good consideration which will support the conveyance").

11. *Magniac v. Thompson*, 32 U.S. 348, 393 (1833) (marriage "is a consideration of the highest value, and from motive of the soundest policy").

12. See, e.g., *Jewell's Lessee v. Jewell*, 42 U.S. 219, 233–234 (1843) (though a marriage might have been prohibited under the religious law of one of the parties, marriage is a "civil contract," and access to it is governed by the civil law); *Maynard v. Hill*, 125 U.S. 190, 210–211 (1888) ("while marriage is often termed by text writers and in decisions of courts as a civil contract, generally to indicate that it must be founded upon the agreement of the parties, and does not require any religious ceremony for its solemnization, it is something more than a mere contract").

13. *Barber v. Barber*, 62 U.S. 582, 602 (1858) (Daniel, J., dissenting). See also *Ogden v. Saunders*, 25 U.S. 213, 289–290 (1827) ("Why may not the community declare that, . . . 'we have an interest in the happiness, and services, and families in this community, which shall not be superceded by individual views?'").

14. *Barber v. Barber*.

15. *National Bank v. Commonwealth of Kentucky*, 76 U.S. 353, 362 (1869). In other contexts, two Justices claimed that the Reconstruction amendments to the Constitution authorized Congress to protect African American families; significantly, however, both suggestions appeared in dissents: *Blyew v. U.S.* 80 U.S. 581, 598–599 (1871) (reading the Thirteenth Amendment and the Civil Rights Act of 1866 to include a right to assist in criminal prosecutions: "To deprive a whole class of the community of this right . . . is to brand them with a badge of slavery; . . . is to leave their lives, their families, and their property unprotected by law" [Bradley, J., dissenting]); *U.S. v. Cruikshank*, 92 U.S. 542, 559–560 (1875) (reading the Fourteenth Amendment and the Enforcement Act as authorizing Congress to prohibit "threats of violence" against a newly enfranchised African American citizen or his family [Clifford, J., dissenting]).

16. 125 U.S. 190, 211 (1888).

17. Ibid., at 213.

18. Ibid., at 211.

19. 96 U.S. 76 (1877), at 78, 80–81.

20. See, for example, *Slaughter-House Cases*, 83 U.S. 36, 102–106 (1872) (linking the constitutional right to the common law [Field, J., dissenting]).

21. See *Ex Parte Bradley*, 74 U.S. 364, 376 (1868) (justifying issuing a writ of mandamus to reinstate an attorney, for reason inter alia that he is "suddenly deprived of the only means of an honorable support of himself and family"); *Bradley v. Fisher*, 80 U.S. 335, 355 (1871) ("To most persons who enter the profession, it is the means of support to themselves and their families"); *Ex Parte Wall*, 107 U.S. 265, 318 (1883) ("To disbar him having such a practice . . . would often entail poverty upon himself and destitution upon his family" [Field, J., dissenting]).

22. See *Slaughter-House Cases*, 83 U.S. 36, 104 (1872) (noting that the source of the

common law's antipathy to monopolies was "their interference with the liberty of the subject to pursue for his maintenance and that of his family any lawful trade or employment" [Field, J., dissenting]); *Oregon Steam Navigation Co. v. Winsor,* 87 U.S. 64, 68 (1873) (noting that the doctrine under which agreements in restraint of trade are illegal is supported by "the injury to the party himself by being precluded from pursuing his occupation and thus being prevented from supporting himself and his family"); *Butcher's Union Co. v. Crescent City Co.,* 111 U.S. 746, 761–762 (1884) (upholding Louisiana's new constitution, which abolished all monopolies, including the Crescent City Co. of *Slaughter-House* fame: monopolies violate common-law rights that "enable men to maintain themselves and their families" [Bradley, J., concurring]); *Gibbs v. Consolidated Gas Co. of Baltimore,* 130 U.S. 396, 409 (1889) (affirming the doctrine of *Winsor, supra*).

23. *U.S. v. Trans-Missouri Freight Ass'n,* 166 U.S. 290, 323–324 (1897).

24. *Pollock v. Farmers' Loan & Trust Co.,* 158 U.S. 601, 694 (1895) (arguing that differential treatment was justified *inter alia* by the protection of families [Brown, J., dissenting]).

25. *Bradwell v. State of Illinois,* 83 U.S. 130 (1870).

26. Ibid., 141–142.

27. *Chae Chan Ping v. U.S.,* 130 U.S. 581 (1889), 594–595.

28. *Davis v. Beason,* 133 U.S. 333, 341 (1890).

29. *Reynolds v. U.S.,* 98 U.S. 145, 165–166 (1878).

30. 125 U.S. 190, 213.

31. James Kent, *Commentaries on American Law,* II: 159–168 (New York: O. Halsted, 1827).

32. *State of Virginia v. State of Tennessee (No. 3, Original),* 148 U.S. 503 (1893), at 524.

33. Carl N. Degler, *At Odds: Women and the Family in America from the Revolution to the Present* (Oxford: Oxford University Press, 1980), 8–15, 168.

34. Lawrence M. Friedman, *Private Lives: Families, Individuals, and the Law* (Cambridge, MA: Harvard University Press, 2004), 27–37.

35. Lawrence M. Friedman, *A History of American Law,* 2nd ed. (New York: Simon & Schuster, 1985), 211–212.

36. 262 U.S. 390 (1923).

37. 268 U.S. 510 (1925).

38. *Meyer,* 399.

39. *Pierce,* 535.

40. *Meyer,* 400.

41. Ibid., 400–402.

42. *Pierce,* 534–535.

43. William E. Leuchtenburg, *The Supreme Court Reborn: The Constitutional Revolution in the Age of Roosevelt* (New York: Oxford University Press, 1995), 5–6.

44. Leuchtenburg, 6–9; Stephen Jay Gould, *The Flamingo's Smile: Reflections in Natural History* (New York: W. W. Norton, 1985), 308–309.

45. Leuchtenburg, 9–10; Gould, 313–317.

46. Leuchtenburg, 9–11.

47. *Buck v. Bell,* 274 U.S. 200 (1927), 201–202, 206–207.

48. Ibid., 205–206.

49. Ibid., 207.

50. Ibid., 208.

51. *Missouri v. Holland,* 252 U.S. 416 (1920), 433.

52. Mark A. Largent, *Breeding Contempt: The History of Coerced Sterilization in the United States* (New Brunswick, NJ: Rutgers University Press, 2008), 102–110.

53. *Skinner v. Oklahoma*, 316 U.S. 535 (1942).

54. Walter F. Murphy et al., *American Constitutional Interpretation*, 4th ed. (New York: Foundation Press, 2008), 158.

55. *Poe v. Ullman*, 367 U.S. 497 (1961).

56. *Griswold v. Connecticut*, 381 U.S. 479 (1965).

57. *Eisenstadt v. Baird*, 405 U.S. 438, 452–453 (1972).

58. Ibid., 453.

59. *Roe v. Wade*, 410 U.S. 113 (1973), 153.

60. *Planned Parenthood of Central Missouri v. Danforth*, 428 U.S. 52 (1976); *Belotti v. Baird (Belotti I)*, 428 U.S. 132 (1976); *Belotti v. Baird (Belotti II)*, 443 U.S. 622 (1979); *Planned Parenthood Association of Kansas City v. Ashcroft*, 462 U.S. 476 (1983).

61. *H. L. v. Matheson*, 450 U.S. 398 (1981); *Hodgson v. Minnesota*, 497 U.S. 417 (1990); *Ohio v. Akron Center for Reproductive Health (Akron II)*, 497 U.S. 502 (1990).

62. *Planned Parenthood v. Danforth* (1976).

63. *Planned Parenthood of Southeastern Pennsylvania v. Casey*, 505 U.S. 833 (1992).

64. *Roe v. Wade*, 162–164.

65. *Akron v. Akron Center for Reproductive Health (Akron I)*, 462 U.S. 416 (1983), 458 (O'Connor dissenting).

66. *Planned Parenthood v. Casey*, 877–879 (quoting from *Roe v. Wade*).

67. *Gonzales v. Carhart*, 550 U.S. 124 (2007).

68. *Planned Parenthood v. Casey*, 846–853.

69. Ibid., 852.

70. *Planned Parenthood v. Casey*, 979–1002 (Scalia, dissenting); *Lawrence v. Texas*, 539 U.S. 123 (2003), 588, 593–598 (Scalia, dissenting).

71. 77 Stat. 56 (June 10, 1963).

72. 78 Stat. 241 (July 2, 1964).

73. 429 U.S. 125 (1976).

74. Pub. L. 95–555 (October 31, 1978).

75. *Bradwell v. Illinois*, 141 (Bradley, dissenting).

76. *Goesaert v. Cleary*, 335 U.S. 464 (1948), 465–466.

77. *Reed v. Reed*, 404 U.S. 71 (1971), 76–77.

78. Amy Leigh Campbell, "Raising the Bar: Ruth Bader Ginsburg and the ACLU Women's Rights Project," 11 *Texas Journal of Women and the Law* 157 (2002), 168–179; Joan C. Williams, "Jumpstarting the Stalled Gender Revolution: Justice Ginsburg and Reconstructive Feminism," 63 *Hastings Law Journal* 1267 (2012), 1270.

79. *Frontiero v. Richardson*, 411 U.S. 677 (1973).

80. For a fascinating account of how Ginsburg came to file and argue her brief, despite resistance from counsel representing Lt. Frontiero, see Campbell, "Raising the Bar," 182–184; Williams, "Jumpstarting the Stalled Gender Revolution," 1270.

81. Campbell, "Raising the Bar," 184–193. For a transcript of the oral argument, see http://www.oyez.org/cases/19701979/1972/1972_71_1694.

82. Campbell, "Raising the Bar," 196–199; Karen O'Connor, *Women's Organizations' Use of the Courts* (Lexington, MA: Lexington Books, 1980), 124; "An Advocate for Women's Rights," Facts-on-File, http://www.fofweb.com/History/MainPrintPage.asp?iPin =WARG05&DataType=Women&WinType=Free.

83. *Kahn v. Shevin*, 416 U.S. 351 (1974).

84. Brief for Appellee, *Weinberger v. Wiesenfeld* (No. 73—1892), 13–14. For a transcript of the oral argument, see http://www.oyez.org/cases/19701979/1974/1974_73_1892.

85. *Weinberger v. Wiesenfeld*, 420 U.S. 636 (1975).

86. *Craig v. Boren*, 429 U.S. 190 (1976).

87. Catharine A. MacKinnon, *Toward a Feminist Theory of the State* (Cambridge, MA: Harvard University Press, 1989), 215–234.

88. Susan Hirschmann, Testimony re: Ruth Bader Ginsburg, to the Senate Judiciary Committee (July 23, 1993), appearing at http://www.gpoaccess.gov/congress/senate/judiciary/sh103482/517529.pdf.

89. *Duren v. Missouri*, 439 U.S. 357 (1979).

90. *Mississippi University for Women v. Hogan*, 458 U.S. 718 (1982).

91. *United States v. Virginia*, 518 U.S. 515 (1996).

92. *Rostker v. Goldberg*, 453 U.S. 57 (1981).

93. *Michael M. v. Superior Court*, 450 U.S. 464 (1981).

94. 29 U.S.C. §§2601 et seq.

95. *Nevada Department of Human Resources v. Hibbs*, 538 U.S. 721 (2003).

96. Lawrence M. Friedman, *Private Lives: Families, Individuals, and the Law* (Cambridge, MA: Harvard University Press, 2004), 4–6.

97. *Ankenbrandt v. Richards*, 504 U.S. 689 (1992).

98. Among the scores of decisions are these: *Atherton v. Atherton*, 181 U.S. 155 (1901); *Williams v. North Carolina [Williams I]*, 317 U.S. 287 (1942); *Williams v. North Carolina [Williams II]*, 325 U.S. 226 (1945); *Boddie v. Connecticut*, 401 U.S. 371 (1971); *Sosna v. Iowa*, 419 U.S. 393 (1975).

99. See *In re Gault*, 387 U.S. 1 (1967); *DeBacker v. Brainard*, 396 U.S. 28 (1969); *Little v. Arkansas*, 435 U.S. 957 (1978); *Engle v. Sims*, 450 U.S. 936 (1981); *Thompson v. Oklahoma*, 487 U.S. 815 (1988); *Stanford v. Kentucky*, 492 U.S. 361 (1989). For two recent decisions, see *Roper v. Simmons*, 543 U.S. 551 (2005); *Graham v. Florida*, 560 U.S. ___ (2010).

100. See Friedman, *Private Lives*, 126–127.

101. See *Levy v. Louisiana*, 391 U.S. 68 (1968); *Glona v. American Guarantee & Liability Insurance Co.*, 391 U.S. 73 (1968).

102. *Labine v. Vincent*, 401 U.S. 532 (1971).

103. See *Weber v. Aetna Casualty & Surety Co.*, 406 U.S. 164 (1972); *Trimble v. Gordon*, 430 U.S. 762 (1977); *United States v. Clark*, 445 U.S. 23 (1980); *Reed v. Campbell*, 476 U.S. 852 (1986).

104. *Gomez v. Perez*, 409 U.S. 535 (1973).

105. *Mills v. Habluetzel*, 456 U.S. 91 (1982); *Pickett v. Brown*, 462 U.S. 1 (1983); *Clark v. Jeter*, 486 U.S. 456 (1988); Child Support Enforcement Act (as amended, 1994), 42 U.S.C. § 666(a)(5)(A)(ii).

106. *Stanley v. Illinois*, 405 U.S. 645 (1972); *Quilloin v. Walcott*, 434 U.S. 246 (1978); *Caban v. Mohammed*, 441 U.S. 380 (1979); *Lehr v. Robertson*, 463 U.S. 248 (1983).

107. *Michael H. v. Gerald D.*, 491 U.S. 110 (1989).

108. Ibid., 121–127.

109. Henry of Bratton [Bracton], *De Legibus et Consuetudinibus Angliae;* Sir Harris Nicolas, *Adulterine Bastardy* (London: William Pickering, 1836). Justice Scalia misspells Nicolas as "Nicholas."

110. John Hubback, *A Treatise on the Evidence of Succession to Real and Personal Property and Peerages* (Philadelphia: T. & J. W. Johnson, 1845), 295.

111. See, e.g., *Smith v. Organization of Foster Families,* 431 U.S. 816 (1977); *Quilloin v. Walcott,* 434 U.S. 246 (1978); *Lassiter v. Department of Social Services,* 452 U.S. 18 (1981); *Santosky v. Kramer,* 455 U.S. 745 (1982).

112. *U.S. Department of Agriculture v. Moreno,* 413 U.S. 528 (1973).

113. *Village of Belle Terre v. Boraas,* 416 U.S. 1 (1974).

114. *Moore v. City of East Cleveland,* 431 U.S. 494 (1977).

115. *Troxel v. Granville,* 530 U.S. 57 (2000).

116. Ibid., 60–75.

117. *McDonald v. City of Chicago,* 130 S.Ct. 3020 (2010), quoting *District of Columbia v. Heller,* 128 S.Ct. 2783 (2008).

CONCLUSION: THE MEANINGS OF MARRIAGE

1. Thornton Wilder, *Our Town* (New York: Coward-McCann, 1938, 1939).

2. For additional perspective on the nationalization of family, see Jill Elaine Hasday, "The Canon of Family Law," 57 *Stanford Law Review* 825 (2004).

3. *Maynard v. Hill,* 125 U.S. 219 (1888).

4. *Meister v. Moore,* 96 U.S. 76 (1877).

5. *Davis v. Beason,* 133 U.S. 333 (1890).

6. *Loving v. Virginia,* 388 U.S. 1 (1967).

7. *Pace v. Alabama,* 106 U.S. 583 (1883).

8. *Jackson v. Alabama,* 72 So.2d 144 (Ala., 1954), cert. denied 348 U.S. 888 (1954).

9. *Naim v. Naim,* 87 S.E.2d 749 (Va. 1955), vacated and remanded 350 U.S. 891 (1955), aff'd 90 S.E.2d 849 (Va. 1955), motion to recall mandate denied and appeal dismissed 350 U.S. 985 (1956).

10. *Loving v. Virginia,* 1–12.

11. *Zablocki v. Redhail,* 434 U.S. 374 (1978).

12. *Turner v. Safley,* 482 U.S. 78 (1987).

13. *Butler v. Wilson,* 415 U.S. 953 (1974).

14. Walter L. Williams, *The Spirit and the Flesh: Sexual Diversity in American Indian Culture* (Boston: Beacon Press, 1986), at 1–2; Walter L. Williams, "The Berdache Tradition," from Lecture Notes, http://crl.ucsd.edu/~elman/Courses/HDP1/2000/LectureNotes/williams.pdf, at 73–74, 76. See also Will Roscoe, *The Zuni Man-Woman* (Albuquerque: University of New Mexico Press, 1992); Sue-Ellen Jacobs, Wesley Thomas, and Sabine Lang, eds., *Two-Spirit People: Native American Gender Identity, Sexuality, and Spirituality* (Urbana: University of Illinois Press, 1997); Sabine Lang, *Men as Women, Women as Men: Changing Gender in Native American Cultures* (Austin: University of Texas Press, 1998); Brian Joseph Gilley, *Becoming Two-Spirit: Gay Identity and Social Acceptance in Indian Country* (Lincoln: University of Nebraska Press, 2006).

15. Williams, "The Berdache Tradition," at 75.

16. Ibid., at 73–74.

17. *Bowers v. Hardwick,* 478 U.S. 186 (1986).

18. *Romer v. Evans,* 517 U.S. 620 (1996).

19. *Reitman v. Mulkey,* 387 U.S. 369 (1967). The case involved the repeal, by constitutional referendum, of fair housing laws that California's legislature had enacted to bar racial discrimination in the sale or rental of private houses or apartments. The Court noted

that ordinarily the repeal of legislation was not constitutionally problematic. Here, however, the repeal was tantamount to the state's authorization to discriminate on the basis of race. "The right to discriminate [was] now embodied in the State's basic charter, immune from legislative, executive, or judicial regulation at any level of the state government." The Court struck down the referendum amendment.

20. *Lawrence v. Texas,* 539 U.S. 558 (2003).

21. *Powell v. State of Georgia,* 270 Ga. 327, 510 S.E.2d 18 (1998). The case involved the prosecution of an adult male for consensual oral sex with a female, who was his wife's seventeen-year-old niece.

22. *Lawrence v. Texas,* 578.

23. Ibid., 604–605 (Scalia, J., dissenting).

24. *Baker v. Nelson,* 409 U.S. 810 (1972), dismissing appeal from 191 N.W.2d 185 (1971).

25. *Baehr v. Lewin,* 852 P.2d 44 (Hawaii, 1993).

26. *Baehr v. Miike,* No. 20371 (Hawaii, Dec. 9, 1999).

27. *Baker v. State of Vermont,* 170 Vt. 194, 744 A.2d 864 (1999).

28. Pub. L. No. 104-199, 110 Stat. 2419 (1996).

29. *Perry v. Brown,* No. 10-16696, D.C. No. 3:09-CV-02292-VRW (9th Cir., Feb. 7, 2012).

30. See William N. Eskridge, Jr., *The Case for Same-Sex Marriage: From Sexual Liberty to Civilized Commitment* (New York: The Free Press, 1996); William N. Eskridge, Jr., *Equality Practice: Civil Unions and the Future of Gay Rights* (New York: Routledge, 2002); William N. Eskridge, Jr., "Marriage Equality State by State," SCOTUSblog (August 15, 2011), http://www.scotusblog.com/2011/08/marriage-equality-state-by-state/.

31. For a contrarian view that federalism is obsolete, at least in the United States, see Malcolm M. Feeley and Edward Rubin, *Federalism: Political Identity and Tragic Compromise* (Ann Arbor: University of Michigan Press, 2008).

32. Jeffrey Segal and Harold J. Spaeth, *The Supreme Court and the Attitudinal Model* (New York: Cambridge University Press, 1993).

33. Robert George, Timothy George, and Chuck Colson, "The Manhattan Declaration: A Call of Christian Conscience" (2009), http://www.manhattandeclaration.org/thedeclaration/read.aspx.

34. William H. Rehnquist, "The Notion of a Living Constitution," 54 *Texas Law Review* 693 (1976).

35. See, e.g., William N. Eskridge, Jr., and Darren R. Spedale, *Gay Marriage: For Better or for Worse? What We've Learned from the Evidence* (New York: Oxford University Press, 2006).

36. Having said this, I concede that debate continues on the subject, sometimes strenuously. Compare generally, Eskridge, *Gay Marriage* (arguing that Scandinavian recognition of same-sex marriage has done no harm either to marriage generally or to children), with Mark Regnerus, "How Different Are the Adult Children of Parents Who Have Same-Sex Relationships? Findings from the New Family Structures Study," *Social Science Research* 41 (2012): 752 (arguing that adult children of a parent who has had a same-sex romantic relationship experience worse social, emotional, and relational outcomes than do children raised by still-married heterosexual biological parents).

37. It is worth noting on this point that the Declaration's claim of religious liberty

does not apply to those persons who adhere to religious faiths that command (or merely permit) practices such as polygamy.

38. George, George, and Colson, "The Manhattan Declaration."

39. Georg Simmel refers to this as the symmetry of reciprocal dependence that occurs only in dyads. See Kurt H. Wolff, trans., *The Sociology of Georg Simmel* (Glencoe, IL: The Free Press, 1950), 122–144. I'm grateful for Stephen Macedo's Murphy Lecture on "The Future of Marriage" (Princeton University, May 3, 2012), for this insight.

EPILOGUE

1. Wendy Wong, Kim Parker, and Paul Taylor, *Breadwinner Moms* (Washington, D.C.: Pew Research Center, May 29, 2013), 1–19.

2. http://www.washingtonpost.com/blogs/the-fix/wp/2013/03/18.

3. *United States v. Windsor,* 570 U.S. ___, No. 12–307 (June 26, 2013).

4. On this point, Justice Alito cited Sherif Girgis, Ryan T. Anderson, and Robert P. George, *What Is Marriage? Man and Woman: A Defense* (New York: Encounter Books, 2012).

5. Indeed a possible signal that the Obama administration is prepared to enforce a unitary policy came within a week of the decision in *Windsor.* The Department of Homeland Security issued a green card for permanent residence to a gay couple, one spouse an American residing in Florida, the other a Bulgarian. See Julia Preston, "Gay Married Man in Florida Approved for Green Card," in http://www.nytimes.com/2013/07/01/us/gay-married-man-in-florida-is-approved-for-green-card.html.

6. *Hollingsworth v. Perry,* 570 U.S. ___, No. 12–144 (June 26, 2013).

7. *Perry v. Schwarzenegger,* 704 F. Supp. 2d 921 (ND Cal. 2010).

8. Michael Klarman, *From the Closet to the Altar: Courts, Backlash, and the Struggle for Same-Sex Marriage* (New York: Oxford University Press, 2013).

9. Perhaps an anticipatory hint of "the other shoe" comes from a U.S. District Court in Michigan. The state of Michigan bars same-sex marriage. By state statute, public employers are prohibited "from providing medical or other fringe benefits to any person cohabiting with a public employee unless the person is legally married to the employee, a legal dependent, or eligible to inherit under the State's intestacy laws." Plaintiffs challenged the statute, claiming that it was designed "to prohibit public employers from furnishing benefits to same-sex partners of their employees," in violation of the equal protection clause of the Constitution of the United States. Two days after *Windsor* was decided, the district court issued a preliminary injunction against enforcement of the state's statute (citing *United States v. Windsor*). Opinion and Order, *Bassett v. Snyder,* Case No. 12–10038 (U.S. District Court for the Eastern District of Michigan, Southern Division, June 28, 2013). The American Civil Liberties Union has filed a separate suit in federal court, challenging directly Pennsylvania's prohibition of same-sex marriage. Trip Gabriel, "A.C.L.U. Lawsuit Aims to Overturn Pennsylvania's Ban on Gay Marriage," http://www.nytimes.com/2013/07/10/us/aclu-lawsuit-aims-to-overturn-pennsylvanias-ban-on-gay-marriage.html. Doubtless, other challenges will follow.

Index

abortion
  and Comstock Law, 177
  in family values rhetoric, 1, 4, 5
  and morality, 224
  and right of privacy, 224
  Supreme Court cases and, 223–226,
    244, 249, 252
  See also reproduction
ACLU Women's Rights Project, 229
adoption, 12, 216, 234, 237
adultery
  Edmunds-Tucker Act and, 207–208
  in English law, 56–57, 184, 310n10
  in family values rhetoric, 1, 4–5
  in religious scripture, 18–19, 20
  Mormonism and, 192, 194, 196, 207
  slavery and, 91, 97
  state regulation of, 104, 207, 241, 252
agrarian republicanism, 71–72, 108–114,
  116–117, 118, 123–124, 147,
  263–264, 289n101, 296n7, 297n13,
  302n114. *See also* Jefferson, Thomas
Alito, Samuel, 239, 268–270, 272
American Civil Liberties Union (ACLU),
  321–322
American political ideology, 67–68, 69–73
American Revolution, 69–73, 74, 288n86,
  289n88
Anti-Trespassing Act of 1807, 118

Antifederalists, 75, 77–78, 113, 291n129,
  292n149
Aristotle
  and familial household, 9, 35–36, 82,
    83, 126, 178, 277–20
  and Jefferson's agrarian republicanism,
    110–111, 112
  and mixed government, 73–74,
    290n115
  and natural law, 87, 264
  and state and family hierarchy, 78,
    80, 112, 113, 292n152, 292n154,
    293n156

Banbury's Case, 235
Bassett v. Snyder, 231–322n9
bastardy. *See* illegitimacy
Beissel, Johann Conrad, 153–157, 170,
  178
"berdache" tradition, 246–248
bigamy, 54, 55, 56, 203, 205, 206, 208,
  214, 252. *See also* polygamy
birth control. *See* contraception
Blackmun, Harry, 224, 248
Blackstone, William
  on canonical law in marriage, 54, 56, 57
  and *Commentaries on the Laws of
    England*, 33–35
  on dualist concept of marriage, 52–54

Shakers (*continued*)
  membership in, 162, 167, 178
  North America arrival of, 157–159
  and production, 178, 179
  and property, 159, 163, 179, 264
  sexual equality among, 160–161, 179, 264
  as "Shaking Quakers," 157–158
  tenets of, 161–163
  See also Lee, Ann
Sharfstein, Dan, 102
Skinner v. Oklahoma, 221–222, 224, 234,
    242–243
slaveholding family
  as constitutionally protected, 81
  and miscegenation, 95–97
  patriarchy of, 9, 89–90, 94, 95
  and sexual predation, 95–96
  and social control, 94, 98
  See also slave marital family; slavery
slave marital family, 90–94, 95–96, 97–99,
    101–102. *See also* Genovese, Eugene;
    Stampp, Kenneth
slavery
  ancient roots of, 81–83
  Blackstone on, 36, 83
  and capitalism, 88, 90, 94
  in Constitution, 9, 77, 84, 88, 292n147
  in constitutional order, 83–84, 88,
    99–101
  defenses of, 86–89
  and *Dred Scott v. Sandford,* 100–101,
    106, 302n130
  and emancipation, 81, 82, 102–103
  inheritable status of, 82
  and Missouri Compromise, 100
  and natural law, 36, 86–87, 264
  and Northwest Ordinance, 99–100, 118,
    294n45, 301n93
  and religion, 84–86, 293n9
  and separation of family members, 95–99
  and territorial expansion, 10, 100–101,
    108–109, 120–121, 122, 134, 295n51
  See also slaveholding family; slave
    marital family
Sluyter, Peter, 152
Smith, Joseph, 185–188, 189–190, 191–
    193, 194–196, 197, 310n6

social evolution. *See* conceptual
    frameworks of family
socialism, 87, 89, 166–167, 303n133,
    308n55
Society of Free Brethren and Sisters. *See*
    Cochranites
Spyer, Thea, 268
Stampp, Kenneth, 90–91, 92, 95, 96, 98–99
Stanley, Abraham, 158
Staves, Susan, 40, 47
Stephenson, George M., 119
sterilization, forced, 218–220, 221–222
Stinchfield, Ephraim, 182–183
"stirpiculture," 170, 175–176
Stringfellow, Thornton, 84–86, 293n9
suffrage, 130, 134, 206, 280n22,
    303nn135–136
Supreme Court, U.S.
  and abortion, 223–226, 227, 244, 249, 252
  and constitutionalization of the family,
    1, 2, 17, 216–220, 220–226, 265–266,
    268–273
  and constitutional right to marriage,
    244–246, 268–273
  and contraception, 15, 222–223, 226
  and divorce, 232, 242
  and English law, 205, 211, 215, 228,
    233, 235, 313nn1–2
  and livelihood right, 213–215, 217,
    313n2
  and morality, 214–215, 222, 224, 226,
    236–237, 242, 248–249, 250, 251,
    252–253, 259
  in nineteenth-century family law,
    211–216, 265, 313nn4–6, 314nn7–10,
    315nn11–13, 315n15, 315nn21–22,
    316n24
  and polygamy, 204–207, 208–209, 211,
    214, 226, 242, 250–251
  and privacy right, 2, 15, 16, 222–223,
    224, 237, 244, 248, 251–252
  and race, 104, 214, 243, 250, 311–
    320n19
  and same-sex marriage, 253–254, 255,
    256–257, 259–260, 262–263, 268–273
  and sex-based inequality, 228–231
  and sexual orientation, 240, 246–253, 259